The Complete

ELFQUEST®

Graphic Novel™

Book Five:
Siege at Blue Mountain

by Wendy and Richard Pini

coloring by Chelsea Animation Studio, New York
supervised by Wendy Pini

FATHER TREE PRESS • Poughkeepsie, New York • 1988

The Complete Elfquest Graphic Novel

Book Five: Siege at Blue Mountain

Published by
Father Tree Press,
a division of
Warp Graphics, Inc.

Color separations by
Colorifics, Inc.,
San Antonio, Texas
Printed in the United States of America
by Hart Graphics, Austin, Texas

For
Janet Scagnelli, Judy Stillway, Gordon Harris, Julia Kidd, Sono Kuwayama, Donnarae Aiello, Michael Zoderozny, Laura Rommereim, Tina Paratore and Tracy Aiello
colorful characters all

First printing December 1988
10 9 8 7 6 5 4 3
ISBN 0-936861-10-X (pbk.)

Introduction
by Len Wein

I'm about to let you in on a little secret. It may cost me dearly to reveal this to you, but in the immortal words of John Wayne (or was it Woody Allen?) sometimes a man's gotta do what a man's gotta do. Okay, ready? Good. Now listen up close, because I'm only going to say this once.

Everything you've read in the past four volumes of *The Complete Elfquest*, everything you are going to read in this volume and the next — is a complete and utter lie.

No. Whoa. Hey, wait, oh ye of too much faith. Before you light those oil-soaked torches and finish braiding that uncomfortable noose, before you assault these frail suburban battlements screaming for my pale, anemic blood, please allow me to explain. After all, I've seen all the same old movies you have and I know that every dying man is allowed one final request, right?

For the past decade, Wendy and Richard Pini have moved among us, all bright-eyed and fresh-faced, dressed like the enterprising entrepreneurs they have since become (but still, oh, for the day's of Wendy's silver-dollar-strewn Hyrkanian bikini) purporting to tell us the saga of an adventurous elf called Cutter, Blood of Ten Chiefs, his brave and loyal band of Wolfriders, and their quest to find a home. Coldly and cunningly, the Pinis led us to believe we were merely reading tales of grotesque Trolls and cocoon-spinning Preservers, of "sending" and "Recognition", of High Ones and Gliders and Go-Backs. In short, the stuff of fantasy, the wisp-thin gossamer from which the brightest dreams are spun.

After all this time, we have come to know well the likes of Picknose and Petalwing, Savah and Suntop, Winnowill and Kahvi, until their distant World of Two Moons has become as close to us as the home-grown garden next door. We have come to understand each character's motivation, to care about each one's triumphs and tragedies. When any member of *Elfquest*'s constantly growing, constantly changing cast becomes lost to us, no matter how small his or her role in the overall epic might be, we grieve, almost as if we have lost some member of our own family.

And that, dear friends, is the terrible lie of it all, the great deception. For all this elvin magic and melodrama is merely a devious front to mask the Pinis' true purpose. You see, they're not really telling tales of elves at all. What they're talking about here, and most eloquently I might add, is that fragile thing we call the human condition.

That, above all, is what has endeared the *Elfquest* saga to us over these past ten years. Without our ever being truly aware of how we were being manipulated, the Pinis have held a mirror up before us. With the smallest bit of effort, by tilting our heads just slightly to one side, we can see ourselves reflected in the faces of these tiny adventurers.

And that too is a part of the magic of *Elfquest*. Among the seemingly limitless players in the epic drama, we can find echoes of each of us. The tenacity and vision of Cutter, the eternal optimism and curiosity of Skywise, the sobriety of Rayek, the childish enthusiasm of Ember and Suntop, we can find all of this and more merely by looking into the eyes of those who touch our lives every day.

That, I think, is why *Elfquest* has acquired such a devoted following, because it speaks to the basic truths that ultimately affect all of us. Jealousy, loyalty, laughter, fear, the flickering flame of courage, the unquenchable spark of love. In our time, we have known all these things and more, and yet Richard and Wendy show them to us from a new perspective, an acute angle from which we have never seen them before, but which brings them into sharp, or at least new, focus. The Pinis seem to know instinctively the secrets we hold closest to our hearts.

And that, dear friends, makes them dangerous.

So the question remaining is this: Do we really want to leave two people on the loose who know us so well? Do we really want them to continue to show us those sides of ourselves that we sometimes would rather stay hidden? That's a decision each of us will have to deal with on his or her own. I can only suggest that you read all of the stories collected in these volumes and make your decision when you're ready. For my part, I've already made mine.

As far as I'm concerned, Wendy and Richard can lie to me any time.

P.S. Now that we've gotten the astute observations out of the way, I suppose I should tell you the real reason I enjoy *Elfquest*. And, trust me, it's a decidedly personal one. You see, my dog Gonzo (a Labrador Deceiver of great heart and very little brain) is the model for one of the wolves featured herein. All you need do is to check the back cover of Warp Graphics's *Elfquest* #12 (in the Gallery section of Volume 3) for details. See the wolf with the floppy left ear? Well, switch ears so it's the right ear that flops, steal a little of the ferocity from the eyes, and that's my dog.

Who said there were no more secrets behind the comics?

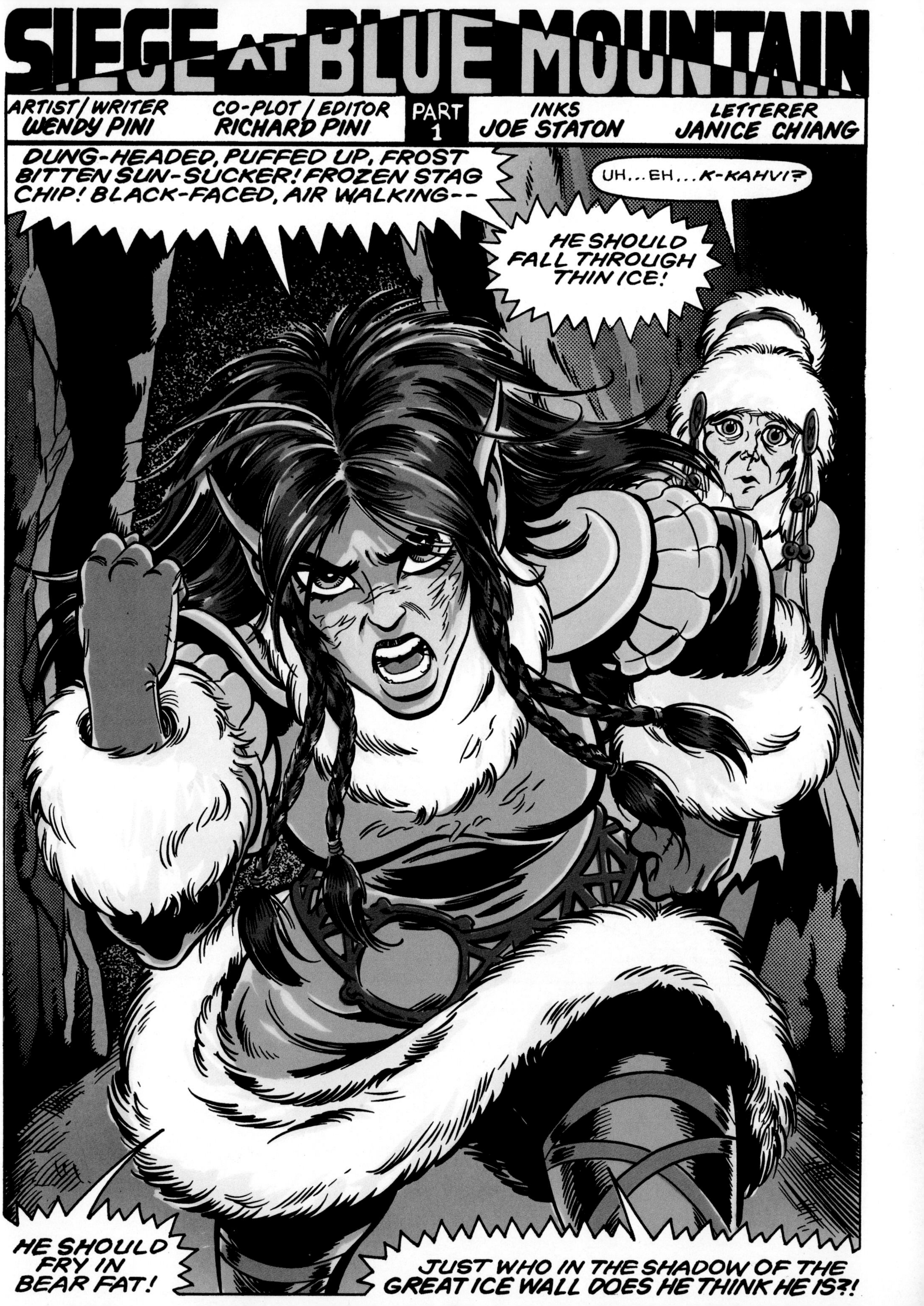
SIEGE AT BLUE MOUNTAIN
ARTIST / WRITER WENDY PINI
CO-PLOT / EDITOR RICHARD PINI
PART 1
INKS JOE STATON
LETTERER JANICE CHIANG
DUNG-HEADED, PUFFED UP, FROST BITTEN SUN-SUCKER! FROZEN STAG CHIP! BLACK-FACED, AIR WALKING--
UH... EH... K-KAHVI?
HE SHOULD FALL THROUGH THIN ICE!
HE SHOULD FRY IN BEAR FAT!
JUST WHO IN THE SHADOW OF THE GREAT ICE WALL DOES HE THINK HE IS?!

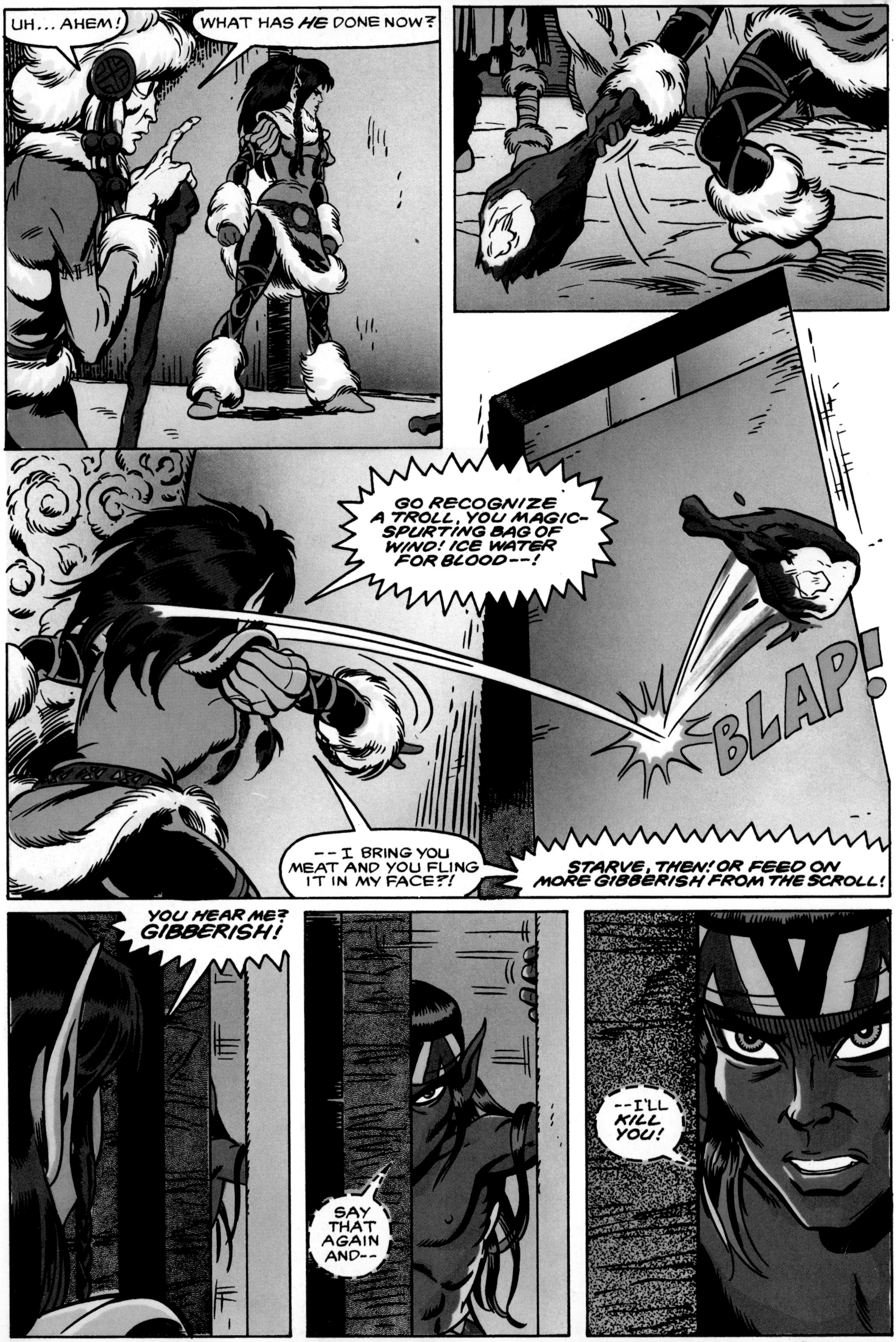
UH... AHEM!
WHAT HAS HE DONE NOW?
GO RECOGNIZE A TROLL, YOU MAGIC-SPURTING BAG OF WIND! ICE WATER FOR BLOOD--!
BLAP!
--I BRING YOU MEAT AND YOU FLING IT IN MY FACE?!
STARVE, THEN! OR FEED ON MORE GIBBERISH FROM THE SCROLL!
YOU HEAR ME? GIBBERISH!
SAY THAT AGAIN AND--
--I'LL KILL YOU!

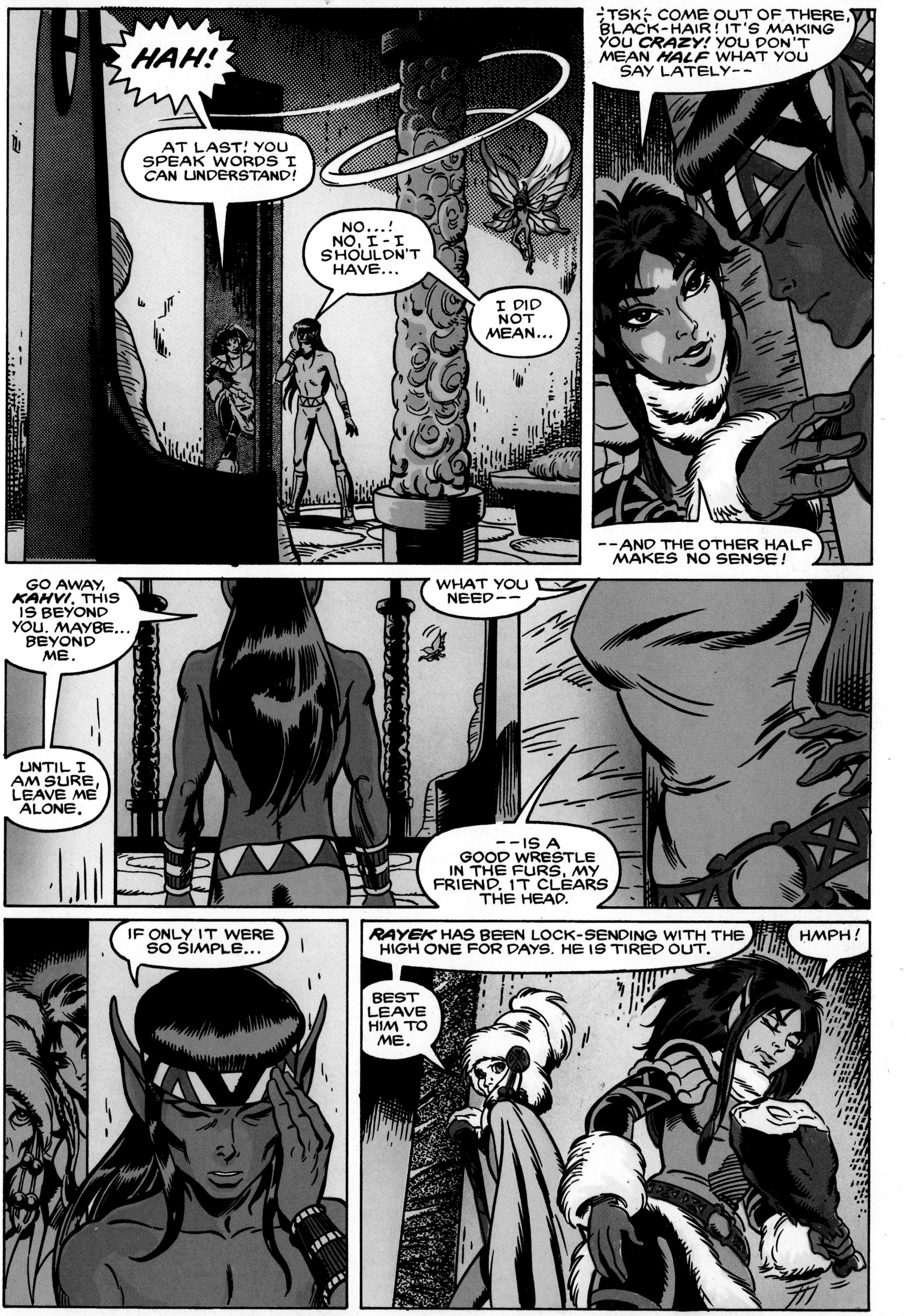
HAH!
AT LAST! YOU SPEAK WORDS I CAN UNDERSTAND!
NO...! NO, I-I SHOULDN'T HAVE...
I DID NOT MEAN...
-TSK- COME OUT OF THERE, BLACK-HAIR! IT'S MAKING YOU CRAZY! YOU DON'T MEAN HALF WHAT YOU SAY LATELY--
--AND THE OTHER HALF MAKES NO SENSE!
GO AWAY, KAHVI. THIS IS BEYOND YOU. MAYBE... BEYOND ME.
UNTIL I AM SURE, LEAVE ME ALONE.
WHAT YOU NEED--
--IS A GOOD WRESTLE IN THE FURS, MY FRIEND. IT CLEARS THE HEAD.
IF ONLY IT WERE SO SIMPLE...
RAYEK HAS BEEN LOCK-SENDING WITH THE HIGH ONE FOR DAYS. HE IS TIRED OUT.
BEST LEAVE HIM TO ME.
HMPH!

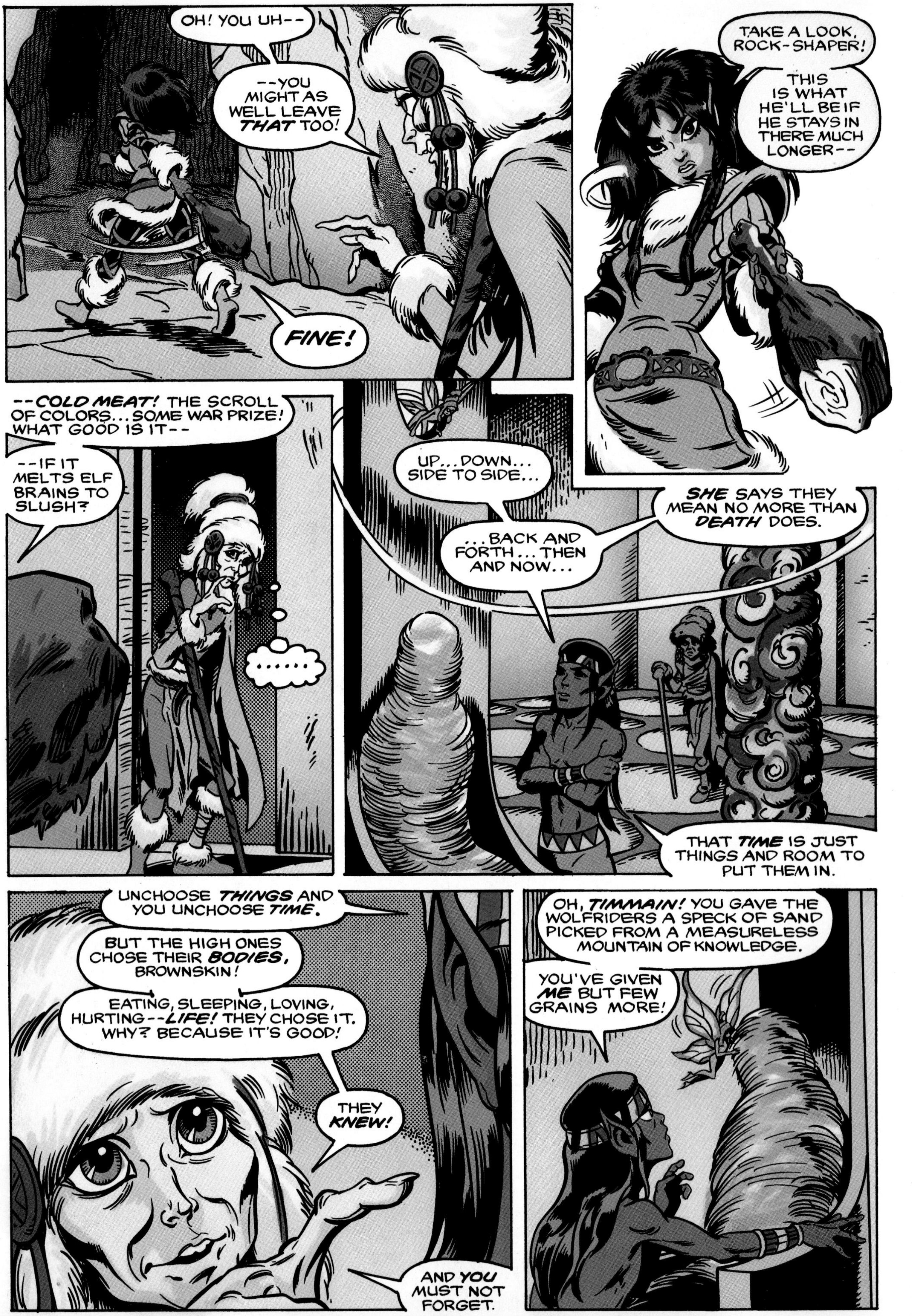
OH! YOU UH--
--YOU MIGHT AS WELL LEAVE THAT TOO!
FINE!
TAKE A LOOK, ROCK-SHAPER!
THIS IS WHAT HE'LL BE IF HE STAYS IN THERE MUCH LONGER--
--COLD MEAT! THE SCROLL OF COLORS... SOME WAR PRIZE! WHAT GOOD IS IT--
--IF IT MELTS ELF BRAINS TO SLUSH?
......
UP... DOWN... SIDE TO SIDE...
...BACK AND FORTH... THEN AND NOW...
SHE SAYS THEY MEAN NO MORE THAN DEATH DOES.
THAT TIME IS JUST THINGS AND ROOM TO PUT THEM IN.
UNCHOOSE THINGS AND YOU UNCHOOSE TIME.
BUT THE HIGH ONES CHOSE THEIR BODIES, BROWNSKIN!
EATING, SLEEPING, LOVING, HURTING--LIFE! THEY CHOSE IT. WHY? BECAUSE IT'S GOOD!
THEY KNEW!
AND YOU MUST NOT FORGET.
OH, TIMMAIN! YOU GAVE THE WOLFRIDERS A SPECK OF SAND PICKED FROM A MEASURELESS MOUNTAIN OF KNOWLEDGE.
YOU'VE GIVEN ME BUT FEW GRAINS MORE!

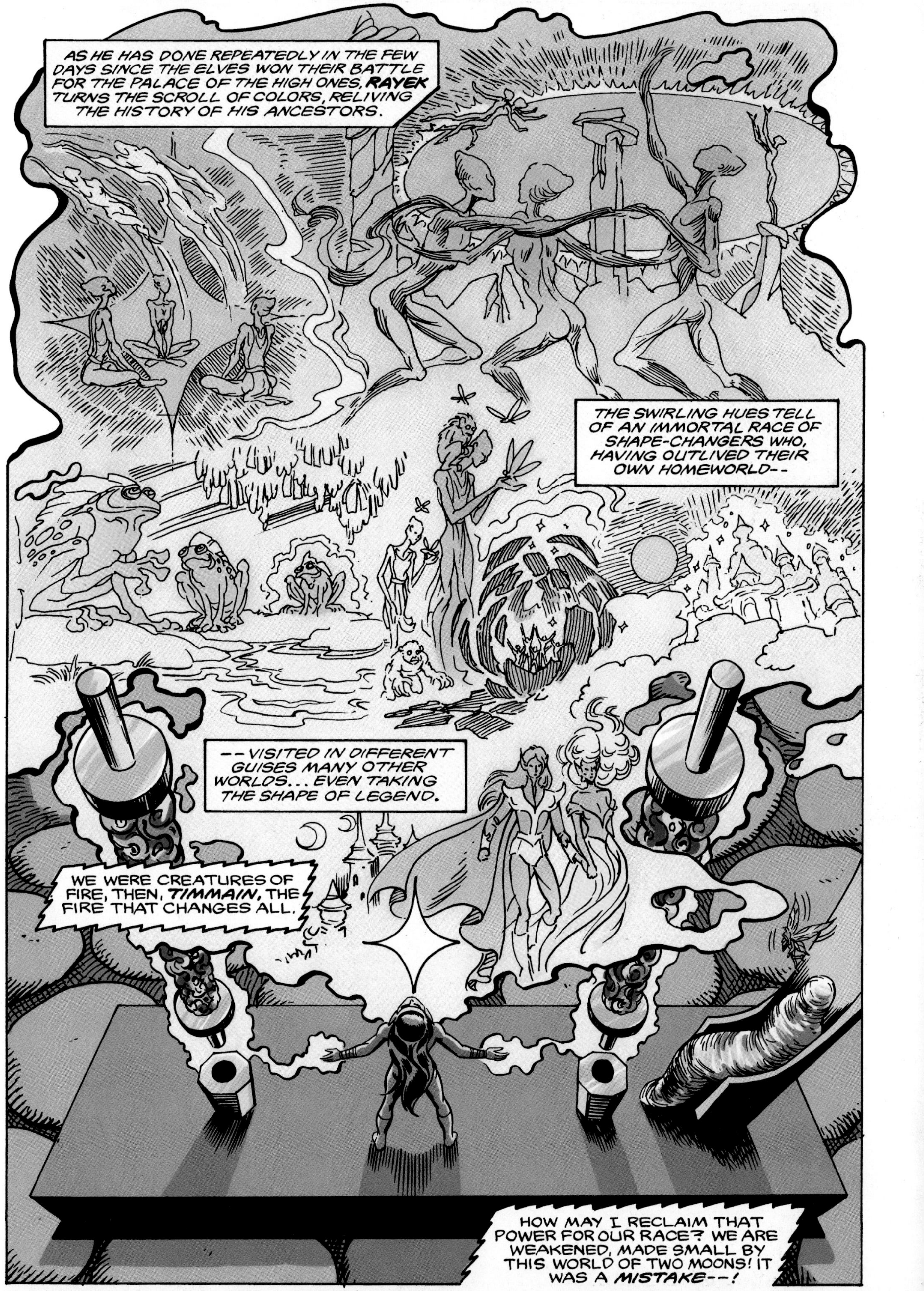
AS HE HAS DONE REPEATEDLY IN THE FEW DAYS SINCE THE ELVES WON THEIR BATTLE FOR THE PALACE OF THE HIGH ONES, RAYEK TURNS THE SCROLL OF COLORS, RELIVING THE HISTORY OF HIS ANCESTORS.
THE SWIRLING HUES TELL OF AN IMMORTAL RACE OF SHAPE-CHANGERS WHO, HAVING OUTLIVED THEIR OWN HOMEWORLD--
--VISITED IN DIFFERENT GUISES MANY OTHER WORLDS... EVEN TAKING THE SHAPE OF LEGEND.
WE WERE CREATURES OF FIRE, THEN, TIMMAIN, THE FIRE THAT CHANGES ALL.
HOW MAY I RECLAIM THAT POWER FOR OUR RACE? WE ARE WEAKENED, MADE SMALL BY THIS WORLD OF TWO MOONS! IT WAS A MISTAKE--!

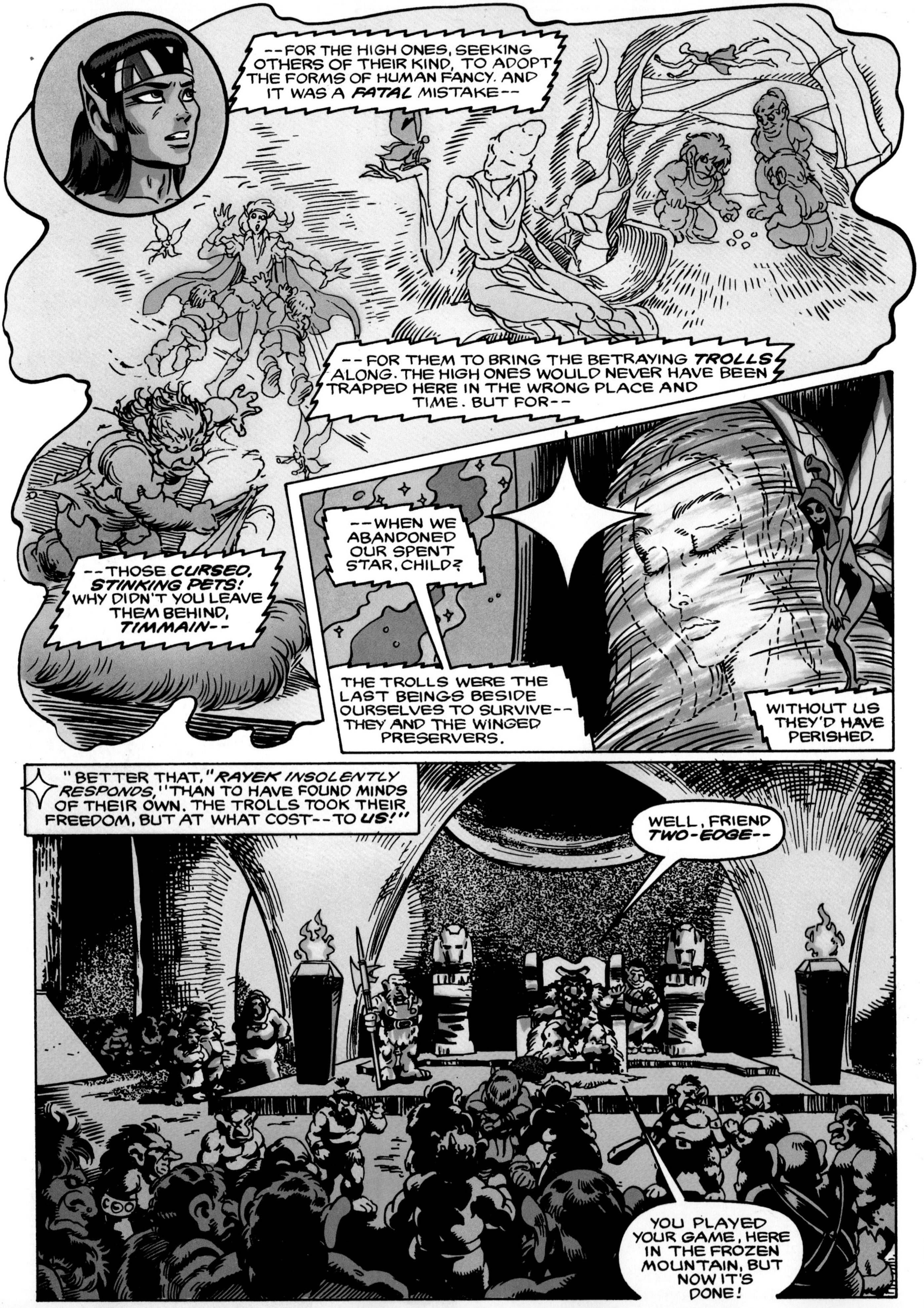
--FOR THE HIGH ONES, SEEKING OTHERS OF THEIR KIND, TO ADOPT THE FORMS OF HUMAN FANCY. AND IT WAS A FATAL MISTAKE--
--FOR THEM TO BRING THE BETRAYING TROLLS ALONG. THE HIGH ONES WOULD NEVER HAVE BEEN TRAPPED HERE IN THE WRONG PLACE AND TIME. BUT FOR--
--THOSE CURSED, STINKING PETS! WHY DIDN'T YOU LEAVE THEM BEHIND, TIMMAIN--
--WHEN WE ABANDONED OUR SPENT STAR, CHILD?
THE TROLLS WERE THE LAST BEINGS BESIDE OURSELVES TO SURVIVE-- THEY AND THE WINGED PRESERVERS.
WITHOUT US THEY'D HAVE PERISHED.
"BETTER THAT," RAYEK INSOLENTLY RESPONDS, "THAN TO HAVE FOUND MINDS OF THEIR OWN. THE TROLLS TOOK THEIR FREEDOM, BUT AT WHAT COST--TO US!"
WELL, FRIEND TWO-EDGE--
YOU PLAYED YOUR GAME, HERE IN THE FROZEN MOUNTAIN, BUT NOW IT'S DONE!

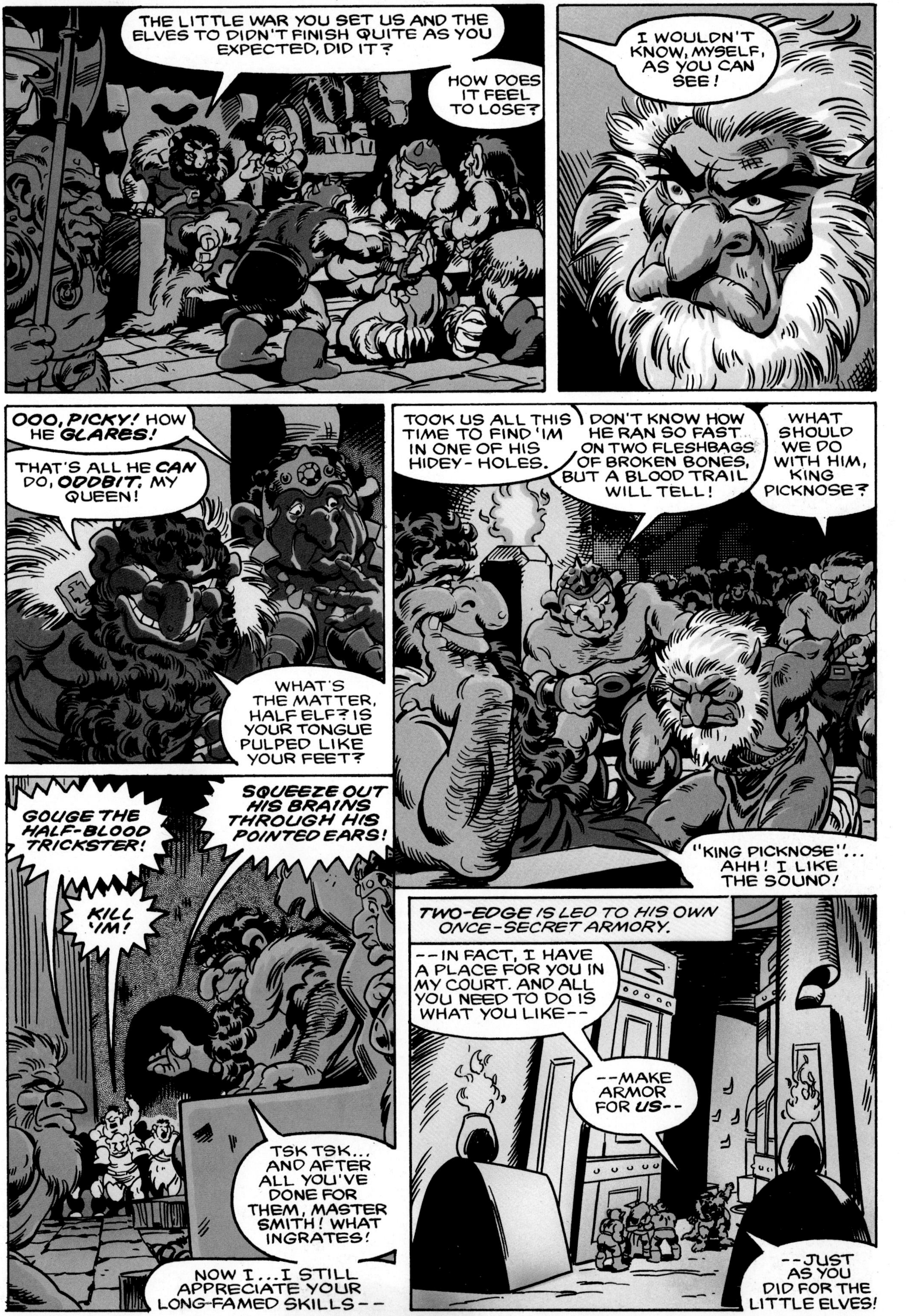

THE LITTLE WAR YOU SET US AND THE ELVES TO DIDN'T FINISH QUITE AS YOU EXPECTED, DID IT?
HOW DOES IT FEEL TO LOSE?
I WOULDN'T KNOW, MYSELF, AS YOU CAN SEE!
OOO, PICKY! HOW HE GLARES!
THAT'S ALL HE CAN DO, ODDBIT, MY QUEEN!
WHAT'S THE MATTER, HALF ELF? IS YOUR TONGUE PULPED LIKE YOUR FEET?
TOOK US ALL THIS TIME TO FIND 'IM IN ONE OF HIS HIDEY-HOLES.
DON'T KNOW HOW HE RAN SO FAST ON TWO FLESHBAGS OF BROKEN BONES, BUT A BLOOD TRAIL WILL TELL!
WHAT SHOULD WE DO WITH HIM, KING PICKNOSE?
"KING PICKNOSE"... AHH! I LIKE THE SOUND!
GOUGE THE HALF-BLOOD TRICKSTER!
SQUEEZE OUT HIS BRAINS THROUGH HIS POINTED EARS!
KILL 'IM!
TSK TSK... AND AFTER ALL YOU'VE DONE FOR THEM, MASTER SMITH! WHAT INGRATES!
NOW I... I STILL APPRECIATE YOUR LONG-FAMED SKILLS --
TWO-EDGE IS LED TO HIS OWN ONCE-SECRET ARMORY.
-- IN FACT, I HAVE A PLACE FOR YOU IN MY COURT. AND ALL YOU NEED TO DO IS WHAT YOU LIKE --
-- MAKE ARMOR FOR US --
-- JUST AS YOU DID FOR THE LITTLE ELVES!

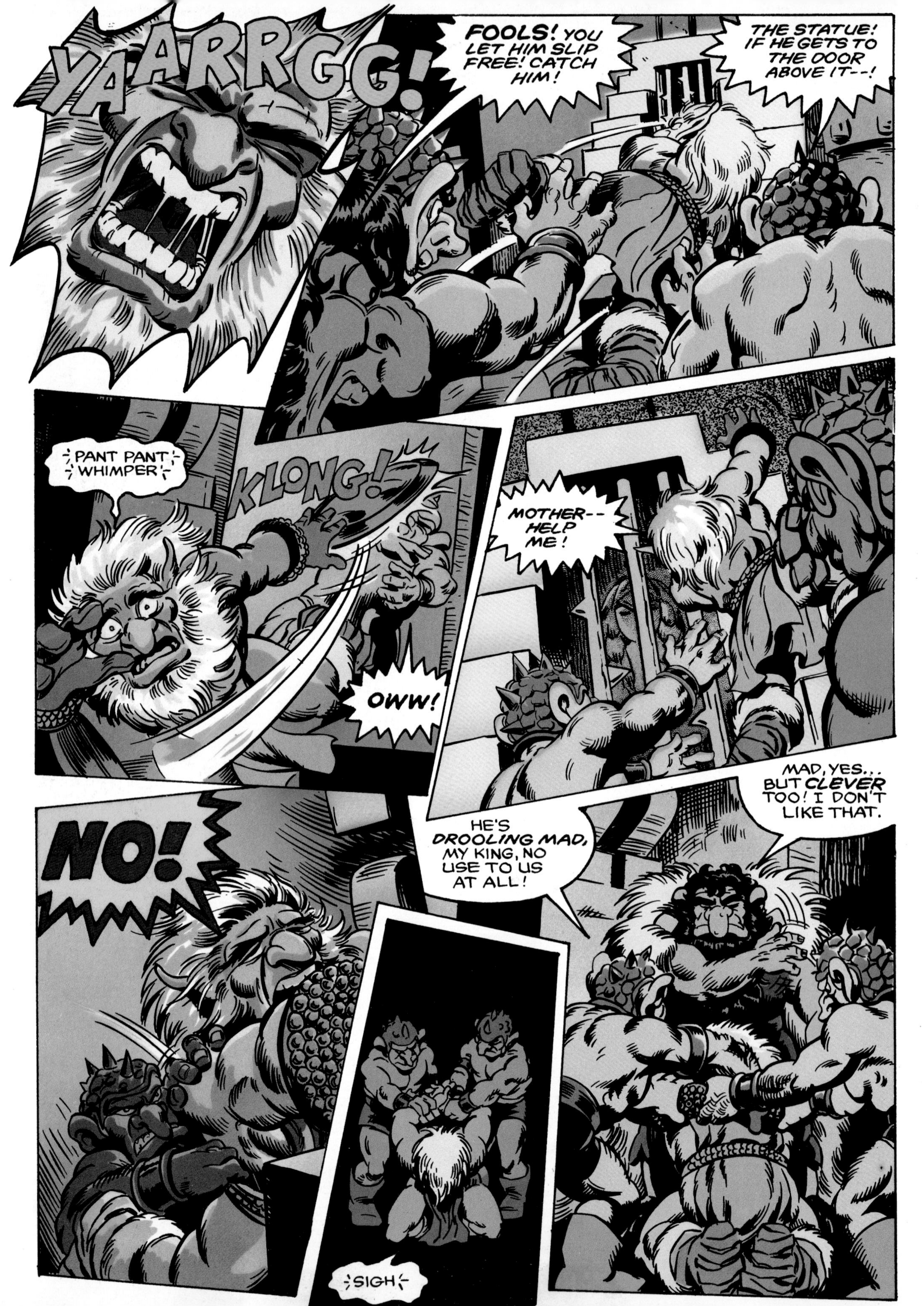
YAARRGG!
FOOLS! YOU LET HIM SLIP FREE! CATCH HIM!
THE STATUE! IF HE GETS TO THE DOOR ABOVE IT--!
PANT PANT WHIMPER
KLONG!
OWW!
MOTHER-- HELP ME!
NO!
HE'S DROOLING MAD, MY KING, NO USE TO US AT ALL!
MAD, YES... BUT CLEVER TOO! I DON'T LIKE THAT.
SIGH

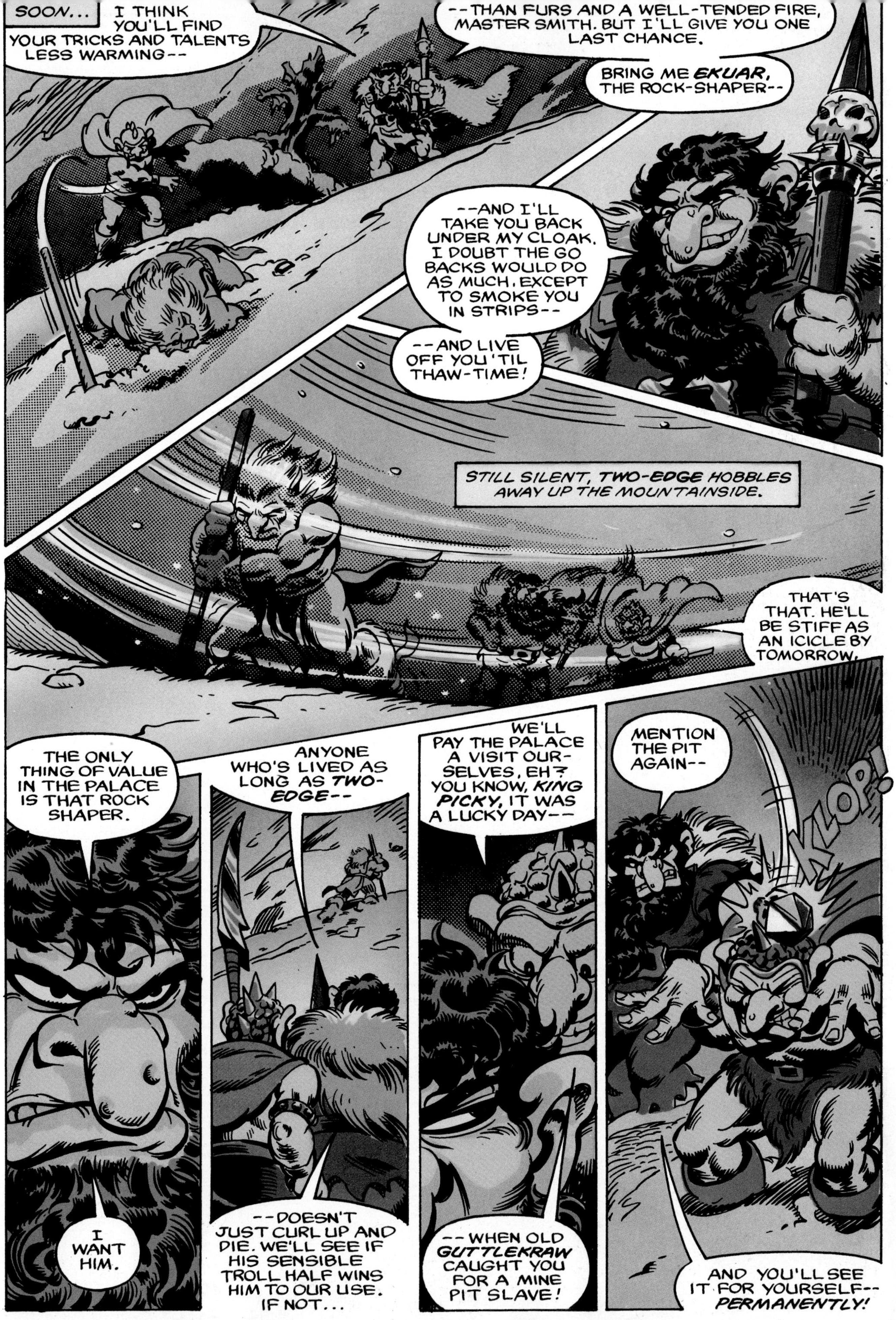
SOON...
I THINK YOU'LL FIND YOUR TRICKS AND TALENTS LESS WARMING--
--THAN FURS AND A WELL-TENDED FIRE, MASTER SMITH. BUT I'LL GIVE YOU ONE LAST CHANCE.
BRING ME EKUAR, THE ROCK-SHAPER--
--AND I'LL TAKE YOU BACK UNDER MY CLOAK. I DOUBT THE GO BACKS WOULD DO AS MUCH, EXCEPT TO SMOKE YOU IN STRIPS--
--AND LIVE OFF YOU 'TIL THAW-TIME!
STILL SILENT, TWO-EDGE HOBBLES AWAY UP THE MOUNTAINSIDE.
THAT'S THAT. HE'LL BE STIFF AS AN ICICLE BY TOMORROW.
THE ONLY THING OF VALUE IN THE PALACE IS THAT ROCK SHAPER.
I WANT HIM.
ANYONE WHO'S LIVED AS LONG AS TWO-EDGE--
--DOESN'T JUST CURL UP AND DIE. WE'LL SEE IF HIS SENSIBLE TROLL HALF WINS HIM TO OUR USE. IF NOT...
WE'LL PAY THE PALACE A VISIT OURSELVES, EH? YOU KNOW, KING PICKY, IT WAS A LUCKY DAY--
--WHEN OLD GUTTLEKRAW CAUGHT YOU FOR A MINE PIT SLAVE!
MENTION THE PIT AGAIN--
KLOP!
AND YOU'LL SEE IT FOR YOURSELF--PERMANENTLY!

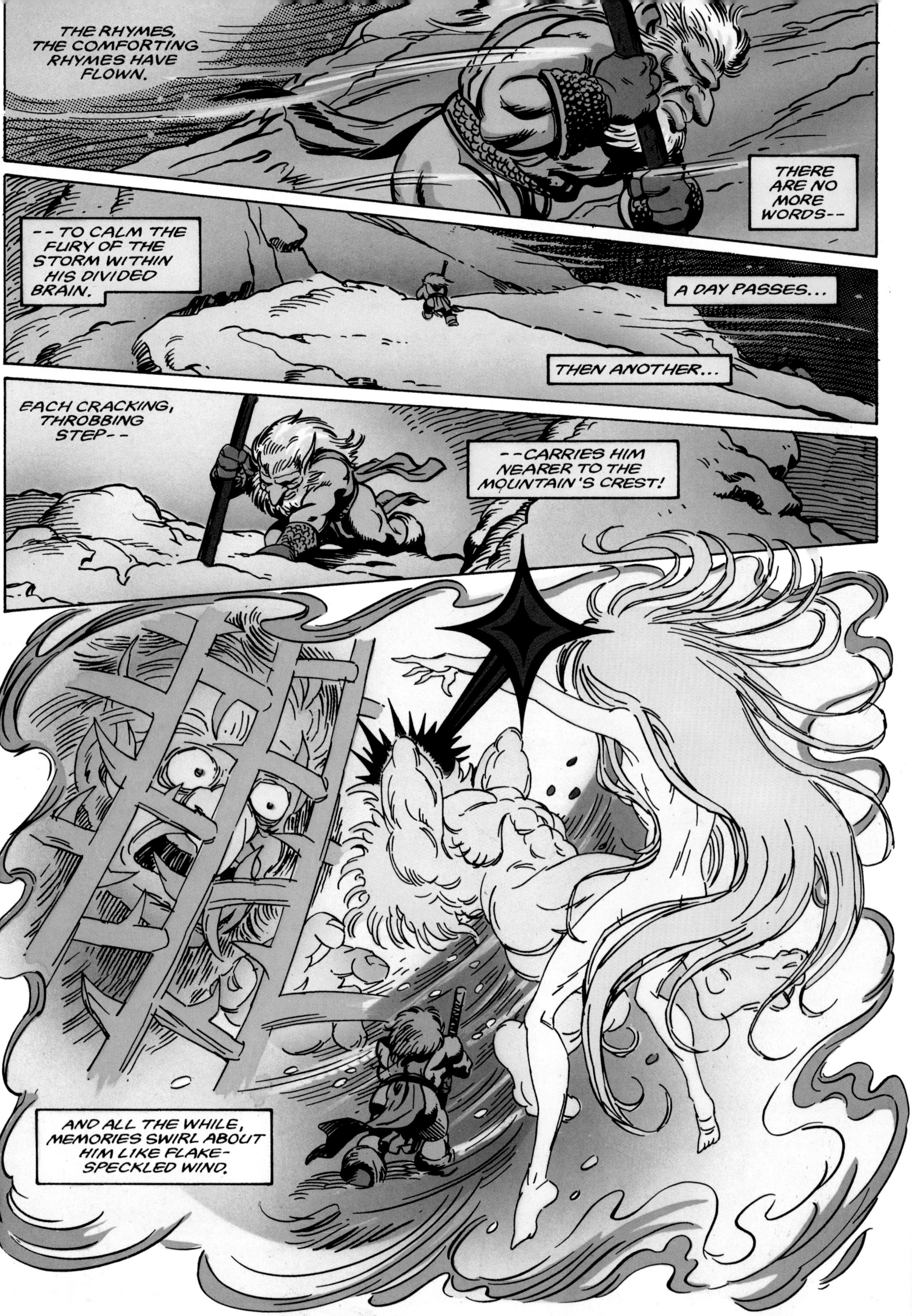
THE RHYMES, THE COMFORTING RHYMES HAVE FLOWN.
THERE ARE NO MORE WORDS--
--TO CALM THE FURY OF THE STORM WITHIN HIS DIVIDED BRAIN.
A DAY PASSES...
THEN ANOTHER...
EACH CRACKING, THROBBING STEP--
--CARRIES HIM NEARER TO THE MOUNTAIN'S CREST!
AND ALL THE WHILE, MEMORIES SWIRL ABOUT HIM LIKE FLAKE-SPECKLED WIND.

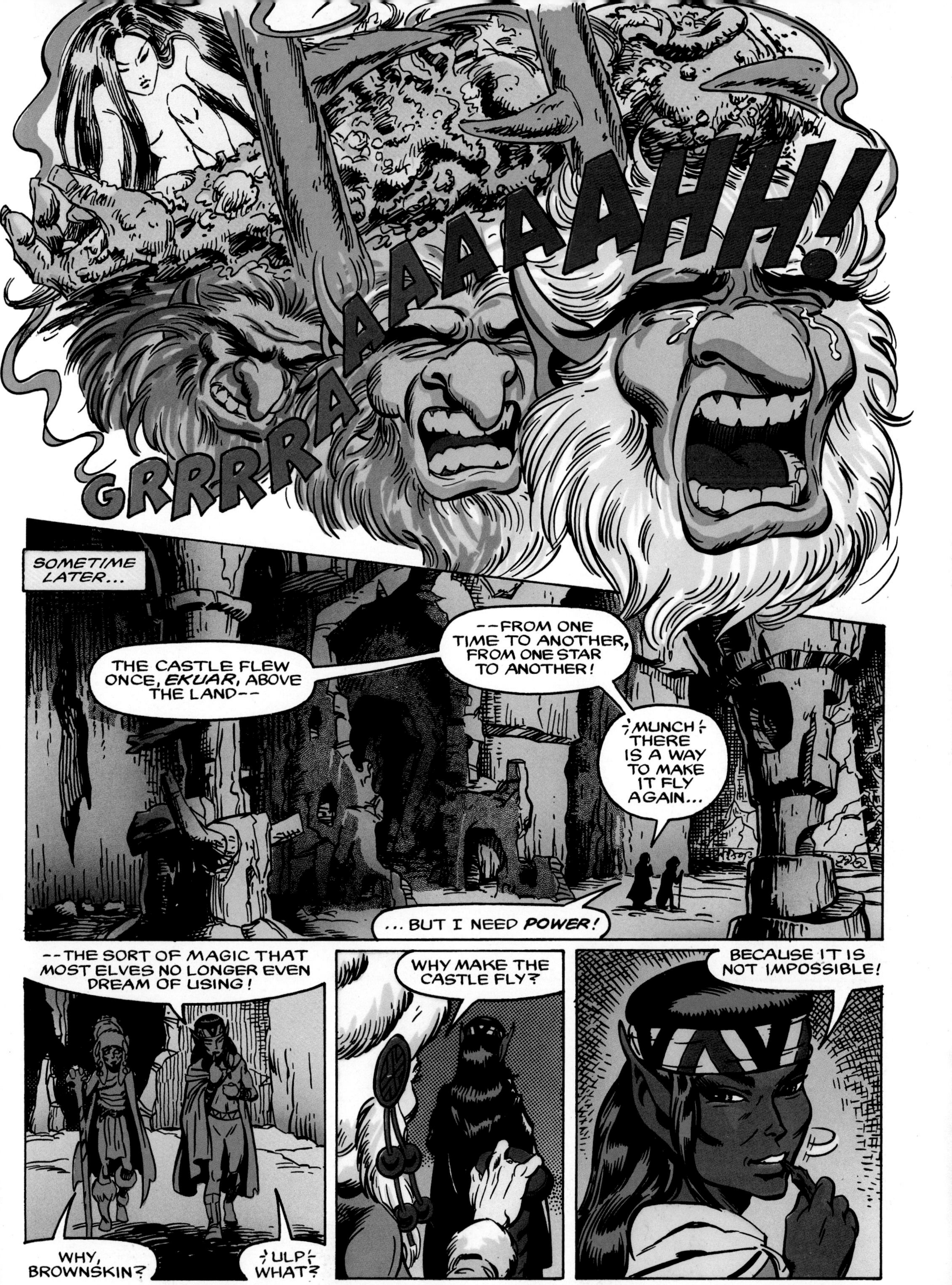

GRRRRAAAAAAAHH!!
SOMETIME LATER...
THE CASTLE FLEW ONCE, EKUAR, ABOVE THE LAND--
--FROM ONE TIME TO ANOTHER, FROM ONE STAR TO ANOTHER!
-MUNCH- THERE IS A WAY TO MAKE IT FLY AGAIN...
...BUT I NEED POWER!
--THE SORT OF MAGIC THAT MOST ELVES NO LONGER EVEN DREAM OF USING!
WHY, BROWNSKIN?
-ULP- WHAT?
WHY MAKE THE CASTLE FLY?
BECAUSE IT IS NOT IMPOSSIBLE!

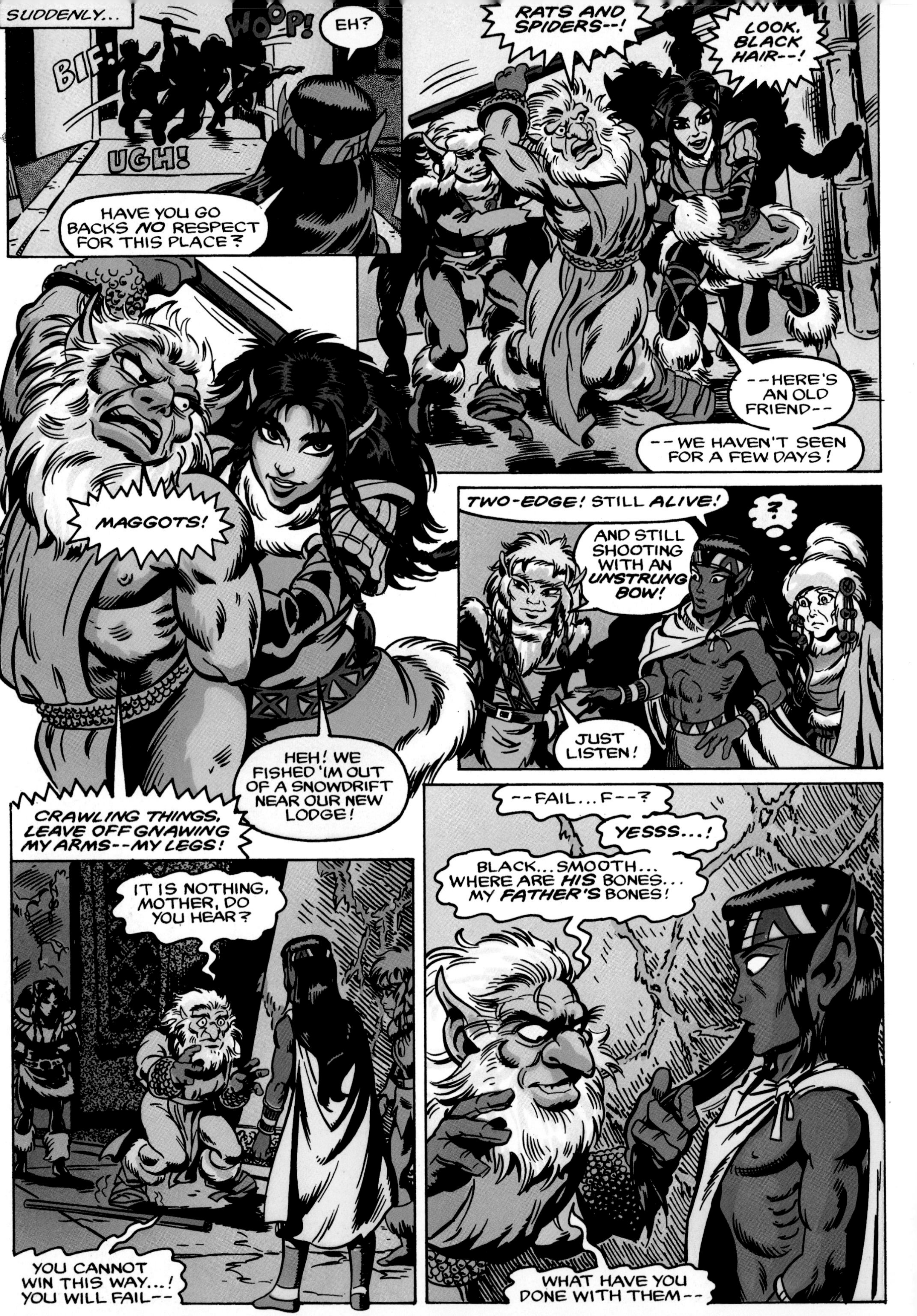

SUDDENLY...
BIF!
WOOP!
EH?
UGH!
HAVE YOU GO BACKS NO RESPECT FOR THIS PLACE?
RATS AND SPIDERS--!
LOOK, BLACK HAIR--!
--HERE'S AN OLD FRIEND--
--WE HAVEN'T SEEN FOR A FEW DAYS!
MAGGOTS!
HEH! WE FISHED 'IM OUT OF A SNOWDRIFT NEAR OUR NEW LODGE!
CRAWLING THINGS, LEAVE OFF GNAWING MY ARMS--MY LEGS!
TWO-EDGE! STILL ALIVE!
AND STILL SHOOTING WITH AN UNSTRUNG BOW!
?
JUST LISTEN!
IT IS NOTHING, MOTHER, DO YOU HEAR?
YOU CANNOT WIN THIS WAY...! YOU WILL FAIL--
--FAIL... F--?
YESSS...!
BLACK... SMOOTH... WHERE ARE HIS BONES... MY FATHER'S BONES!
WHAT HAVE YOU DONE WITH THEM--

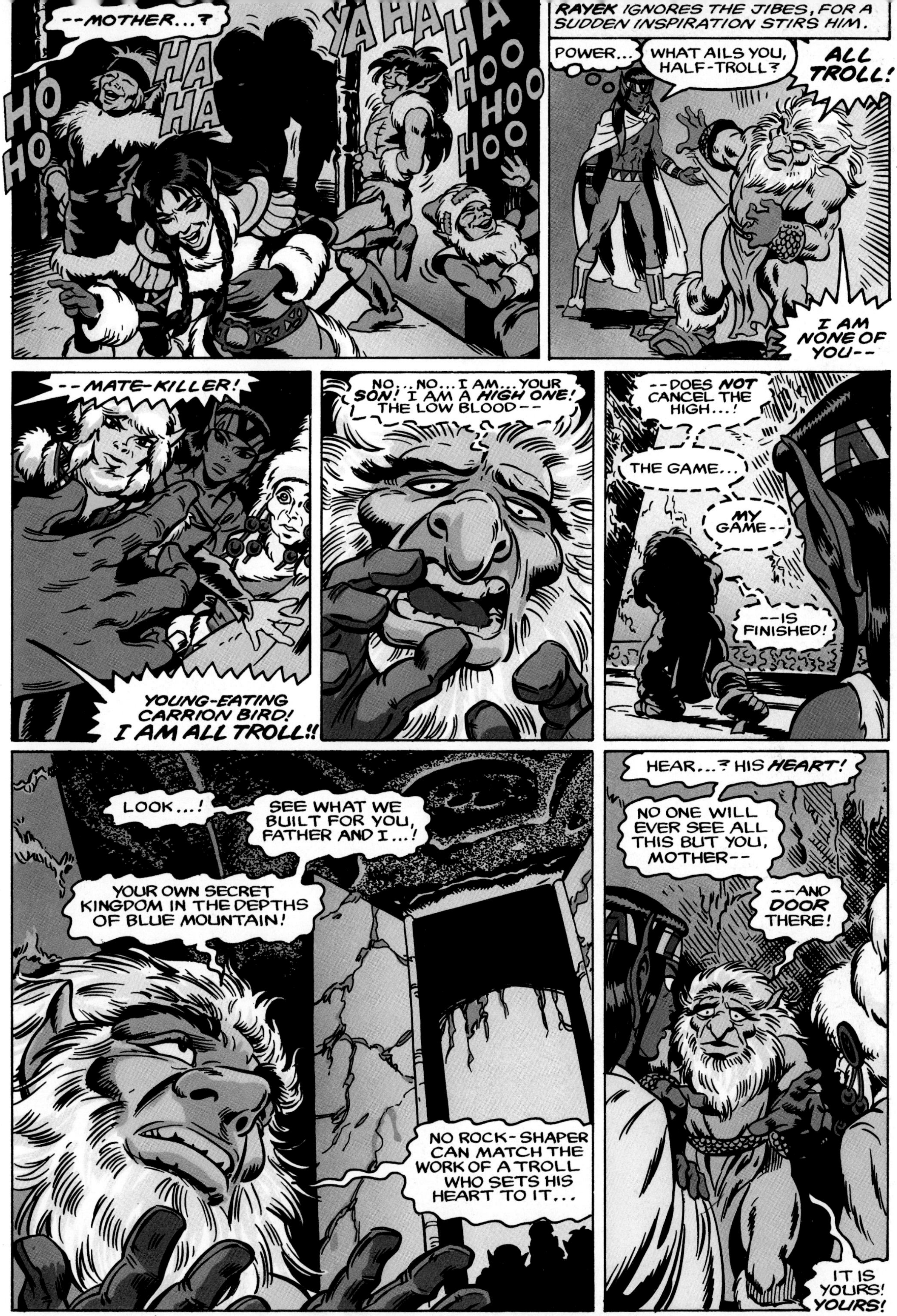
--MOTHER...?
HO HO
HA HA
YA HA HA HA
HOO HOO HOO HOO
RAYEK IGNORES THE JIBES, FOR A SUDDEN INSPIRATION STIRS HIM.
POWER...
WHAT AILS YOU, HALF-TROLL?
ALL TROLL!
I AM NONE OF YOU--
--MATE-KILLER!
YOUNG-EATING CARRION BIRD! I AM ALL TROLL!!
NO...NO...I AM...YOUR SON! I AM A HIGH ONE! THE LOW BLOOD--
--DOES NOT CANCEL THE HIGH...!
THE GAME...
MY GAME--
--IS FINISHED!
LOOK...!
SEE WHAT WE BUILT FOR YOU, FATHER AND I...!
YOUR OWN SECRET KINGDOM IN THE DEPTHS OF BLUE MOUNTAIN!
NO ROCK-SHAPER CAN MATCH THE WORK OF A TROLL WHO SETS HIS HEART TO IT...
HEAR...? HIS HEART!
NO ONE WILL EVER SEE ALL THIS BUT YOU, MOTHER--
--AND DOOR THERE!
IT IS YOURS! YOURS!

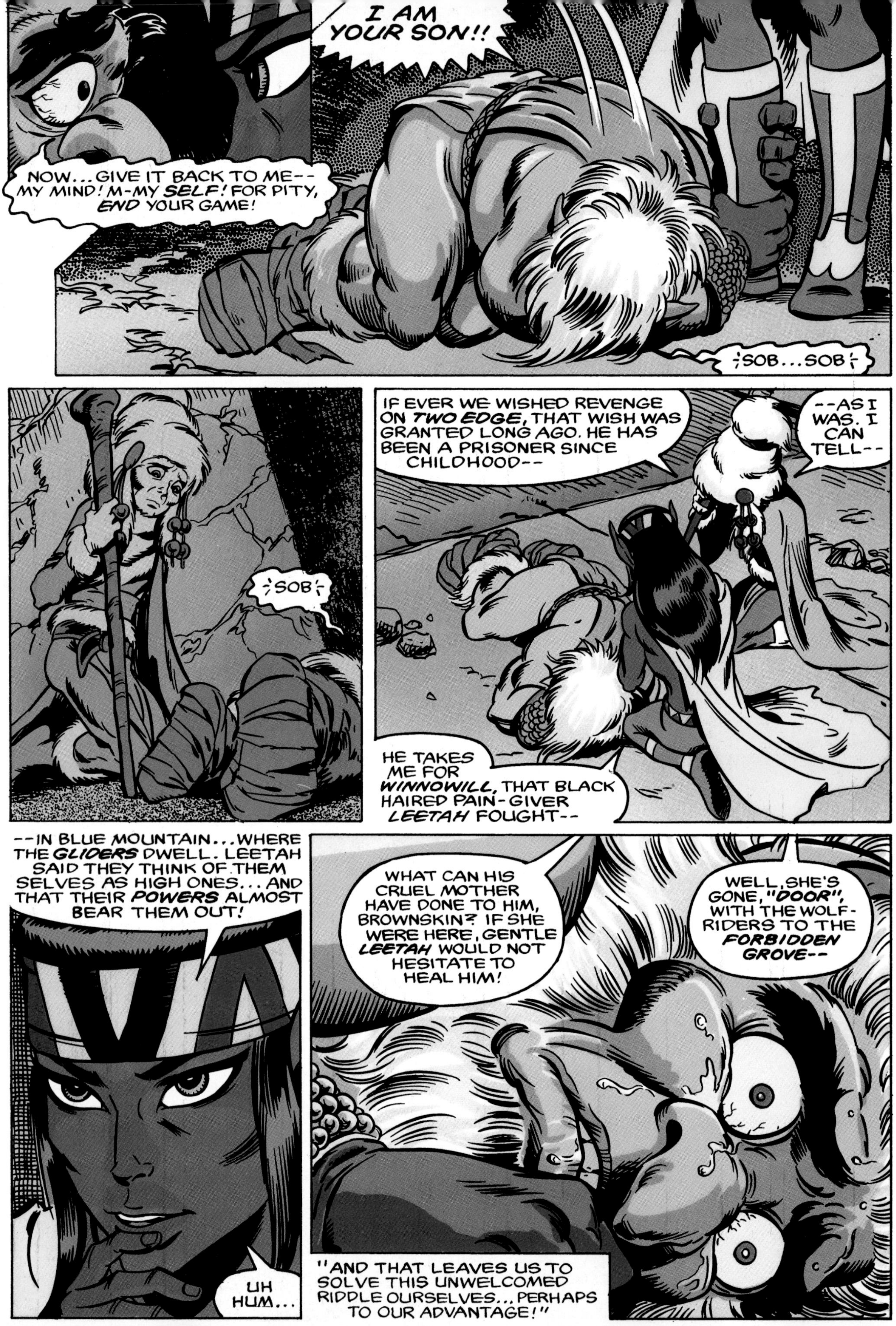
I AM YOUR SON!!
NOW... GIVE IT BACK TO ME-- MY MIND! M-MY SELF! FOR PITY, END YOUR GAME!
SOB... SOB
SOB
IF EVER WE WISHED REVENGE ON TWO EDGE, THAT WISH WAS GRANTED LONG AGO. HE HAS BEEN A PRISONER SINCE CHILDHOOD--
--AS I WAS. I CAN TELL--
HE TAKES ME FOR WINNOWILL, THAT BLACK HAIRED PAIN-GIVER LEETAH FOUGHT--
--IN BLUE MOUNTAIN... WHERE THE GLIDERS DWELL. LEETAH SAID THEY THINK OF THEM SELVES AS HIGH ONES... AND THAT THEIR POWERS ALMOST BEAR THEM OUT!
UH HUM...
WHAT CAN HIS CRUEL MOTHER HAVE DONE TO HIM, BROWNSKIN? IF SHE WERE HERE, GENTLE LEETAH WOULD NOT HESITATE TO HEAL HIM!
WELL, SHE'S GONE, "DOOR", WITH THE WOLF-RIDERS TO THE FORBIDDEN GROVE--
"AND THAT LEAVES US TO SOLVE THIS UNWELCOMED RIDDLE OURSELVES... PERHAPS TO OUR ADVANTAGE!"

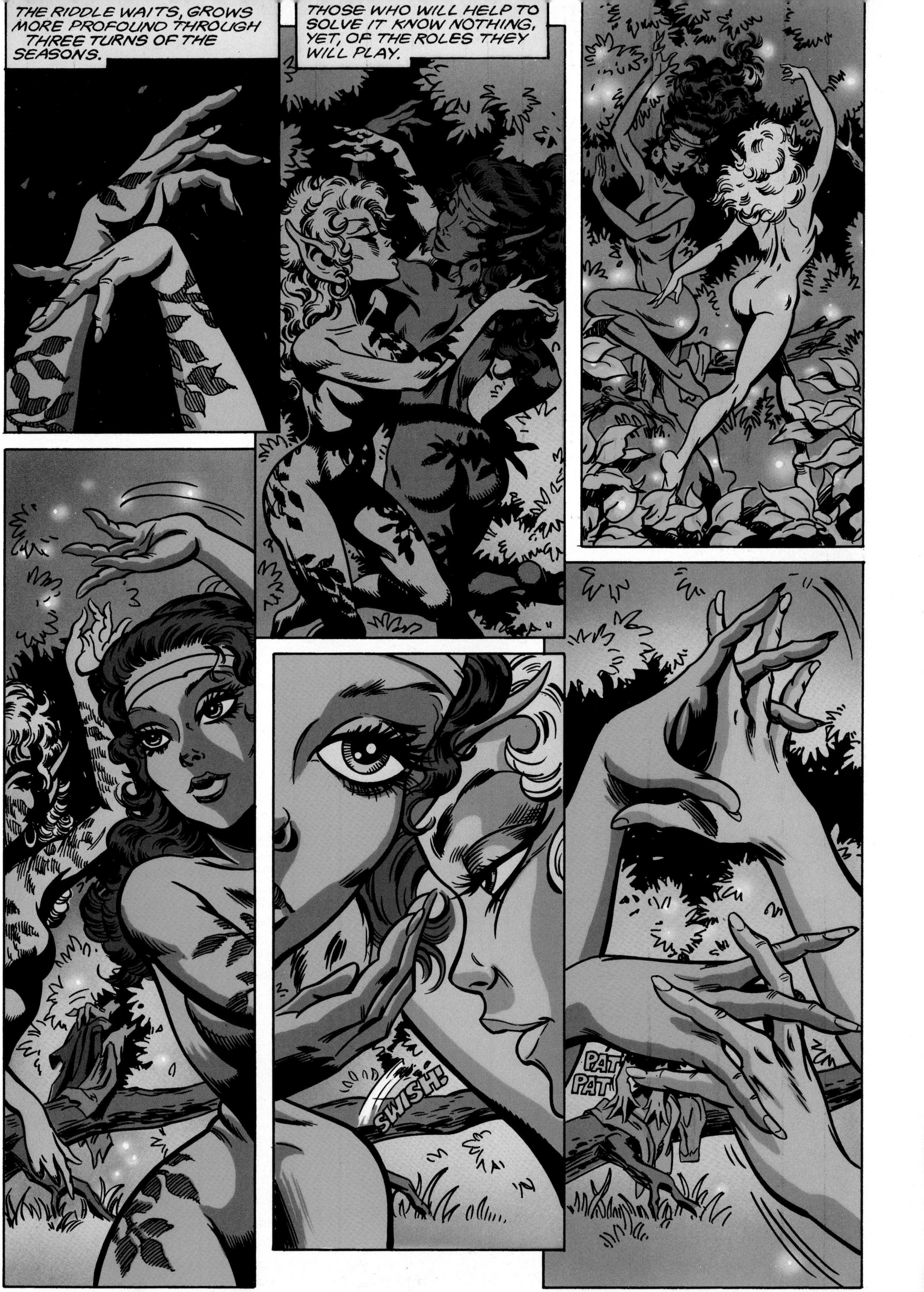
THE RIDDLE WAITS, GROWS MORE PROFOUND THROUGH THREE TURNS OF THE SEASONS.
THOSE WHO WILL HELP TO SOLVE IT KNOW NOTHING, YET, OF THE ROLES THEY WILL PLAY.
SWISH!
PAT PAT

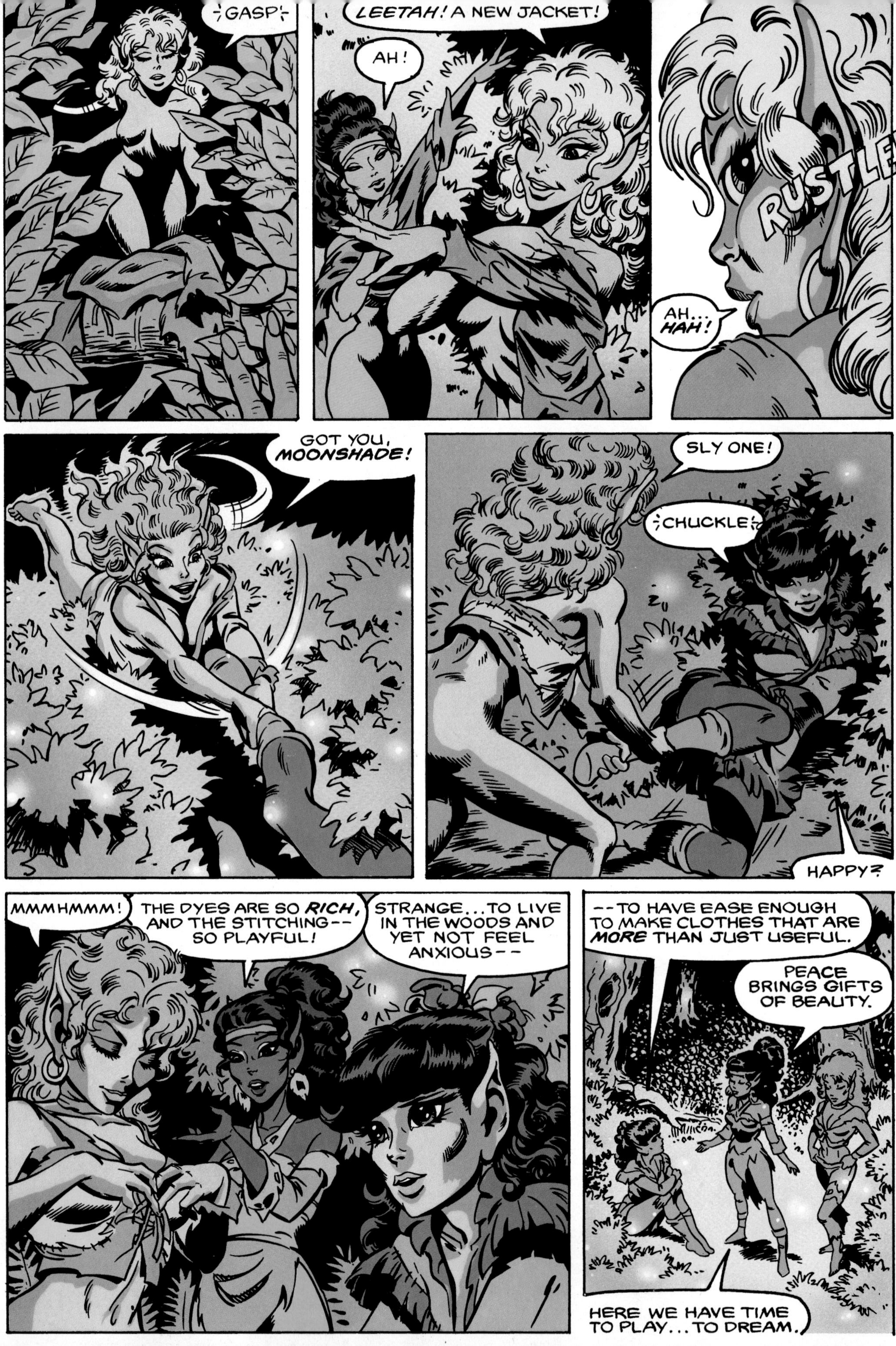

GASP
LEETAH! A NEW JACKET!
AH!
RUSTLE!
AH... HAH!
GOT YOU, MOONSHADE!
SLY ONE!
CHUCKLE
HAPPY?
MMMHMMM!
THE DYES ARE SO RICH, AND THE STITCHING-- SO PLAYFUL!
STRANGE...TO LIVE IN THE WOODS AND YET NOT FEEL ANXIOUS--
--TO HAVE EASE ENOUGH TO MAKE CLOTHES THAT ARE MORE THAN JUST USEFUL.
PEACE BRINGS GIFTS OF BEAUTY.
HERE WE HAVE TIME TO PLAY...TO DREAM.

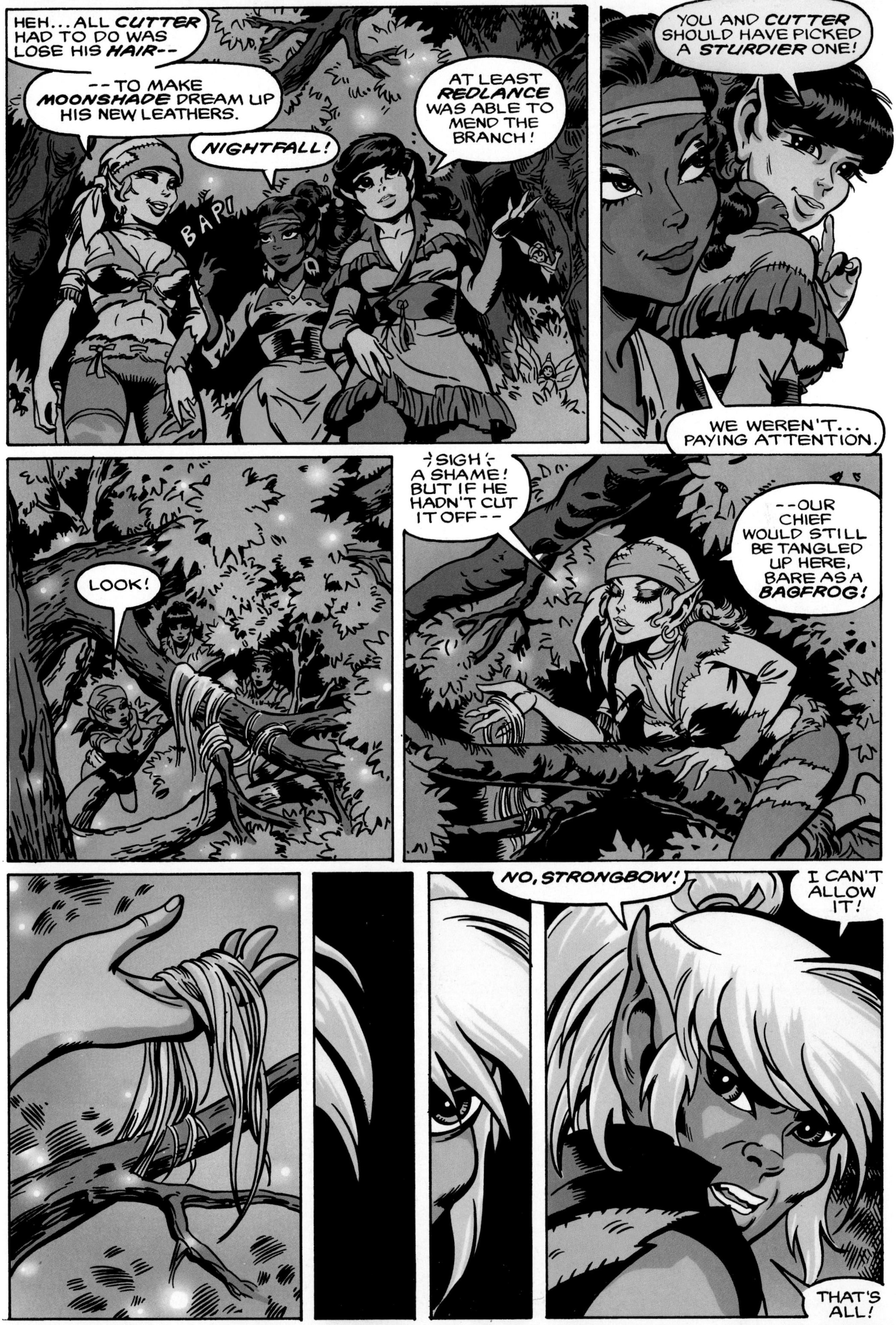

HEH... ALL CUTTER HAD TO DO WAS LOSE HIS HAIR--
--TO MAKE MOONSHADE DREAM UP HIS NEW LEATHERS.
NIGHTFALL!
BAP!
AT LEAST REDLANCE WAS ABLE TO MEND THE BRANCH!
YOU AND CUTTER SHOULD HAVE PICKED A STURDIER ONE!
WE WEREN'T... PAYING ATTENTION.
LOOK!
-SIGH- A SHAME! BUT IF HE HADN'T CUT IT OFF--
--OUR CHIEF WOULD STILL BE TANGLED UP HERE, BARE AS A BAGFROG!
NO, STRONGBOW!
I CAN'T ALLOW IT!
THAT'S ALL!

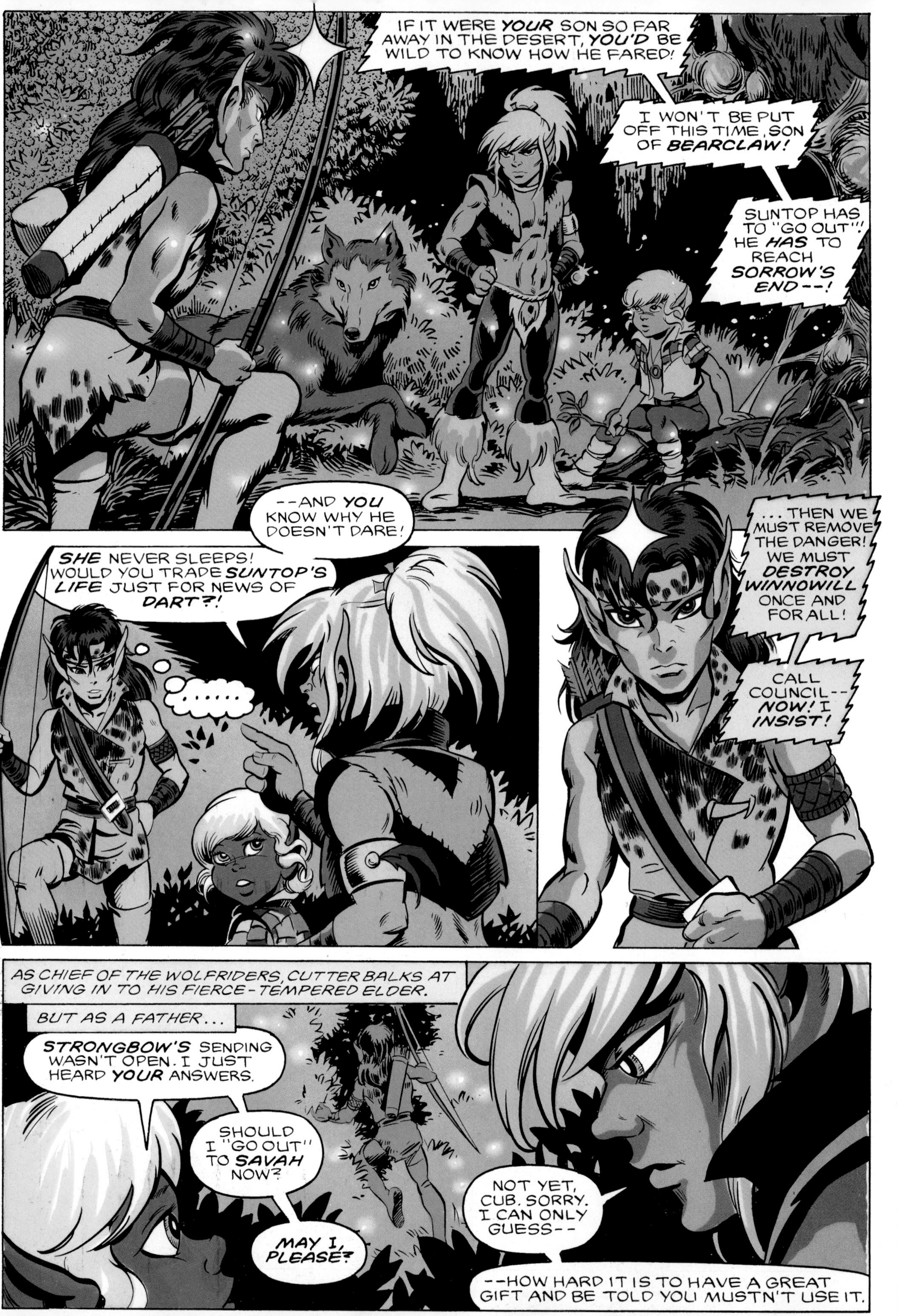
IF IT WERE YOUR SON SO FAR AWAY IN THE DESERT, YOU'D BE WILD TO KNOW HOW HE FARED!
I WON'T BE PUT OFF THIS TIME, SON OF BEARCLAW!
SUNTOP HAS TO "GO OUT"! HE HAS TO REACH SORROW'S END--!
--AND YOU KNOW WHY HE DOESN'T DARE!
SHE NEVER SLEEPS! WOULD YOU TRADE SUNTOP'S LIFE JUST FOR NEWS OF DART?!
......
...THEN WE MUST REMOVE THE DANGER! WE MUST DESTROY WINNOWILL ONCE AND FOR ALL!
CALL COUNCIL--NOW! I INSIST!
AS CHIEF OF THE WOLFRIDERS, CUTTER BALKS AT GIVING IN TO HIS FIERCE-TEMPERED ELDER.
BUT AS A FATHER...
STRONGBOW'S SENDING WASN'T OPEN. I JUST HEARD YOUR ANSWERS.
SHOULD I "GO OUT" TO SAVAH NOW?
MAY I, PLEASE?
NOT YET, CUB. SORRY. I CAN ONLY GUESS--
--HOW HARD IT IS TO HAVE A GREAT GIFT AND BE TOLD YOU MUSTN'T USE IT.

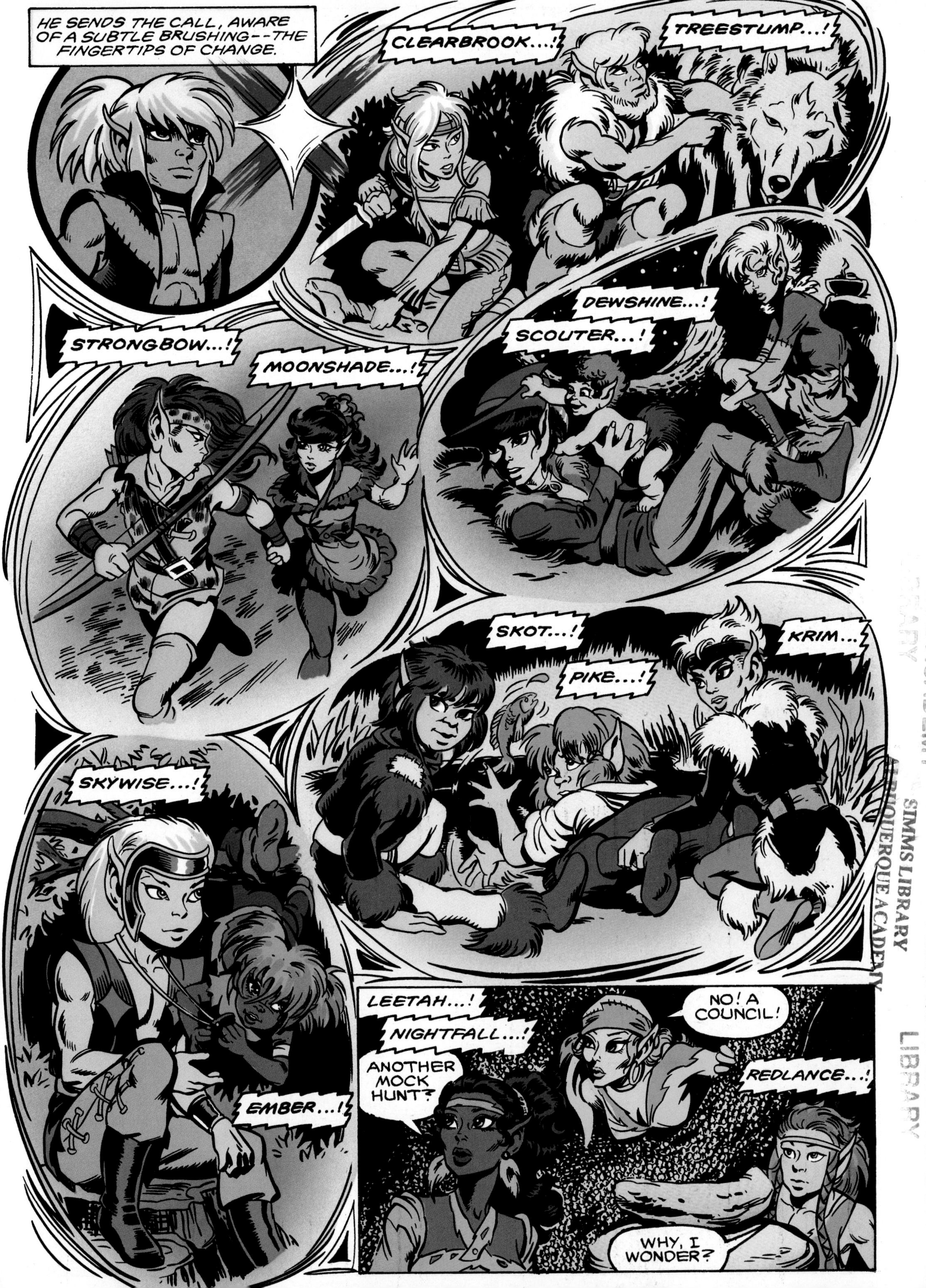
HE SENDS THE CALL, AWARE OF A SUBTLE BRUSHING--THE FINGERTIPS OF CHANGE.
CLEARBROOK...!
TREESTUMP...!
DEWSHINE...!
SCOUTER...!
STRONGBOW...!
MOONSHADE...!
SKOT...!
PIKE...!
KRIM...
SKYWISE...!
EMBER...!
LEETAH...!
NIGHTFALL...!
ANOTHER MOCK HUNT?
NO! A COUNCIL!
REDLANCE...!
WHY, I WONDER?

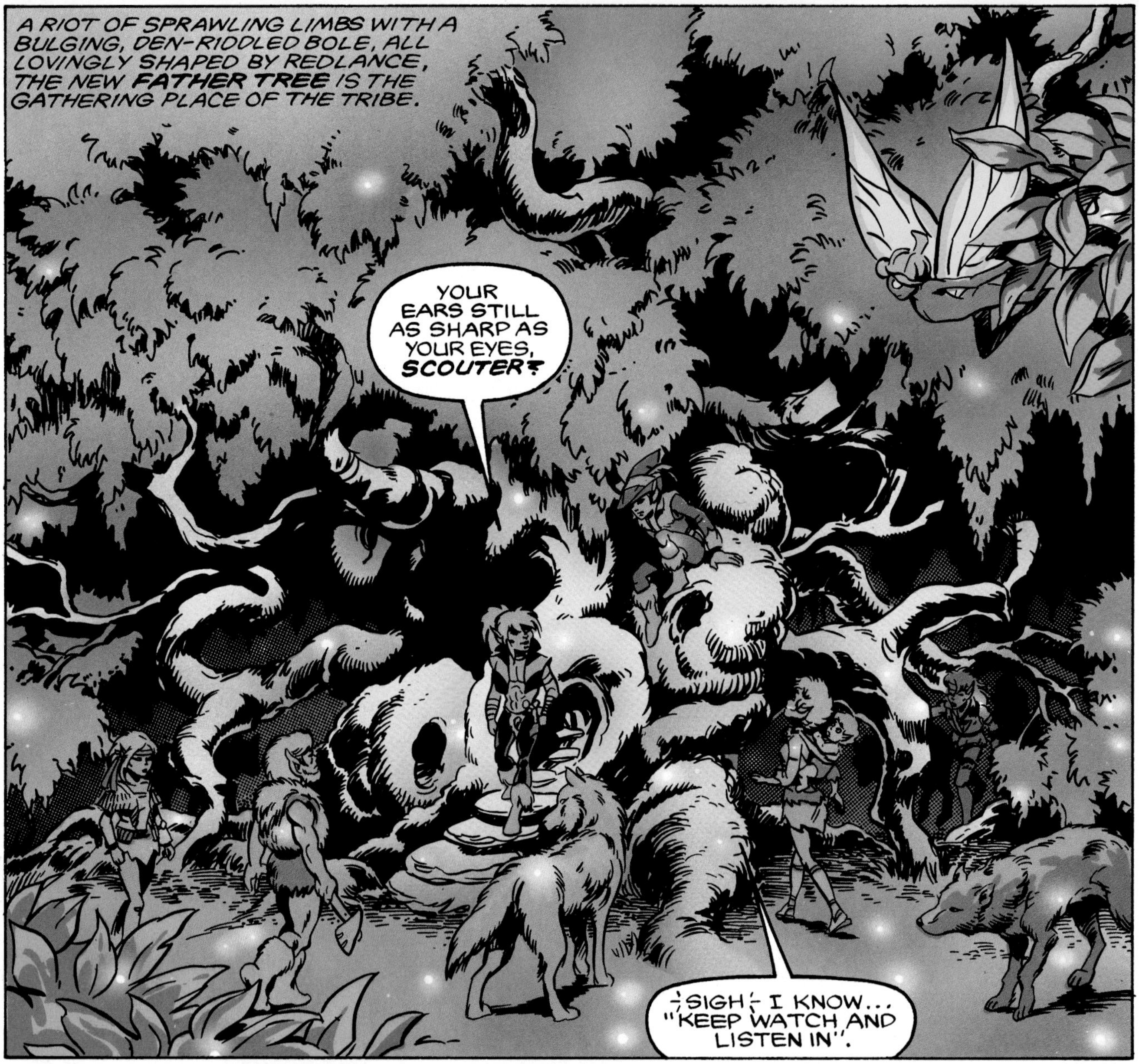
A RIOT OF SPRAWLING LIMBS WITH A BULGING, DEN-RIDDLED BOLE, ALL LOVINGLY SHAPED BY REDLANCE, THE NEW FATHER TREE IS THE GATHERING PLACE OF THE TRIBE.
YOUR EARS STILL AS SHARP AS YOUR EYES, SCOUTER?
-SIGH- I KNOW... "KEEP WATCH AND LISTEN IN".

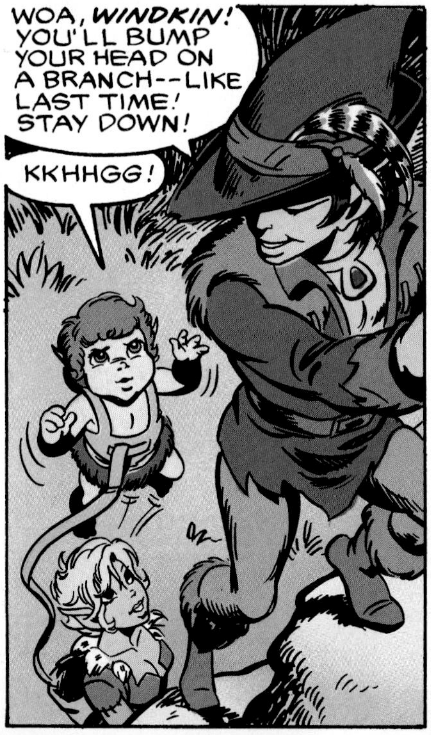
WOA, WINDKIN! YOU'LL BUMP YOUR HEAD ON A BRANCH--LIKE LAST TIME! STAY DOWN!
KKHHGG!

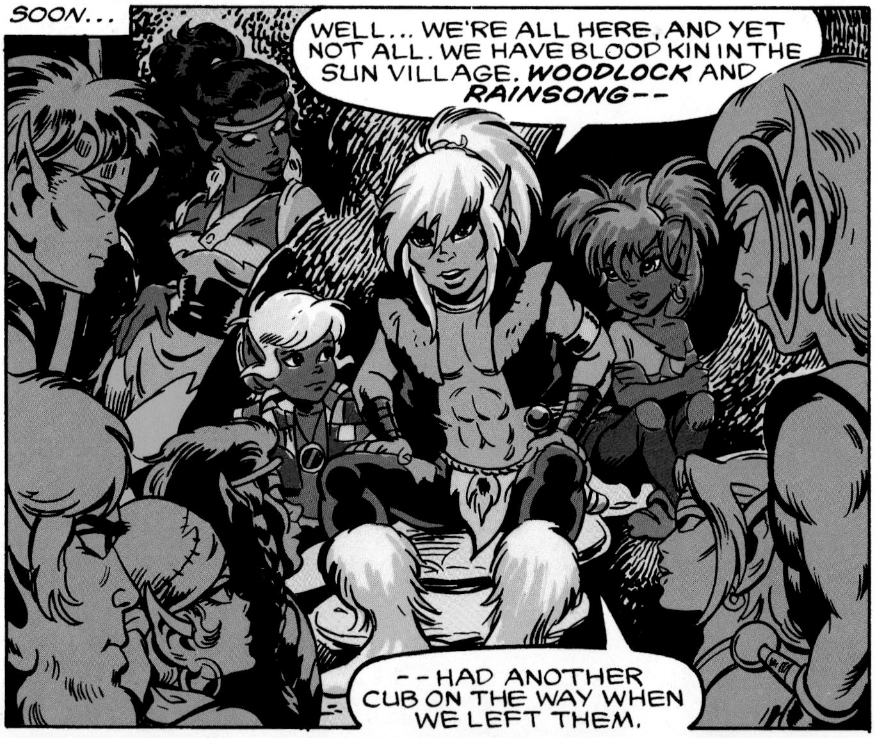
SOON...
WELL... WE'RE ALL HERE, AND YET NOT ALL. WE HAVE BLOOD KIN IN THE SUN VILLAGE. WOODLOCK AND RAINSONG--
--HAD ANOTHER CUB ON THE WAY WHEN WE LEFT THEM.

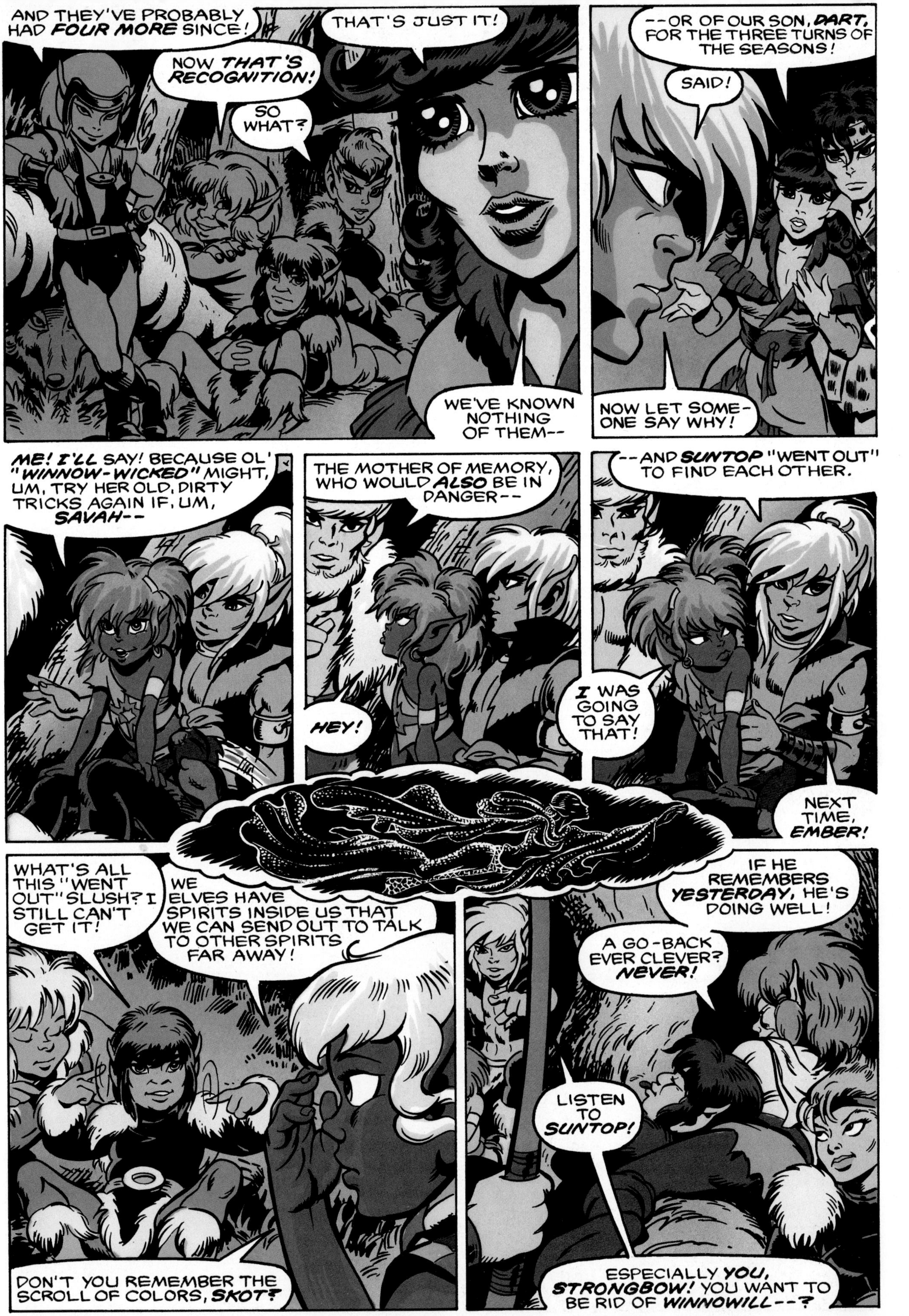
AND THEY'VE PROBABLY HAD FOUR MORE SINCE!
NOW THAT'S RECOGNITION!
SO WHAT?
THAT'S JUST IT!
WE'VE KNOWN NOTHING OF THEM--
--OR OF OUR SON, DART, FOR THE THREE TURNS OF THE SEASONS!
SAID!
NOW LET SOME-ONE SAY WHY!
ME! I'LL SAY! BECAUSE OL' "WINNOW-WICKED" MIGHT, UM, TRY HER OLD, DIRTY TRICKS AGAIN IF, UM, SAVAH--
THE MOTHER OF MEMORY, WHO WOULD ALSO BE IN DANGER--
HEY!
--AND SUNTOP "WENT OUT" TO FIND EACH OTHER.
I WAS GOING TO SAY THAT!
NEXT TIME, EMBER!
WHAT'S ALL THIS "WENT OUT" SLUSH? I STILL CAN'T GET IT!
WE ELVES HAVE SPIRITS INSIDE US THAT WE CAN SEND OUT TO TALK TO OTHER SPIRITS FAR AWAY!
DON'T YOU REMEMBER THE SCROLL OF COLORS, SKOT?
IF HE REMEMBERS YESTERDAY, HE'S DOING WELL!
A GO-BACK EVER CLEVER? NEVER!
LISTEN TO SUNTOP!
ESPECIALLY YOU, STRONGBOW! YOU WANT TO BE RID OF WINNOWILL--?

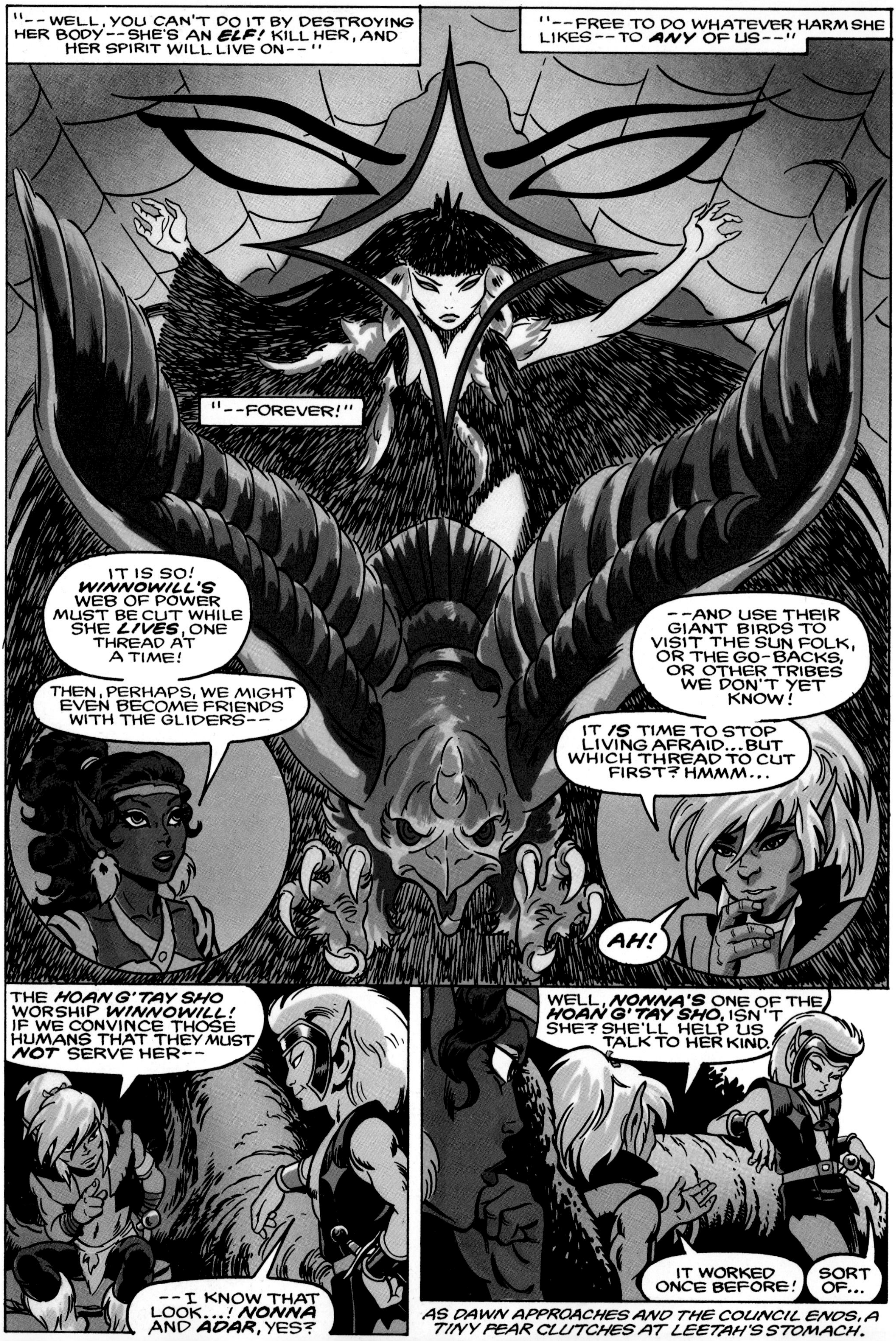
"--WELL, YOU CAN'T DO IT BY DESTROYING HER BODY--SHE'S AN *ELF!* KILL HER, AND HER SPIRIT WILL LIVE ON--"
"--FREE TO DO WHATEVER HARM SHE LIKES--TO *ANY* OF US--"
"--FOREVER!"
IT IS SO! *WINNOWILL'S* WEB OF POWER MUST BE CUT WHILE SHE *LIVES*, ONE THREAD AT A TIME!
THEN, PERHAPS, WE MIGHT EVEN BECOME FRIENDS WITH THE GLIDERS--
--AND USE THEIR GIANT BIRDS TO VISIT THE SUN FOLK, OR THE GO-BACKS, OR OTHER TRIBES WE DON'T YET KNOW!
IT *IS* TIME TO STOP LIVING AFRAID...BUT WHICH THREAD TO CUT FIRST? HMMM...
AH!
THE *HOAN G'TAY SHO* WORSHIP *WINNOWILL!* IF WE CONVINCE THOSE HUMANS THAT THEY MUST *NOT* SERVE HER--
--I KNOW THAT LOOK...! *NONNA* AND *ADAR*, YES?
WELL, *NONNA'S* ONE OF THE *HOAN G'TAY SHO*, ISN'T SHE? SHE'LL HELP US TALK TO HER KIND.
IT WORKED ONCE BEFORE!
SORT OF...
AS DAWN APPROACHES AND THE COUNCIL ENDS, A TINY FEAR CLUTCHES AT LEETAH'S STOMACH.

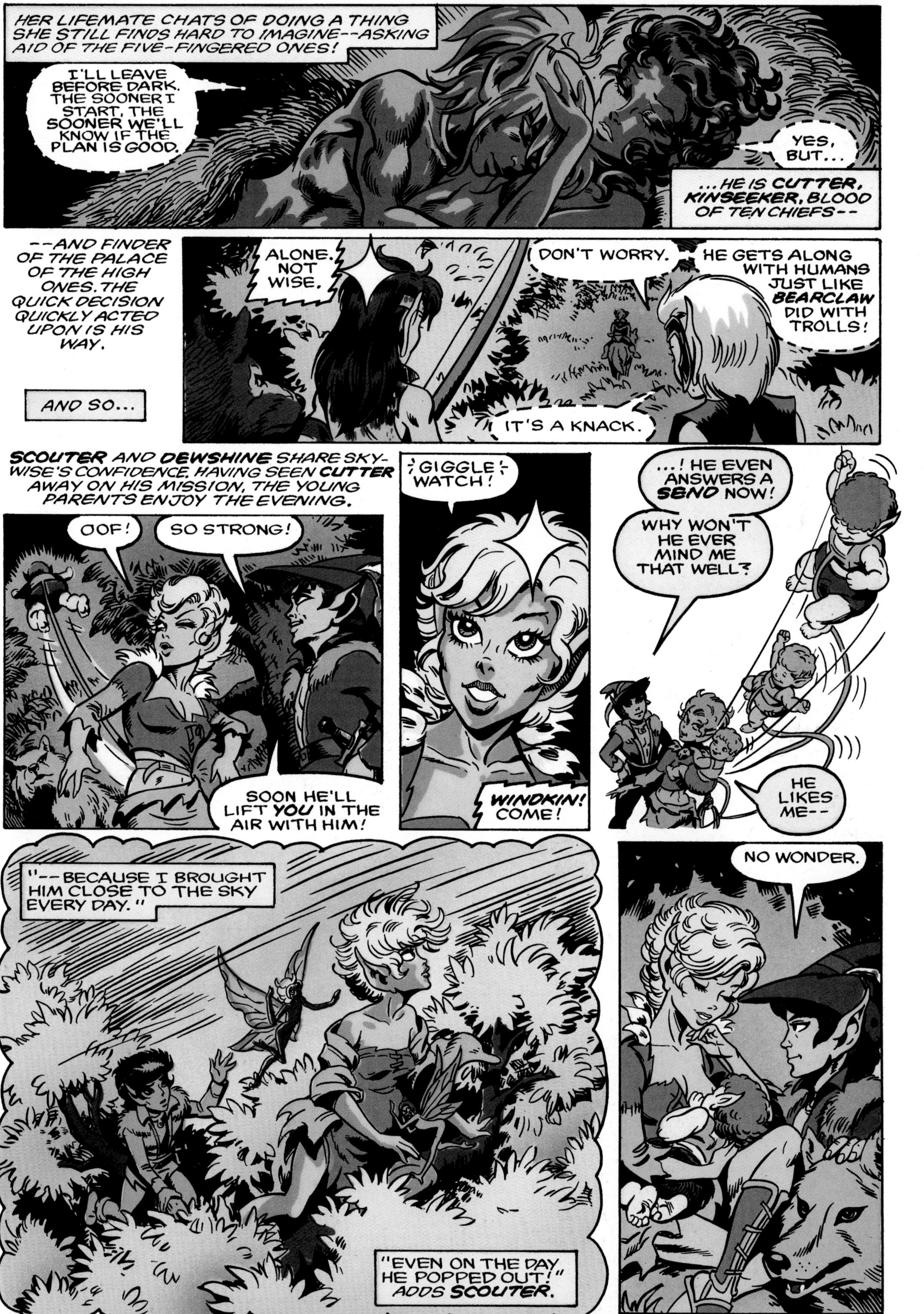
HER LIFEMATE CHATS OF DOING A THING SHE STILL FINDS HARD TO IMAGINE--ASKING AID OF THE FIVE-FINGERED ONES!
I'LL LEAVE BEFORE DARK. THE SOONER I START, THE SOONER WE'LL KNOW IF THE PLAN IS GOOD.
YES, BUT...
...HE IS CUTTER, KINSEEKER, BLOOD OF TEN CHIEFS--
--AND FINDER OF THE PALACE OF THE HIGH ONES. THE QUICK DECISION QUICKLY ACTED UPON IS HIS WAY.
AND SO...
ALONE. NOT WISE.
DON'T WORRY.
HE GETS ALONG WITH HUMANS JUST LIKE BEARCLAW DID WITH TROLLS!
IT'S A KNACK.
SCOUTER AND DEWSHINE SHARE SKYWISE'S CONFIDENCE. HAVING SEEN CUTTER AWAY ON HIS MISSION, THE YOUNG PARENTS ENJOY THE EVENING.
OOF!
SO STRONG!
SOON HE'LL LIFT YOU IN THE AIR WITH HIM!
GIGGLE WATCH!
WINDKIN! COME!
...! HE EVEN ANSWERS A SEND NOW!
WHY WON'T HE EVER MIND ME THAT WELL?
HE LIKES ME--
"--BECAUSE I BROUGHT HIM CLOSE TO THE SKY EVERY DAY."
"EVEN ON THE DAY HE POPPED OUT!" ADDS SCOUTER.
NO WONDER.

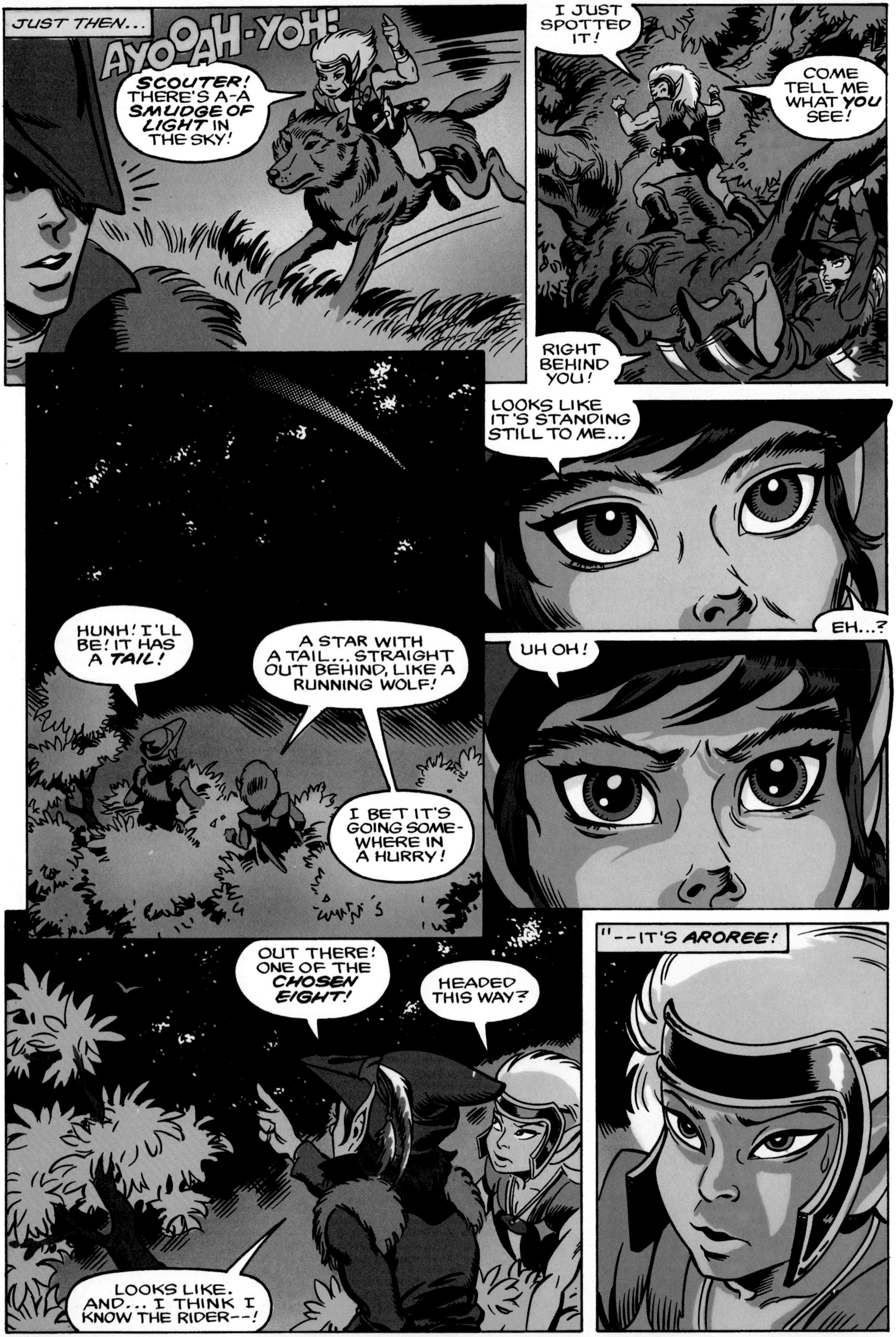
JUST THEN...
AYOOAH-YOH!
SCOUTER! THERE'S A-A SMUDGE OF LIGHT IN THE SKY!
I JUST SPOTTED IT!
COME TELL ME WHAT YOU SEE!
RIGHT BEHIND YOU!
LOOKS LIKE IT'S STANDING STILL TO ME...
EH...?
HUNH! I'LL BE! IT HAS A TAIL!
A STAR WITH A TAIL... STRAIGHT OUT BEHIND, LIKE A RUNNING WOLF!
I BET IT'S GOING SOMEWHERE IN A HURRY!
UH OH!
OUT THERE! ONE OF THE CHOSEN EIGHT!
HEADED THIS WAY?
LOOKS LIKE. AND... I THINK I KNOW THE RIDER--!
"--IT'S AROREE!

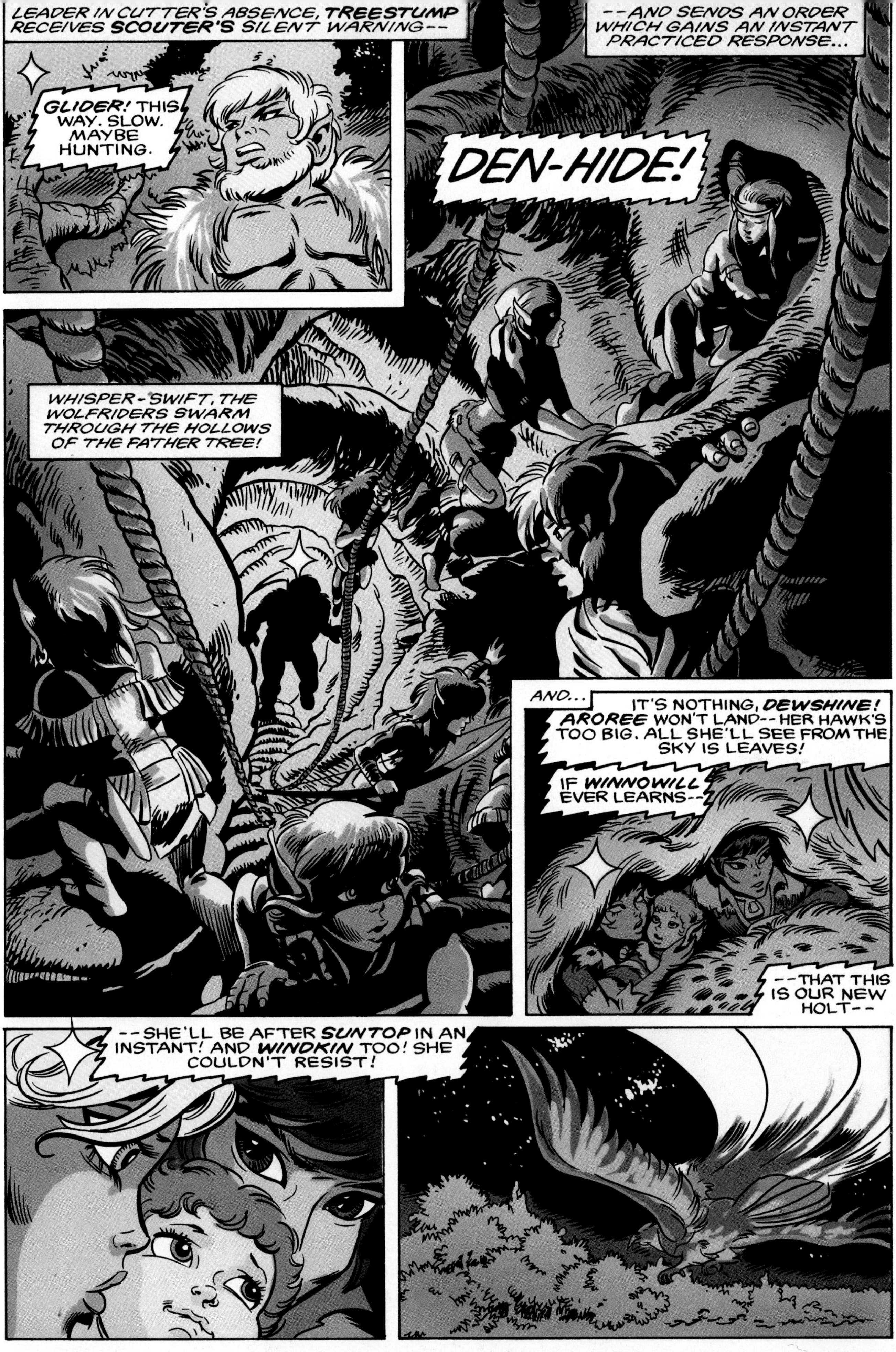
LEADER IN CUTTER'S ABSENCE, TREESTUMP RECEIVES SCOUTER'S SILENT WARNING--
GLIDER! THIS WAY. SLOW. MAYBE HUNTING.
--AND SENDS AN ORDER WHICH GAINS AN INSTANT PRACTICED RESPONSE...
DEN-HIDE!
WHISPER-SWIFT, THE WOLFRIDERS SWARM THROUGH THE HOLLOWS OF THE FATHER TREE!
AND...
IT'S NOTHING, DEWSHINE! AROREE WON'T LAND--HER HAWK'S TOO BIG. ALL SHE'LL SEE FROM THE SKY IS LEAVES!
IF WINNOWILL EVER LEARNS--
--THAT THIS IS OUR NEW HOLT--
--SHE'LL BE AFTER SUNTOP IN AN INSTANT! AND WINDKIN TOO! SHE COULDN'T RESIST!

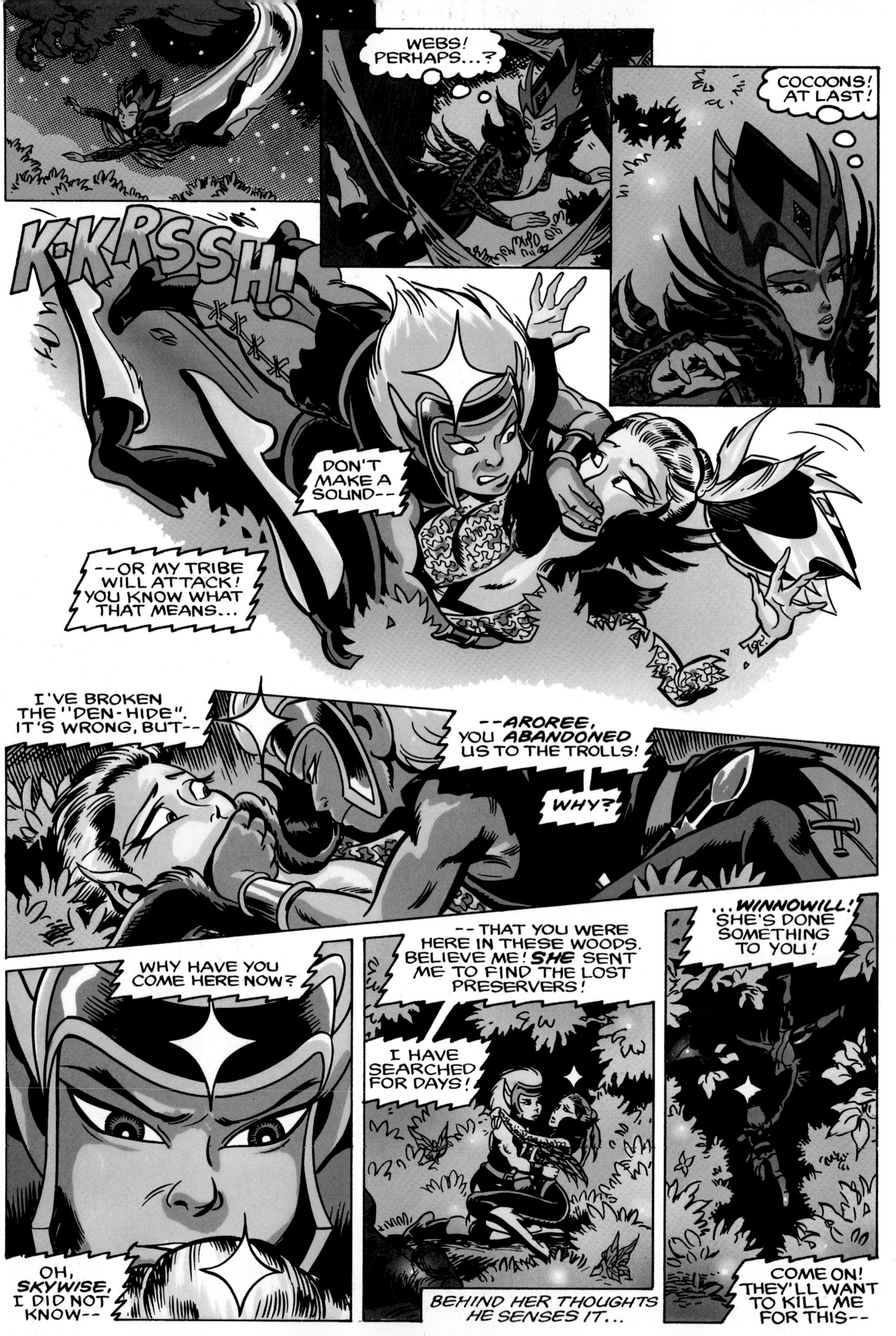

WEBS! PERHAPS...?
COCOONS! AT LAST!
K-KRSSSH!
DON'T MAKE A SOUND--
--OR MY TRIBE WILL ATTACK! YOU KNOW WHAT THAT MEANS...
I'VE BROKEN THE "DEN-HIDE". IT'S WRONG, BUT--
--AROREE, YOU ABANDONED US TO THE TROLLS!
WHY?
WHY HAVE YOU COME HERE NOW?
OH, SKYWISE, I DID NOT KNOW--
--THAT YOU WERE HERE IN THESE WOODS. BELIEVE ME! SHE SENT ME TO FIND THE LOST PRESERVERS!
I HAVE SEARCHED FOR DAYS!
BEHIND HER THOUGHTS HE SENSES IT...
...WINNOWILL! SHE'S DONE SOMETHING TO YOU!
COME ON! THEY'LL WANT TO KILL ME FOR THIS--

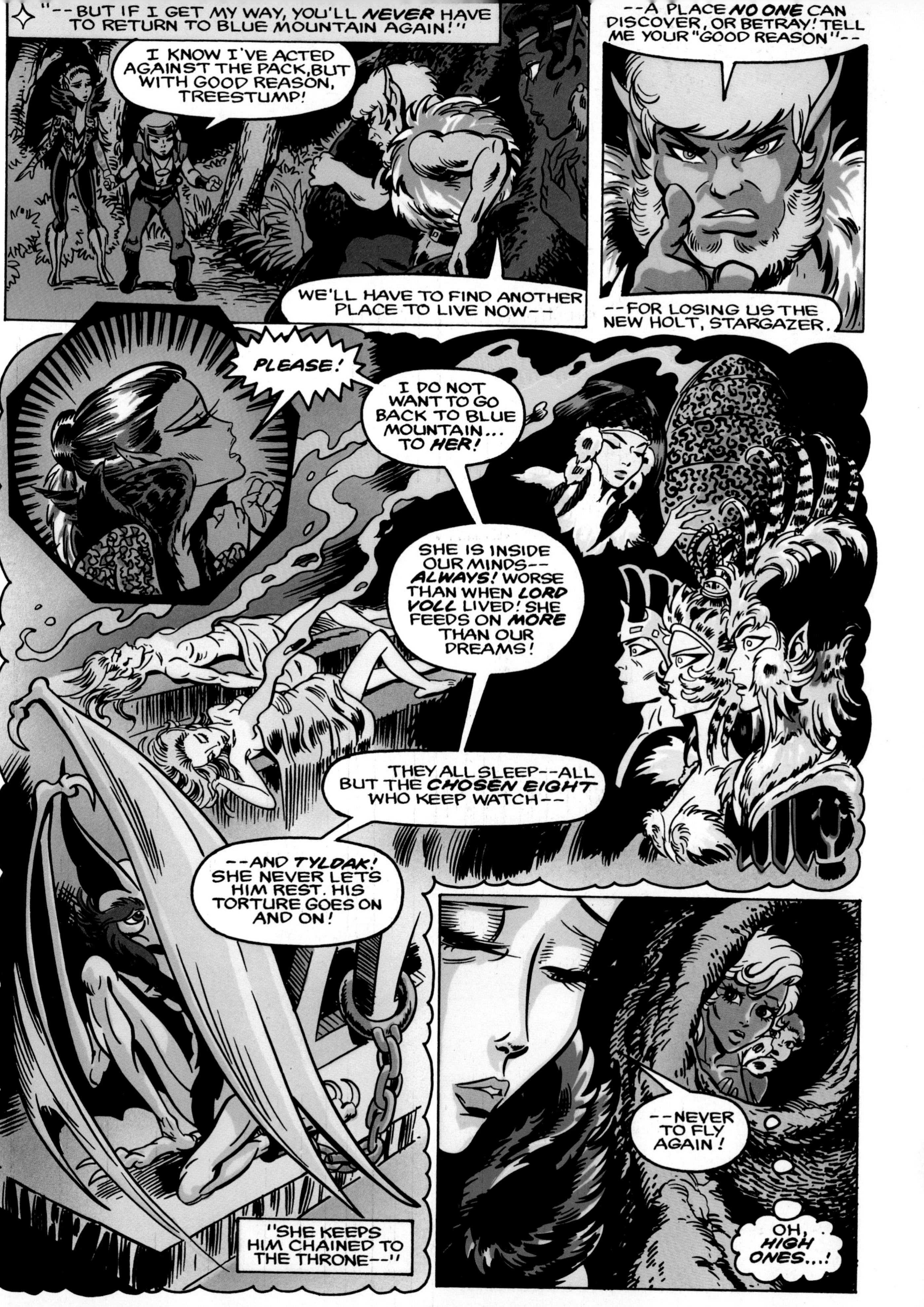
"--BUT IF I GET MY WAY, YOU'LL NEVER HAVE TO RETURN TO BLUE MOUNTAIN AGAIN!"
I KNOW I'VE ACTED AGAINST THE PACK, BUT WITH GOOD REASON, TREESTUMP!
WE'LL HAVE TO FIND ANOTHER PLACE TO LIVE NOW--
--A PLACE NO ONE CAN DISCOVER, OR BETRAY! TELL ME YOUR "GOOD REASON"--
--FOR LOSING US THE NEW HOLT, STARGAZER.
PLEASE!
I DO NOT WANT TO GO BACK TO BLUE MOUNTAIN... TO HER!
SHE IS INSIDE OUR MINDS--ALWAYS! WORSE THAN WHEN LORD VOLL LIVED! SHE FEEDS ON MORE THAN OUR DREAMS!
THEY ALL SLEEP--ALL BUT THE CHOSEN EIGHT WHO KEEP WATCH--
--AND TYLDAK! SHE NEVER LETS HIM REST. HIS TORTURE GOES ON AND ON!
"SHE KEEPS HIM CHAINED TO THE THRONE--"
--NEVER TO FLY AGAIN!
OH, HIGH ONES...!

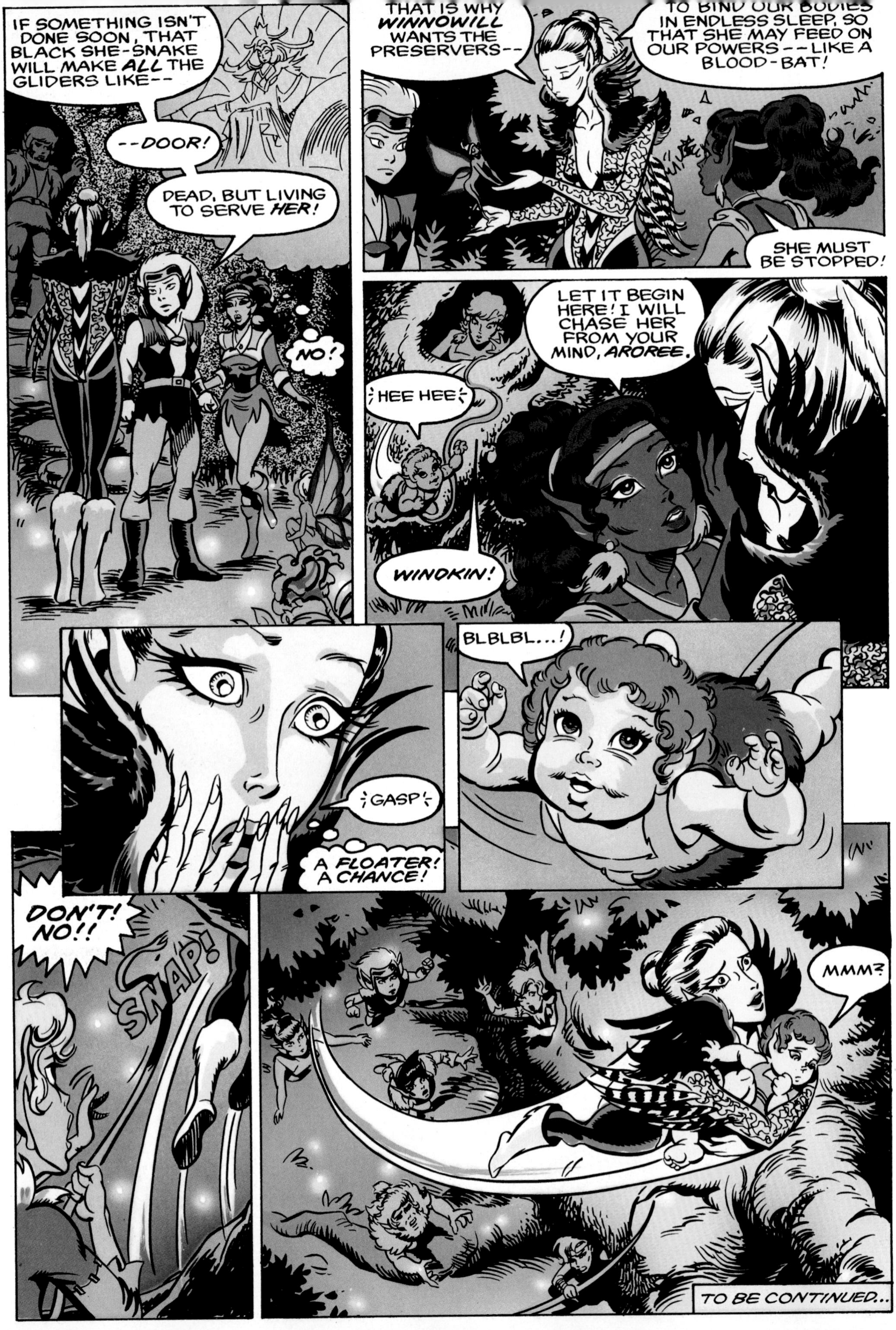

IF SOMETHING ISN'T DONE SOON, THAT BLACK SHE-SNAKE WILL MAKE ALL THE GLIDERS LIKE--
--DOOR!
DEAD, BUT LIVING TO SERVE HER!
NO!
THAT IS WHY WINNOWILL WANTS THE PRESERVERS--
TO BIND OUR BODIES IN ENDLESS SLEEP, SO THAT SHE MAY FEED ON OUR POWERS--LIKE A BLOOD-BAT!
SHE MUST BE STOPPED!
LET IT BEGIN HERE! I WILL CHASE HER FROM YOUR MIND, AROREE.
HEE HEE
WINDKIN!
GASP
A FLOATER! A CHANCE!
BLBLBL...!
DON'T! NO!!
SNAP!
MMM?
TO BE CONTINUED...

SIEGE AT BLUE MOUNTAIN

ARTIST / WRITER WENDY PINI | CO-PLOT / EDITOR RICHARD PINI | PART 2 | INKS JOE STATON | LETTERER JANICE CHIANG

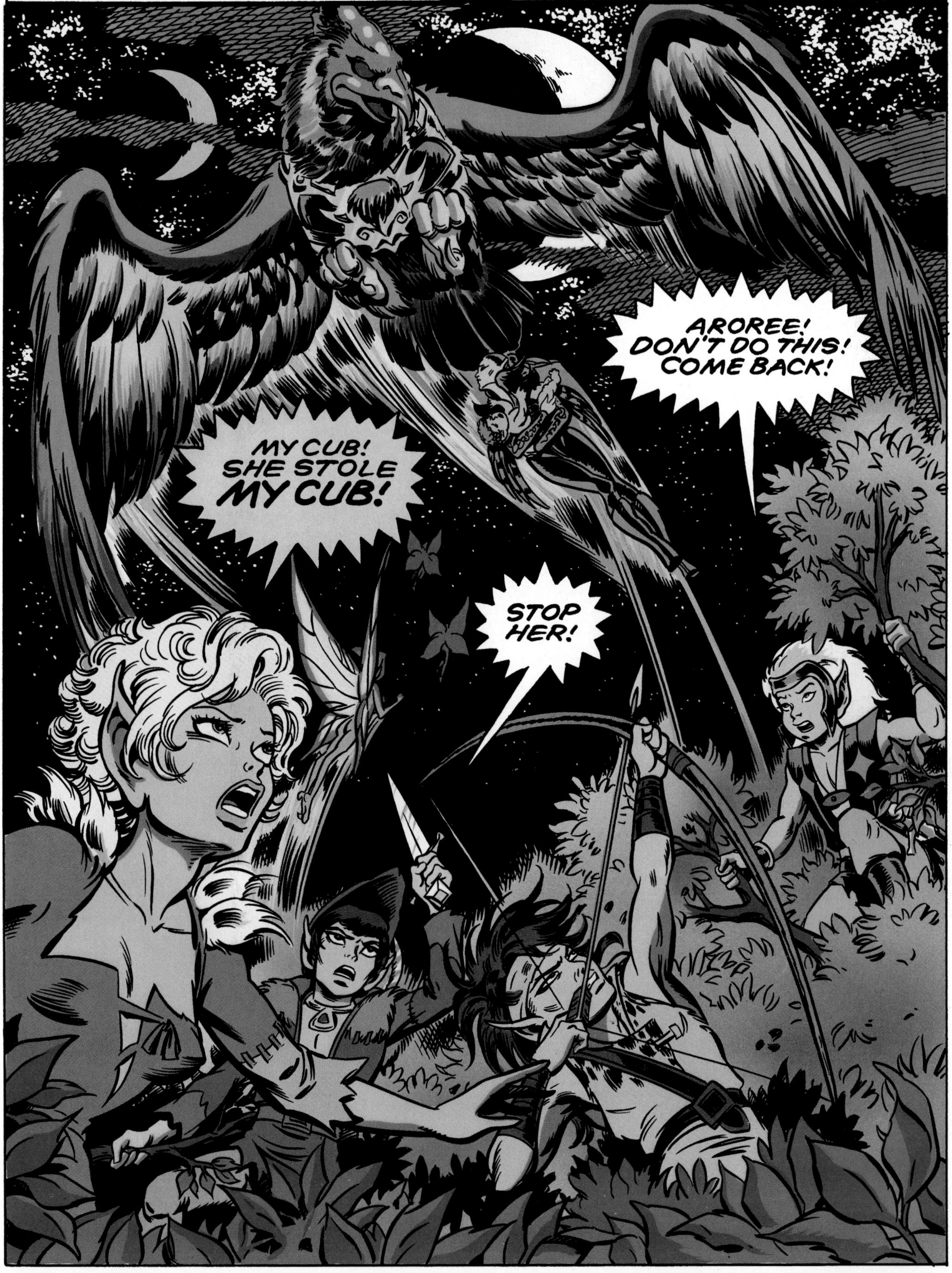
AROREE! DON'T DO THIS! COME BACK!
MY CUB! SHE STOLE MY CUB!
STOP HER!

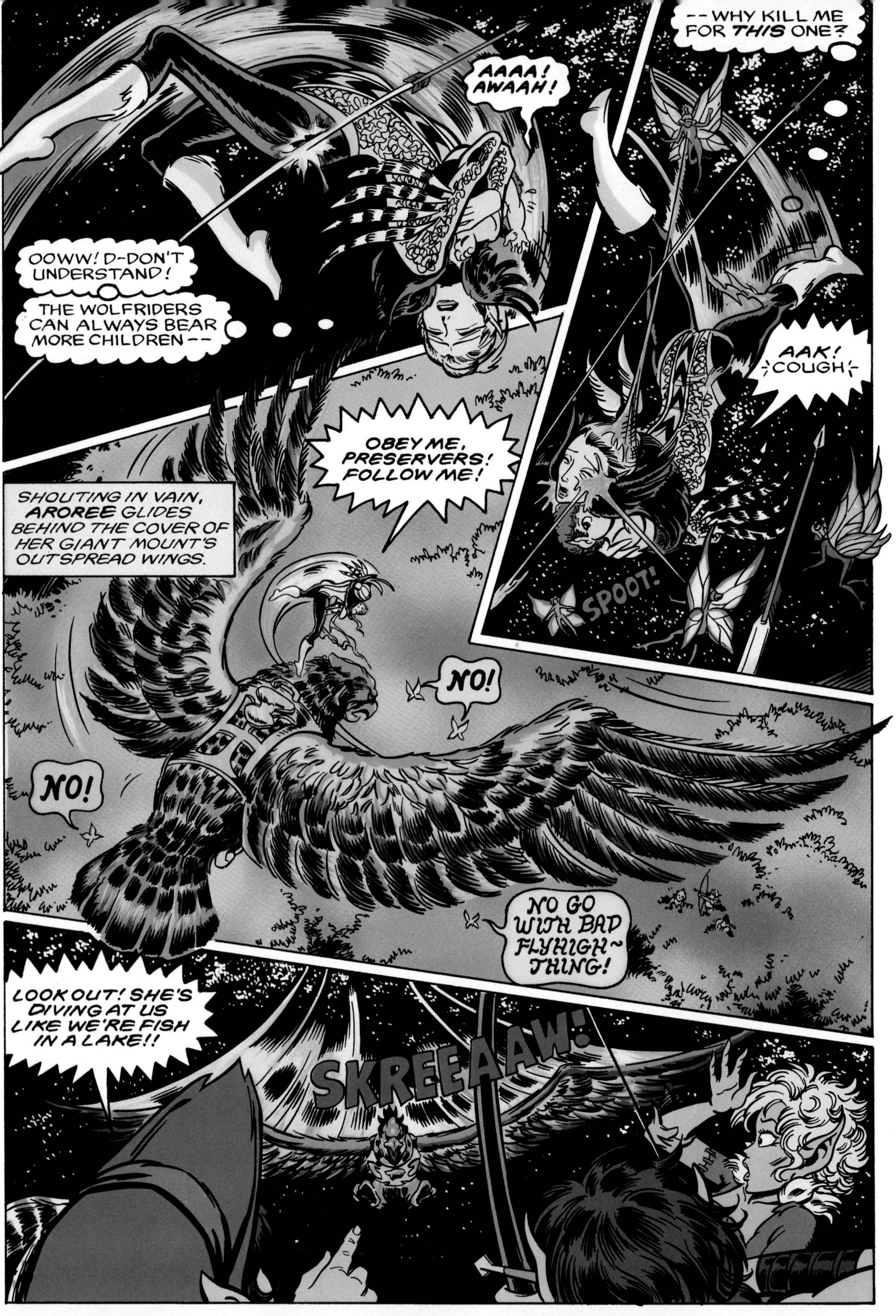
AAAA! AWAAH!
OOWW! D-DON'T UNDERSTAND!
THE WOLFRIDERS CAN ALWAYS BEAR MORE CHILDREN--
--WHY KILL ME FOR THIS ONE?
AAK! -COUGH-
SPOOT!
OBEY ME, PRESERVERS! FOLLOW ME!
SHOUTING IN VAIN, AROREE GLIDES BEHIND THE COVER OF HER GIANT MOUNT'S OUTSPREAD WINGS.
NO!
NO!
NO GO WITH BAD FLYHIGH~THING!
LOOK OUT! SHE'S DIVING AT US LIKE WE'RE FISH IN A LAKE!!
SKREEAAW!

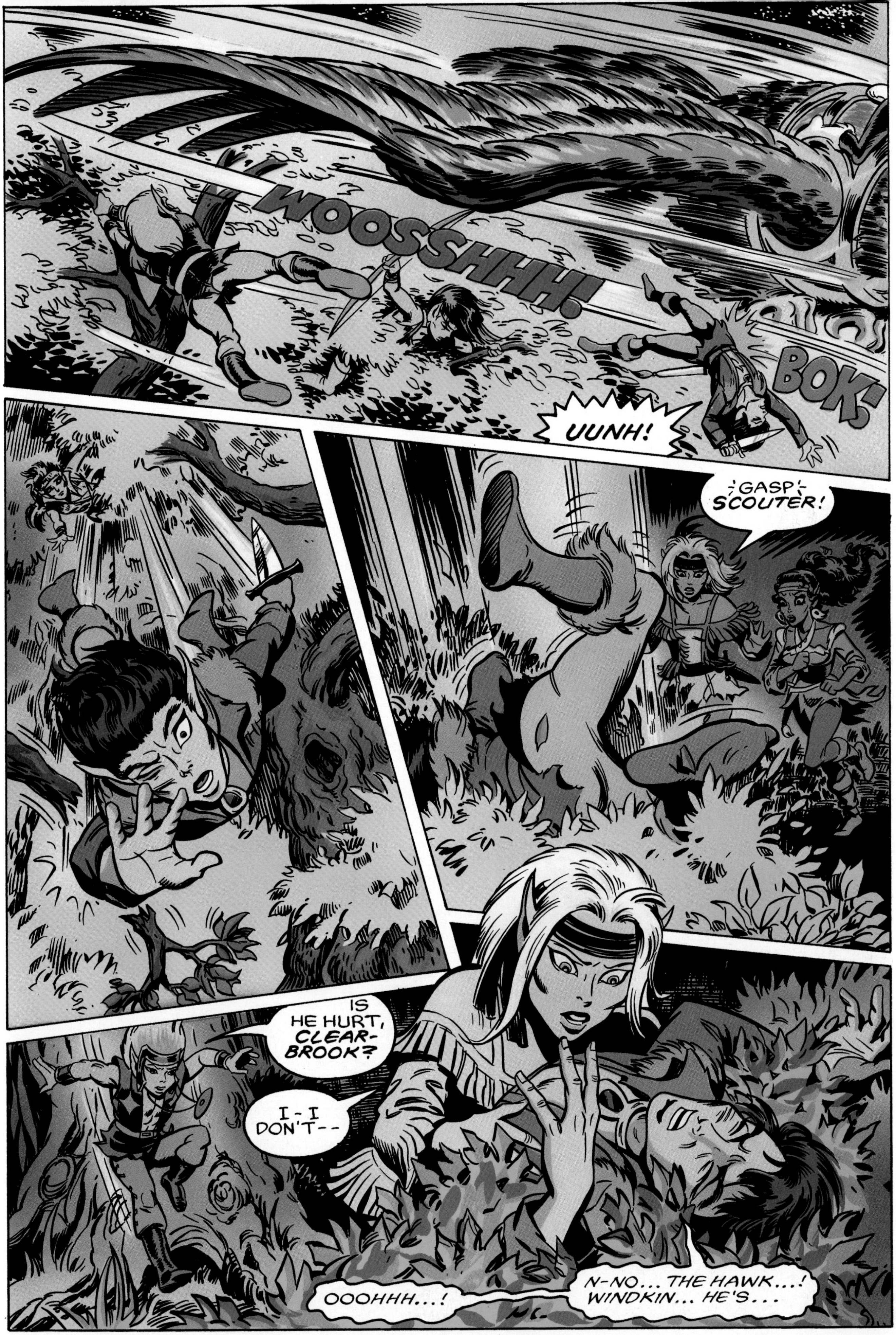
WOOSSHHH!
BOK!
UUNH!
GASP SCOUTER!
IS HE HURT, CLEARBROOK?
I-I DON'T--
OOOHHH...!
N-NO... THE HAWK...! WINDKIN... HE'S...

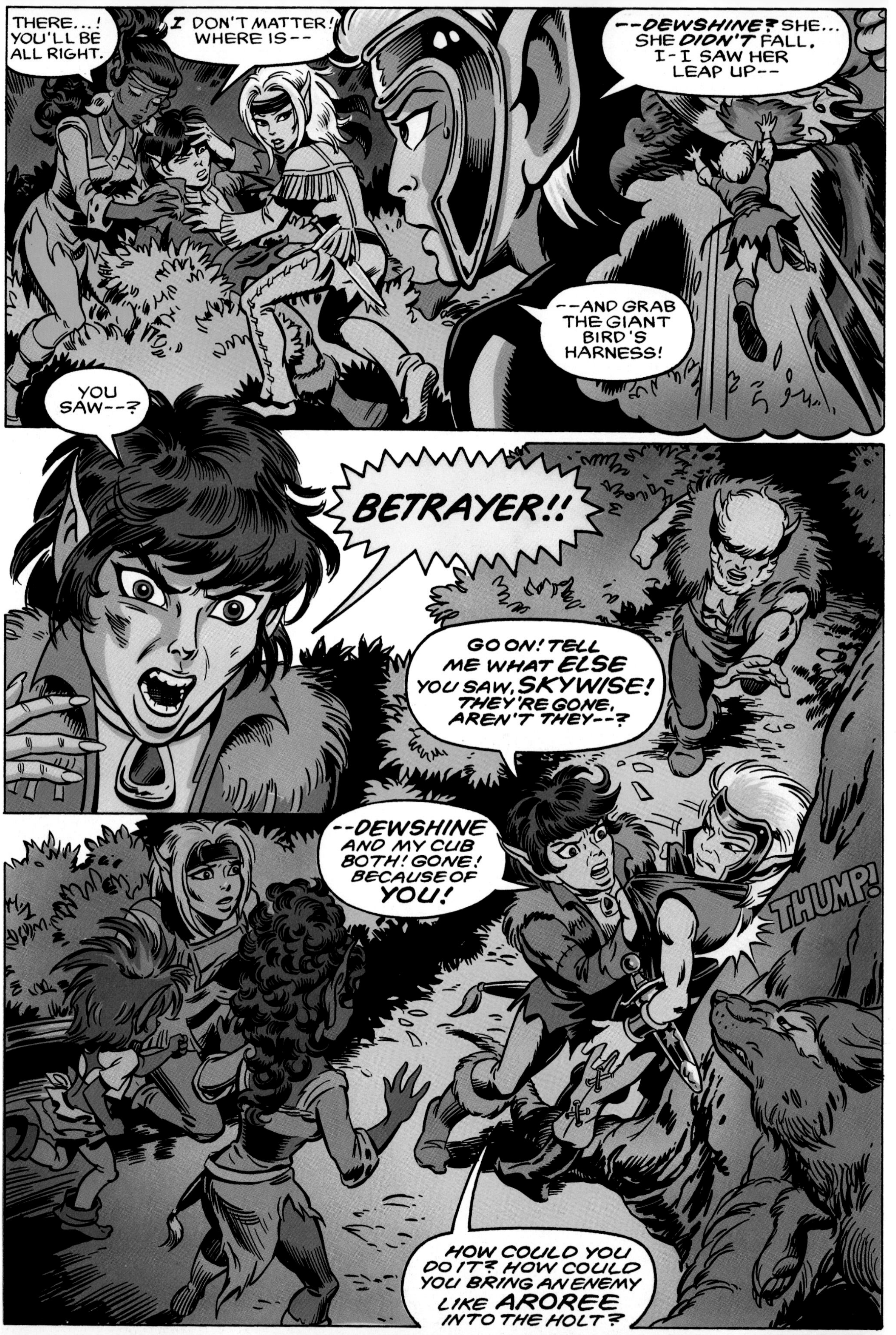

THERE...! YOU'LL BE ALL RIGHT.
I DON'T MATTER! WHERE IS --
--DEWSHINE? SHE... SHE DIDN'T FALL. I-I SAW HER LEAP UP--
--AND GRAB THE GIANT BIRD'S HARNESS!
YOU SAW--?
BETRAYER!!
GO ON! TELL ME WHAT ELSE YOU SAW, SKYWISE! THEY'RE GONE, AREN'T THEY--?
--DEWSHINE AND MY CUB BOTH! GONE! BECAUSE OF YOU!
THUMP!
HOW COULD YOU DO IT? HOW COULD YOU BRING AN ENEMY LIKE AROREE INTO THE HOLT?

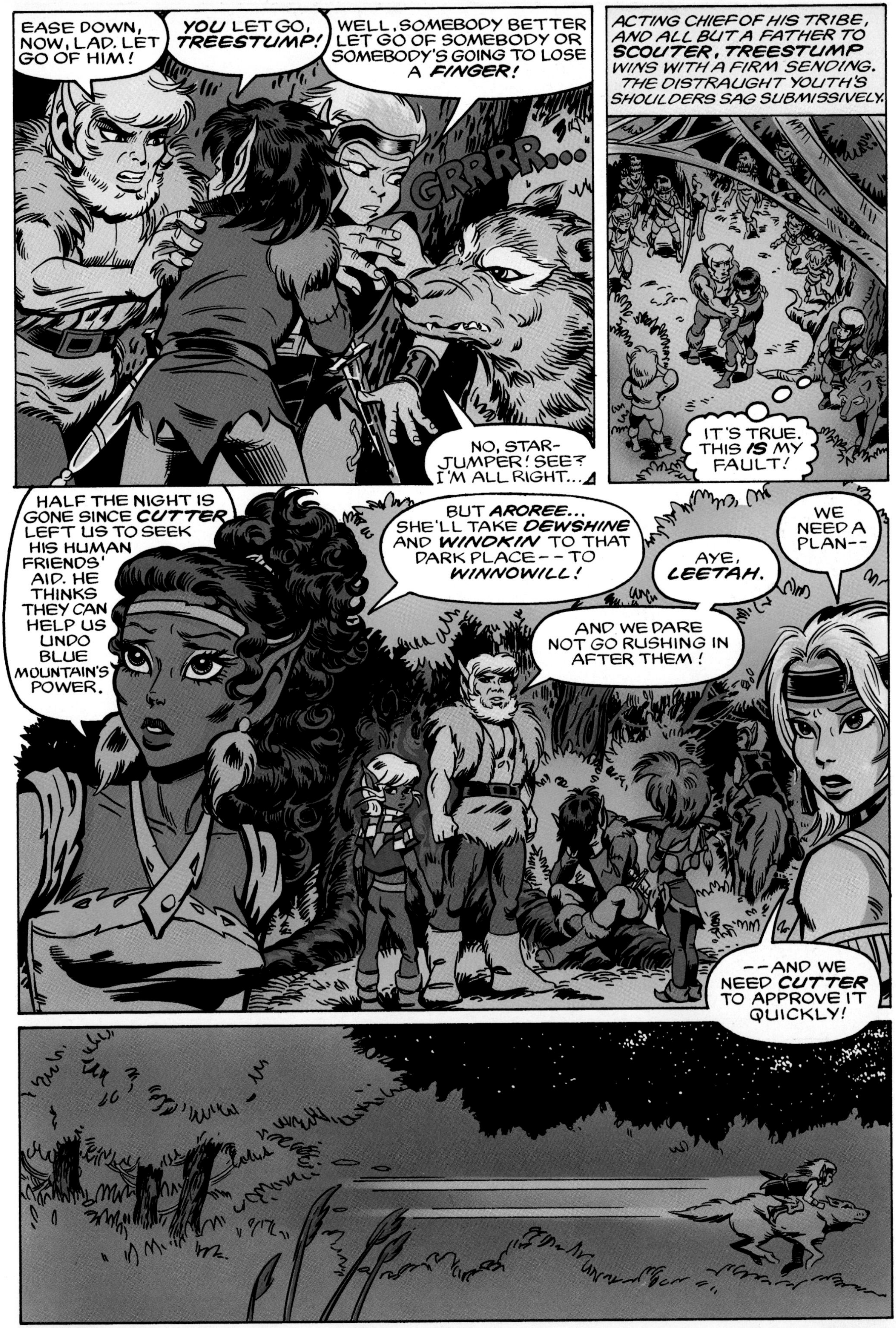

EASE DOWN, NOW, LAD. LET GO OF HIM!
YOU LET GO, TREESTUMP!
WELL, SOMEBODY BETTER LET GO OF SOMEBODY OR SOMEBODY'S GOING TO LOSE A FINGER!
GRRRR...
NO, STAR-JUMPER! SEE? I'M ALL RIGHT...
ACTING CHIEF OF HIS TRIBE, AND ALL BUT A FATHER TO SCOUTER, TREESTUMP WINS WITH A FIRM SENDING. THE DISTRAUGHT YOUTH'S SHOULDERS SAG SUBMISSIVELY.
IT'S TRUE. THIS IS MY FAULT!
HALF THE NIGHT IS GONE SINCE CUTTER LEFT US TO SEEK HIS HUMAN FRIENDS' AID. HE THINKS THEY CAN HELP US UNDO BLUE MOUNTAIN'S POWER.
BUT AROREE... SHE'LL TAKE DEWSHINE AND WINOKIN TO THAT DARK PLACE--TO WINNOWILL!
AYE, LEETAH.
AND WE DARE NOT GO RUSHING IN AFTER THEM!
WE NEED A PLAN--
--AND WE NEED CUTTER TO APPROVE IT QUICKLY!

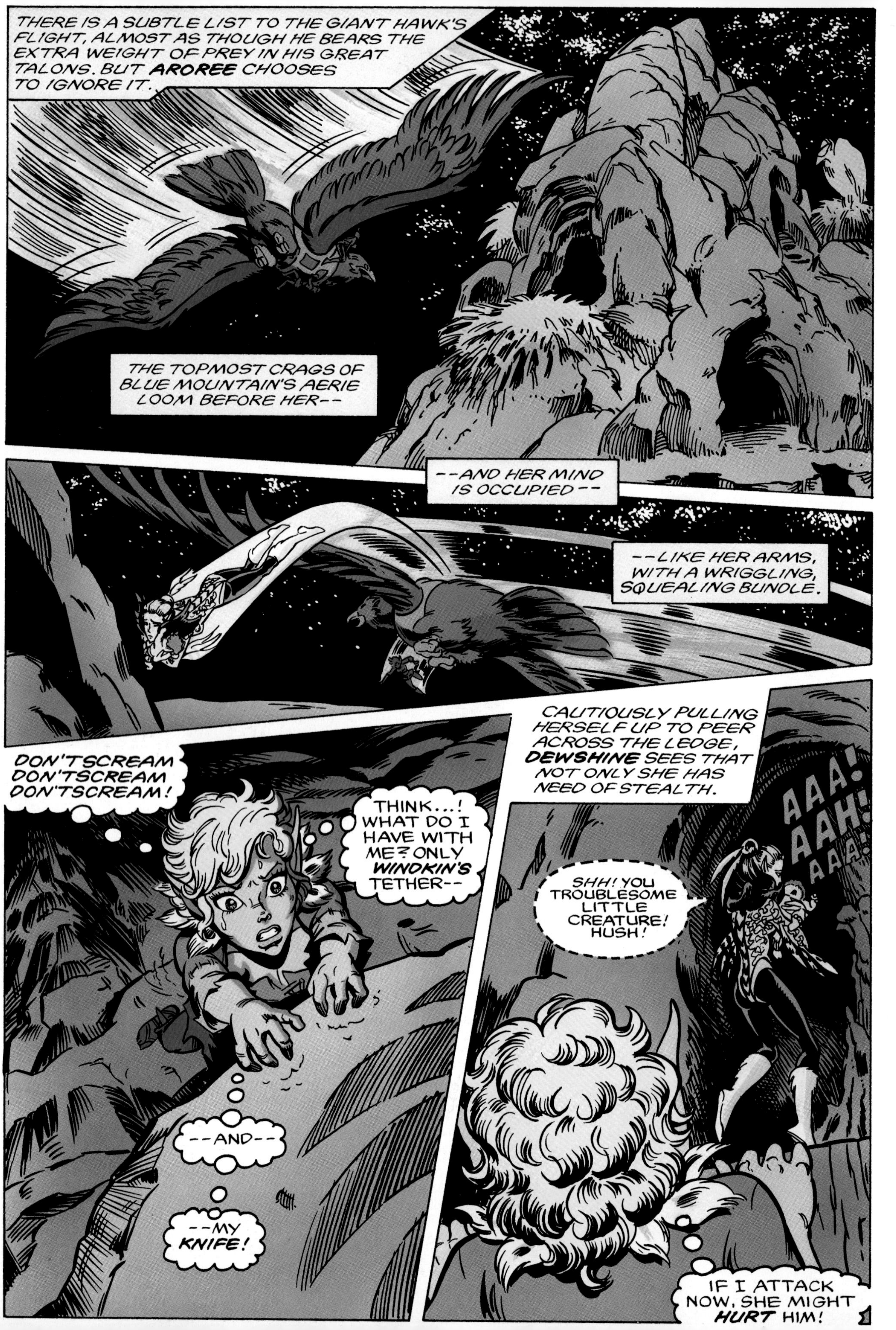
THERE IS A SUBTLE LIST TO THE GIANT HAWK'S FLIGHT, ALMOST AS THOUGH HE BEARS THE EXTRA WEIGHT OF PREY IN HIS GREAT TALONS. BUT **AROREE** CHOOSES TO IGNORE IT.
THE TOPMOST CRAGS OF BLUE MOUNTAIN'S AERIE LOOM BEFORE HER--
--AND HER MIND IS OCCUPIED--
--LIKE HER ARMS, WITH A WRIGGLING, SQUEALING BUNDLE.
DON'TSCREAM DON'TSCREAM DON'TSCREAM!
THINK...! WHAT DO I HAVE WITH ME? ONLY **WINDKIN'S** TETHER--
--AND--
--MY **KNIFE**!
CAUTIOUSLY PULLING HERSELF UP TO PEER ACROSS THE LEDGE, **DEWSHINE** SEES THAT NOT ONLY SHE HAS NEED OF STEALTH.
AAA! AAH! AAA!
SHH! YOU TROUBLESOME LITTLE CREATURE! HUSH!
IF I ATTACK NOW, SHE MIGHT **HURT** HIM!

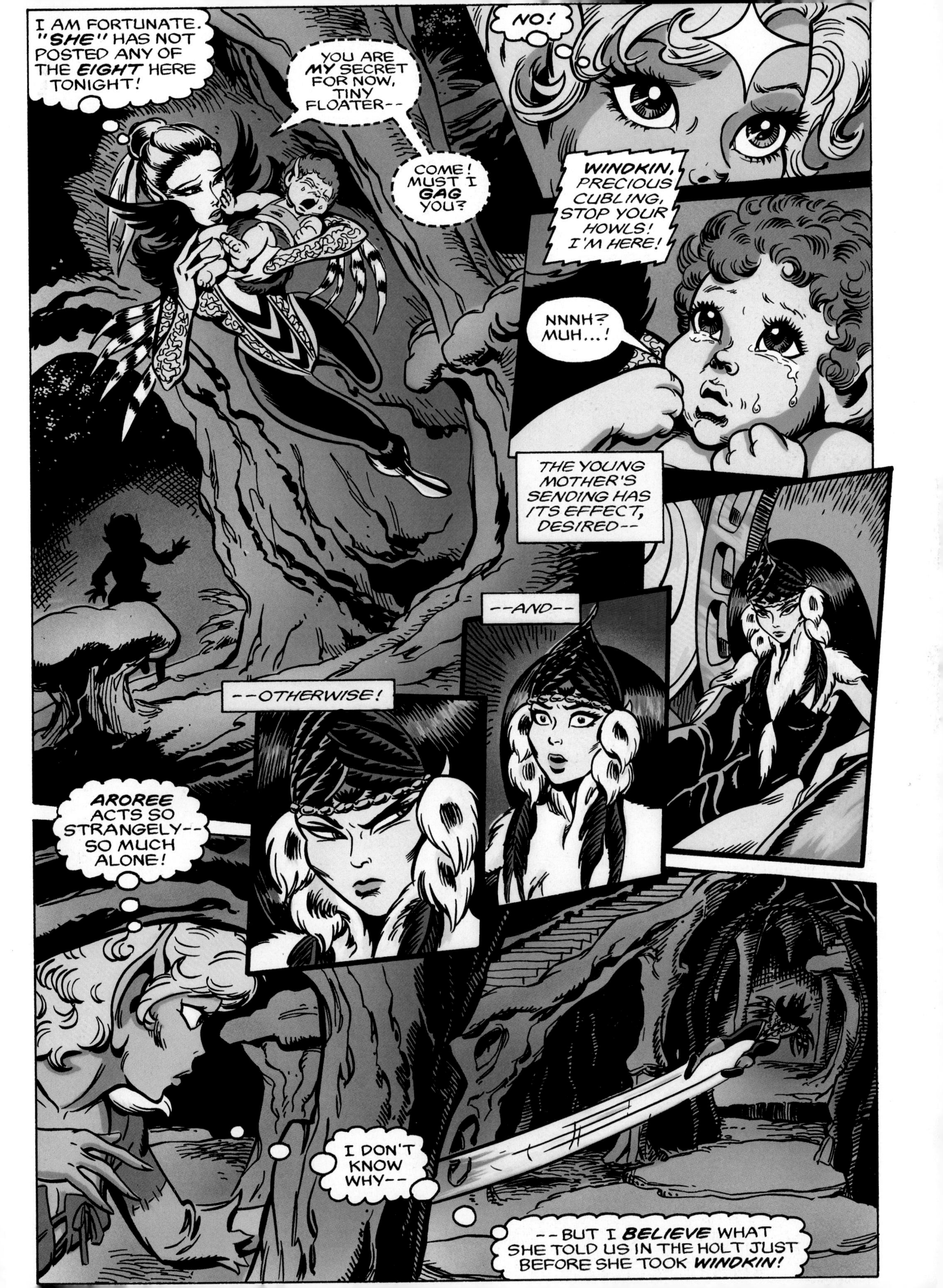
I AM FORTUNATE. "SHE" HAS NOT POSTED ANY OF THE EIGHT HERE TONIGHT!
YOU ARE MY SECRET FOR NOW, TINY FLOATER--
COME! MUST I GAG YOU?
NO!
WINDKIN, PRECIOUS CUBLING, STOP YOUR HOWLS! I'M HERE!
NNNH? MUH...!
THE YOUNG MOTHER'S SENDING HAS ITS EFFECT, DESIRED--
--AND--
--OTHERWISE!
AROREE ACTS SO STRANGELY--SO MUCH ALONE!
I DON'T KNOW WHY--
--BUT I BELIEVE WHAT SHE TOLD US IN THE HOLT JUST BEFORE SHE TOOK WINDKIN!

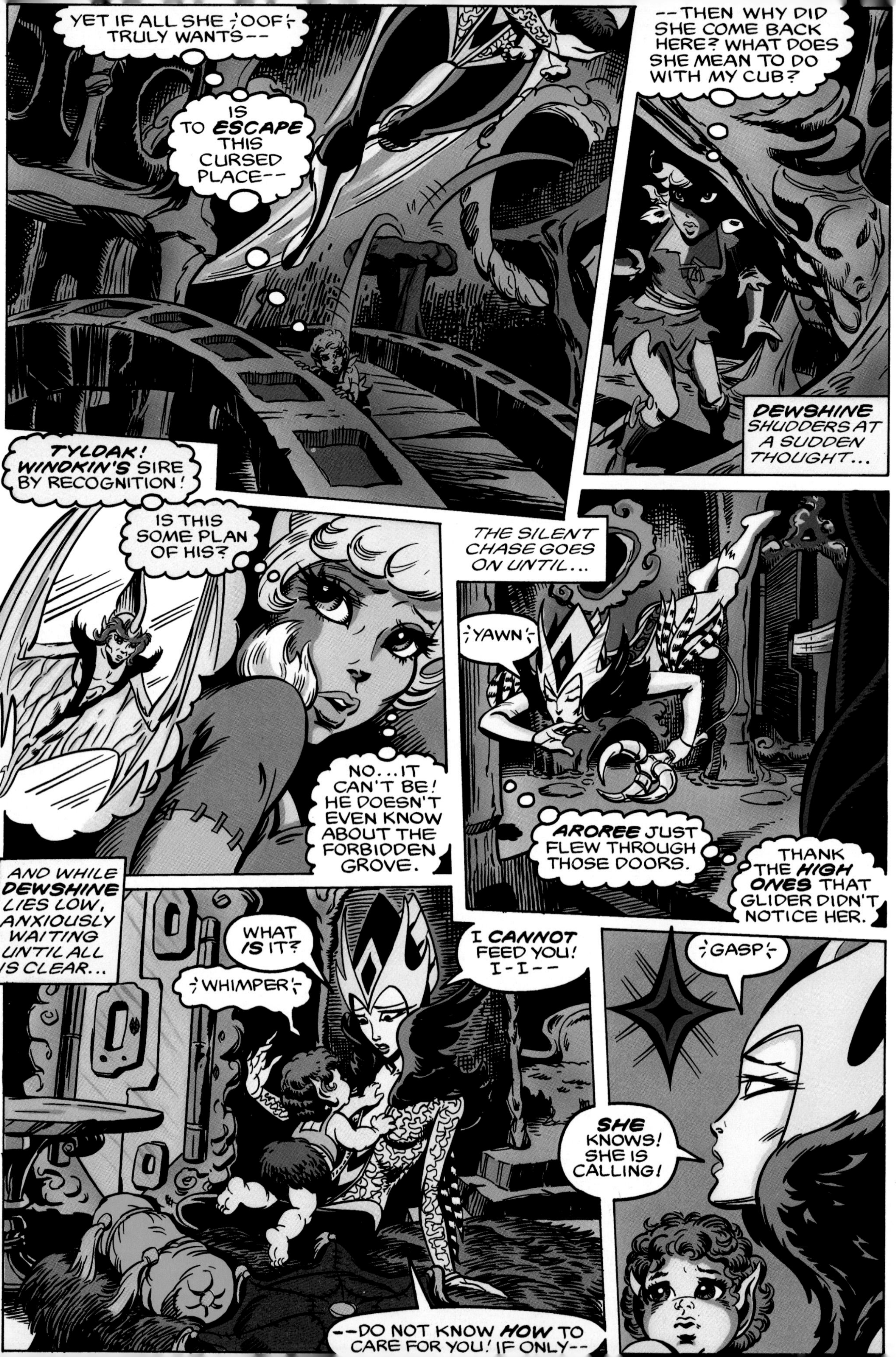
YET IF ALL SHE -OOF- TRULY WANTS--
IS TO ESCAPE THIS CURSED PLACE--
--THEN WHY DID SHE COME BACK HERE? WHAT DOES SHE MEAN TO DO WITH MY CUB?
DEWSHINE SHUDDERS AT A SUDDEN THOUGHT...
TYLDAK! WINOKIN'S SIRE BY RECOGNITION!
IS THIS SOME PLAN OF HIS?
NO...IT CAN'T BE! HE DOESN'T EVEN KNOW ABOUT THE FORBIDDEN GROVE.
THE SILENT CHASE GOES ON UNTIL...
-YAWN-
AROREE JUST FLEW THROUGH THOSE DOORS.
THANK THE HIGH ONES THAT GLIDER DIDN'T NOTICE HER.
AND WHILE DEWSHINE LIES LOW, ANXIOUSLY WAITING UNTIL ALL IS CLEAR...
WHAT IS IT?
-WHIMPER-
I CANNOT FEED YOU! I-I--
--DO NOT KNOW HOW TO CARE FOR YOU! IF ONLY--
-GASP-
SHE KNOWS! SHE IS CALLING!

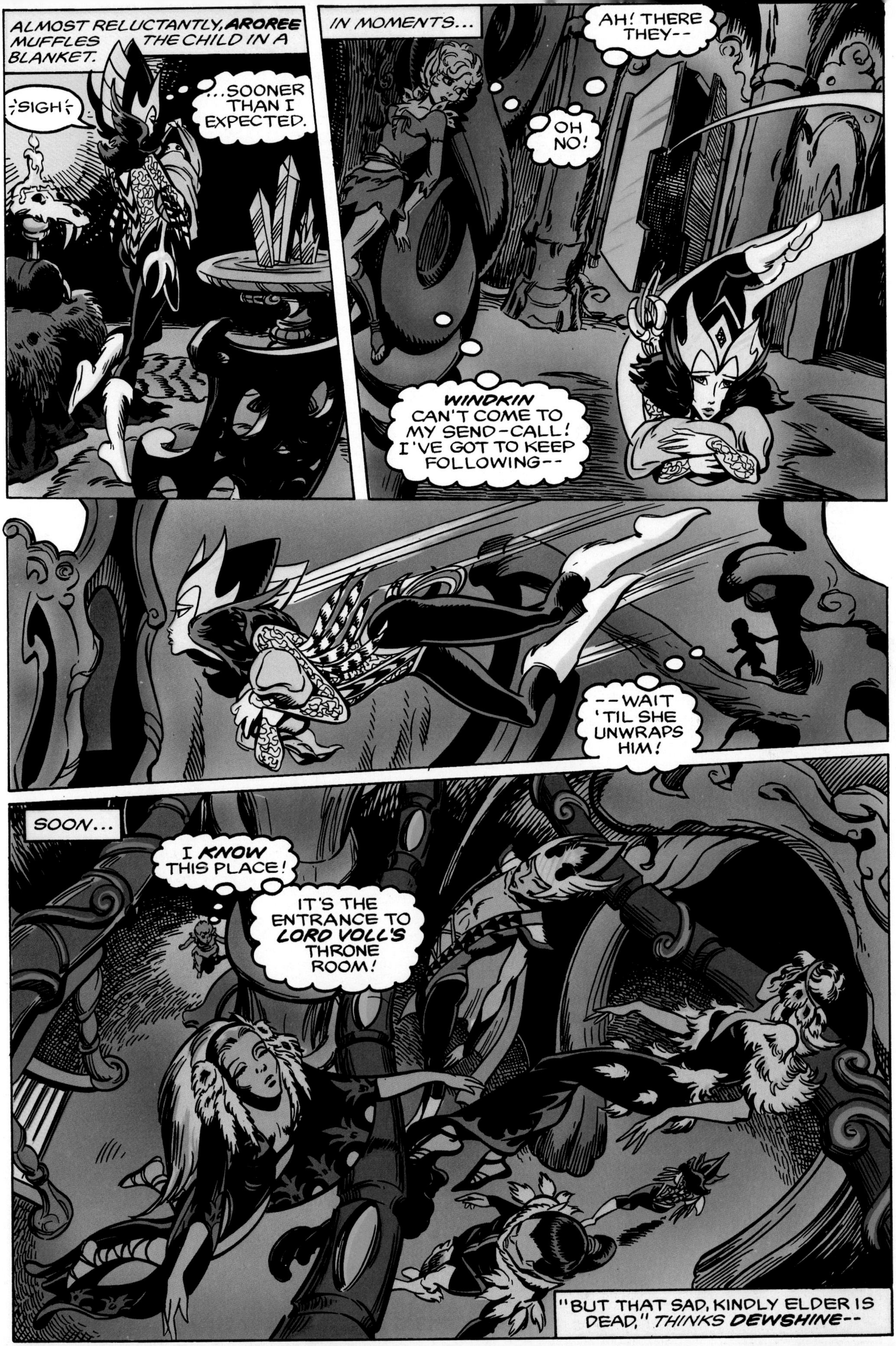

ALMOST RELUCTANTLY, AROREE MUFFLES THE CHILD IN A BLANKET.
-;SIGH;-
...SOONER THAN I EXPECTED.
IN MOMENTS...
AH! THERE THEY--
OH NO!
WINDKIN CAN'T COME TO MY SEND-CALL! I'VE GOT TO KEEP FOLLOWING--
--WAIT 'TIL SHE UNWRAPS HIM!
SOON...
I KNOW THIS PLACE!
IT'S THE ENTRANCE TO LORD VOLL'S THRONE ROOM!
"BUT THAT SAD, KINDLY ELDER IS DEAD," THINKS DEWSHINE--

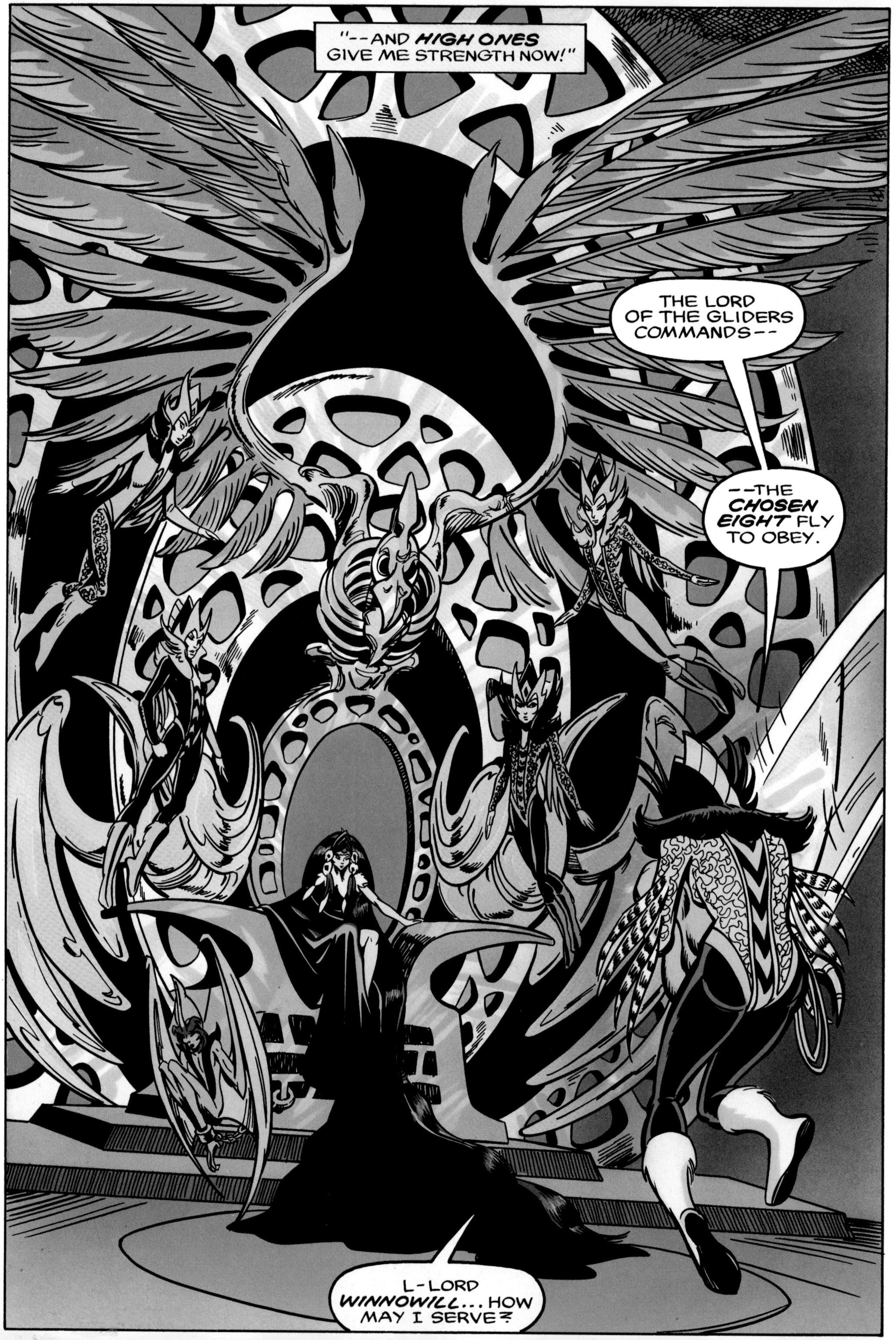
"--AND HIGH ONES GIVE ME STRENGTH NOW!"
THE LORD OF THE GLIDERS COMMANDS--
--THE CHOSEN EIGHT FLY TO OBEY.
L-LORD WINNOWILL... HOW MAY I SERVE?

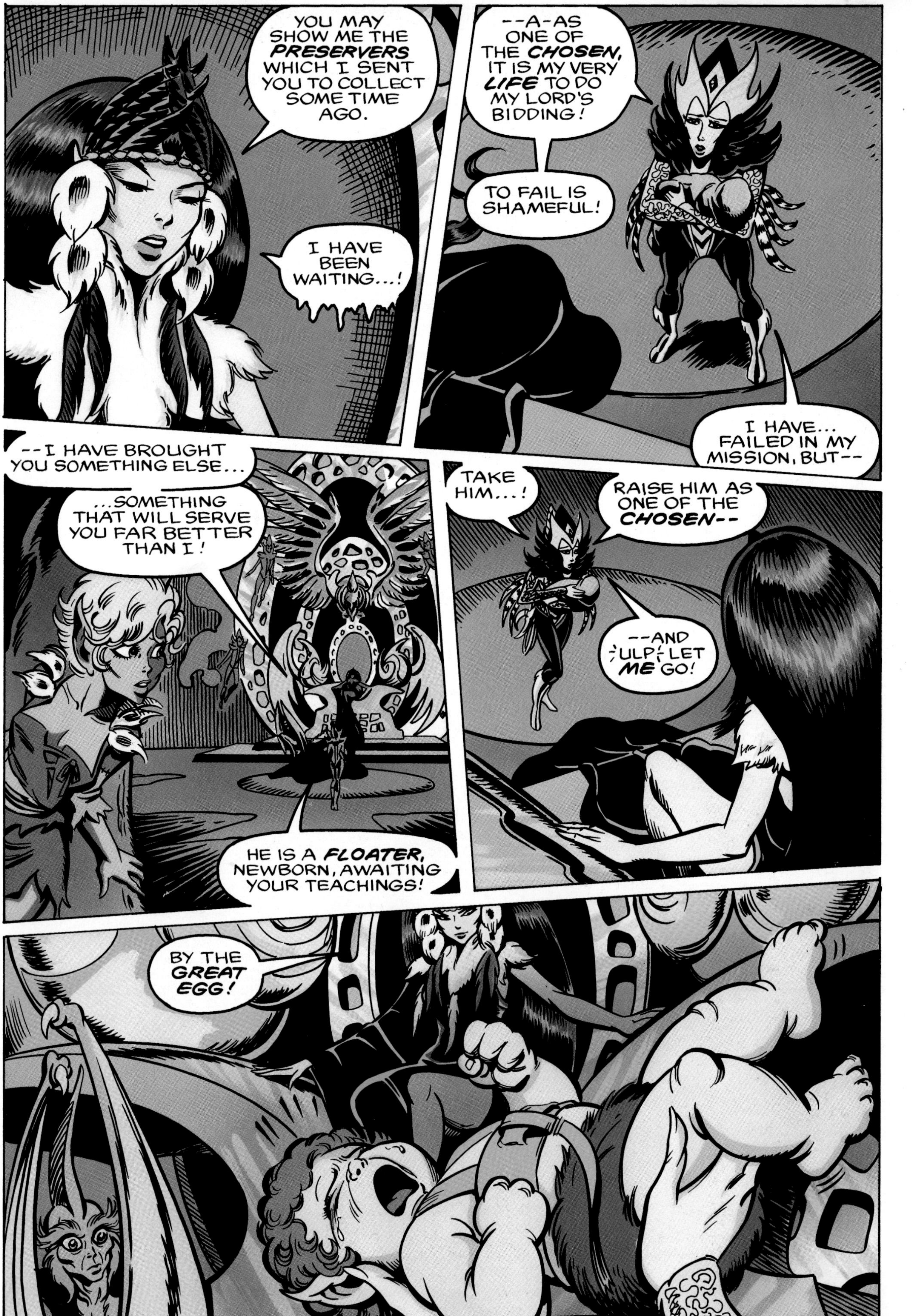
YOU MAY SHOW ME THE PRESERVERS WHICH I SENT YOU TO COLLECT SOME TIME AGO.
I HAVE BEEN WAITING...!
--A-AS ONE OF THE CHOSEN, IT IS MY VERY LIFE TO DO MY LORD'S BIDDING!
TO FAIL IS SHAMEFUL!
I HAVE... FAILED IN MY MISSION, BUT--
--I HAVE BROUGHT YOU SOMETHING ELSE...
...SOMETHING THAT WILL SERVE YOU FAR BETTER THAN I!
HE IS A FLOATER, NEWBORN, AWAITING YOUR TEACHINGS!
TAKE HIM...!
RAISE HIM AS ONE OF THE CHOSEN--
--AND ULP LET ME GO!
BY THE GREAT EGG!

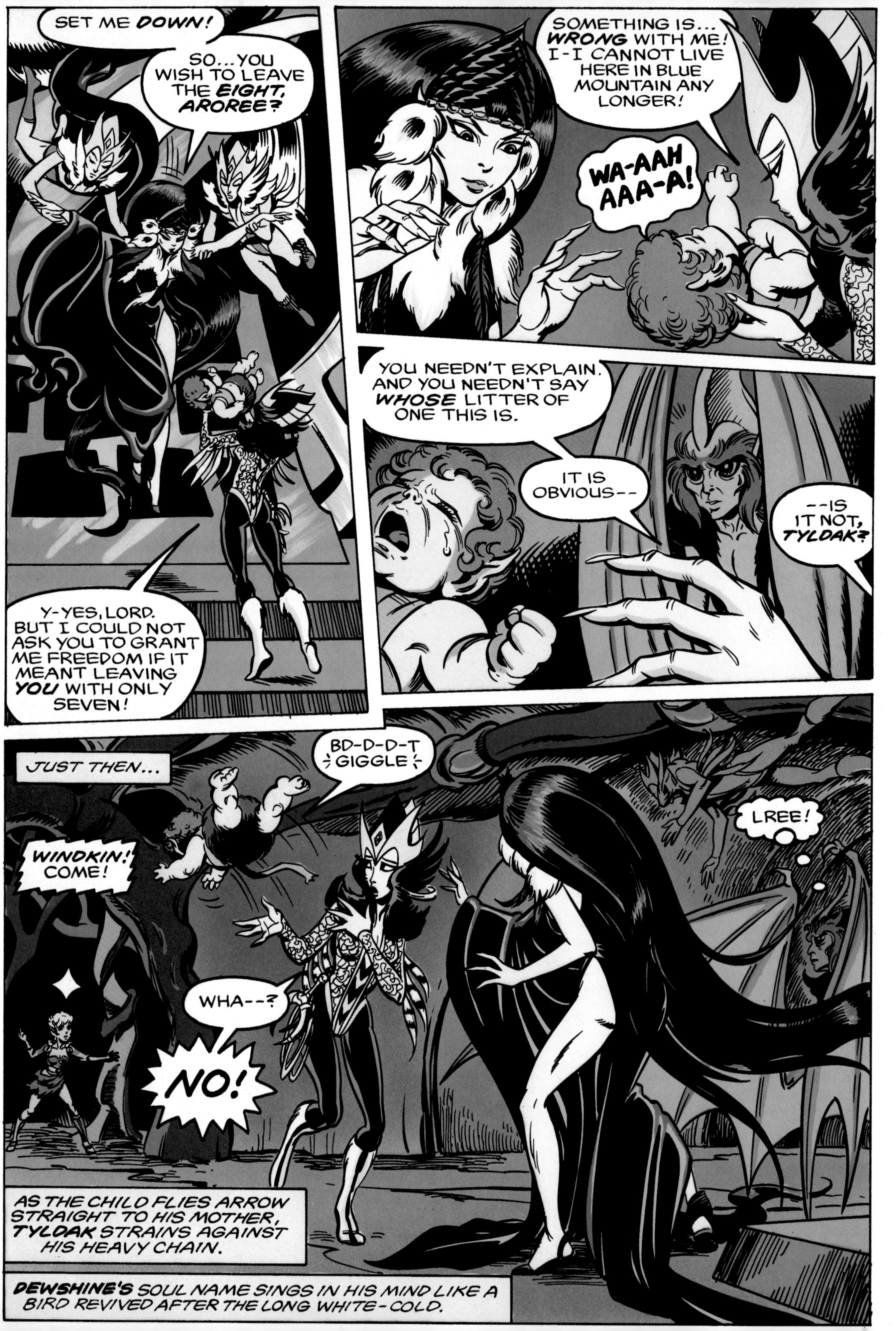
SET ME DOWN!
SO... YOU WISH TO LEAVE THE EIGHT, AROREE?
Y-YES, LORD. BUT I COULD NOT ASK YOU TO GRANT ME FREEDOM IF IT MEANT LEAVING YOU WITH ONLY SEVEN!
SOMETHING IS... WRONG WITH ME! I-I CANNOT LIVE HERE IN BLUE MOUNTAIN ANY LONGER!
WA-AAH AAA-A!
YOU NEEDN'T EXPLAIN. AND YOU NEEDN'T SAY WHOSE LITTER OF ONE THIS IS.
IT IS OBVIOUS--
--IS IT NOT, TYLDAK?
JUST THEN...
BD-D-D-T GIGGLE
LREE!
WINDKIN! COME!
WHA--?
NO!
AS THE CHILD FLIES ARROW STRAIGHT TO HIS MOTHER, TYLDAK STRAINS AGAINST HIS HEAVY CHAIN.
DEWSHINE'S SOUL NAME SINGS IN HIS MIND LIKE A BIRD REVIVED AFTER THE LONG WHITE-COLD.

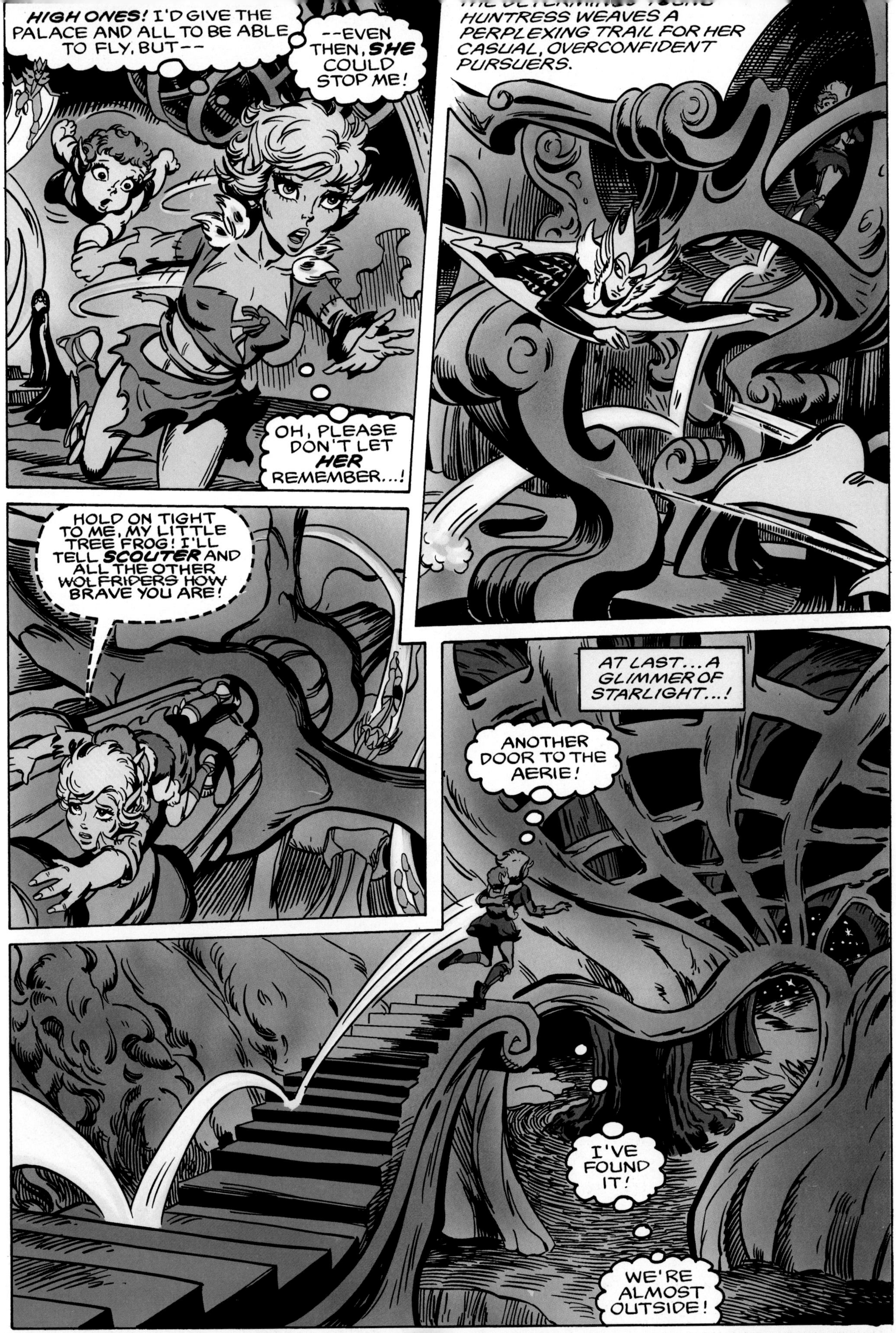
HIGH ONES! I'D GIVE THE PALACE AND ALL TO BE ABLE TO FLY, BUT--
--EVEN THEN, SHE COULD STOP ME!
OH, PLEASE DON'T LET HER REMEMBER...!
HUNTRESS WEAVES A PERPLEXING TRAIL FOR HER CASUAL, OVERCONFIDENT PURSUERS.
HOLD ON TIGHT TO ME, MY LITTLE TREE FROG! I'LL TELL SCOUTER AND ALL THE OTHER WOLFRIDERS HOW BRAVE YOU ARE!
AT LAST... A GLIMMER OF STARLIGHT...!
ANOTHER DOOR TO THE AERIE!
I'VE FOUND IT!
WE'RE ALMOST OUTSIDE!

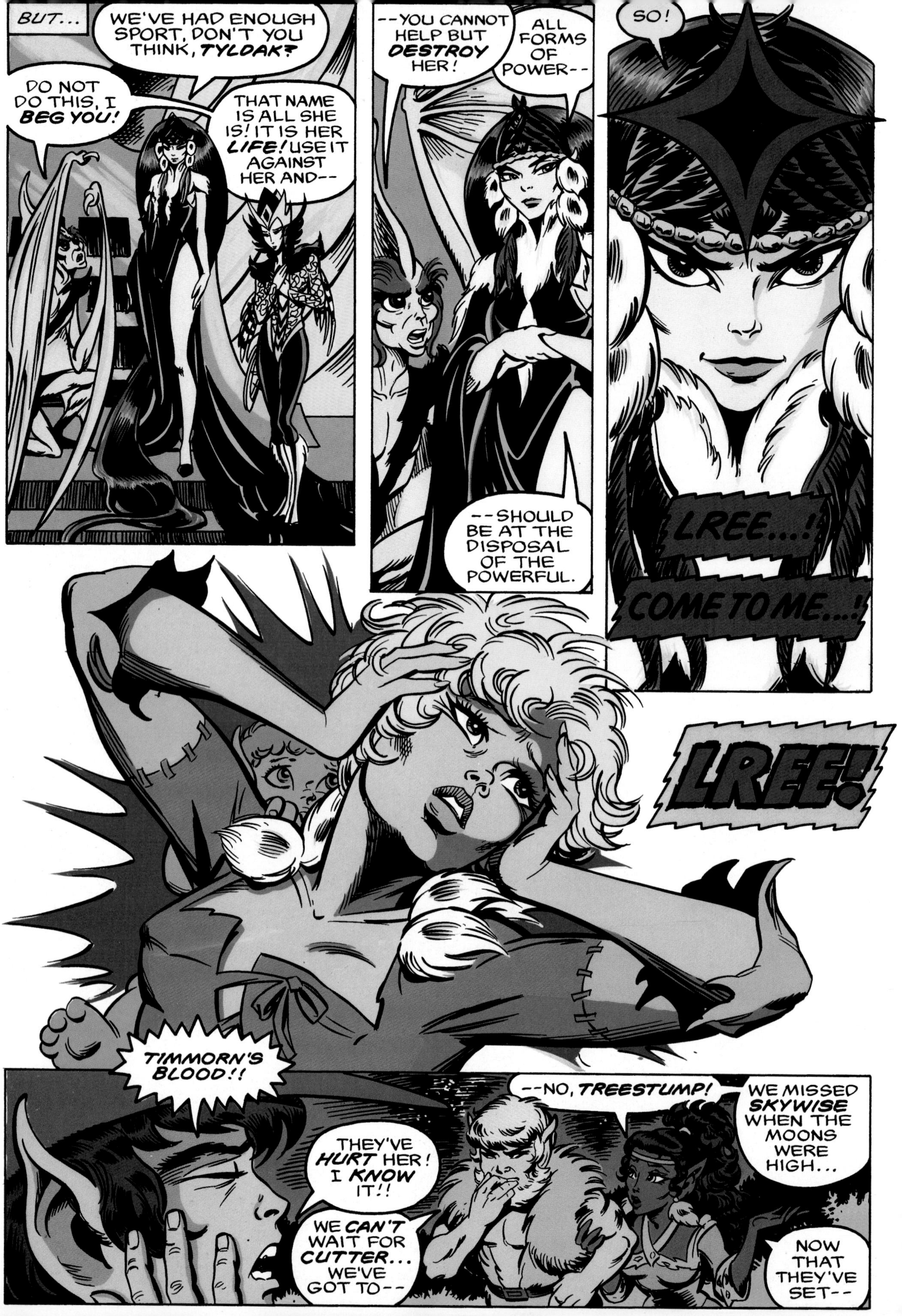
BUT...
WE'VE HAD ENOUGH SPORT, DON'T YOU THINK, TYLDAK?
DO NOT DO THIS, I BEG YOU!
THAT NAME IS ALL SHE IS! IT IS HER LIFE! USE IT AGAINST HER AND--
--YOU CANNOT HELP BUT DESTROY HER!
ALL FORMS OF POWER--
--SHOULD BE AT THE DISPOSAL OF THE POWERFUL.
SO!
LREE...!
COME TO ME...!
LREE!
TIMMORN'S BLOOD!!
THEY'VE HURT HER! I KNOW IT!!
WE CAN'T WAIT FOR CUTTER... WE'VE GOT TO--
--NO, TREESTUMP!
WE MISSED SKYWISE WHEN THE MOONS WERE HIGH...
NOW THAT THEY'VE SET--

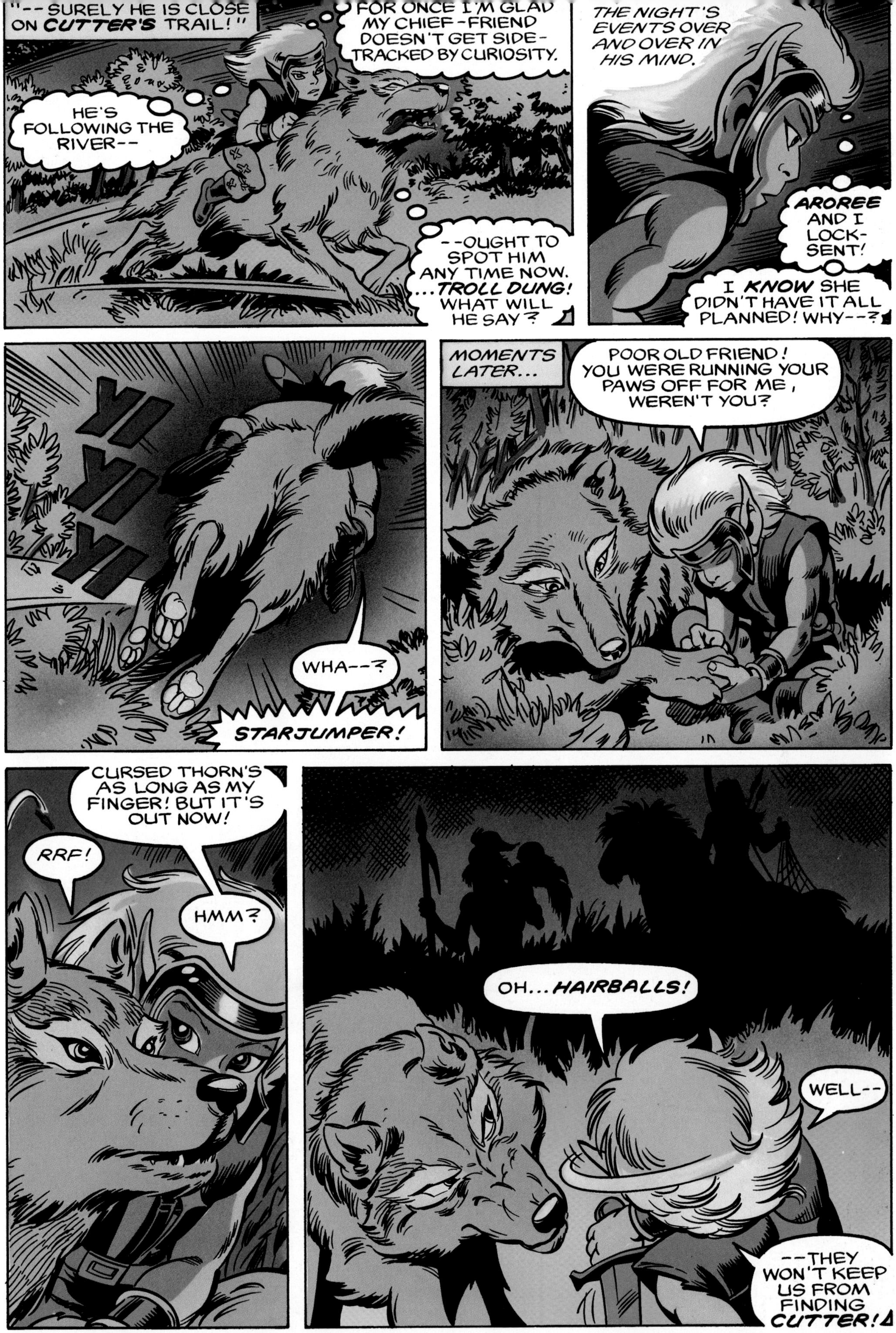
"--SURELY HE IS CLOSE ON CUTTER'S TRAIL!"
FOR ONCE I'M GLAD MY CHIEF-FRIEND DOESN'T GET SIDE-TRACKED BY CURIOSITY.
HE'S FOLLOWING THE RIVER--
--OUGHT TO SPOT HIM ANY TIME NOW. ...TROLL DUNG! WHAT WILL HE SAY?
THE NIGHT'S EVENTS OVER AND OVER IN HIS MIND.
AROREE AND I LOCK-SENT!
I KNOW SHE DIDN'T HAVE IT ALL PLANNED! WHY--?
YI YI YI
WHA--?
STARJUMPER!
MOMENTS LATER...
POOR OLD FRIEND! YOU WERE RUNNING YOUR PAWS OFF FOR ME, WEREN'T YOU?
CURSED THORN'S AS LONG AS MY FINGER! BUT IT'S OUT NOW!
RRF!
HMM?
OH... HAIRBALLS!
WELL--
--THEY WON'T KEEP US FROM FINDING CUTTER!

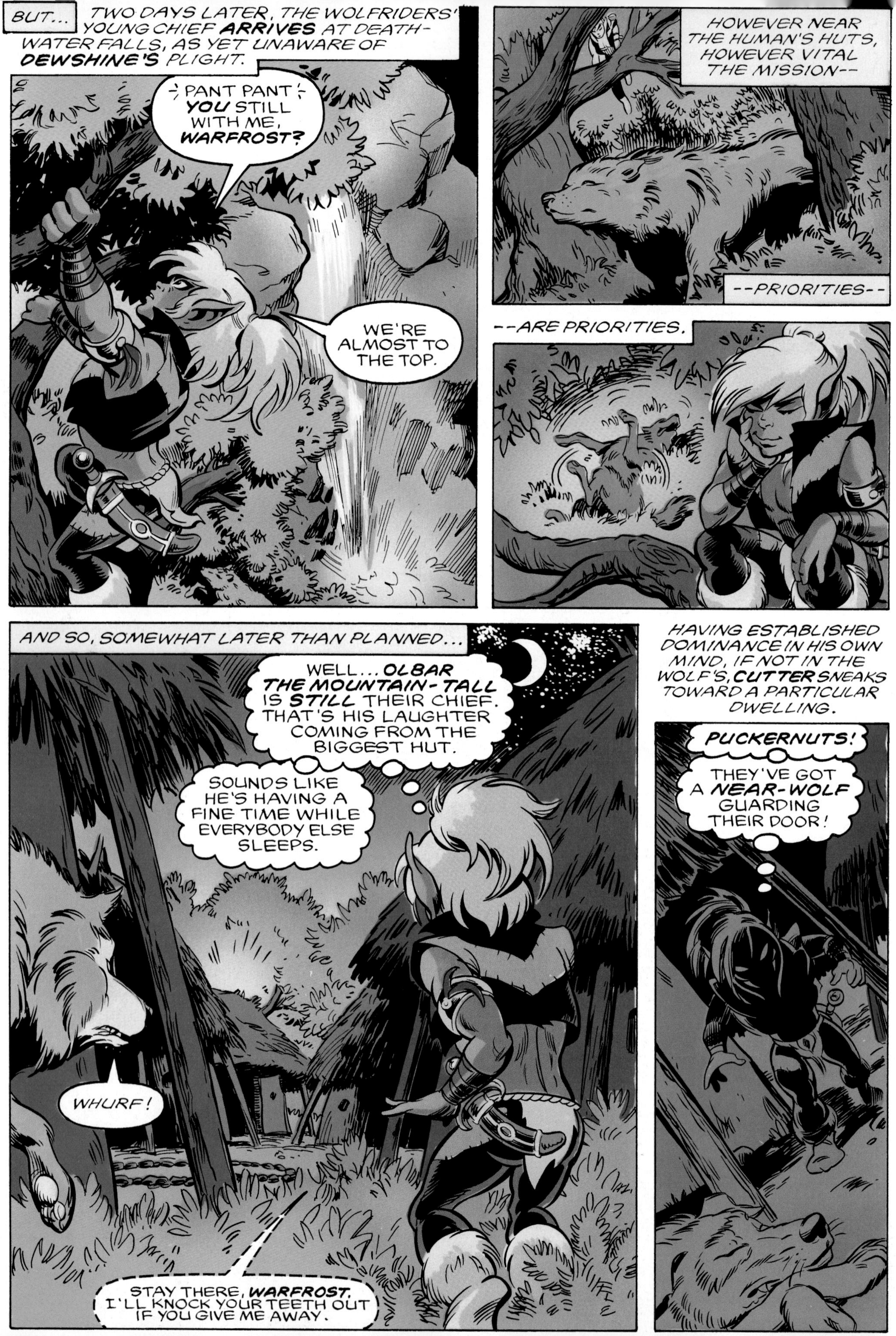

BUT... TWO DAYS LATER, THE WOLFRIDERS' YOUNG CHIEF ARRIVES AT DEATH-WATER FALLS, AS YET UNAWARE OF DEWSHINE'S PLIGHT.
PANT PANT YOU STILL WITH ME, WARFROST?
WE'RE ALMOST TO THE TOP.
HOWEVER NEAR THE HUMAN'S HUTS, HOWEVER VITAL THE MISSION--
--PRIORITIES--
--ARE PRIORITIES.
AND SO, SOMEWHAT LATER THAN PLANNED...
WELL... OLBAR THE MOUNTAIN-TALL IS STILL THEIR CHIEF. THAT'S HIS LAUGHTER COMING FROM THE BIGGEST HUT.
SOUNDS LIKE HE'S HAVING A FINE TIME WHILE EVERYBODY ELSE SLEEPS.
WHURF!
STAY THERE, WARFROST. I'LL KNOCK YOUR TEETH OUT IF YOU GIVE ME AWAY.
HAVING ESTABLISHED DOMINANCE IN HIS OWN MIND, IF NOT IN THE WOLF'S, CUTTER SNEAKS TOWARD A PARTICULAR DWELLING.
PUCKERNUTS!
THEY'VE GOT A NEAR-WOLF GUARDING THEIR DOOR!

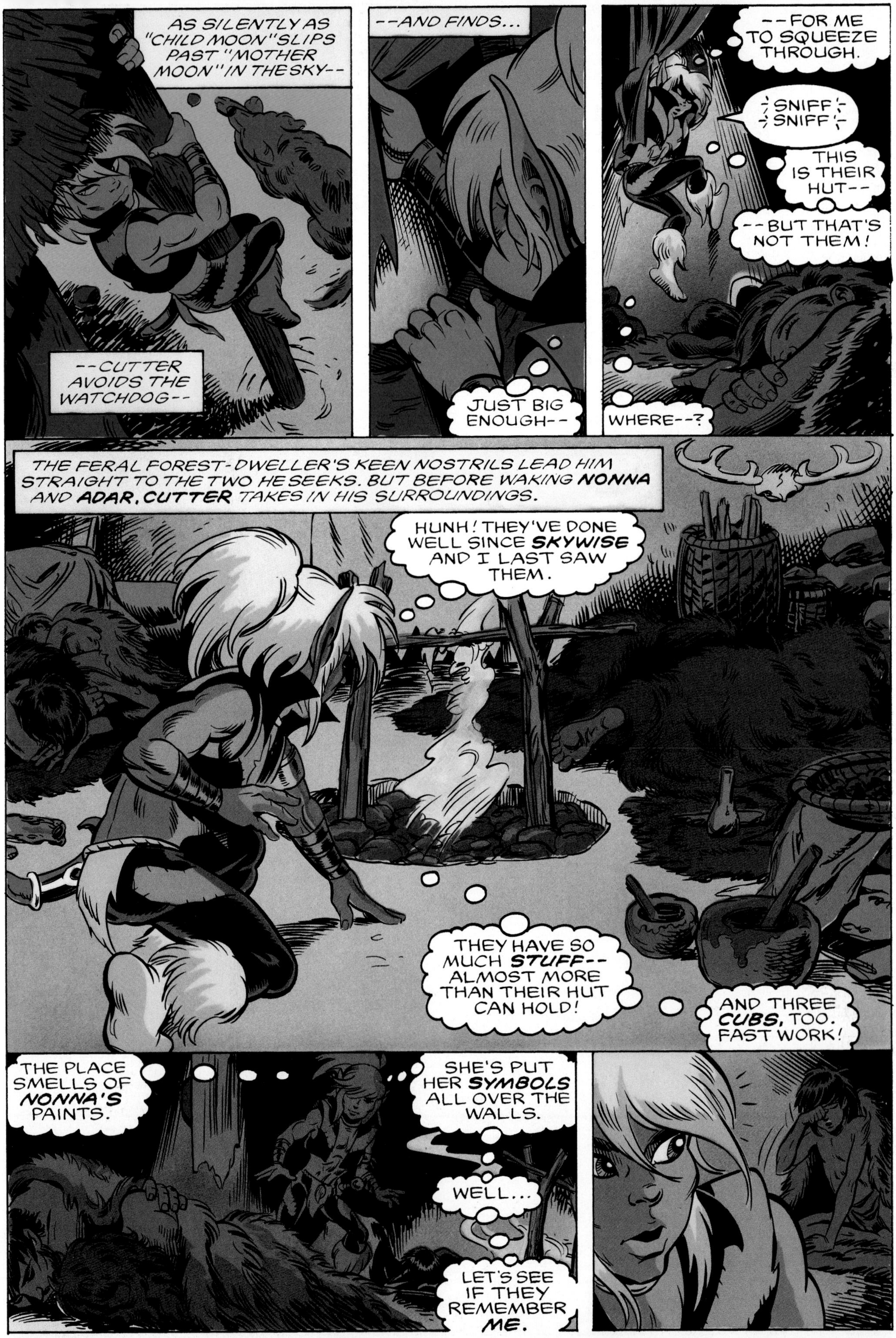
AS SILENTLY AS "CHILD MOON" SLIPS PAST "MOTHER MOON" IN THE SKY--
--CUTTER AVOIDS THE WATCHDOG--
--AND FINDS...
JUST BIG ENOUGH--
--FOR ME TO SQUEEZE THROUGH.
SNIFF SNIFF
THIS IS THEIR HUT--
--BUT THAT'S NOT THEM!
WHERE--?
THE FERAL FOREST-DWELLER'S KEEN NOSTRILS LEAD HIM STRAIGHT TO THE TWO HE SEEKS. BUT BEFORE WAKING NONNA AND ADAR, CUTTER TAKES IN HIS SURROUNDINGS.
HUNH! THEY'VE DONE WELL SINCE SKYWISE AND I LAST SAW THEM.
THEY HAVE SO MUCH STUFF-- ALMOST MORE THAN THEIR HUT CAN HOLD!
AND THREE CUBS, TOO. FAST WORK!
THE PLACE SMELLS OF NONNA'S PAINTS.
SHE'S PUT HER SYMBOLS ALL OVER THE WALLS.
WELL...
LET'S SEE IF THEY REMEMBER ME.

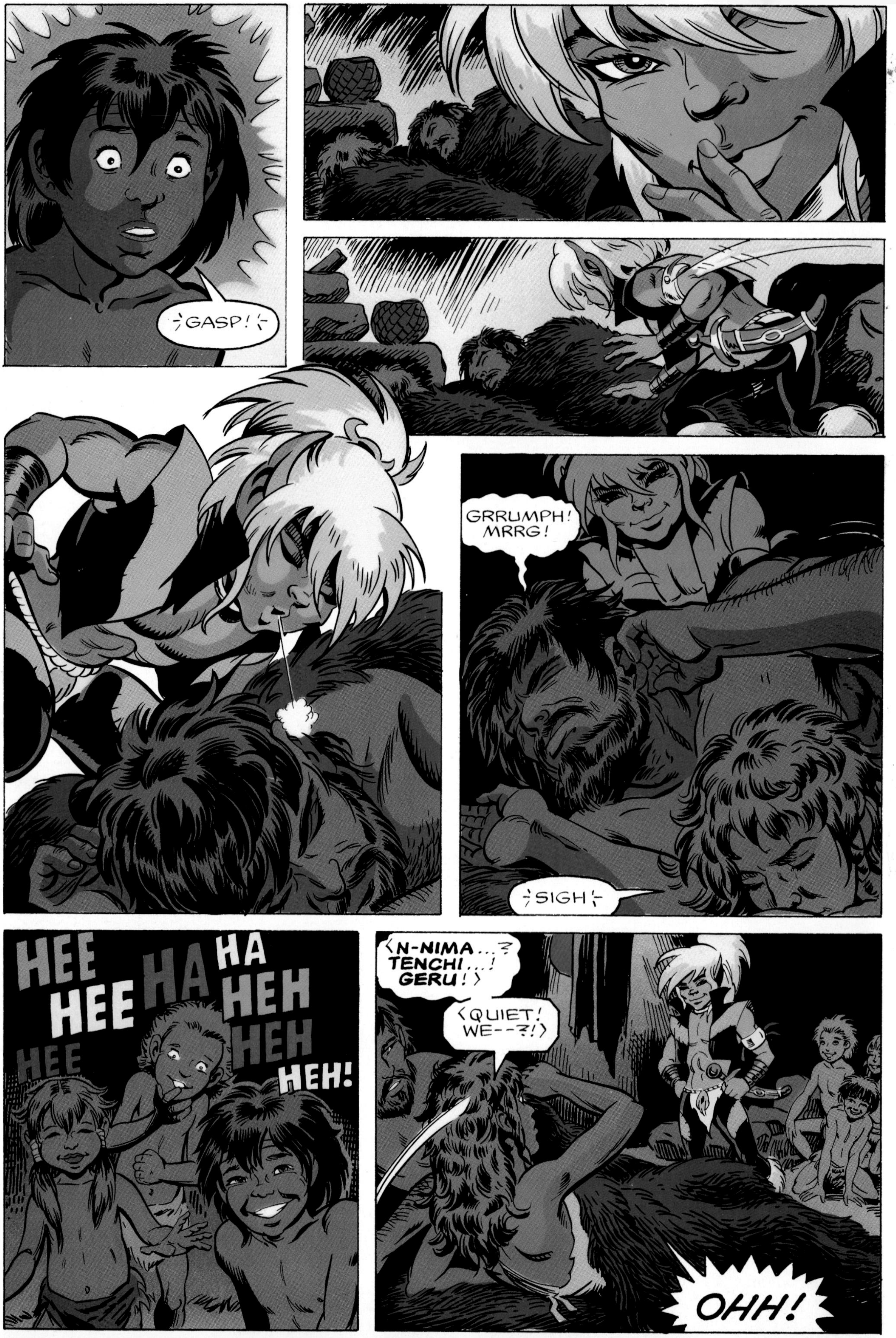
GASP!
GRRUMPH! MRRG!
SIGH
HEE HEE HEE HA HA HEH HEH HEH!
‹N-NIMA...? TENCHI...! GERU!›
‹QUIET! WE--?!›
OHH!

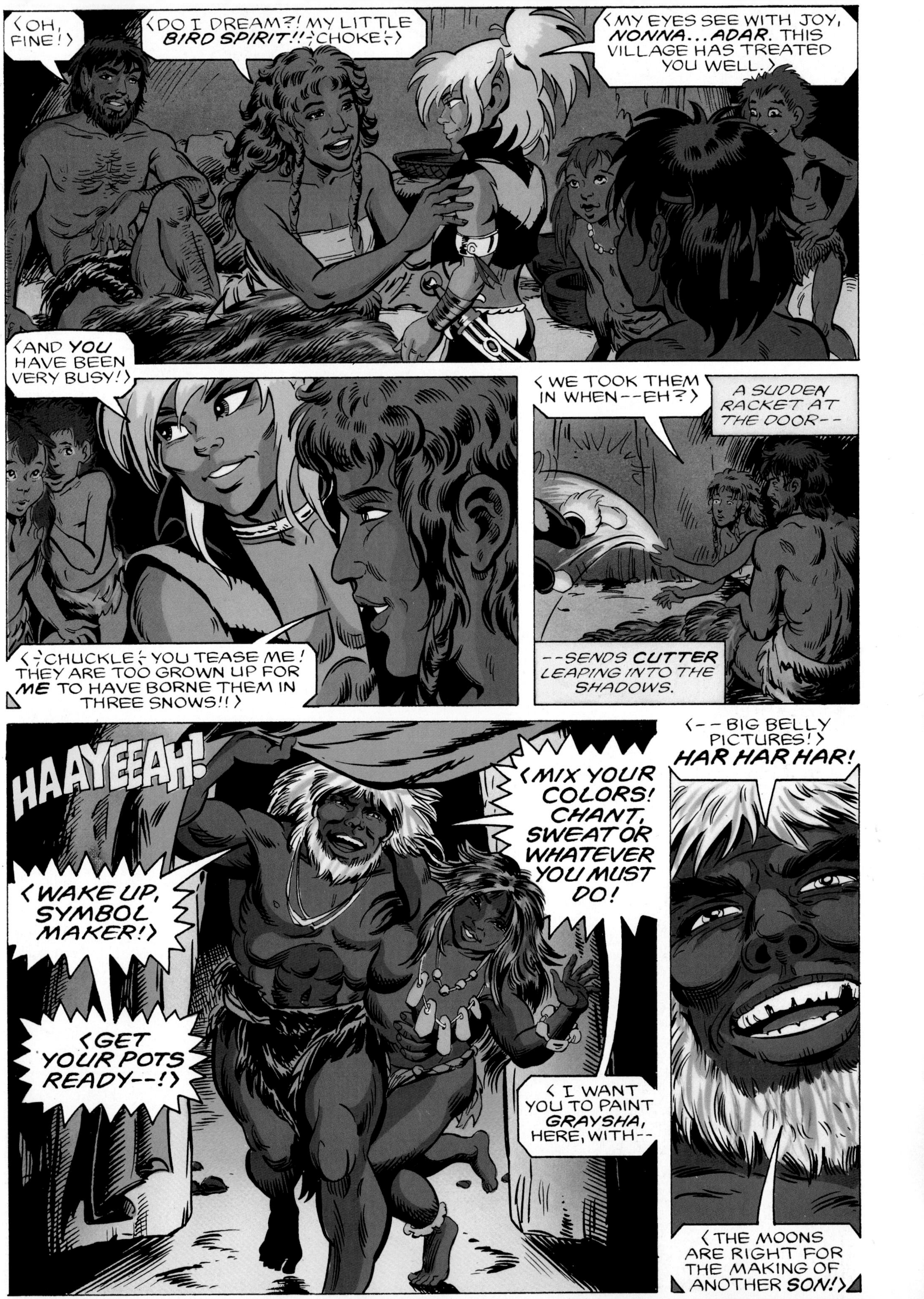

<OH, FINE!>
<DO I DREAM?! MY LITTLE BIRD SPIRIT!! -CHOKE->
<MY EYES SEE WITH JOY, NONNA...ADAR. THIS VILLAGE HAS TREATED YOU WELL.>
<AND YOU HAVE BEEN VERY BUSY!>
<-CHUCKLE- YOU TEASE ME! THEY ARE TOO GROWN UP FOR ME TO HAVE BORNE THEM IN THREE SNOWS!!>
<WE TOOK THEM IN WHEN--EH?>
A SUDDEN RACKET AT THE DOOR--
--SENDS CUTTER LEAPING INTO THE SHADOWS.
HAAYEEAH!
<WAKE UP, SYMBOL MAKER!>
<GET YOUR POTS READY--!>
<MIX YOUR COLORS! CHANT, SWEAT OR WHATEVER YOU MUST DO!
<I WANT YOU TO PAINT GRAYSHA, HERE, WITH--
<--BIG BELLY PICTURES!> HAR HAR HAR!
<THE MOONS ARE RIGHT FOR THE MAKING OF ANOTHER SON!>

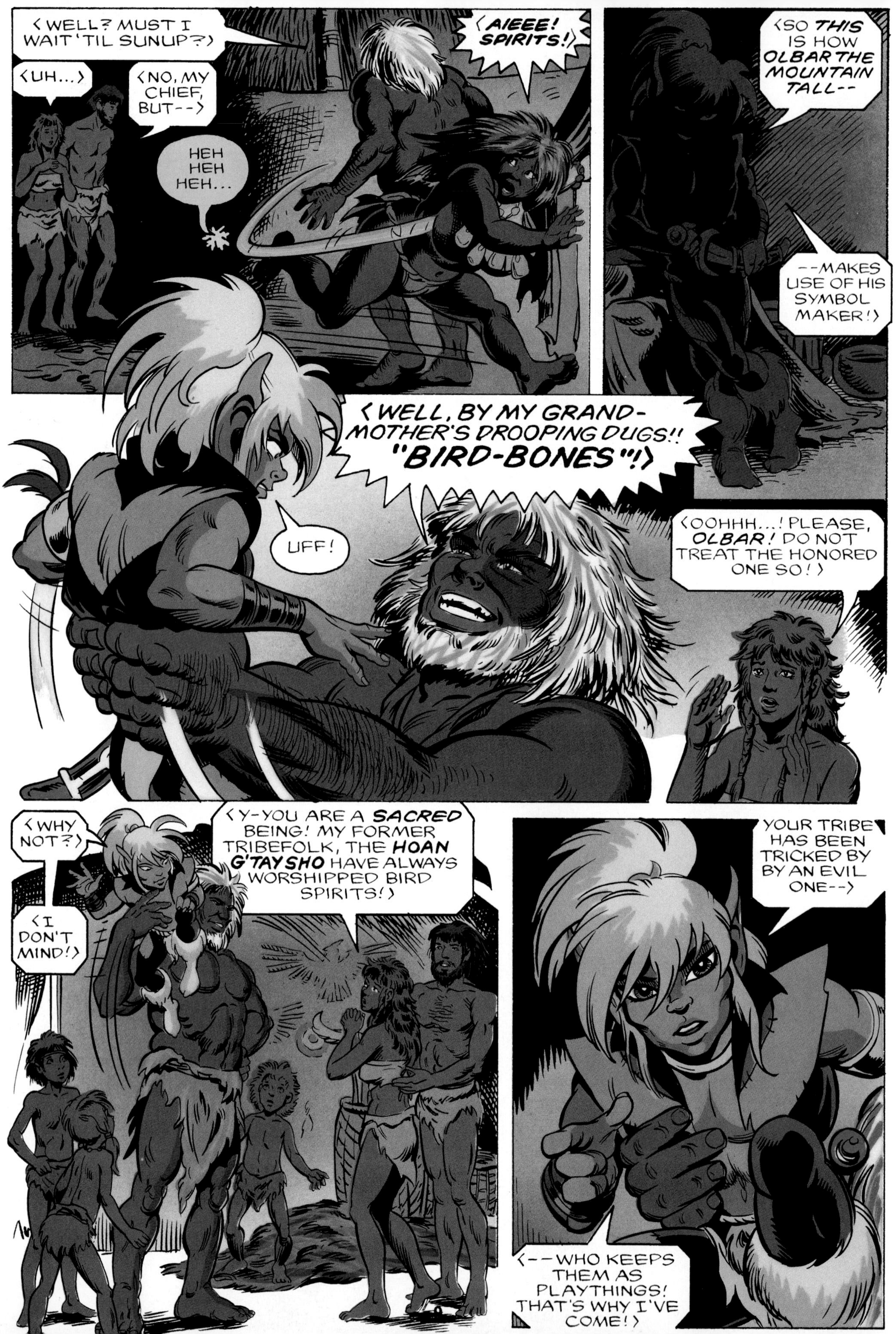
〈WELL? MUST I WAIT 'TIL SUNUP?〉
〈UH...〉
〈NO, MY CHIEF, BUT--〉
HEH HEH HEH...
〈AIEEE! SPIRITS!〉
〈SO THIS IS HOW OLBAR THE MOUNTAIN TALL--
--MAKES USE OF HIS SYMBOL MAKER!〉
〈WELL, BY MY GRANDMOTHER'S DROOPING DUGS!! "BIRD-BONES"!〉
UFF!
〈OOHHH...! PLEASE, OLBAR! DO NOT TREAT THE HONORED ONE SO!〉
〈WHY NOT?〉
〈I DON'T MIND!〉
〈Y-YOU ARE A SACRED BEING! MY FORMER TRIBEFOLK, THE HOAN G'TAYSHO HAVE ALWAYS WORSHIPPED BIRD SPIRITS!〉
YOUR TRIBE HAS BEEN TRICKED BY BY AN EVIL ONE--〉
〈--WHO KEEPS THEM AS PLAYTHINGS! THAT'S WHY I'VE COME!〉

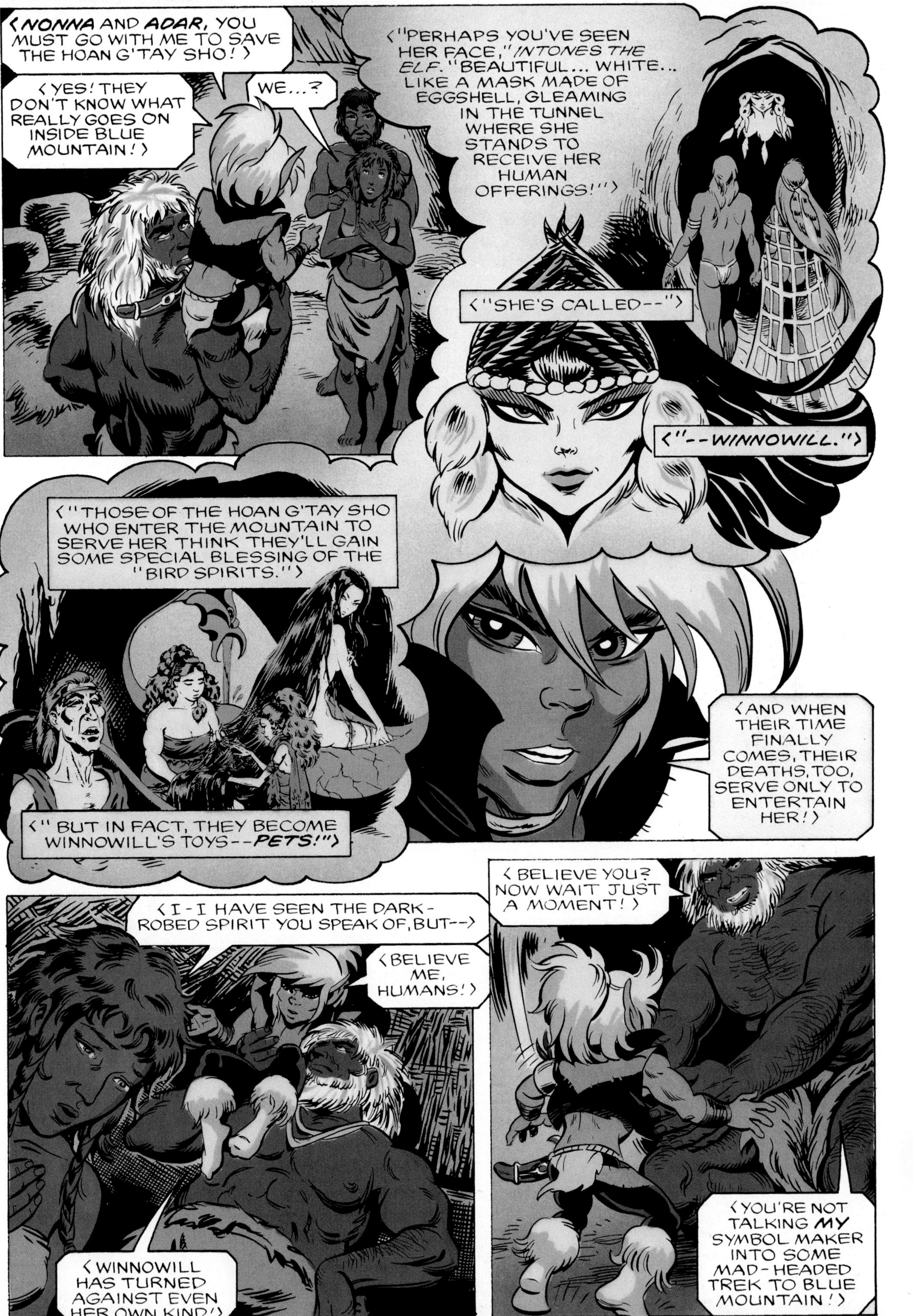

⟨NONNA AND ADAR, YOU MUST GO WITH ME TO SAVE THE HOAN G'TAY SHO!⟩
⟨YES! THEY DON'T KNOW WHAT REALLY GOES ON INSIDE BLUE MOUNTAIN!⟩
WE...?
⟨"PERHAPS YOU'VE SEEN HER FACE," INTONES THE ELF. "BEAUTIFUL... WHITE... LIKE A MASK MADE OF EGGSHELL, GLEAMING IN THE TUNNEL WHERE SHE STANDS TO RECEIVE HER HUMAN OFFERINGS!"⟩
⟨"SHE'S CALLED--"⟩
⟨"--WINNOWILL."⟩
⟨"THOSE OF THE HOAN G'TAY SHO WHO ENTER THE MOUNTAIN TO SERVE HER THINK THEY'LL GAIN SOME SPECIAL BLESSING OF THE "BIRD SPIRITS."⟩
⟨" BUT IN FACT, THEY BECOME WINNOWILL'S TOYS--PETS!"⟩
⟨AND WHEN THEIR TIME FINALLY COMES, THEIR DEATHS, TOO, SERVE ONLY TO ENTERTAIN HER!⟩
⟨I-I HAVE SEEN THE DARK-ROBED SPIRIT YOU SPEAK OF, BUT--⟩
⟨BELIEVE ME, HUMANS!⟩
⟨WINNOWILL HAS TURNED AGAINST EVEN HER OWN KIND!⟩
⟨BELIEVE YOU? NOW WAIT JUST A MOMENT!⟩
⟨YOU'RE NOT TALKING MY SYMBOL MAKER INTO SOME MAD-HEADED TREK TO BLUE MOUNTAIN!⟩

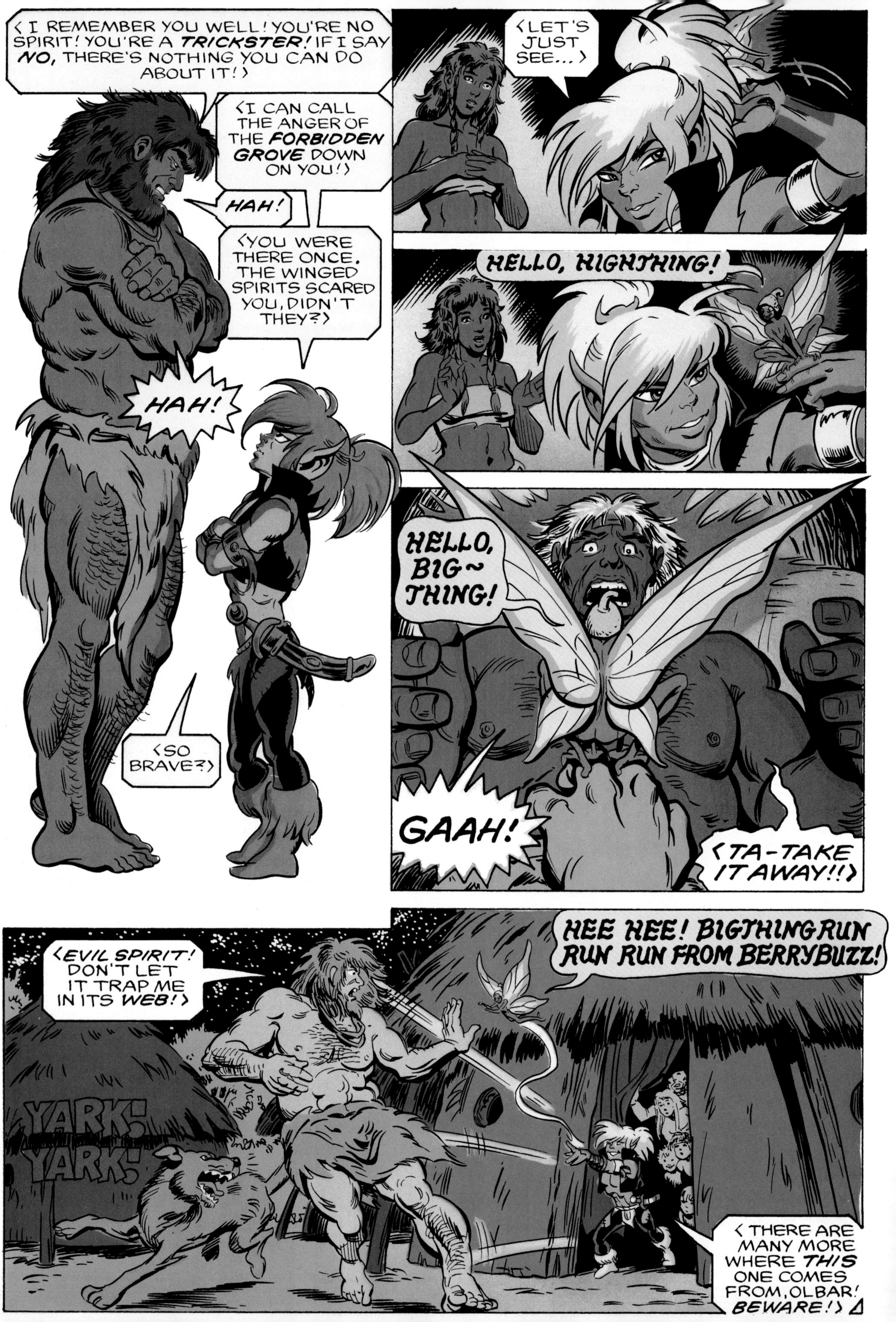
< I REMEMBER YOU WELL! YOU'RE NO SPIRIT! YOU'RE A TRICKSTER! IF I SAY NO, THERE'S NOTHING YOU CAN DO ABOUT IT! >
< I CAN CALL THE ANGER OF THE FORBIDDEN GROVE DOWN ON YOU! >
HAH!
< YOU WERE THERE ONCE. THE WINGED SPIRITS SCARED YOU, DIDN'T THEY? >
HAH!
< SO BRAVE? >
< LET'S JUST SEE... >
HELLO, HIGHTHING!
HELLO, BIG~THING!
GAAH!
< TA-TAKE IT AWAY!! >
< EVIL SPIRIT! DON'T LET IT TRAP ME IN ITS WEB! >
HEE HEE! BIGTHING RUN RUN RUN FROM BERRYBUZZ!
YARK! YARK!
< THERE ARE MANY MORE WHERE THIS ONE COMES FROM, OLBAR! BEWARE! >

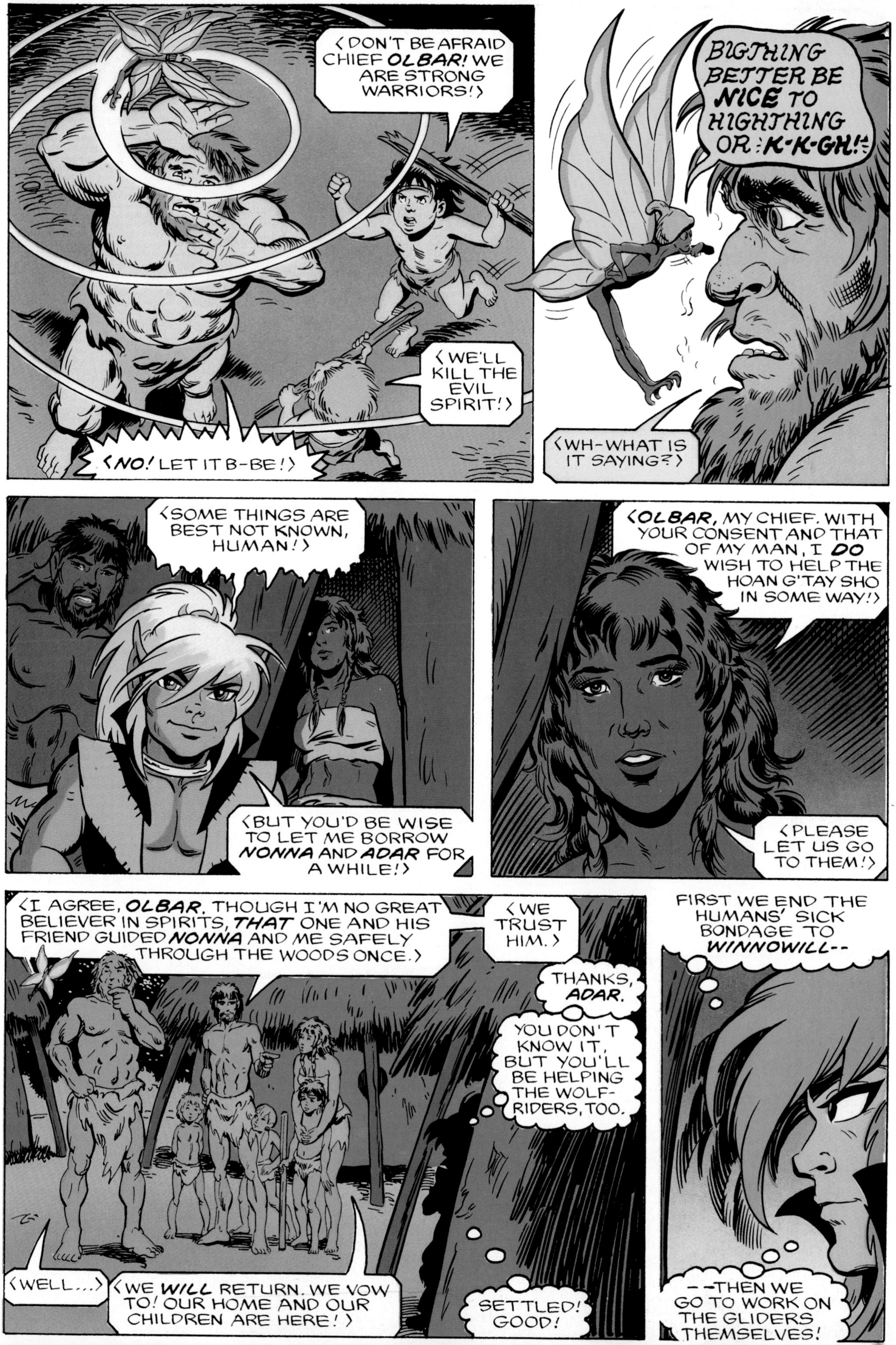

<DON'T BE AFRAID CHIEF OLBAR! WE ARE STRONG WARRIORS!>
<WE'LL KILL THE EVIL SPIRIT!>
<NO! LET IT B-BE!>
BIGTHING BETTER BE NICE TO HIGHTHING OR :K-K-GH!:
<WH-WHAT IS IT SAYING?>
<SOME THINGS ARE BEST NOT KNOWN, HUMAN!>
<BUT YOU'D BE WISE TO LET ME BORROW NONNA AND ADAR FOR A WHILE!>
<OLBAR, MY CHIEF. WITH YOUR CONSENT AND THAT OF MY MAN, I DO WISH TO HELP THE HOAN G'TAY SHO IN SOME WAY!>
<PLEASE LET US GO TO THEM!>
<I AGREE, OLBAR. THOUGH I'M NO GREAT BELIEVER IN SPIRITS, THAT ONE AND HIS FRIEND GUIDED NONNA AND ME SAFELY THROUGH THE WOODS ONCE.>
<WE TRUST HIM.>
THANKS, ADAR.
YOU DON'T KNOW IT, BUT YOU'LL BE HELPING THE WOLF-RIDERS, TOO.
<WELL...>
<WE WILL RETURN. WE VOW TO! OUR HOME AND OUR CHILDREN ARE HERE!>
SETTLED! GOOD!
FIRST WE END THE HUMANS' SICK BONDAGE TO WINNOWILL--
--THEN WE GO TO WORK ON THE GLIDERS THEMSELVES!

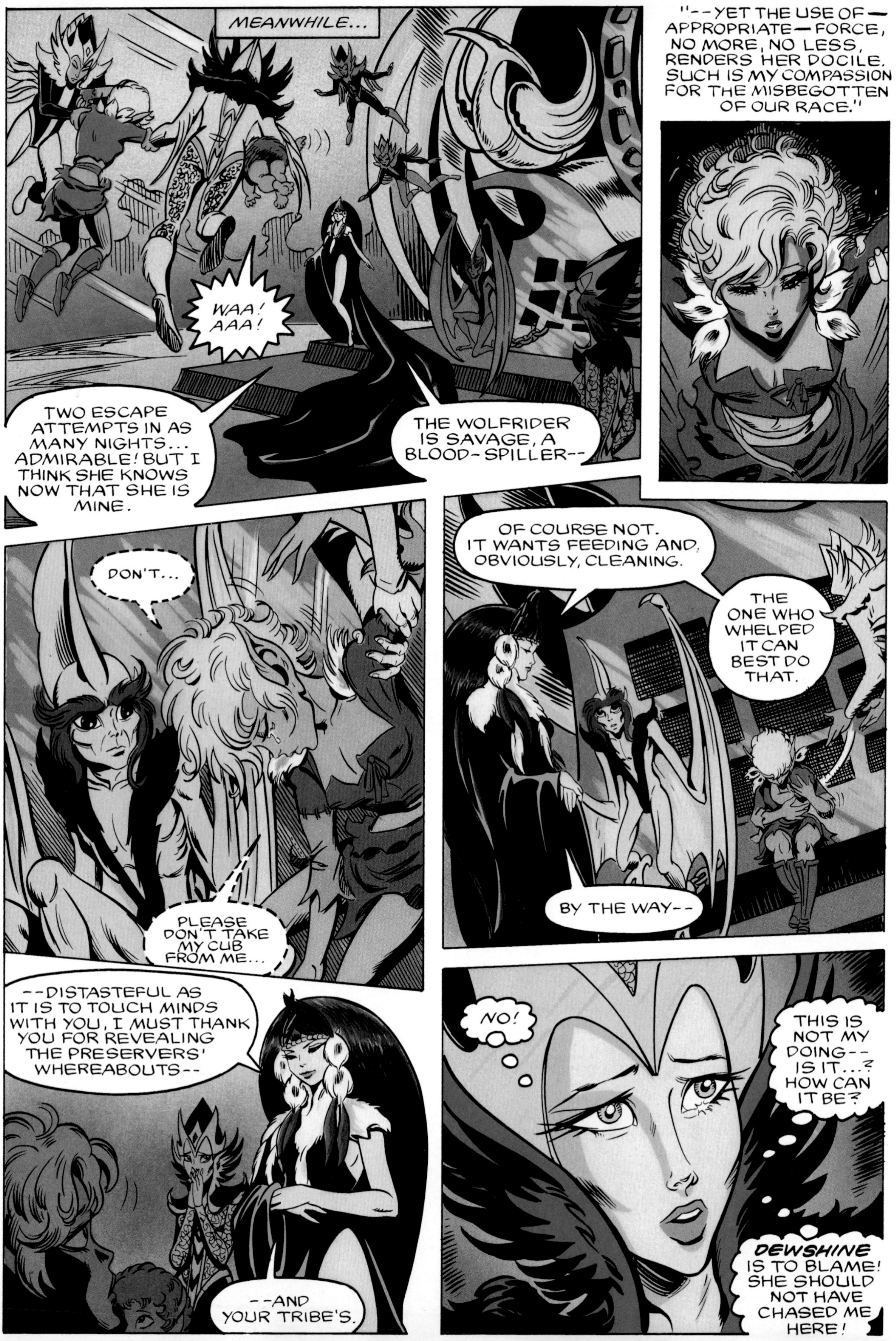
MEANWHILE...
WAA! AAA!
TWO ESCAPE ATTEMPTS IN AS MANY NIGHTS... ADMIRABLE! BUT I THINK SHE KNOWS NOW THAT SHE IS MINE.
THE WOLFRIDER IS SAVAGE, A BLOOD-SPILLER--
"--YET THE USE OF--APPROPRIATE--FORCE, NO MORE, NO LESS, RENDERS HER DOCILE. SUCH IS MY COMPASSION FOR THE MISBEGOTTEN OF OUR RACE."
DON'T...
PLEASE DON'T TAKE MY CUB FROM ME...
OF COURSE NOT. IT WANTS FEEDING AND, OBVIOUSLY, CLEANING.
THE ONE WHO WHELPED IT CAN BEST DO THAT.
BY THE WAY--
--DISTASTEFUL AS IT IS TO TOUCH MINDS WITH YOU, I MUST THANK YOU FOR REVEALING THE PRESERVERS' WHEREABOUTS--
--AND YOUR TRIBE'S.
NO!
THIS IS NOT MY DOING-- IS IT...? HOW CAN IT BE?
DEWSHINE IS TO BLAME! SHE SHOULD NOT HAVE CHASED ME HERE!

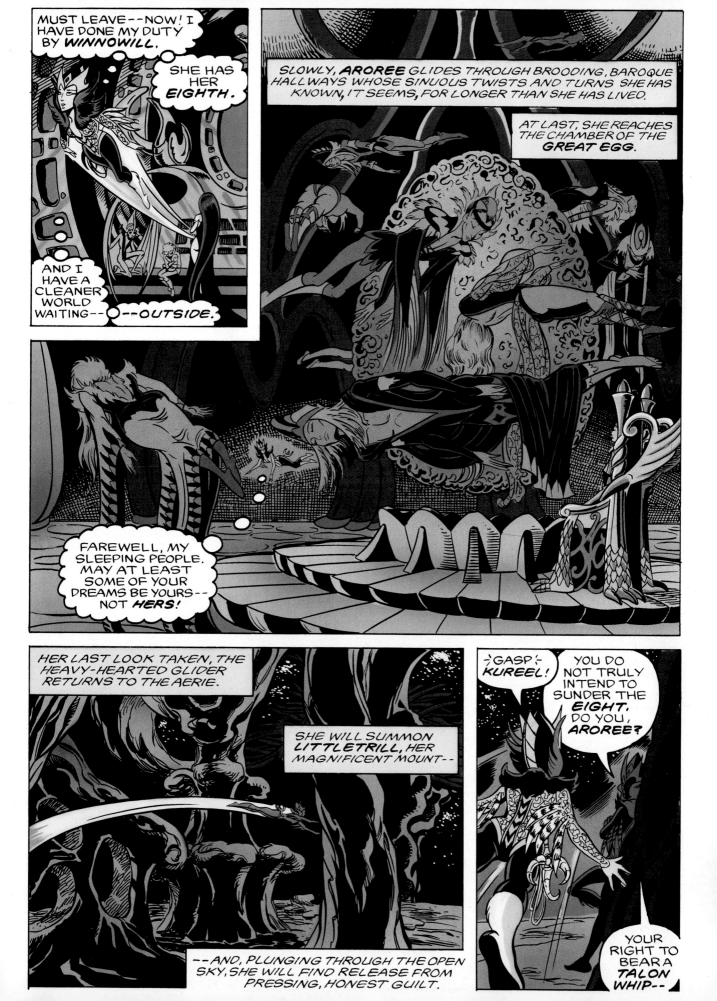

MUST LEAVE--NOW! I HAVE DONE MY DUTY BY *WINNOWILL*.

SHE HAS HER *EIGHTH*.

AND I HAVE A CLEANER WORLD WAITING-- --OUTSIDE.

SLOWLY, *AROREE* GLIDES THROUGH BROODING, BAROQUE HALLWAYS WHOSE SINUOUS TWISTS AND TURNS SHE HAS KNOWN, IT SEEMS, FOR LONGER THAN SHE HAS LIVED.

AT LAST, SHE REACHES THE CHAMBER OF THE *GREAT EGG*.

FAREWELL, MY SLEEPING PEOPLE. MAY AT LEAST SOME OF YOUR DREAMS BE YOURS-- NOT *HERS*!

HER LAST LOOK TAKEN, THE HEAVY-HEARTED GLIDER RETURNS TO THE AERIE.

SHE WILL SUMMON *LITTLETRILL*, HER MAGNIFICENT MOUNT--

--AND, PLUNGING THROUGH THE OPEN SKY, SHE WILL FIND RELEASE FROM PRESSING, HONEST GUILT.

÷GASP÷ *KUREEL*!

YOU DO NOT TRULY INTEND TO SUNDER THE *EIGHT*, DO YOU, *AROREE*?

YOUR RIGHT TO BEAR A *TALON WHIP*--

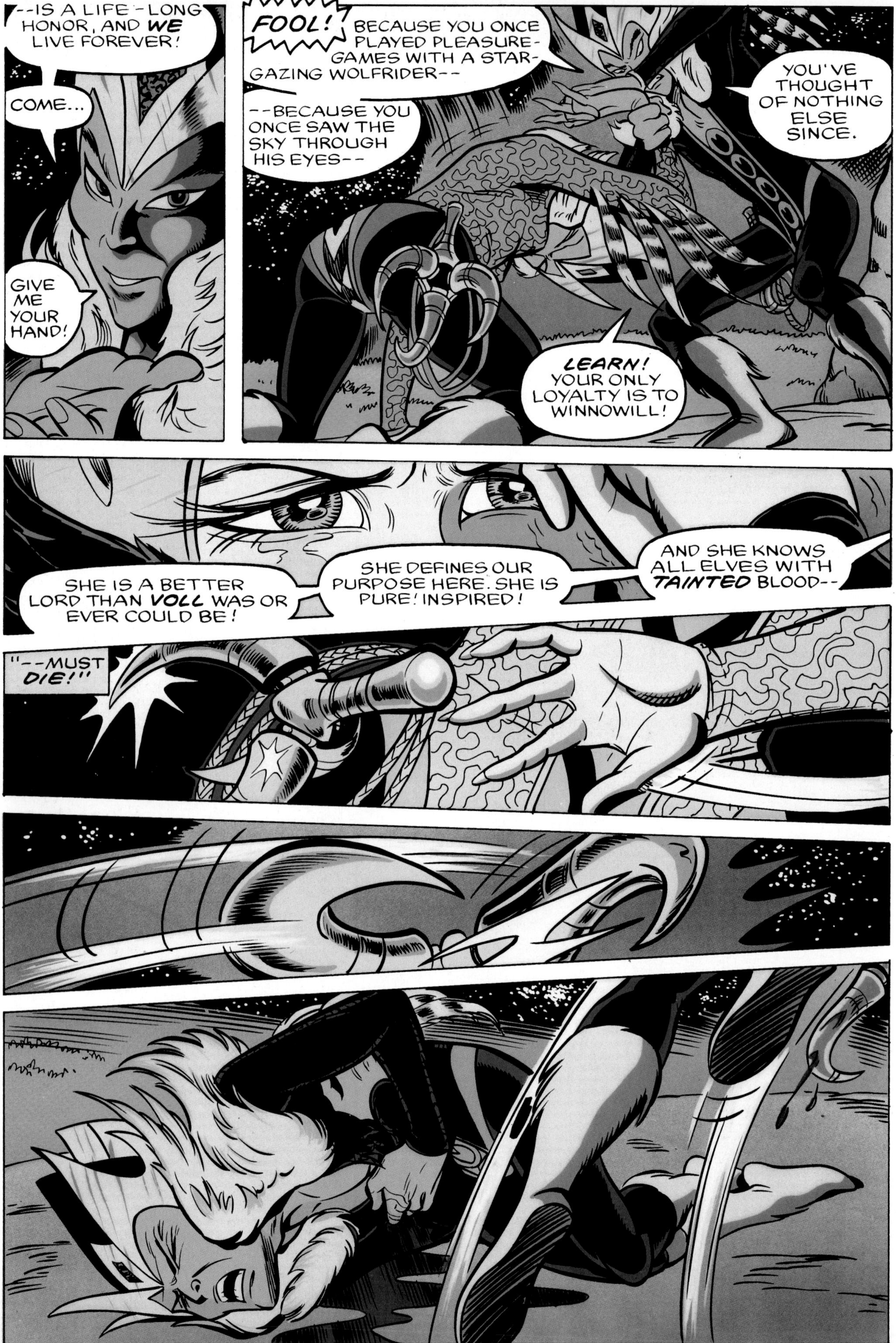

--IS A LIFE-LONG HONOR, AND WE LIVE FOREVER!
COME...
GIVE ME YOUR HAND!
FOOL!
BECAUSE YOU ONCE PLAYED PLEASURE-GAMES WITH A STAR-GAZING WOLFRIDER--
--BECAUSE YOU ONCE SAW THE SKY THROUGH HIS EYES--
YOU'VE THOUGHT OF NOTHING ELSE SINCE.
LEARN! YOUR ONLY LOYALTY IS TO WINNOWILL!
SHE IS A BETTER LORD THAN VOLL WAS OR EVER COULD BE!
SHE DEFINES OUR PURPOSE HERE. SHE IS PURE! INSPIRED!
AND SHE KNOWS ALL ELVES WITH TAINTED BLOOD--
"--MUST DIE!"

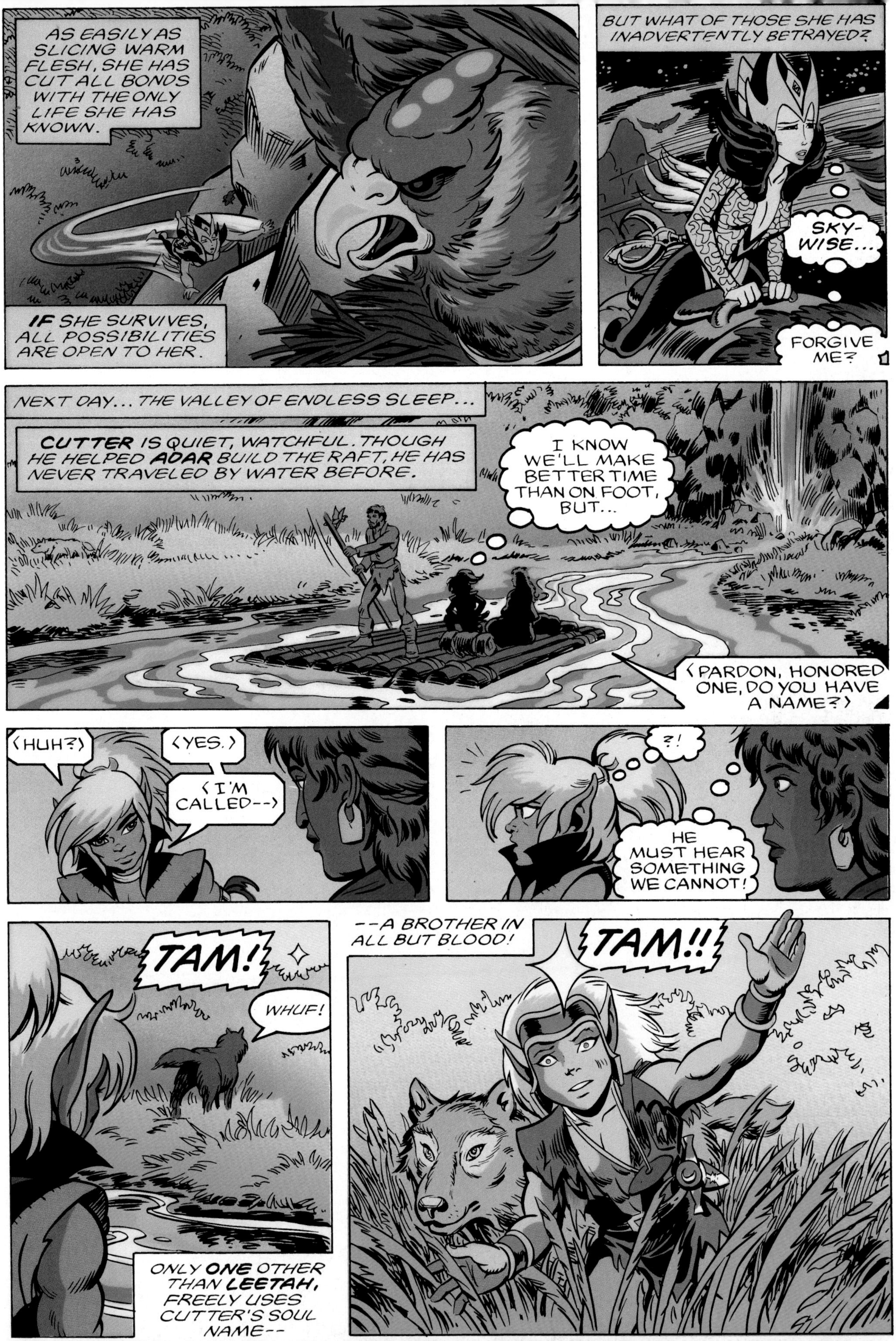
AS EASILY AS SLICING WARM FLESH, SHE HAS CUT ALL BONDS WITH THE ONLY LIFE SHE HAS KNOWN.
IF SHE SURVIVES, ALL POSSIBILITIES ARE OPEN TO HER.
BUT WHAT OF THOSE SHE HAS INADVERTENTLY BETRAYED?
SKY-WISE...
FORGIVE ME?
NEXT DAY... THE VALLEY OF ENDLESS SLEEP...
CUTTER IS QUIET, WATCHFUL. THOUGH HE HELPED ADAR BUILD THE RAFT, HE HAS NEVER TRAVELED BY WATER BEFORE.
I KNOW WE'LL MAKE BETTER TIME THAN ON FOOT, BUT...
‹PARDON, HONORED ONE, DO YOU HAVE A NAME?›
‹HUH?›
‹YES.›
‹I'M CALLED--›
?!
HE MUST HEAR SOMETHING WE CANNOT!
TAM!
WHUF!
ONLY ONE OTHER THAN LEETAH, FREELY USES CUTTER'S SOUL NAME--
--A BROTHER IN ALL BUT BLOOD!
TAM!!

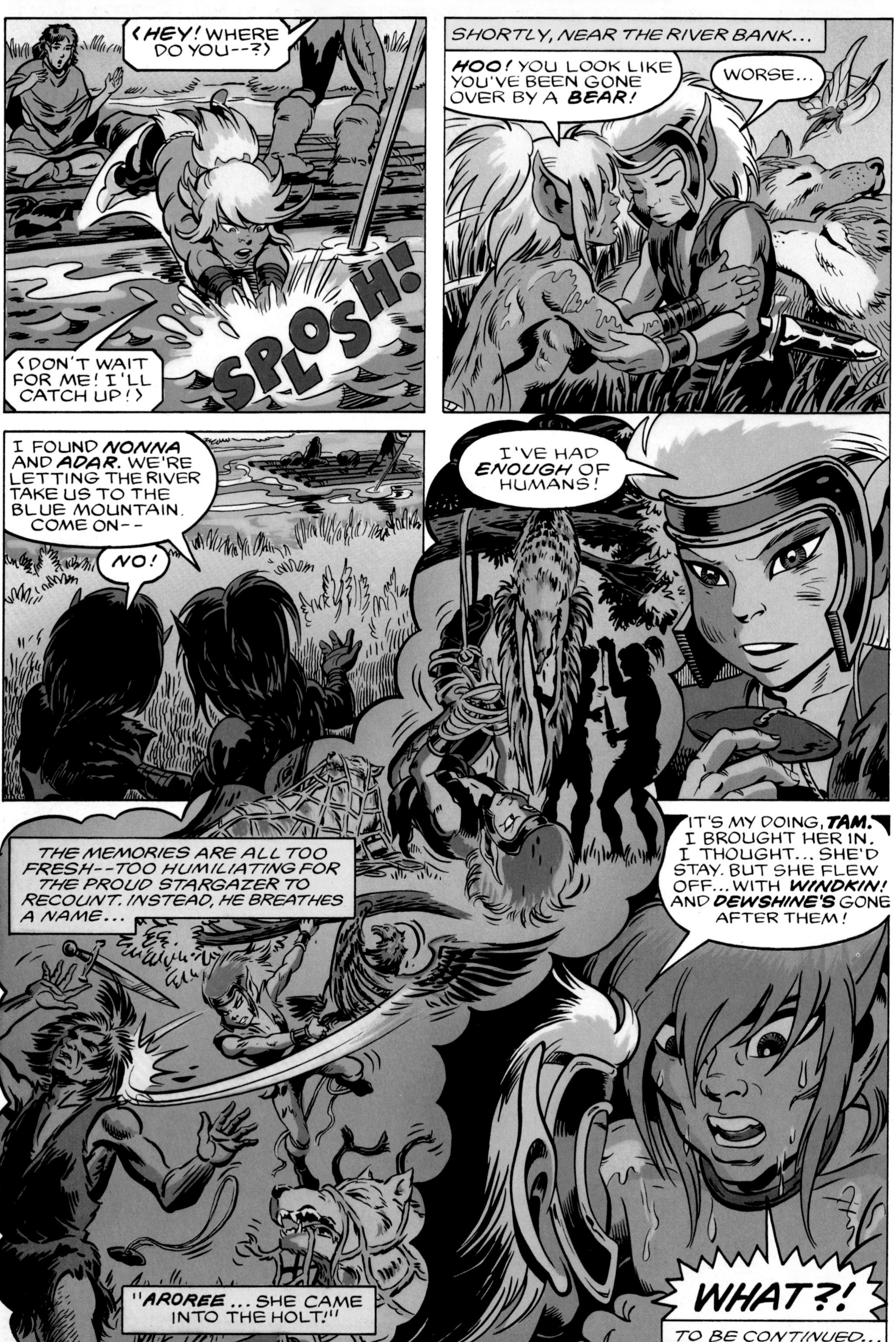
‹HEY! WHERE DO YOU--?›
SPLOSH!
‹DON'T WAIT FOR ME! I'LL CATCH UP!›
SHORTLY, NEAR THE RIVER BANK...
HOO! YOU LOOK LIKE YOU'VE BEEN GONE OVER BY A BEAR!
WORSE...
I FOUND NONNA AND ADAR. WE'RE LETTING THE RIVER TAKE US TO THE BLUE MOUNTAIN. COME ON--
NO!
I'VE HAD ENOUGH OF HUMANS!
THE MEMORIES ARE ALL TOO FRESH--TOO HUMILIATING FOR THE PROUD STARGAZER TO RECOUNT. INSTEAD, HE BREATHES A NAME...
"AROREE... SHE CAME INTO THE HOLT!"
IT'S MY DOING, TAM. I BROUGHT HER IN. I THOUGHT... SHE'D STAY. BUT SHE FLEW OFF... WITH WINDKIN! AND DEWSHINE'S GONE AFTER THEM!
WHAT?!
TO BE CONTINUED...

SIEGE AT BLUE MOUNTAIN

ARTIST/WRITER WENDY PINI | CO-PLOT/EDITOR RICHARD PINI | PART 3 | INKS JOE STATON | LETTERER JANICE CHIANG

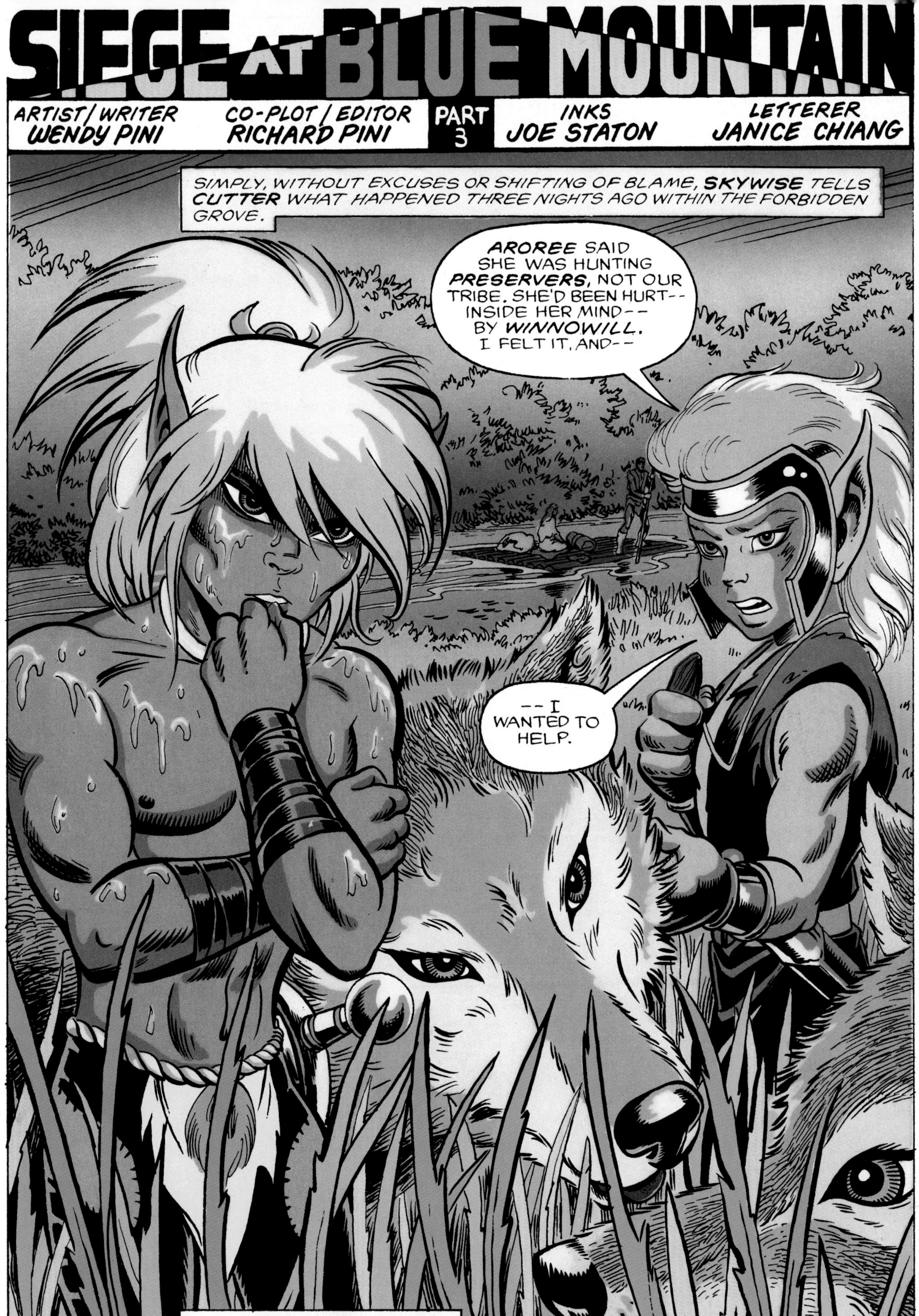
SIMPLY, WITHOUT EXCUSES OR SHIFTING OF BLAME, SKYWISE TELLS CUTTER WHAT HAPPENED THREE NIGHTS AGO WITHIN THE FORBIDDEN GROVE.
AROREE SAID SHE WAS HUNTING PRESERVERS, NOT OUR TRIBE. SHE'D BEEN HURT-- INSIDE HER MIND-- BY WINNOWILL. I FELT IT, AND--
--I WANTED TO HELP.
THE YOUNG WOLFRIDER CHIEF LISTENS... VERY QUIETLY.

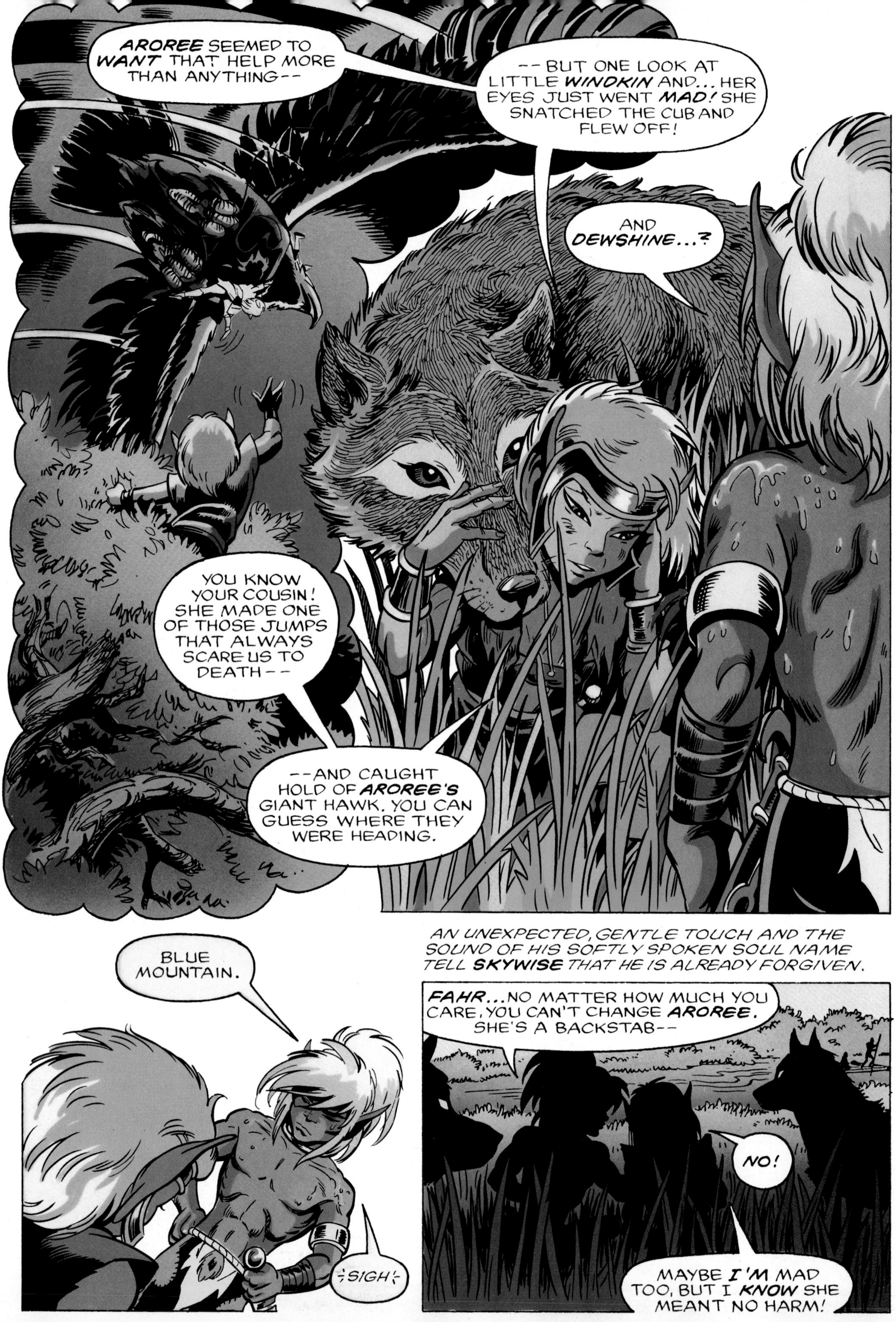
AROREE SEEMED TO WANT THAT HELP MORE THAN ANYTHING--
--BUT ONE LOOK AT LITTLE WINOKIN AND... HER EYES JUST WENT MAD! SHE SNATCHED THE CUB AND FLEW OFF!
AND DEWSHINE...?
YOU KNOW YOUR COUSIN! SHE MADE ONE OF THOSE JUMPS THAT ALWAYS SCARE US TO DEATH--
--AND CAUGHT HOLD OF AROREE'S GIANT HAWK. YOU CAN GUESS WHERE THEY WERE HEADING.
BLUE MOUNTAIN.
SIGH
AN UNEXPECTED, GENTLE TOUCH AND THE SOUND OF HIS SOFTLY SPOKEN SOUL NAME TELL SKYWISE THAT HE IS ALREADY FORGIVEN.
FAHR...NO MATTER HOW MUCH YOU CARE, YOU CAN'T CHANGE AROREE. SHE'S A BACKSTAB--
NO!
MAYBE I'M MAD TOO, BUT I KNOW SHE MEANT NO HARM!

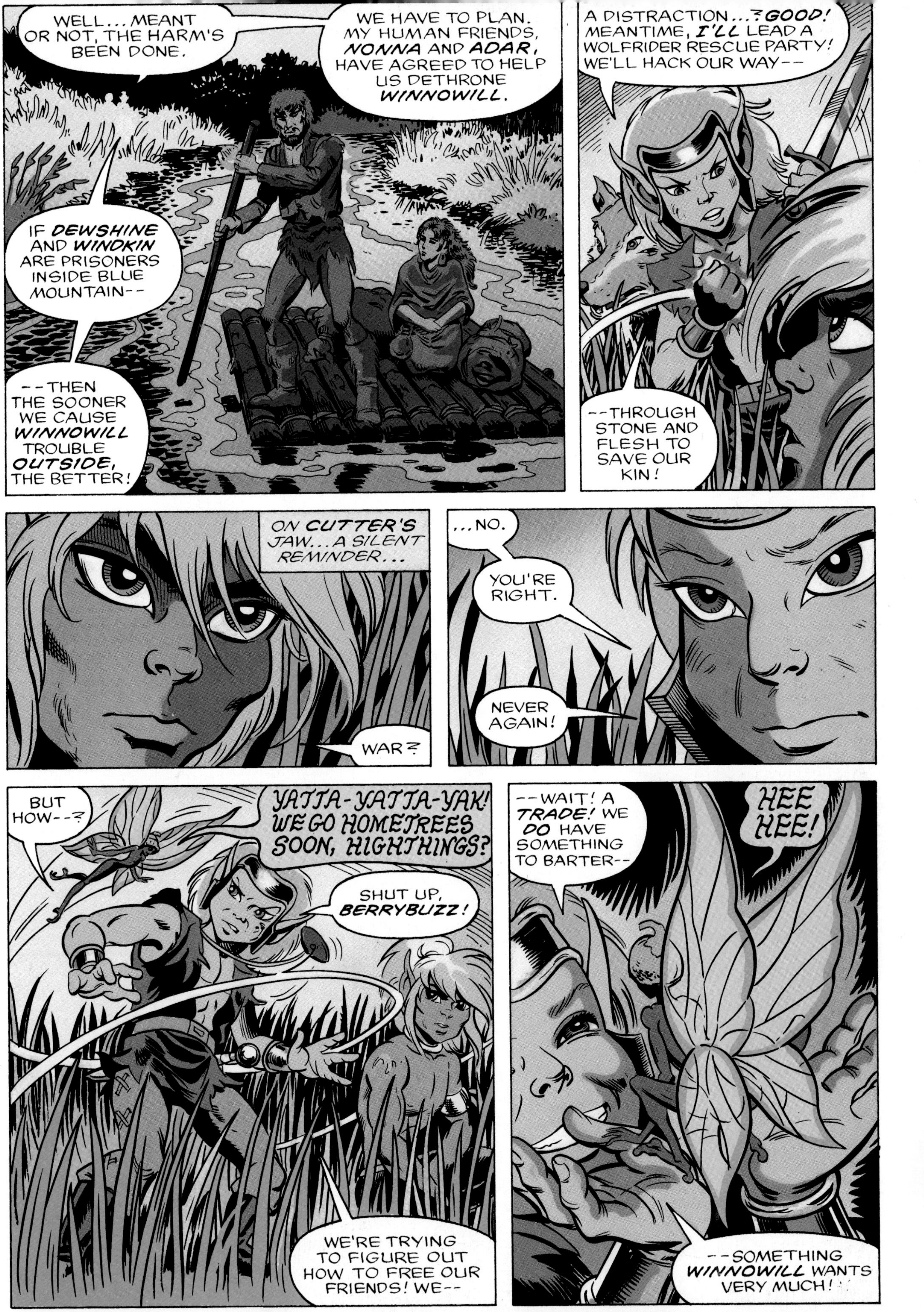

WELL... MEANT OR NOT, THE HARM'S BEEN DONE.
WE HAVE TO PLAN. MY HUMAN FRIENDS, NONNA AND ADAR, HAVE AGREED TO HELP US DETHRONE WINNOWILL.
IF DEWSHINE AND WINDKIN ARE PRISONERS INSIDE BLUE MOUNTAIN--
--THEN THE SOONER WE CAUSE WINNOWILL TROUBLE OUTSIDE, THE BETTER!
A DISTRACTION...? GOOD! MEANTIME, I'LL LEAD A WOLFRIDER RESCUE PARTY! WE'LL HACK OUR WAY--
--THROUGH STONE AND FLESH TO SAVE OUR KIN!
ON CUTTER'S JAW... A SILENT REMINDER...
WAR?
...NO.
YOU'RE RIGHT.
NEVER AGAIN!
BUT HOW--?
YATTA-YATTA-YAK! WE GO HOMETREES SOON, HIGHTHINGS?
SHUT UP, BERRYBUZZ!
WE'RE TRYING TO FIGURE OUT HOW TO FREE OUR FRIENDS! WE--
HEE HEE!
--WAIT! A TRADE! WE DO HAVE SOMETHING TO BARTER--
--SOMETHING WINNOWILL WANTS VERY MUCH!

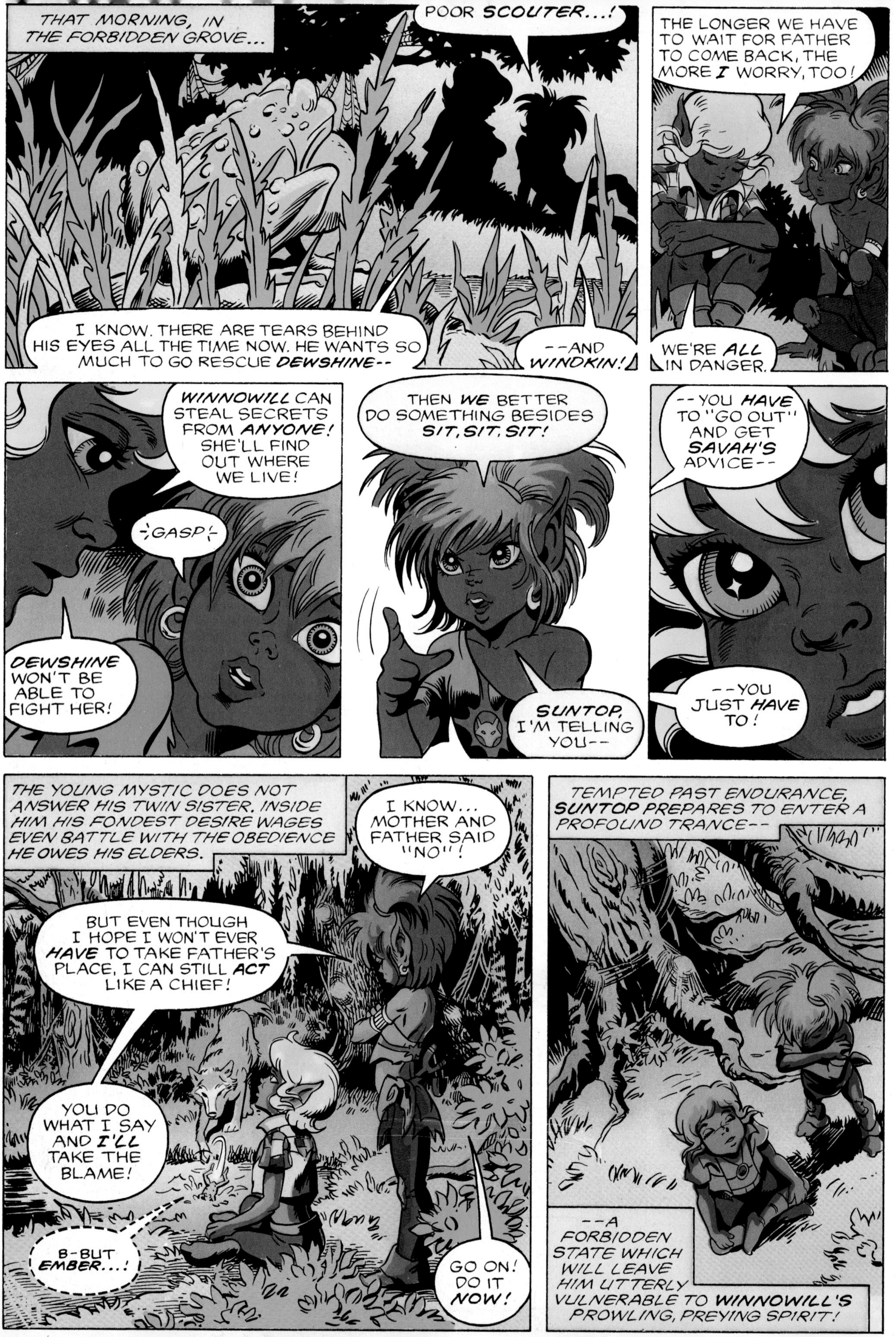
THAT MORNING, IN THE FORBIDDEN GROVE...
POOR SCOUTER...!
I KNOW. THERE ARE TEARS BEHIND HIS EYES ALL THE TIME NOW. HE WANTS SO MUCH TO GO RESCUE DEWSHINE--
--AND WINDKIN!
THE LONGER WE HAVE TO WAIT FOR FATHER TO COME BACK, THE MORE I WORRY, TOO!
WE'RE ALL IN DANGER.
WINNOWILL CAN STEAL SECRETS FROM ANYONE! SHE'LL FIND OUT WHERE WE LIVE!
GASP
DEWSHINE WON'T BE ABLE TO FIGHT HER!
THEN WE BETTER DO SOMETHING BESIDES SIT, SIT, SIT!
SUNTOP, I'M TELLING YOU--
--YOU HAVE TO "GO OUT" AND GET SAVAH'S ADVICE--
--YOU JUST HAVE TO!
THE YOUNG MYSTIC DOES NOT ANSWER HIS TWIN SISTER. INSIDE HIM HIS FONDEST DESIRE WAGES EVEN BATTLE WITH THE OBEDIENCE HE OWES HIS ELDERS.
I KNOW... MOTHER AND FATHER SAID "NO"!
BUT EVEN THOUGH I HOPE I WON'T EVER HAVE TO TAKE FATHER'S PLACE, I CAN STILL ACT LIKE A CHIEF!
YOU DO WHAT I SAY AND I'LL TAKE THE BLAME!
B-BUT EMBER...!
GO ON! DO IT NOW!
TEMPTED PAST ENDURANCE, SUNTOP PREPARES TO ENTER A PROFOUND TRANCE--
--A FORBIDDEN STATE WHICH WILL LEAVE HIM UTTERLY VULNERABLE TO WINNOWILL'S PROWLING, PREYING SPIRIT!

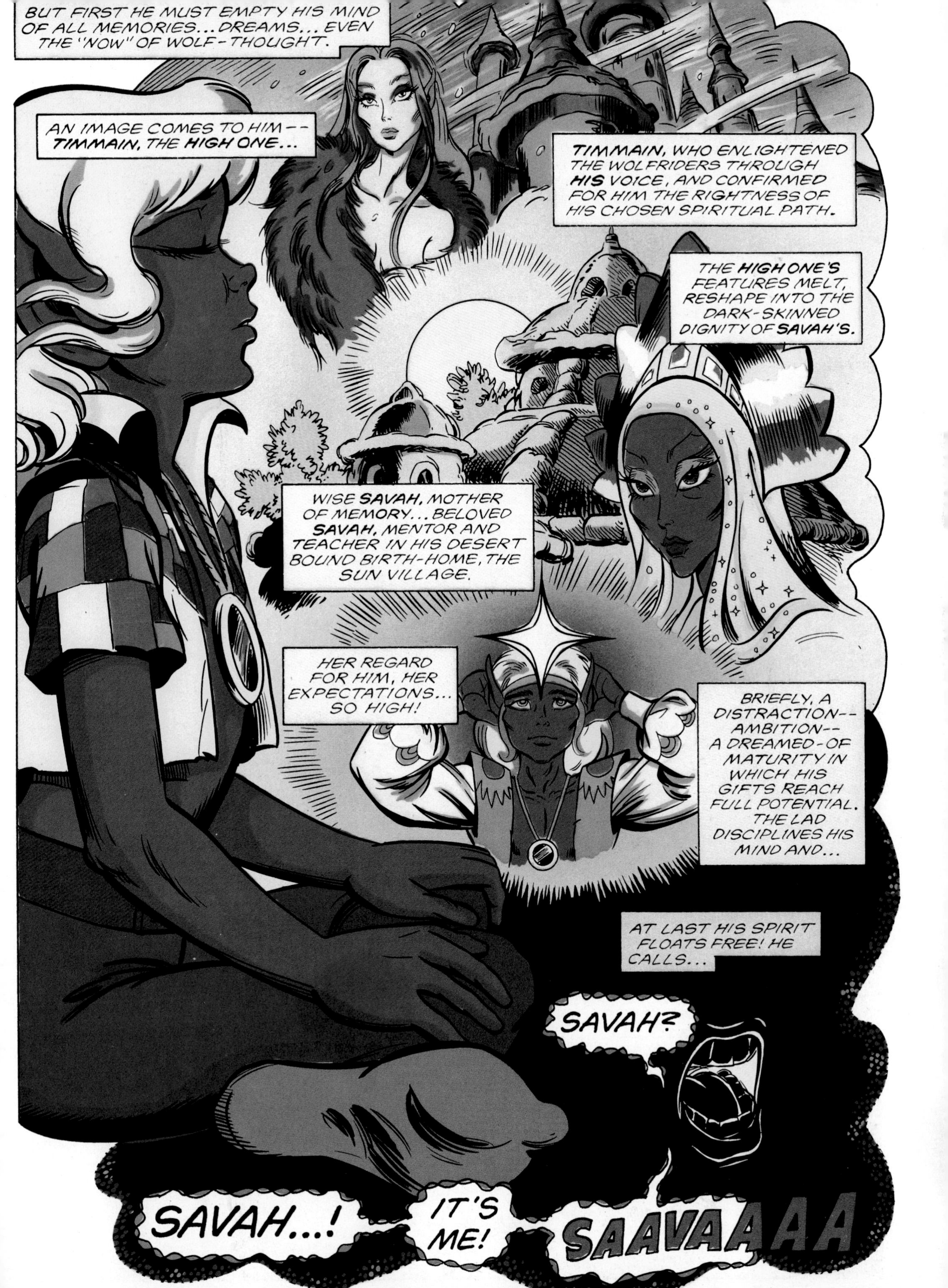
BUT FIRST HE MUST EMPTY HIS MIND OF ALL MEMORIES... DREAMS... EVEN THE "NOW" OF WOLF-THOUGHT.
AN IMAGE COMES TO HIM -- TIMMAIN, THE HIGH ONE...
TIMMAIN, WHO ENLIGHTENED THE WOLFRIDERS THROUGH HIS VOICE, AND CONFIRMED FOR HIM THE RIGHTNESS OF HIS CHOSEN SPIRITUAL PATH.
THE HIGH ONE'S FEATURES MELT, RESHAPE INTO THE DARK-SKINNED DIGNITY OF SAVAH'S.
WISE SAVAH, MOTHER OF MEMORY... BELOVED SAVAH, MENTOR AND TEACHER IN HIS DESERT BOUND BIRTH-HOME, THE SUN VILLAGE.
HER REGARD FOR HIM, HER EXPECTATIONS... SO HIGH!
BRIEFLY, A DISTRACTION-- AMBITION-- A DREAMED-OF MATURITY IN WHICH HIS GIFTS REACH FULL POTENTIAL. THE LAD DISCIPLINES HIS MIND AND...
AT LAST HIS SPIRIT FLOATS FREE! HE CALLS...
SAVAH?
SAVAH...!
IT'S ME!
SAAVAAAAA

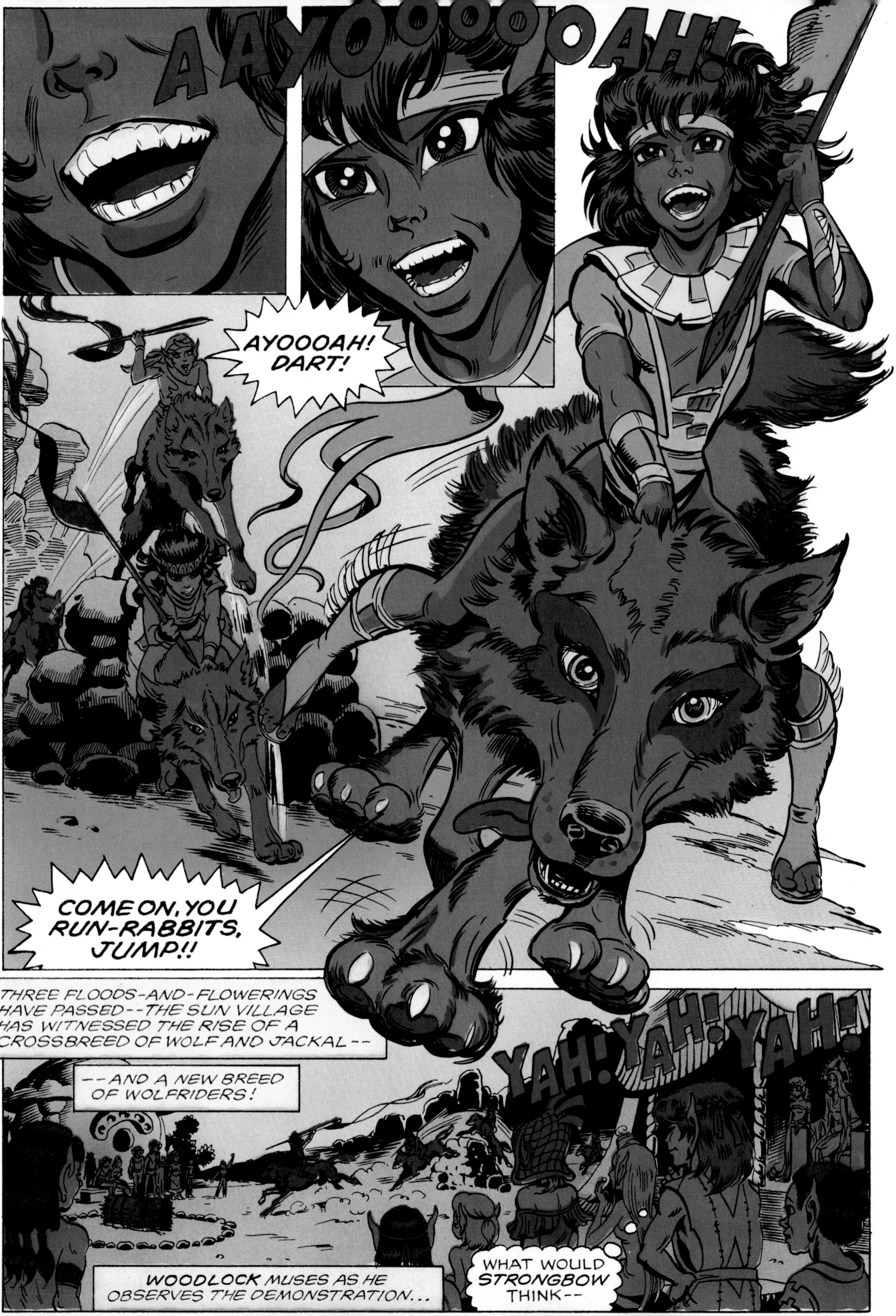

AAYOOOOOOAH!
AYOOOAH! DART!
COME ON, YOU RUN-RABBITS, JUMP!!
THREE FLOODS-AND-FLOWERINGS HAVE PASSED--THE SUN VILLAGE HAS WITNESSED THE RISE OF A CROSSBREED OF WOLF AND JACKAL--
--AND A NEW BREED OF WOLFRIDERS!
YAH! YAH! YAH!
WOODLOCK MUSES AS HE OBSERVES THE DEMONSTRATION...
WHAT WOULD STRONGBOW THINK--

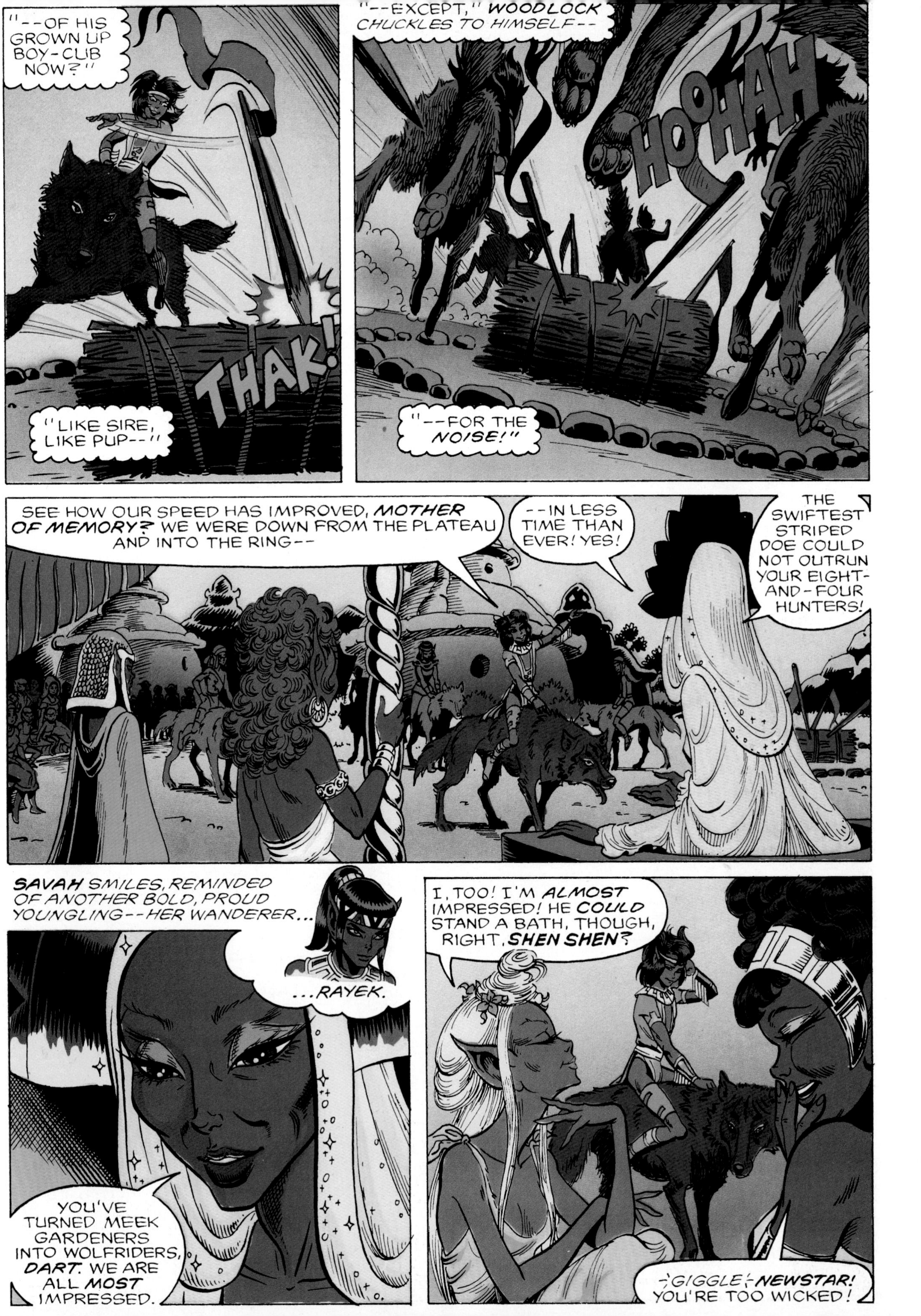
"--OF HIS GROWN UP BOY-CUB NOW?"
THAK!
"LIKE SIRE, LIKE PUP--"
"--EXCEPT," WOODLOCK CHUCKLES TO HIMSELF--
HOOHAH
"--FOR THE NOISE!"
SEE HOW OUR SPEED HAS IMPROVED, MOTHER OF MEMORY? WE WERE DOWN FROM THE PLATEAU AND INTO THE RING--
--IN LESS TIME THAN EVER! YES!
THE SWIFTEST STRIPED DOE COULD NOT OUTRUN YOUR EIGHT-AND-FOUR HUNTERS!
SAVAH SMILES, REMINDED OF ANOTHER BOLD, PROUD YOUNGLING--HER WANDERER...
...RAYEK.
YOU'VE TURNED MEEK GARDENERS INTO WOLFRIDERS, DART. WE ARE ALL MOST IMPRESSED.
I, TOO! I'M ALMOST IMPRESSED! HE COULD STAND A BATH, THOUGH, RIGHT, SHEN SHEN?
-:GIGGLE:- NEWSTAR! YOU'RE TOO WICKED!

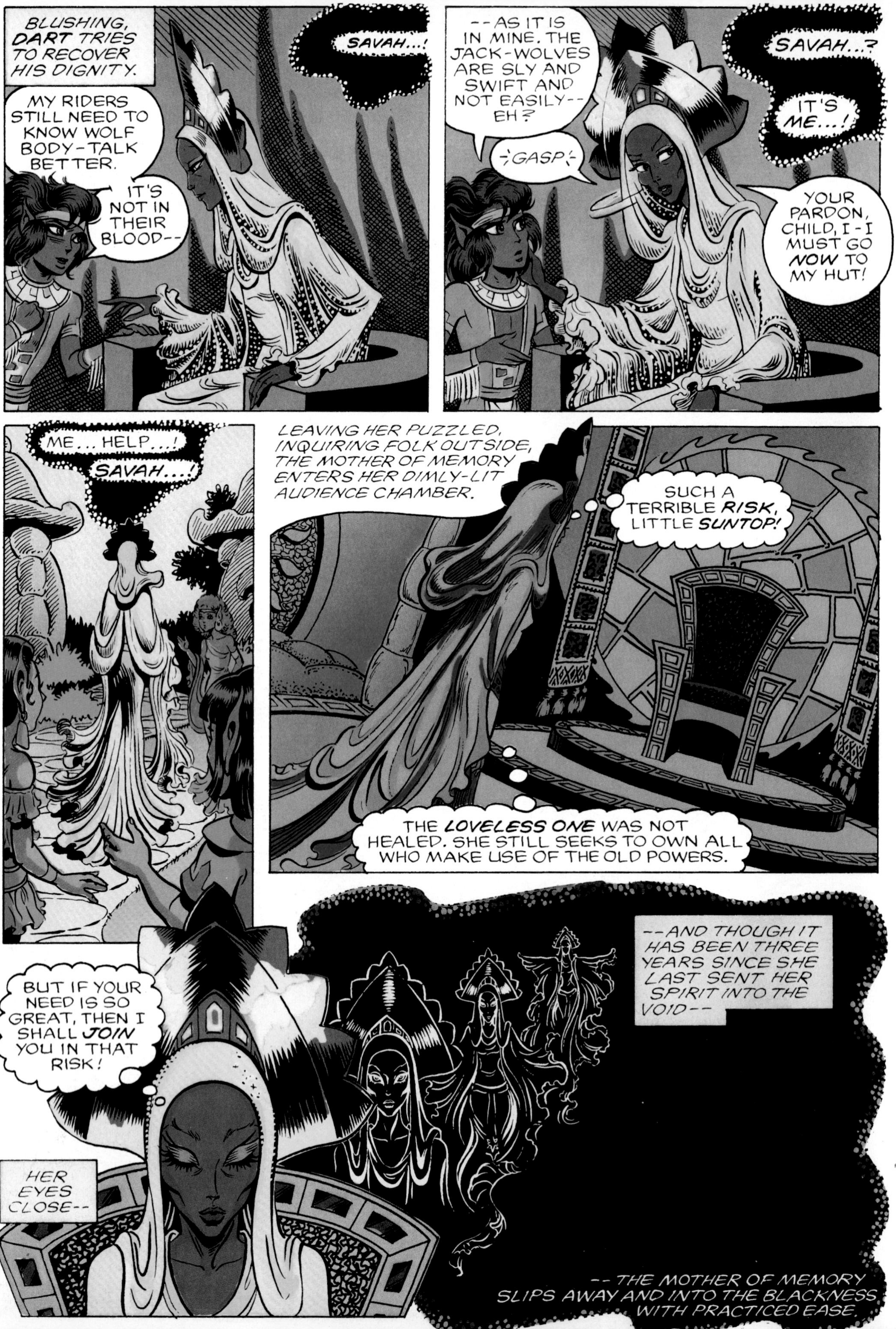
BLUSHING, DART TRIES TO RECOVER HIS DIGNITY.
SAVAH...!
MY RIDERS STILL NEED TO KNOW WOLF BODY-TALK BETTER.
IT'S NOT IN THEIR BLOOD--
--AS IT IS IN MINE. THE JACK-WOLVES ARE SLY AND SWIFT AND NOT EASILY--EH?
SAVAH...?
IT'S ME...!
GASP
YOUR PARDON, CHILD, I-I MUST GO NOW TO MY HUT!
ME... HELP...!
SAVAH...!
LEAVING HER PUZZLED, INQUIRING FOLK OUTSIDE, THE MOTHER OF MEMORY ENTERS HER DIMLY-LIT AUDIENCE CHAMBER.
SUCH A TERRIBLE RISK, LITTLE SUNTOP!
THE LOVELESS ONE WAS NOT HEALED. SHE STILL SEEKS TO OWN ALL WHO MAKE USE OF THE OLD POWERS.
BUT IF YOUR NEED IS SO GREAT, THEN I SHALL JOIN YOU IN THAT RISK!
HER EYES CLOSE--
--AND THOUGH IT HAS BEEN THREE YEARS SINCE SHE LAST SENT HER SPIRIT INTO THE VOID--
--THE MOTHER OF MEMORY SLIPS AWAY AND INTO THE BLACKNESS WITH PRACTICED EASE.

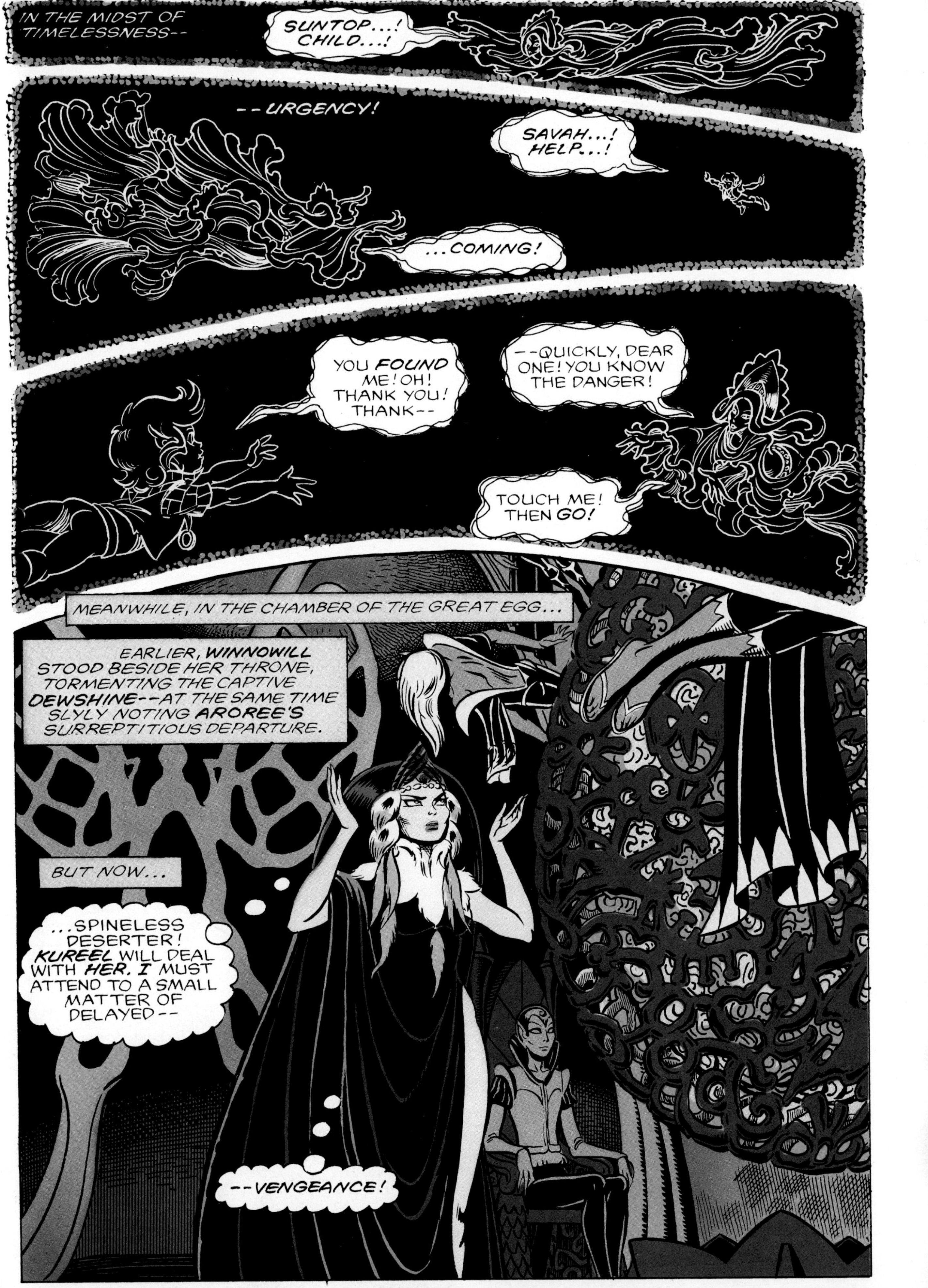
IN THE MIDST OF TIMELESSNESS--
SUNTOP...! CHILD...!
--URGENCY!
SAVAH...! HELP...!
...COMING!
YOU FOUND ME! OH! THANK YOU! THANK--
--QUICKLY, DEAR ONE! YOU KNOW THE DANGER!
TOUCH ME! THEN GO!
MEANWHILE, IN THE CHAMBER OF THE GREAT EGG...
EARLIER, WINNOWILL STOOD BESIDE HER THRONE, TORMENTING THE CAPTIVE DEWSHINE--AT THE SAME TIME SLYLY NOTING AROREE'S SURREPTITIOUS DEPARTURE.
BUT NOW...
...SPINELESS DESERTER! KUREEL WILL DEAL WITH HER. I MUST ATTEND TO A SMALL MATTER OF DELAYED--
--VENGEANCE!

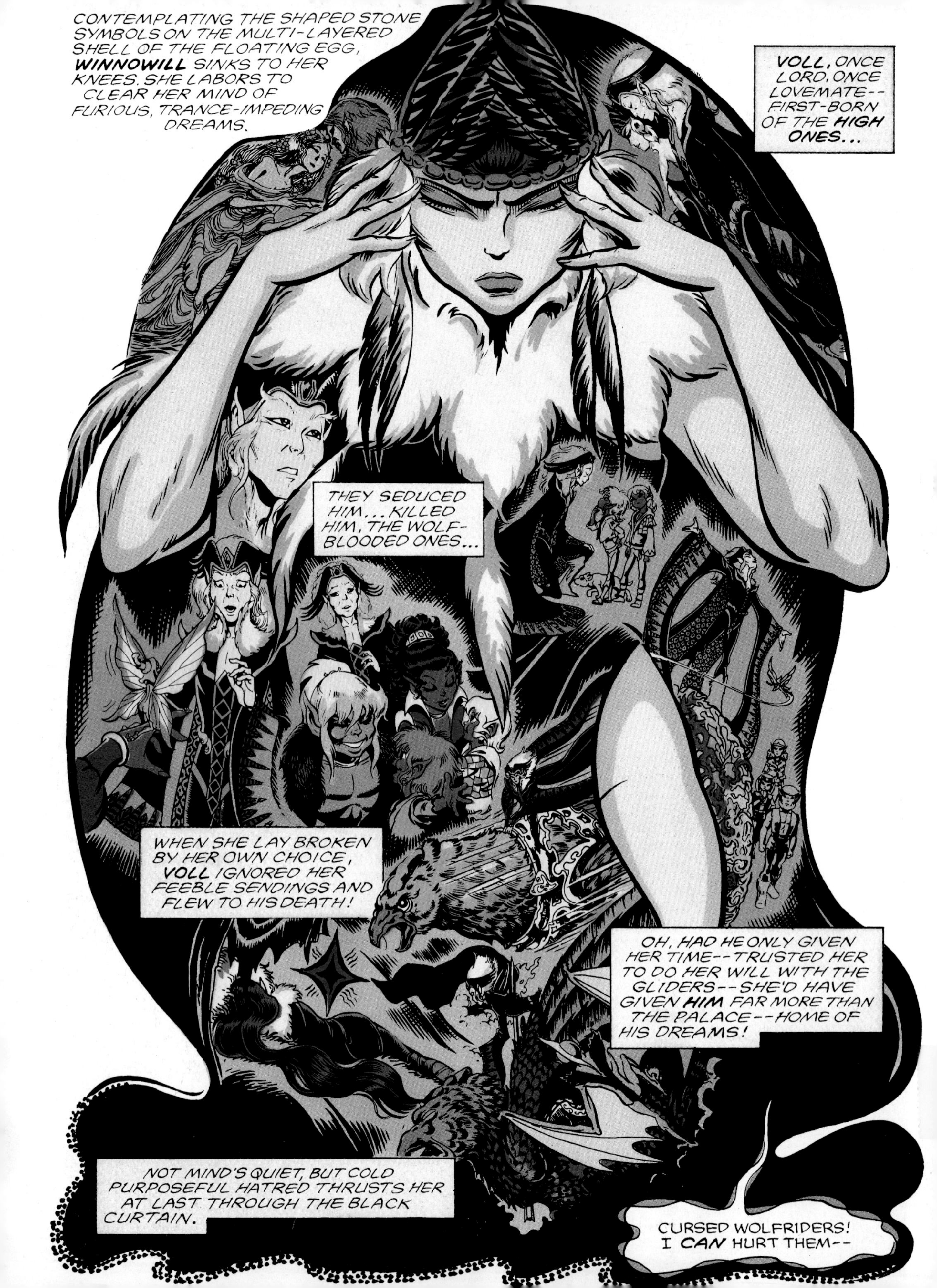
CONTEMPLATING THE SHAPED STONE SYMBOLS ON THE MULTI-LAYERED SHELL OF THE FLOATING EGG, WINNOWILL SINKS TO HER KNEES. SHE LABORS TO CLEAR HER MIND OF FURIOUS, TRANCE-IMPEDING DREAMS.
VOLL, ONCE LORD, ONCE LOVEMATE-- FIRST-BORN OF THE HIGH ONES...
THEY SEDUCED HIM... KILLED HIM, THE WOLF-BLOODED ONES...
WHEN SHE LAY BROKEN BY HER OWN CHOICE, VOLL IGNORED HER FEEBLE SENDINGS AND FLEW TO HIS DEATH!
OH, HAD HE ONLY GIVEN HER TIME-- TRUSTED HER TO DO HER WILL WITH THE GLIDERS-- SHE'D HAVE GIVEN HIM FAR MORE THAN THE PALACE-- HOME OF HIS DREAMS!
NOT MIND'S QUIET, BUT COLD PURPOSEFUL HATRED THRUSTS HER AT LAST THROUGH THE BLACK CURTAIN.
CURSED WOLFRIDERS! I CAN HURT THEM--

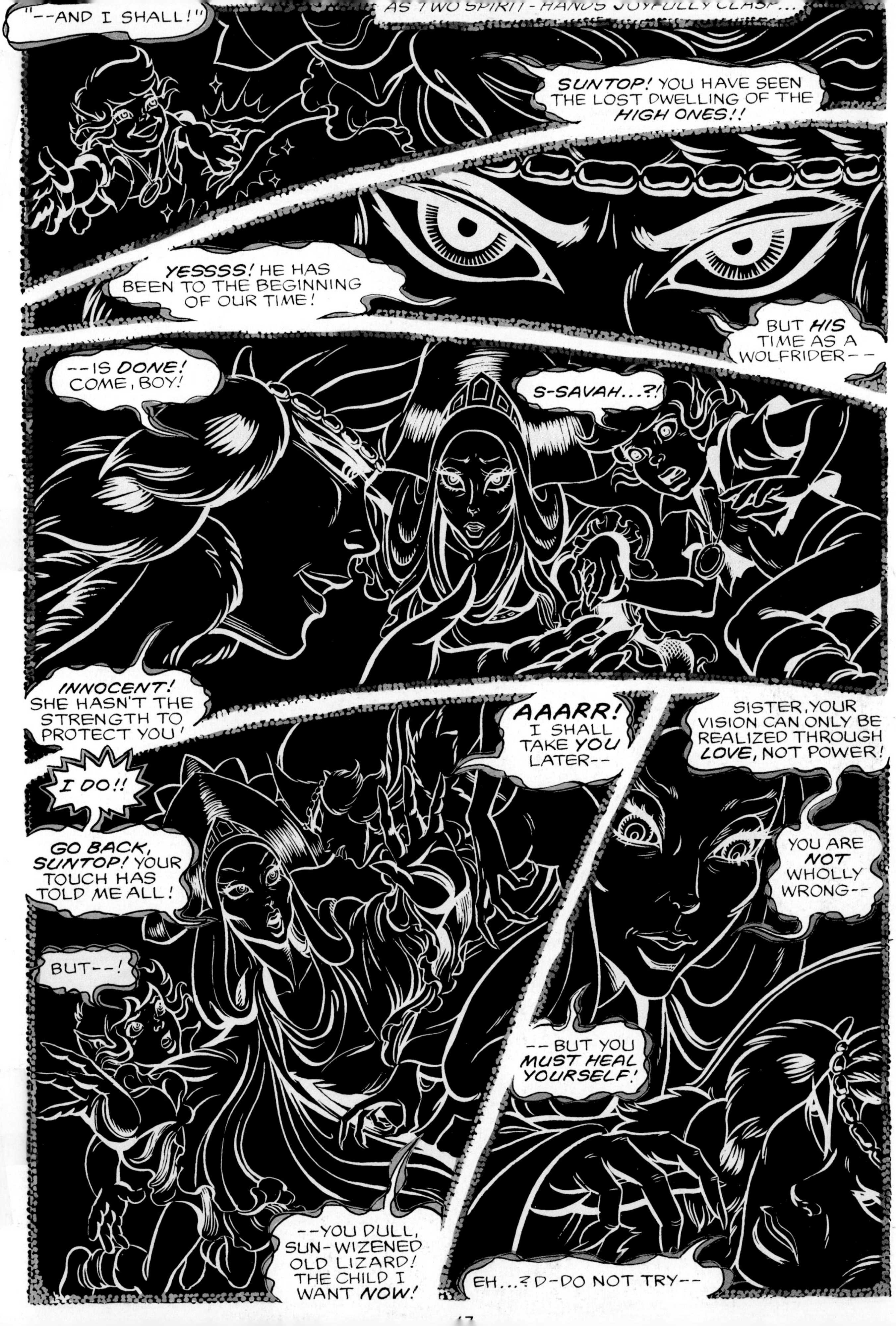
"--AND I SHALL!"
AS TWO SPIRIT-HANDS JOYFULLY CLASP...
SUNTOP! YOU HAVE SEEN THE LOST DWELLING OF THE HIGH ONES!!
YESSSS! HE HAS BEEN TO THE BEGINNING OF OUR TIME!
BUT HIS TIME AS A WOLFRIDER--
--IS DONE! COME, BOY!
S-SAVAH...?!
INNOCENT! SHE HASN'T THE STRENGTH TO PROTECT YOU!
I DO!!
GO BACK, SUNTOP! YOUR TOUCH HAS TOLD ME ALL!
BUT--!
AAARR! I SHALL TAKE YOU LATER--
--YOU DULL, SUN-WIZENED OLD LIZARD! THE CHILD I WANT NOW!
SISTER, YOUR VISION CAN ONLY BE REALIZED THROUGH LOVE, NOT POWER!
YOU ARE NOT WHOLLY WRONG--
--BUT YOU MUST HEAL YOURSELF!
EH...? D-DO NOT TRY--

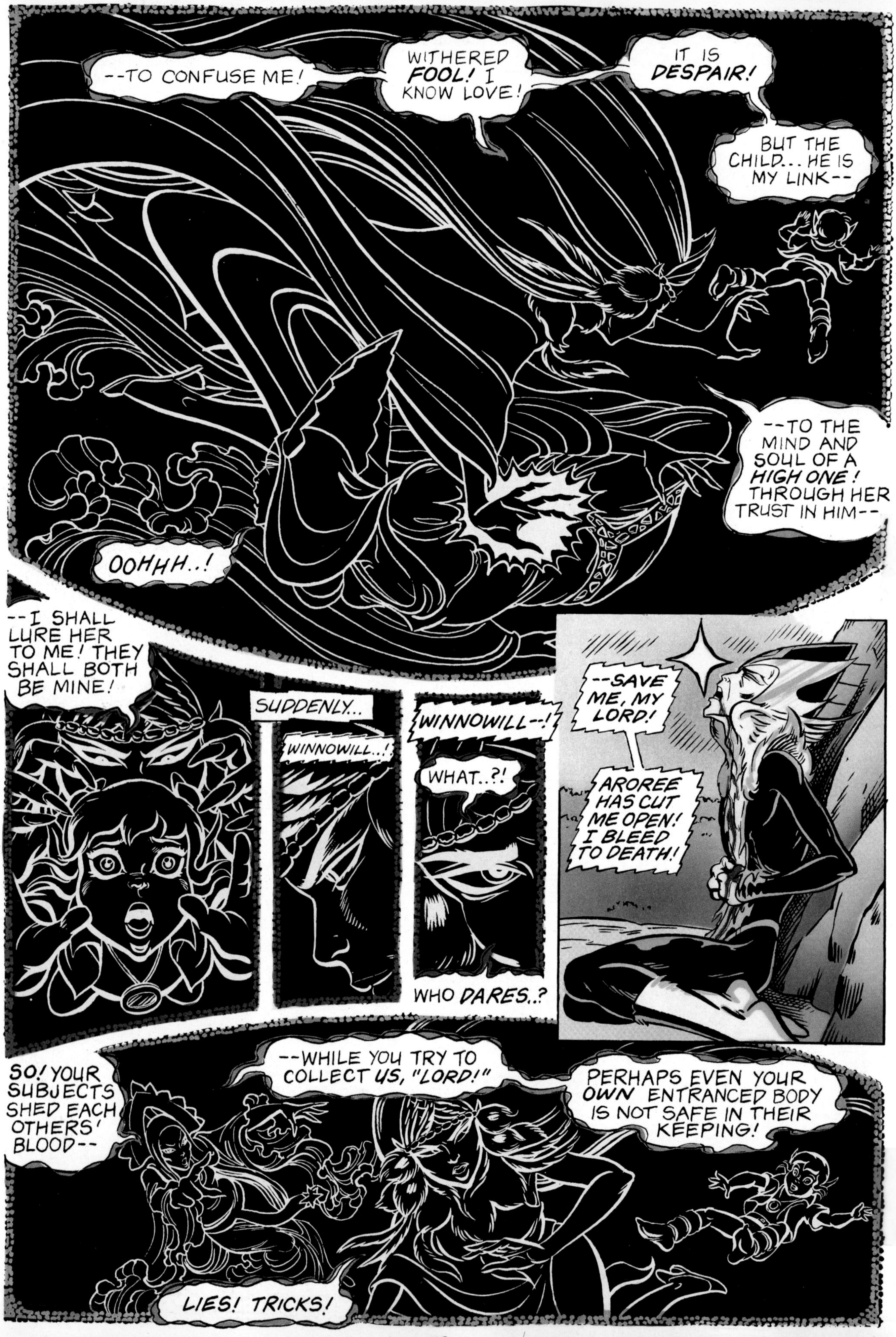
--TO CONFUSE ME!
WITHERED FOOL! I KNOW LOVE!
IT IS DESPAIR!
BUT THE CHILD... HE IS MY LINK--
--TO THE MIND AND SOUL OF A HIGH ONE! THROUGH HER TRUST IN HIM--
OOHHH..!
--I SHALL LURE HER TO ME! THEY SHALL BOTH BE MINE!
SUDDENLY...
WINNOWILL..!
WINNOWILL--!
WHAT..?!
WHO DARES..?
--SAVE ME, MY LORD!
AROREE HAS CUT ME OPEN! I BLEED TO DEATH!
SO! YOUR SUBJECTS SHED EACH OTHERS' BLOOD--
--WHILE YOU TRY TO COLLECT US, "LORD!"
PERHAPS EVEN YOUR OWN ENTRANCED BODY IS NOT SAFE IN THEIR KEEPING!
LIES! TRICKS!

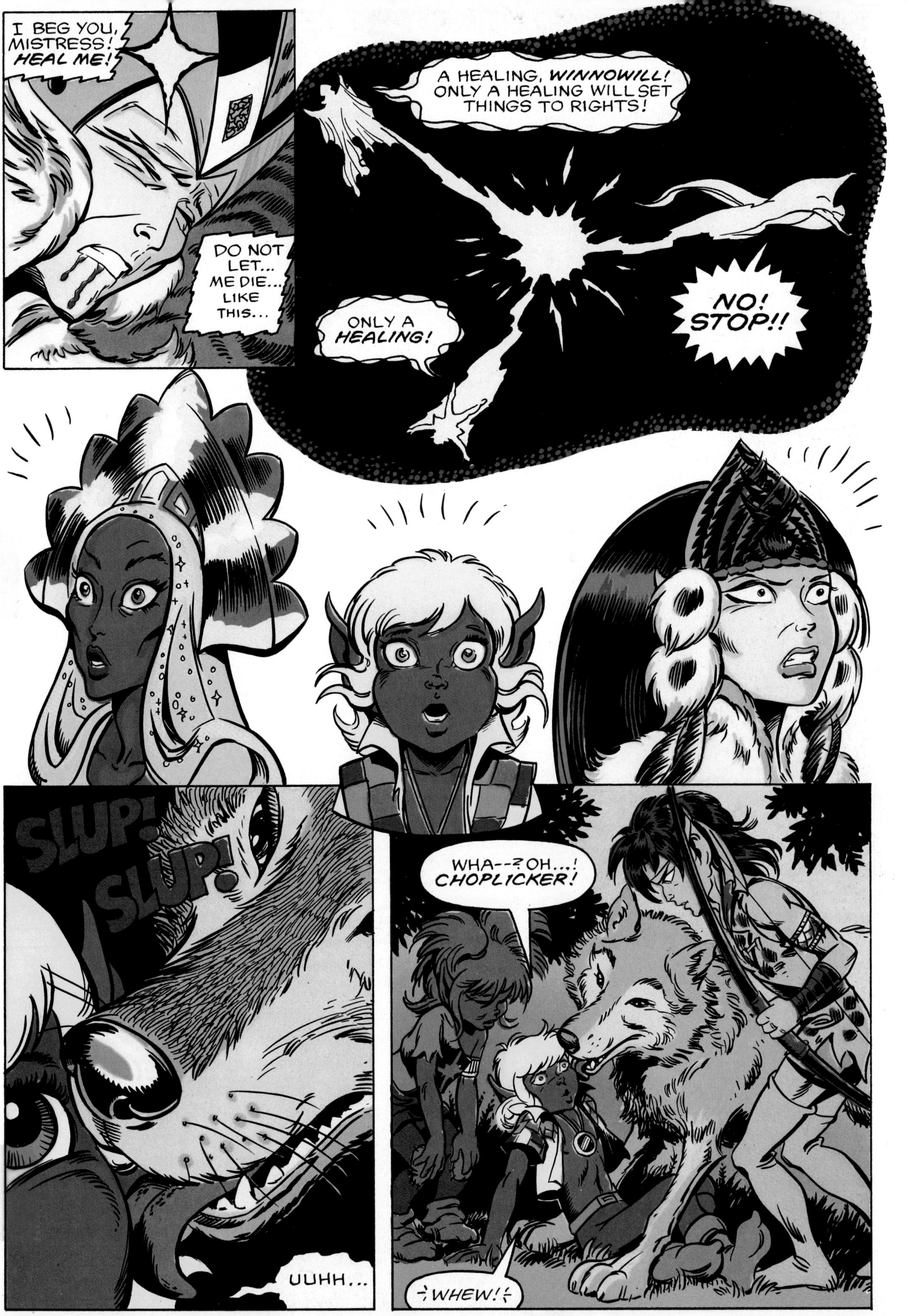
I BEG YOU, MISTRESS! HEAL ME!
DO NOT LET... ME DIE... LIKE THIS...
A HEALING, WINNOWILL! ONLY A HEALING WILL SET THINGS TO RIGHTS!
ONLY A HEALING!
NO! STOP!!
SLUP! SLUP!
UUHH...
WHA--? OH...! CHOPLICKER!
WHEW!

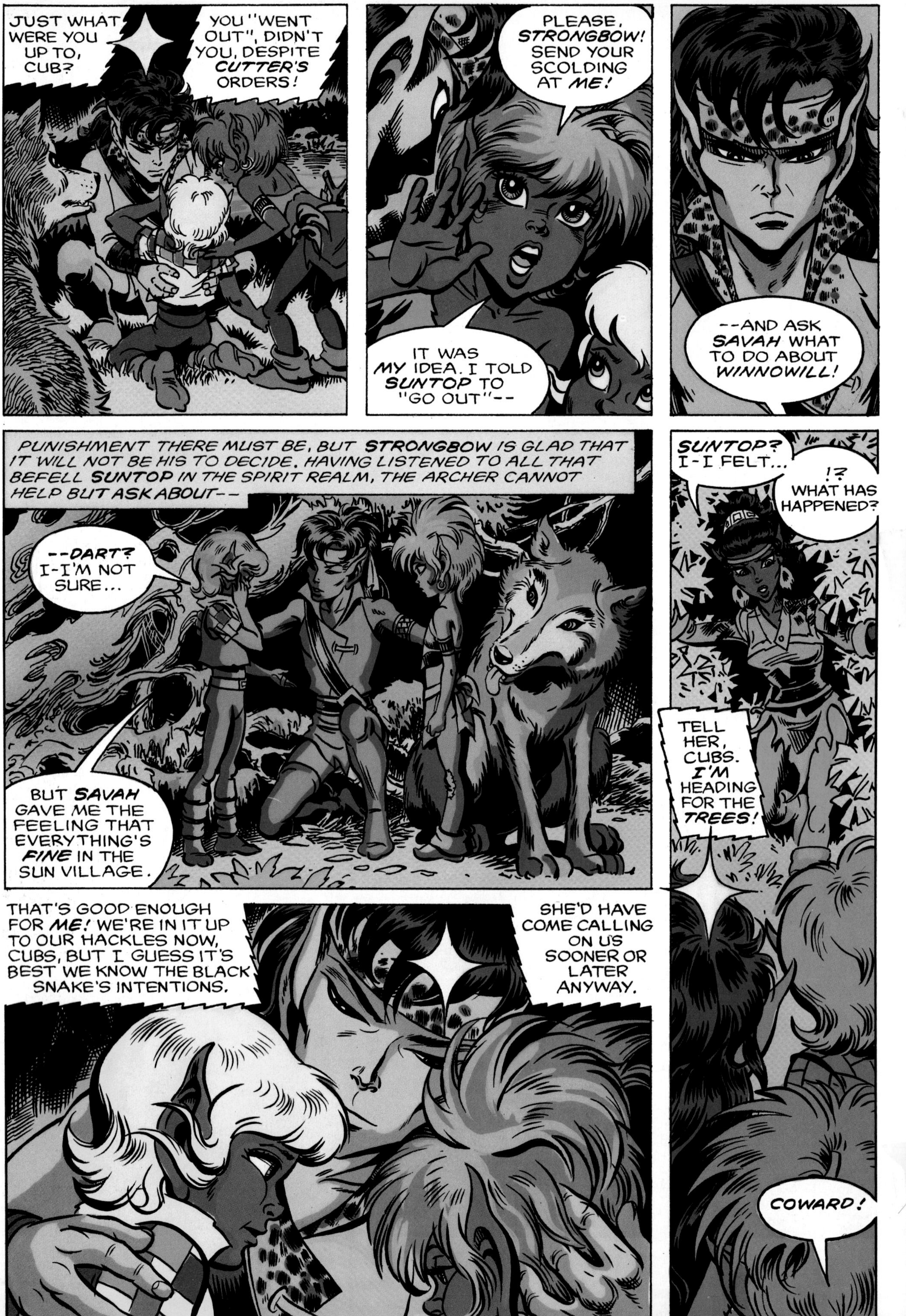
JUST WHAT WERE YOU UP TO, CUB?
YOU "WENT OUT", DIDN'T YOU, DESPITE CUTTER'S ORDERS!
PLEASE, STRONGBOW! SEND YOUR SCOLDING AT ME!
IT WAS MY IDEA. I TOLD SUNTOP TO "GO OUT"--
--AND ASK SAVAH WHAT TO DO ABOUT WINNOWILL!
PUNISHMENT THERE MUST BE, BUT STRONGBOW IS GLAD THAT IT WILL NOT BE HIS TO DECIDE. HAVING LISTENED TO ALL THAT BEFELL SUNTOP IN THE SPIRIT REALM, THE ARCHER CANNOT HELP BUT ASK ABOUT--
--DART? I-I'M NOT SURE...
BUT SAVAH GAVE ME THE FEELING THAT EVERYTHING'S FINE IN THE SUN VILLAGE.
SUNTOP? I-I FELT...
!? WHAT HAS HAPPENED?
TELL HER, CUBS. I'M HEADING FOR THE TREES!
THAT'S GOOD ENOUGH FOR ME! WE'RE IN IT UP TO OUR HACKLES NOW, CUBS, BUT I GUESS IT'S BEST WE KNOW THE BLACK SNAKE'S INTENTIONS.
SHE'D HAVE COME CALLING ON US SOONER OR LATER ANYWAY.
COWARD!

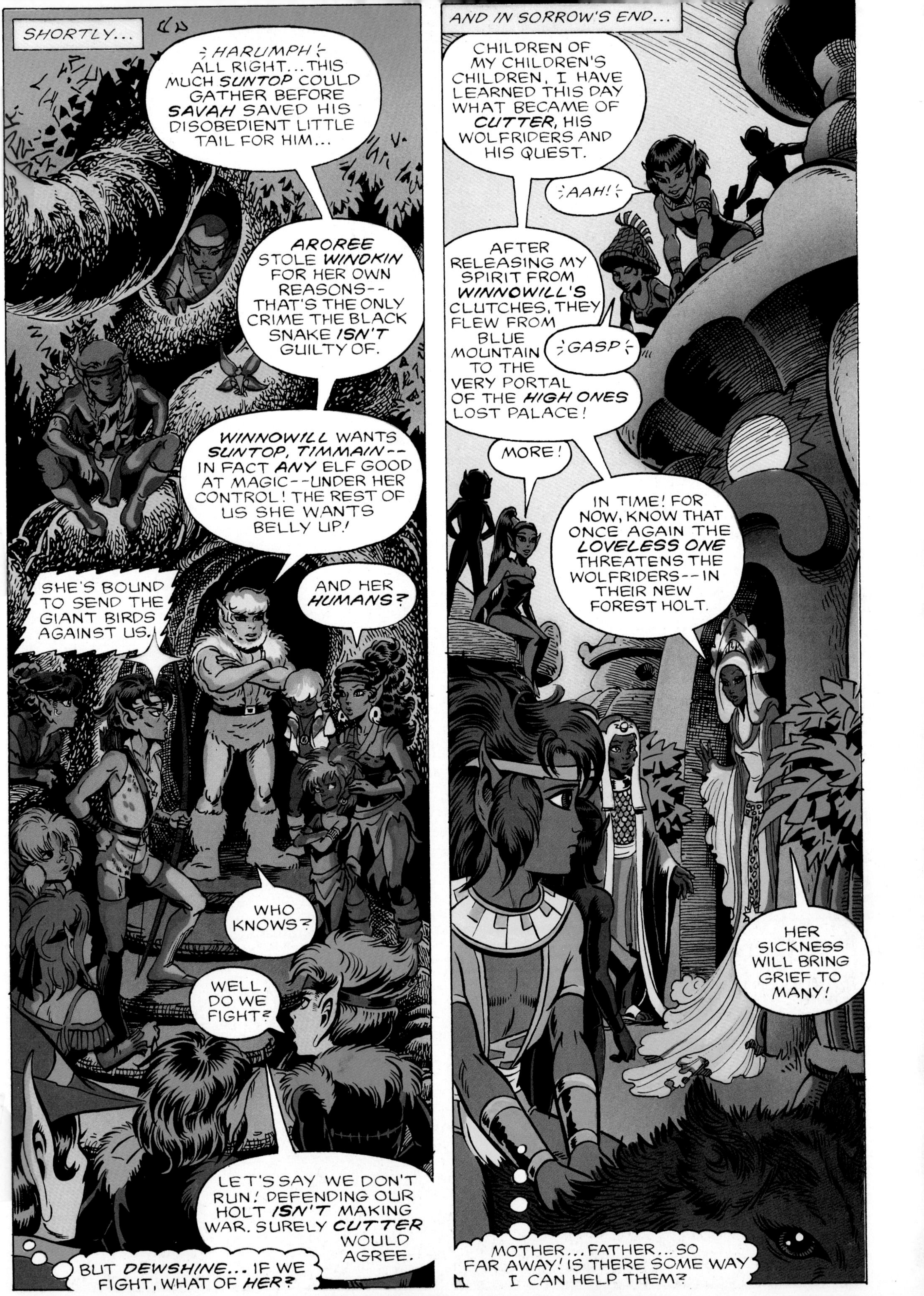
SHORTLY...
HARUMPH! ALL RIGHT... THIS MUCH SUNTOP COULD GATHER BEFORE SAVAH SAVED HIS DISOBEDIENT LITTLE TAIL FOR HIM...
AROREE STOLE WINDKIN FOR HER OWN REASONS-- THAT'S THE ONLY CRIME THE BLACK SNAKE ISN'T GUILTY OF.
WINNOWILL WANTS SUNTOP, TIMMAIN-- IN FACT ANY ELF GOOD AT MAGIC--UNDER HER CONTROL! THE REST OF US SHE WANTS BELLY UP!
SHE'S BOUND TO SEND THE GIANT BIRDS AGAINST US.
AND HER HUMANS?
WHO KNOWS?
WELL, DO WE FIGHT?
LET'S SAY WE DON'T RUN! DEFENDING OUR HOLT ISN'T MAKING WAR. SURELY CUTTER WOULD AGREE.
BUT DEWSHINE... IF WE FIGHT, WHAT OF HER?
AND IN SORROW'S END...
CHILDREN OF MY CHILDREN'S CHILDREN, I HAVE LEARNED THIS DAY WHAT BECAME OF CUTTER, HIS WOLFRIDERS AND HIS QUEST.
AAH!
AFTER RELEASING MY SPIRIT FROM WINNOWILL'S CLUTCHES, THEY FLEW FROM BLUE MOUNTAIN TO THE VERY PORTAL OF THE HIGH ONES LOST PALACE!
GASP
MORE!
IN TIME! FOR NOW, KNOW THAT ONCE AGAIN THE LOVELESS ONE THREATENS THE WOLFRIDERS-- IN THEIR NEW FOREST HOLT.
HER SICKNESS WILL BRING GRIEF TO MANY!
MOTHER... FATHER... SO FAR AWAY! IS THERE SOME WAY I CAN HELP THEM?

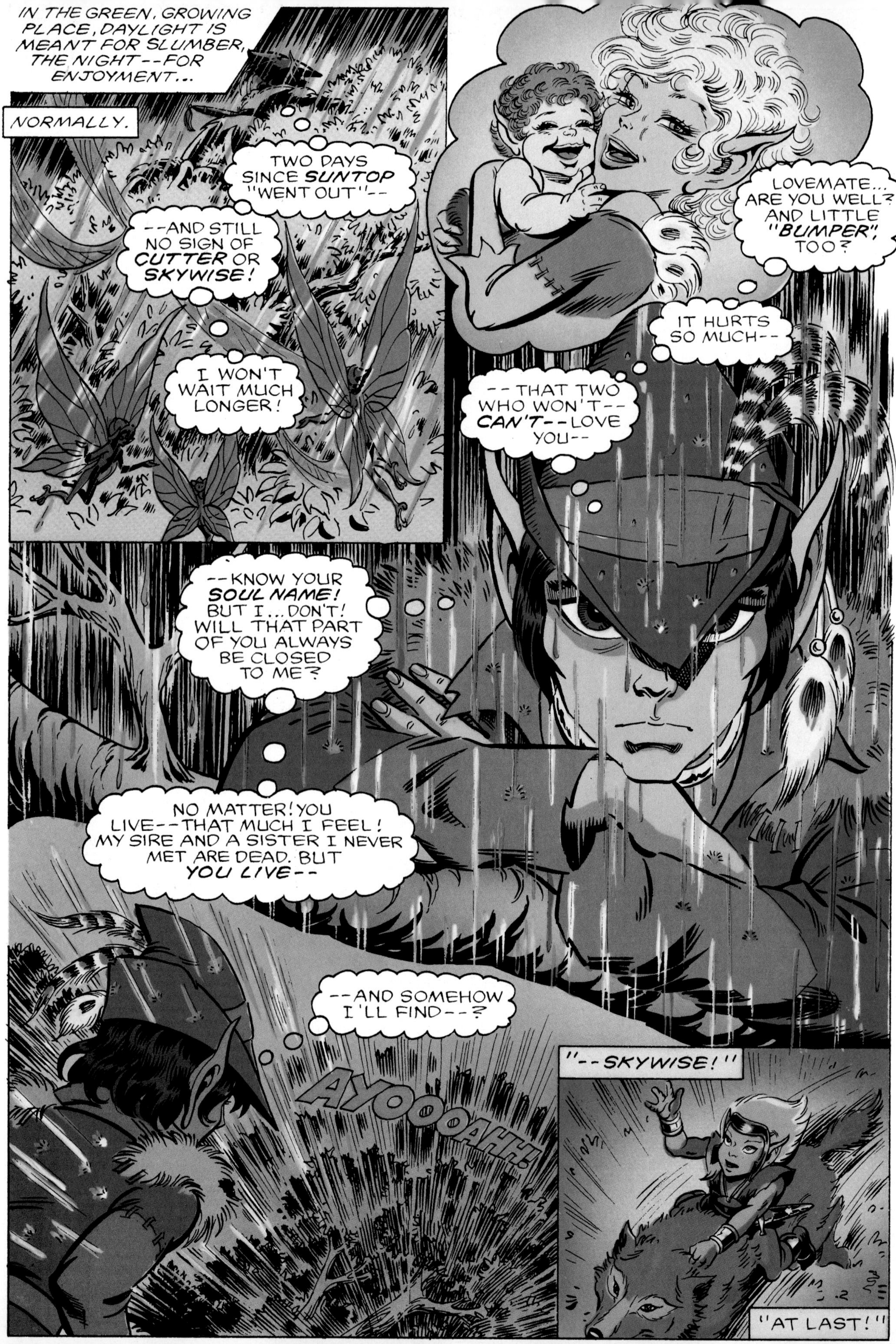
IN THE GREEN, GROWING PLACE, DAYLIGHT IS MEANT FOR SLUMBER, THE NIGHT--FOR ENJOYMENT...
NORMALLY.
TWO DAYS SINCE SUNTOP "WENT OUT"--
--AND STILL NO SIGN OF CUTTER OR SKYWISE!
I WON'T WAIT MUCH LONGER!
LOVEMATE... ARE YOU WELL? AND LITTLE "BUMPER", TOO?
IT HURTS SO MUCH--
--THAT TWO WHO WON'T--CAN'T--LOVE YOU--
--KNOW YOUR SOUL NAME! BUT I...DON'T! WILL THAT PART OF YOU ALWAYS BE CLOSED TO ME?
NO MATTER! YOU LIVE--THAT MUCH I FEEL! MY SIRE AND A SISTER I NEVER MET ARE DEAD. BUT YOU LIVE--
--AND SOMEHOW I'LL FIND--?
AYOOOAHH!
"--SKYWISE!"
"AT LAST!"

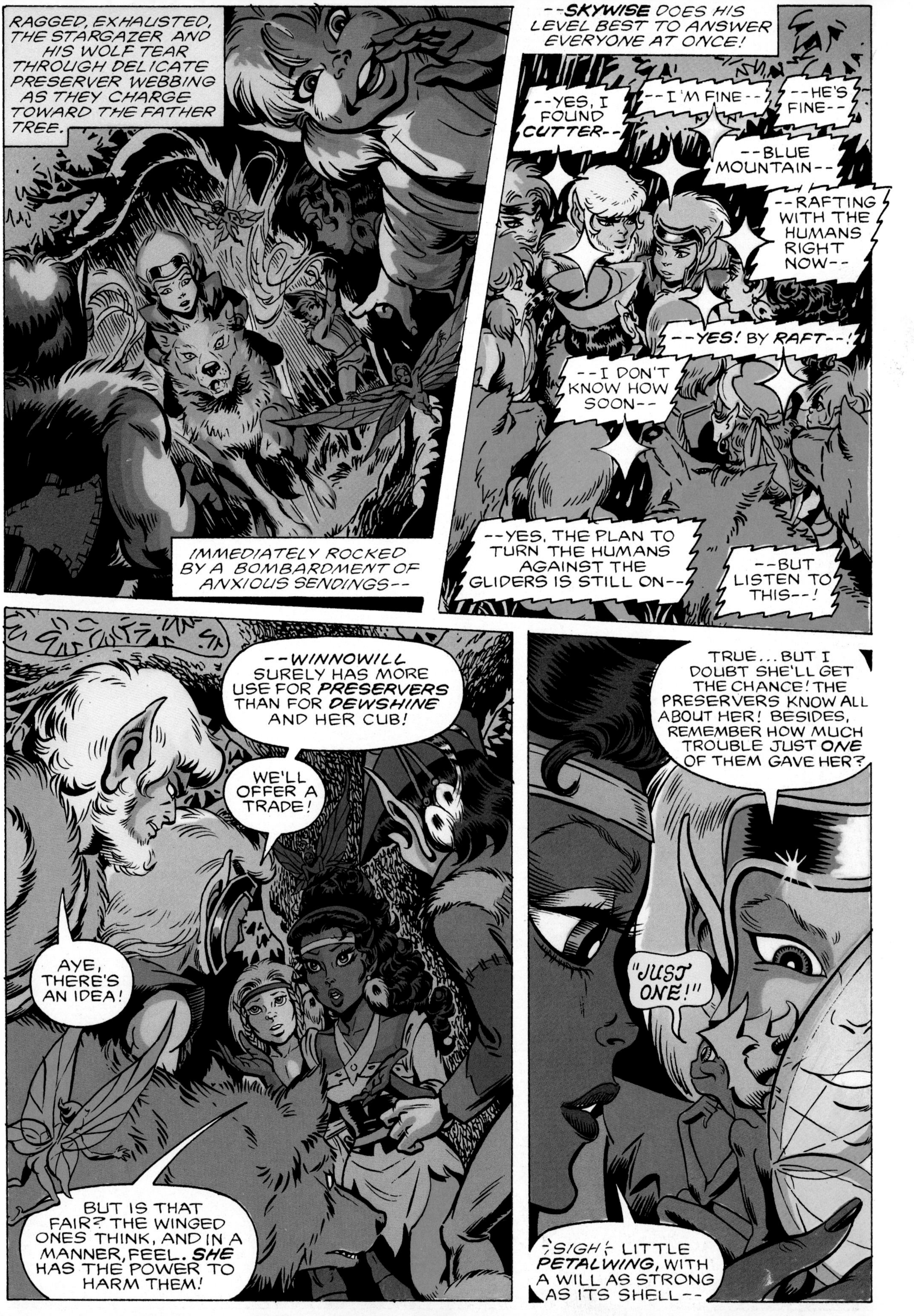

RAGGED, EXHAUSTED, THE STARGAZER AND HIS WOLF TEAR THROUGH DELICATE PRESERVER WEBBING AS THEY CHARGE TOWARD THE FATHER TREE.
IMMEDIATELY ROCKED BY A BOMBARDMENT OF ANXIOUS SENDINGS--
--SKYWISE DOES HIS LEVEL BEST TO ANSWER EVERYONE AT ONCE!
--YES, I FOUND CUTTER--
--I'M FINE--
--HE'S FINE--
--BLUE MOUNTAIN--
--RAFTING WITH THE HUMANS RIGHT NOW--
--YES! BY RAFT--!
--I DON'T KNOW HOW SOON--
--YES, THE PLAN TO TURN THE HUMANS AGAINST THE GLIDERS IS STILL ON--
--BUT LISTEN TO THIS--!
--WINNOWILL SURELY HAS MORE USE FOR PRESERVERS THAN FOR DEWSHINE AND HER CUB!
WE'LL OFFER A TRADE!
AYE, THERE'S AN IDEA!
BUT IS THAT FAIR? THE WINGED ONES THINK, AND IN A MANNER, FEEL. SHE HAS THE POWER TO HARM THEM!
TRUE... BUT I DOUBT SHE'LL GET THE CHANCE! THE PRESERVERS KNOW ALL ABOUT HER! BESIDES, REMEMBER HOW MUCH TROUBLE JUST ONE OF THEM GAVE HER?
"JUST ONE!"
-SIGH- LITTLE PETALWING, WITH A WILL AS STRONG AS ITS SHELL--

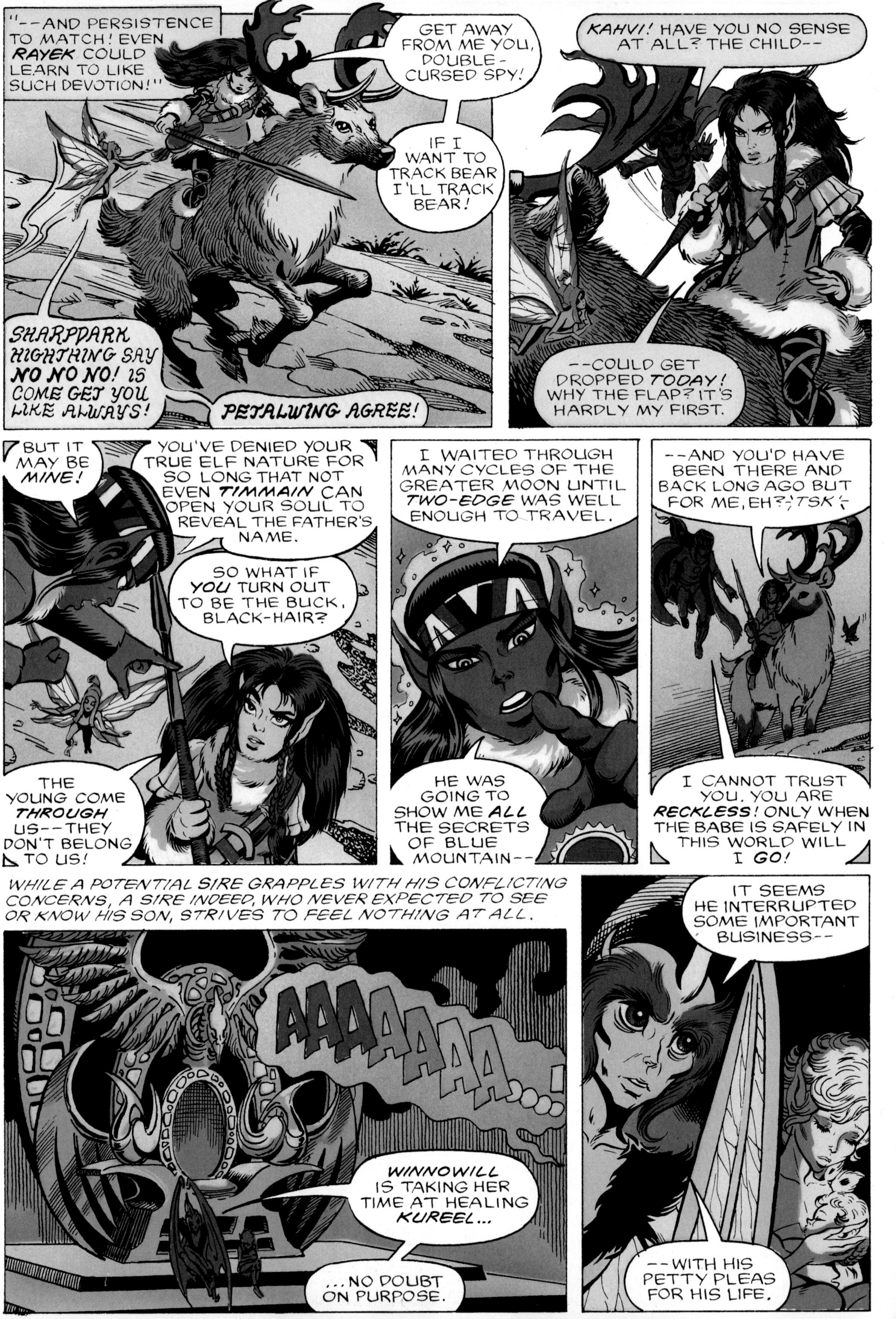
"--AND PERSISTENCE TO MATCH! EVEN RAYEK COULD LEARN TO LIKE SUCH DEVOTION!"
GET AWAY FROM ME YOU, DOUBLE-CURSED SPY!
IF I WANT TO TRACK BEAR I'LL TRACK BEAR!
SHARPDARK HIGHTHING SAY NO NO NO! IS COME GET YOU LIKE ALWAYS!
PETALWING AGREE!
KAHVI! HAVE YOU NO SENSE AT ALL? THE CHILD--
--COULD GET DROPPED TODAY! WHY THE FLAP? IT'S HARDLY MY FIRST.
BUT IT MAY BE MINE!
YOU'VE DENIED YOUR TRUE ELF NATURE FOR SO LONG THAT NOT EVEN TIMMAIN CAN OPEN YOUR SOUL TO REVEAL THE FATHER'S NAME.
SO WHAT IF YOU TURN OUT TO BE THE BUCK, BLACK-HAIR?
THE YOUNG COME THROUGH US--THEY DON'T BELONG TO US!
I WAITED THROUGH MANY CYCLES OF THE GREATER MOON UNTIL TWO-EDGE WAS WELL ENOUGH TO TRAVEL.
HE WAS GOING TO SHOW ME ALL THE SECRETS OF BLUE MOUNTAIN--
--AND YOU'D HAVE BEEN THERE AND BACK LONG AGO BUT FOR ME, EH? TSK
I CANNOT TRUST YOU. YOU ARE RECKLESS! ONLY WHEN THE BABE IS SAFELY IN THIS WORLD WILL I GO!
WHILE A POTENTIAL SIRE GRAPPLES WITH HIS CONFLICTING CONCERNS, A SIRE INDEED, WHO NEVER EXPECTED TO SEE OR KNOW HIS SON, STRIVES TO FEEL NOTHING AT ALL.
AAAAAAAAA...!
WINNOWILL IS TAKING HER TIME AT HEALING KUREEL...
...NO DOUBT ON PURPOSE.
IT SEEMS HE INTERRUPTED SOME IMPORTANT BUSINESS--
--WITH HIS PETTY PLEAS FOR HIS LIFE.

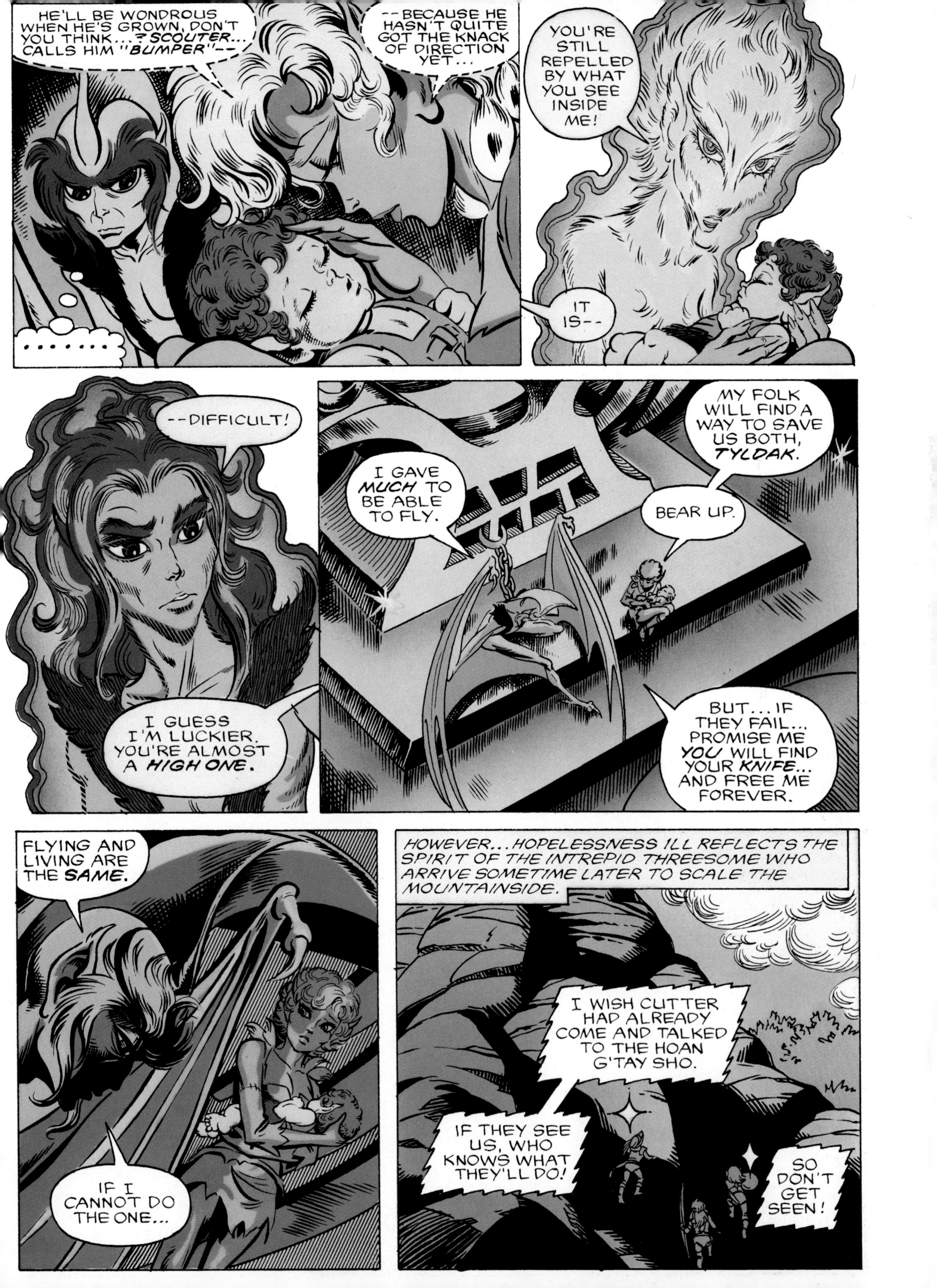
HE'LL BE WONDROUS WHEN HE'S GROWN, DON'T YOU THINK...? SCOUTER... CALLS HIM "BUMPER"--
--BECAUSE HE HASN'T QUITE GOT THE KNACK OF DIRECTION YET...
....
YOU'RE STILL REPELLED BY WHAT YOU SEE INSIDE ME!
IT IS--
--DIFFICULT!
I GUESS I'M LUCKIER. YOU'RE ALMOST A HIGH ONE.
MY FOLK WILL FIND A WAY TO SAVE US BOTH, TYLDAK.
I GAVE MUCH TO BE ABLE TO FLY.
BEAR UP.
BUT... IF THEY FAIL... PROMISE ME YOU WILL FIND YOUR KNIFE... AND FREE ME FOREVER.
FLYING AND LIVING ARE THE SAME.
IF I CANNOT DO THE ONE...
HOWEVER... HOPELESSNESS ILL REFLECTS THE SPIRIT OF THE INTREPID THREESOME WHO ARRIVE SOMETIME LATER TO SCALE THE MOUNTAINSIDE.
I WISH CUTTER HAD ALREADY COME AND TALKED TO THE HOAN G'TAY SHO.
IF THEY SEE US, WHO KNOWS WHAT THEY'LL DO!
SO DON'T GET SEEN!

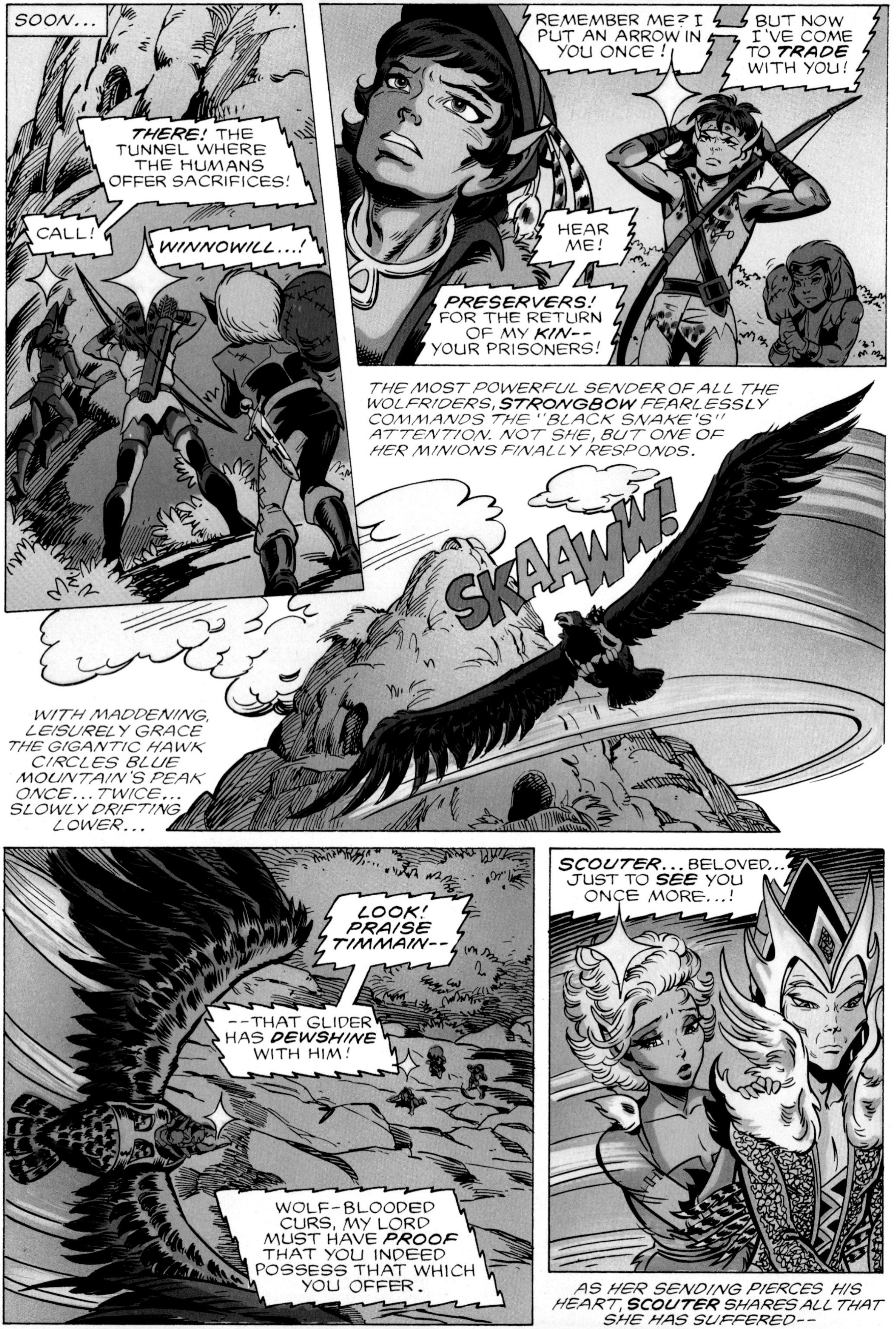
SOON...
THERE! THE TUNNEL WHERE THE HUMANS OFFER SACRIFICES!
CALL!
WINNOWILL...!
REMEMBER ME? I PUT AN ARROW IN YOU ONCE!
BUT NOW I'VE COME TO TRADE WITH YOU!
HEAR ME!
PRESERVERS! FOR THE RETURN OF MY KIN-- YOUR PRISONERS!
THE MOST POWERFUL SENDER OF ALL THE WOLFRIDERS, STRONGBOW FEARLESSLY COMMANDS THE "BLACK SNAKE'S" ATTENTION. NOT SHE, BUT ONE OF HER MINIONS FINALLY RESPONDS.
SKAAWW!
WITH MADDENING, LEISURELY GRACE THE GIGANTIC HAWK CIRCLES BLUE MOUNTAIN'S PEAK ONCE... TWICE... SLOWLY DRIFTING LOWER...
LOOK! PRAISE TIMMAIN--
--THAT GLIDER HAS DEWSHINE WITH HIM!
WOLF-BLOODED CURS, MY LORD MUST HAVE PROOF THAT YOU INDEED POSSESS THAT WHICH YOU OFFER.
SCOUTER... BELOVED... JUST TO SEE YOU ONCE MORE...!
AS HER SENDING PIERCES HIS HEART, SCOUTER SHARES ALL THAT SHE HAS SUFFERED--

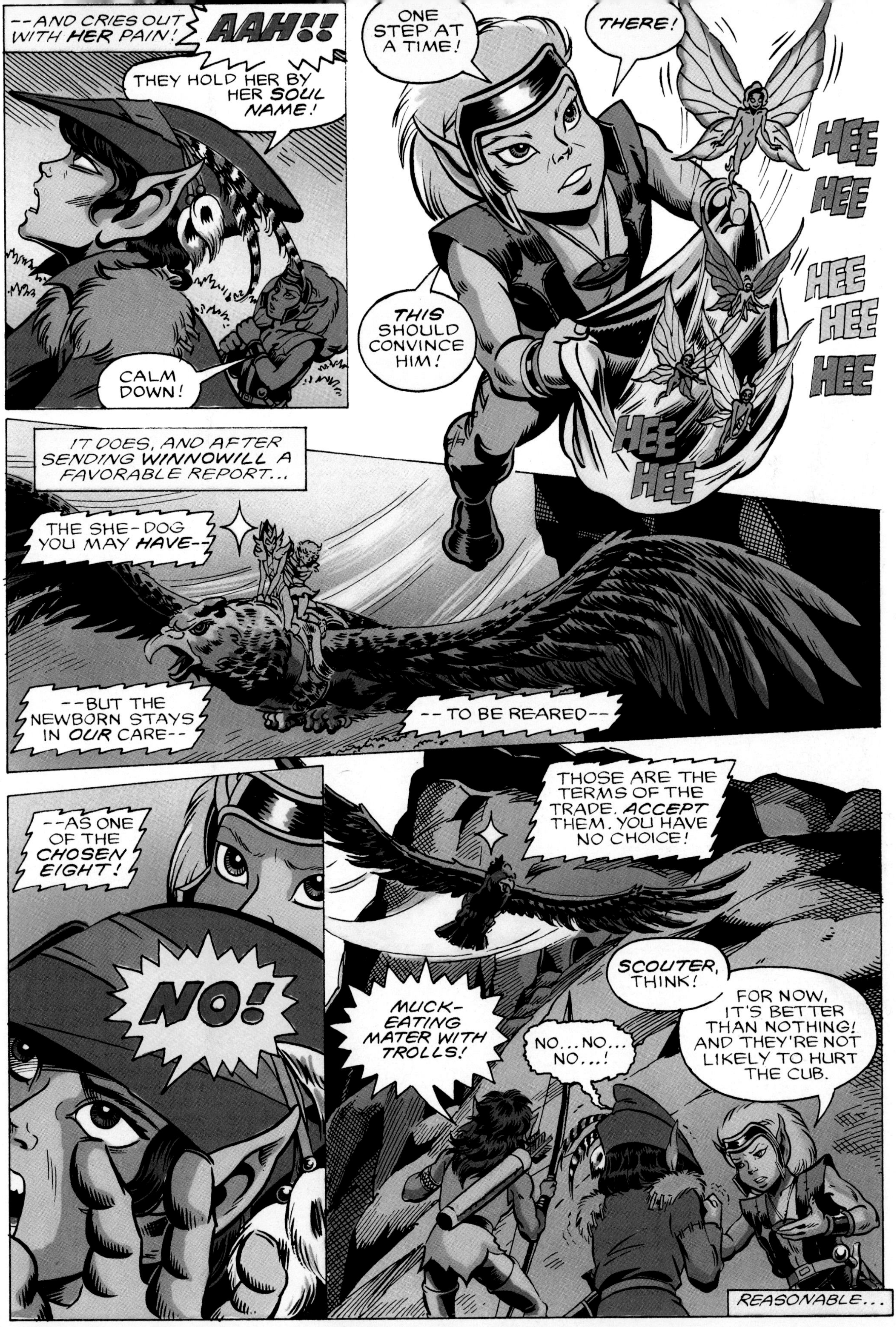

--AND CRIES OUT WITH HER PAIN!
AAH!!
THEY HOLD HER BY HER SOUL NAME!
CALM DOWN!
ONE STEP AT A TIME!
THERE!
THIS SHOULD CONVINCE HIM!
HEE HEE
HEE HEE HEE
HEE HEE
IT DOES, AND AFTER SENDING WINNOWILL A FAVORABLE REPORT...
THE SHE-DOG YOU MAY HAVE--
--BUT THE NEWBORN STAYS IN OUR CARE--
--TO BE REARED--
--AS ONE OF THE CHOSEN EIGHT!
NO!
THOSE ARE THE TERMS OF THE TRADE. ACCEPT THEM. YOU HAVE NO CHOICE!
MUCK-EATING MATER WITH TROLLS!
NO...NO... NO...!
SCOUTER, THINK!
FOR NOW, IT'S BETTER THAN NOTHING! AND THEY'RE NOT LIKELY TO HURT THE CUB.
REASONABLE...

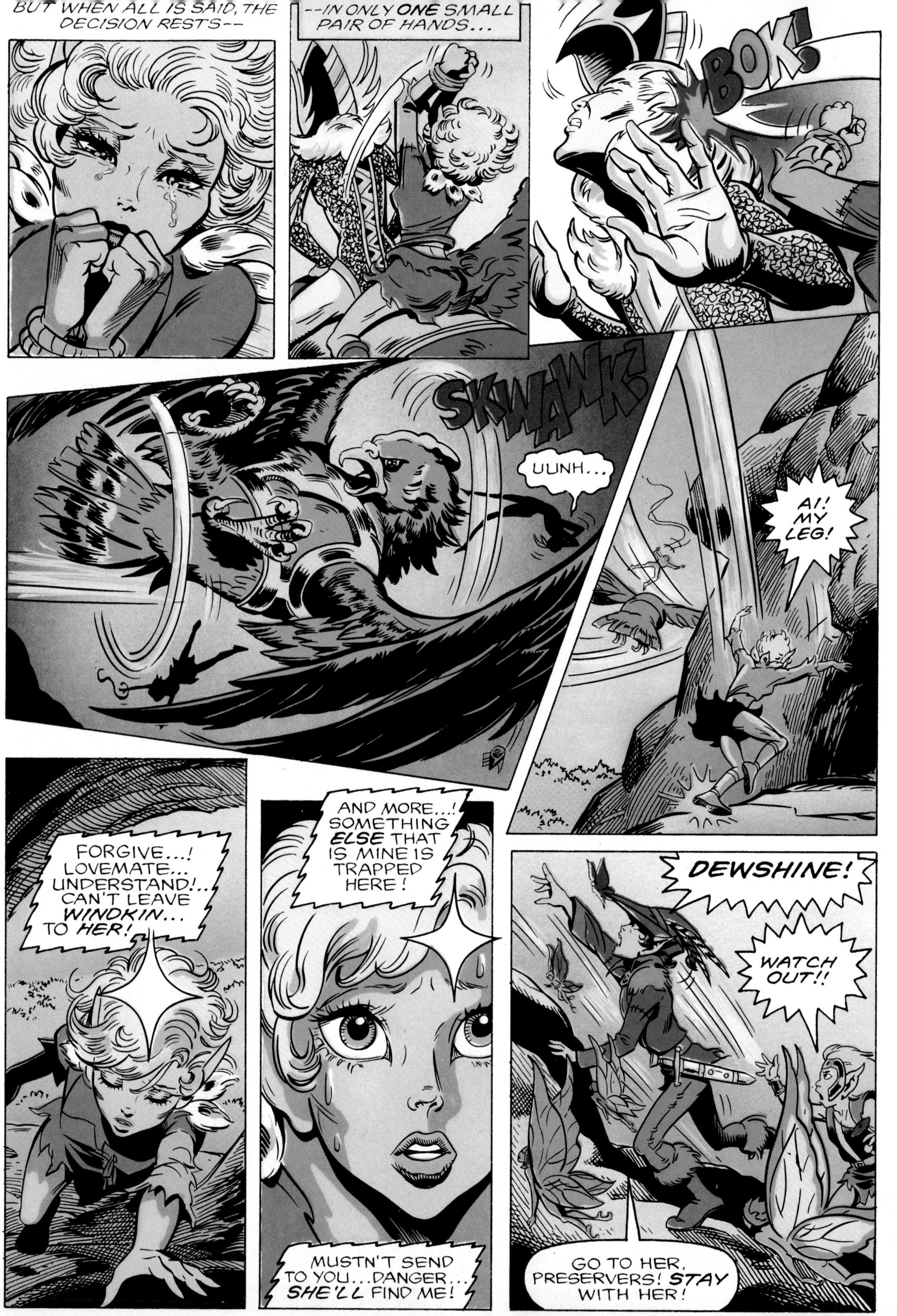

BUT WHEN ALL IS SAID, THE DECISION RESTS--
--IN ONLY ONE SMALL PAIR OF HANDS...
BOK!
SKWAWK!
UUNH...
AI! MY LEG!
FORGIVE...! LOVEMATE... UNDERSTAND!.. CAN'T LEAVE WINDKIN... TO HER!
AND MORE...! SOMETHING ELSE THAT IS MINE IS TRAPPED HERE!
MUSTN'T SEND TO YOU...DANGER... SHE'LL FIND ME!
DEWSHINE!
WATCH OUT!!
GO TO HER, PRESERVERS! STAY WITH HER!

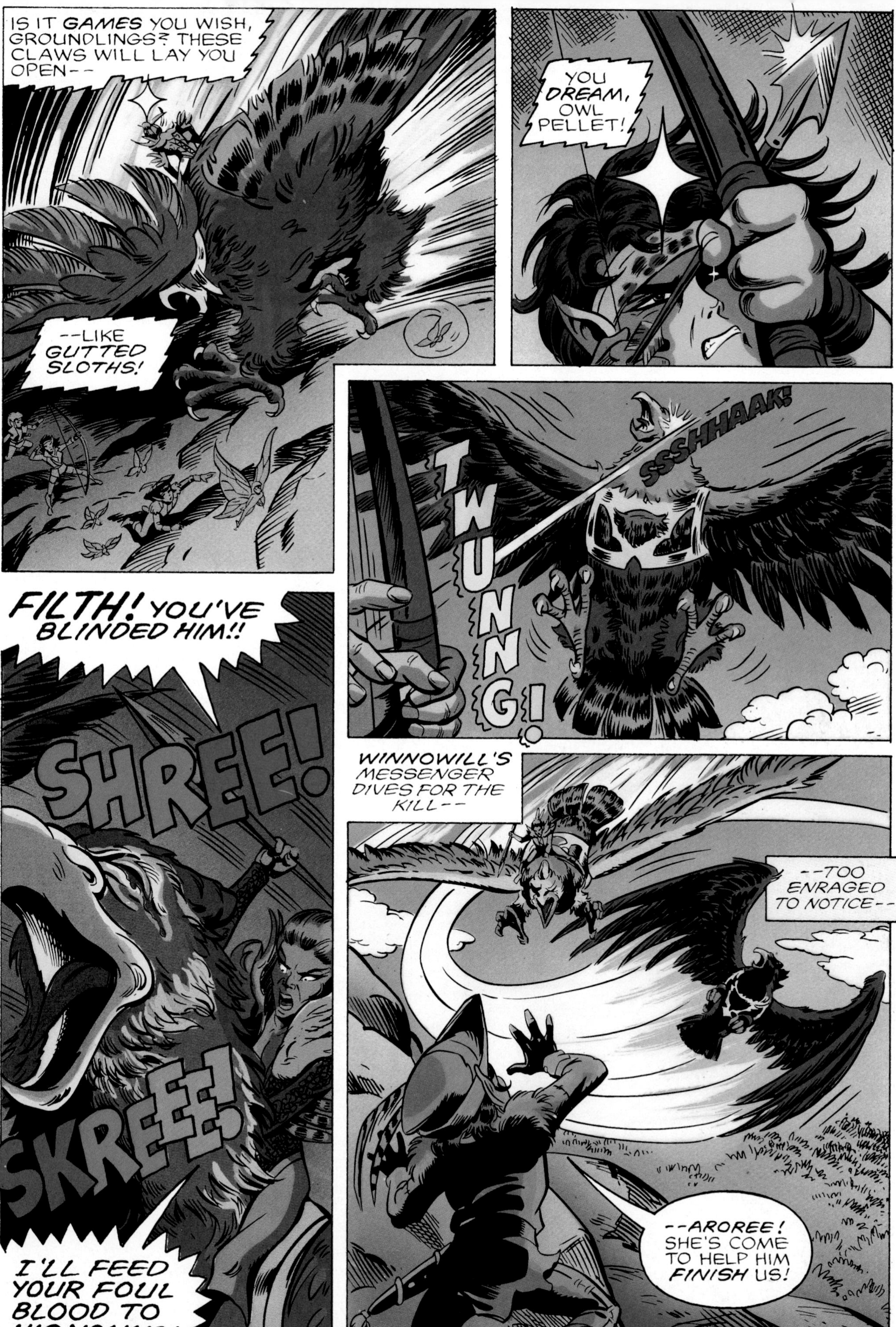

IS IT GAMES YOU WISH, GROUNDLINGS? THESE CLAWS WILL LAY YOU OPEN--
--LIKE GUTTED SLOTHS!
YOU DREAM, OWL PELLET!
TWUNNG!
SSSHHAAK!
FILTH! YOU'VE BLINDED HIM!!
SHREE!
SKREEE!
I'LL FEED YOUR FOUL BLOOD TO HIS YOUNG!
WINNOWILL'S MESSENGER DIVES FOR THE KILL--
--TOO ENRAGED TO NOTICE--
--AROREE! SHE'S COME TO HELP HIM FINISH US!

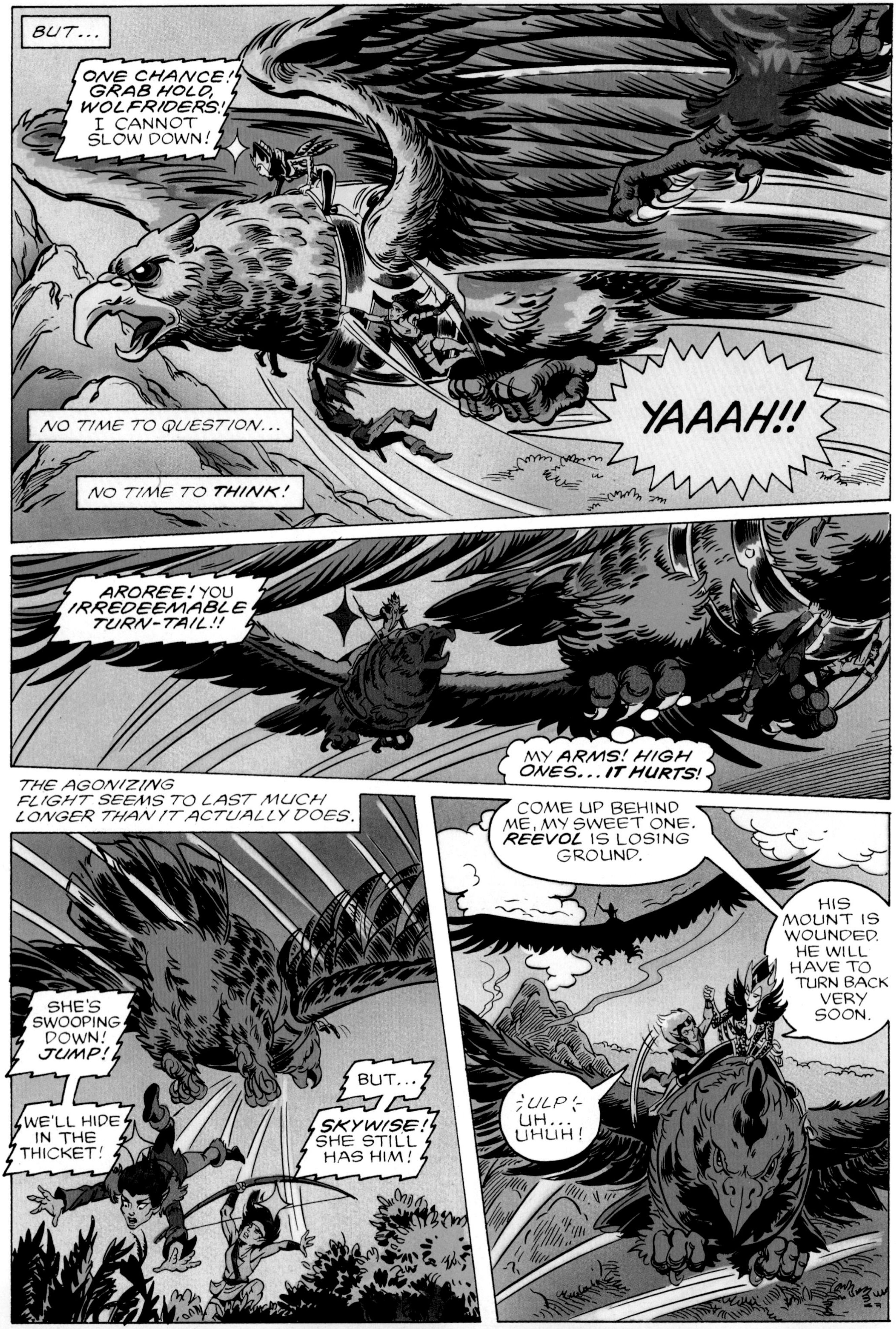

BUT...
ONE CHANCE! GRAB HOLD, WOLFRIDERS! I CANNOT SLOW DOWN!
NO TIME TO QUESTION...
NO TIME TO THINK!
YAAAH!!
AROREE! YOU IRREDEEMABLE TURN-TAIL!!
MY ARMS! HIGH ONES... IT HURTS!
THE AGONIZING FLIGHT SEEMS TO LAST MUCH LONGER THAN IT ACTUALLY DOES.
SHE'S SWOOPING DOWN! JUMP!
WE'LL HIDE IN THE THICKET!
BUT...
SKYWISE! SHE STILL HAS HIM!
COME UP BEHIND ME, MY SWEET ONE. REEVOL IS LOSING GROUND.
HIS MOUNT IS WOUNDED. HE WILL HAVE TO TURN BACK VERY SOON.
ULP
UH... UHUH!

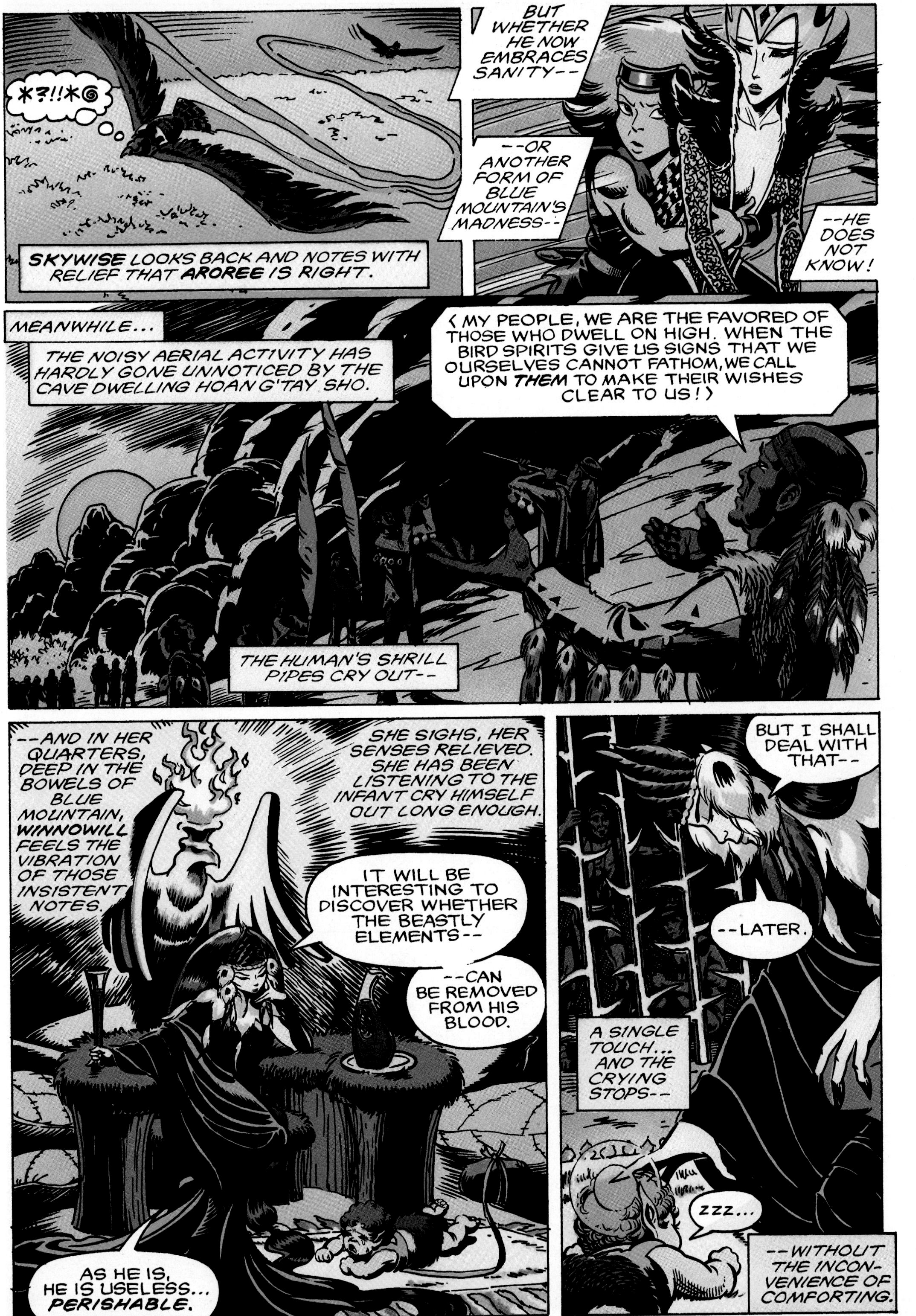
?!!@
SKYWISE LOOKS BACK AND NOTES WITH RELIEF THAT AROREE IS RIGHT.
BUT WHETHER HE NOW EMBRACES SANITY--
--OR ANOTHER FORM OF BLUE MOUNTAIN'S MADNESS--
--HE DOES NOT KNOW!
MEANWHILE...
THE NOISY AERIAL ACTIVITY HAS HARDLY GONE UNNOTICED BY THE CAVE DWELLING HOAN G'TAY SHO.
‹ MY PEOPLE, WE ARE THE FAVORED OF THOSE WHO DWELL ON HIGH. WHEN THE BIRD SPIRITS GIVE US SIGNS THAT WE OURSELVES CANNOT FATHOM, WE CALL UPON THEM TO MAKE THEIR WISHES CLEAR TO US! ›
THE HUMAN'S SHRILL PIPES CRY OUT--
--AND IN HER QUARTERS, DEEP IN THE BOWELS OF BLUE MOUNTAIN, WINNOWILL FEELS THE VIBRATION OF THOSE INSISTENT NOTES.
SHE SIGHS, HER SENSES RELIEVED. SHE HAS BEEN LISTENING TO THE INFANT CRY HIMSELF OUT LONG ENOUGH.
IT WILL BE INTERESTING TO DISCOVER WHETHER THE BEASTLY ELEMENTS--
--CAN BE REMOVED FROM HIS BLOOD.
AS HE IS, HE IS USELESS... PERISHABLE.
BUT I SHALL DEAL WITH THAT--
--LATER.
A SINGLE TOUCH... AND THE CRYING STOPS--
ZZZ...
--WITHOUT THE INCONVENIENCE OF COMFORTING.

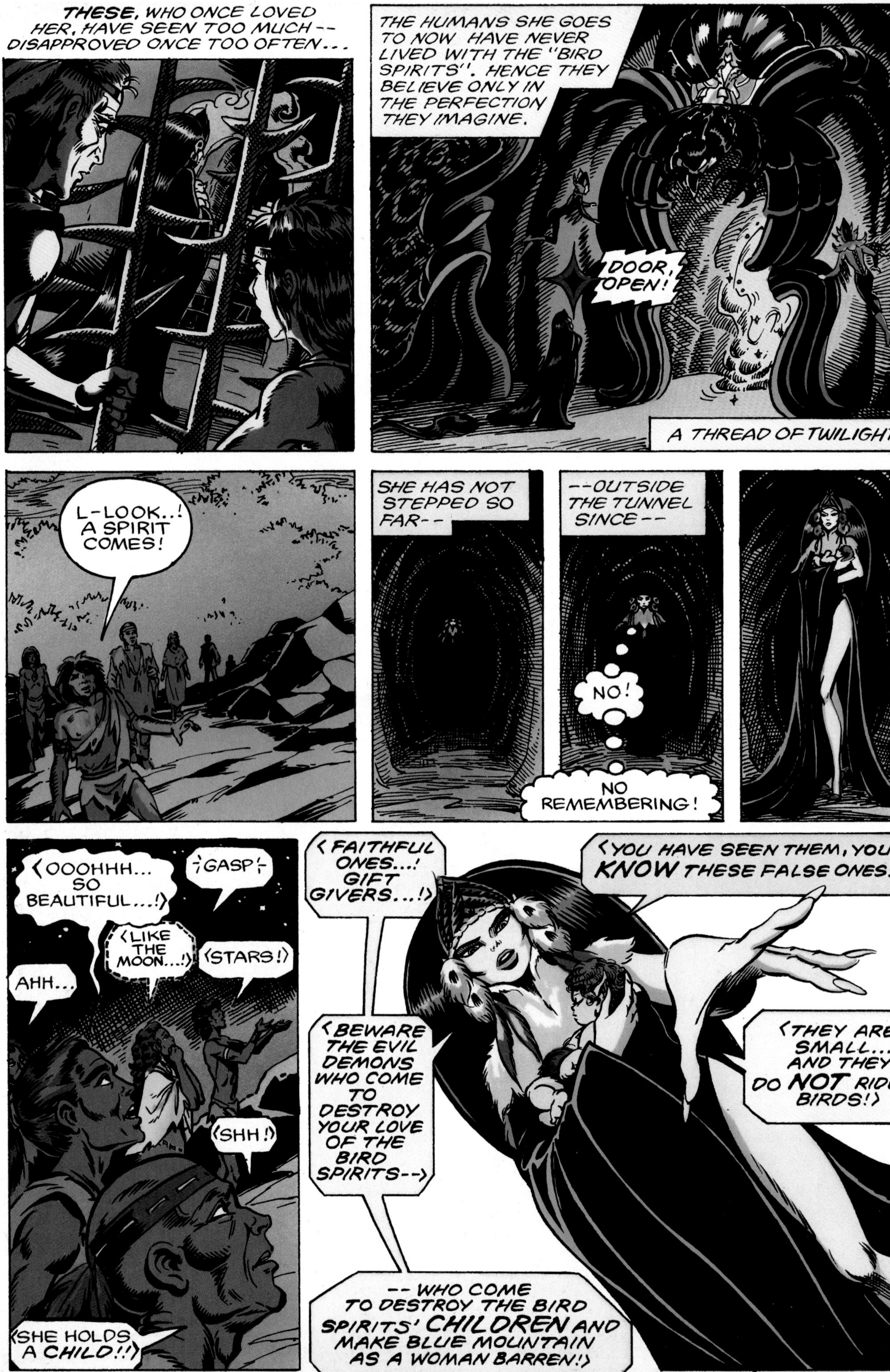
THESE, WHO ONCE LOVED HER, HAVE SEEN TOO MUCH -- DISAPPROVED ONCE TOO OFTEN...
THE HUMANS SHE GOES TO NOW HAVE NEVER LIVED WITH THE "BIRD SPIRITS". HENCE THEY BELIEVE ONLY IN THE PERFECTION THEY IMAGINE.
DOOR, OPEN!
A THREAD OF TWILIGHT...
L-LOOK..! A SPIRIT COMES!
SHE HAS NOT STEPPED SO FAR--
--OUTSIDE THE TUNNEL SINCE--
NO!
NO REMEMBERING!
‹OOOHHH... SO BEAUTIFUL...!›
-GASP-
‹LIKE THE MOON...!›
‹STARS!›
AHH...
‹SHH!›
‹SHE HOLDS A CHILD!!›
‹FAITHFUL ONES...! GIFT GIVERS...!›
‹YOU HAVE SEEN THEM, YOU KNOW THESE FALSE ONES!›
‹BEWARE THE EVIL DEMONS WHO COME TO DESTROY YOUR LOVE OF THE BIRD SPIRITS--›
‹THEY ARE SMALL... AND THEY DO NOT RIDE BIRDS!›
-- WHO COME TO DESTROY THE BIRD SPIRITS' CHILDREN AND MAKE BLUE MOUNTAIN AS A WOMAN BARREN!›

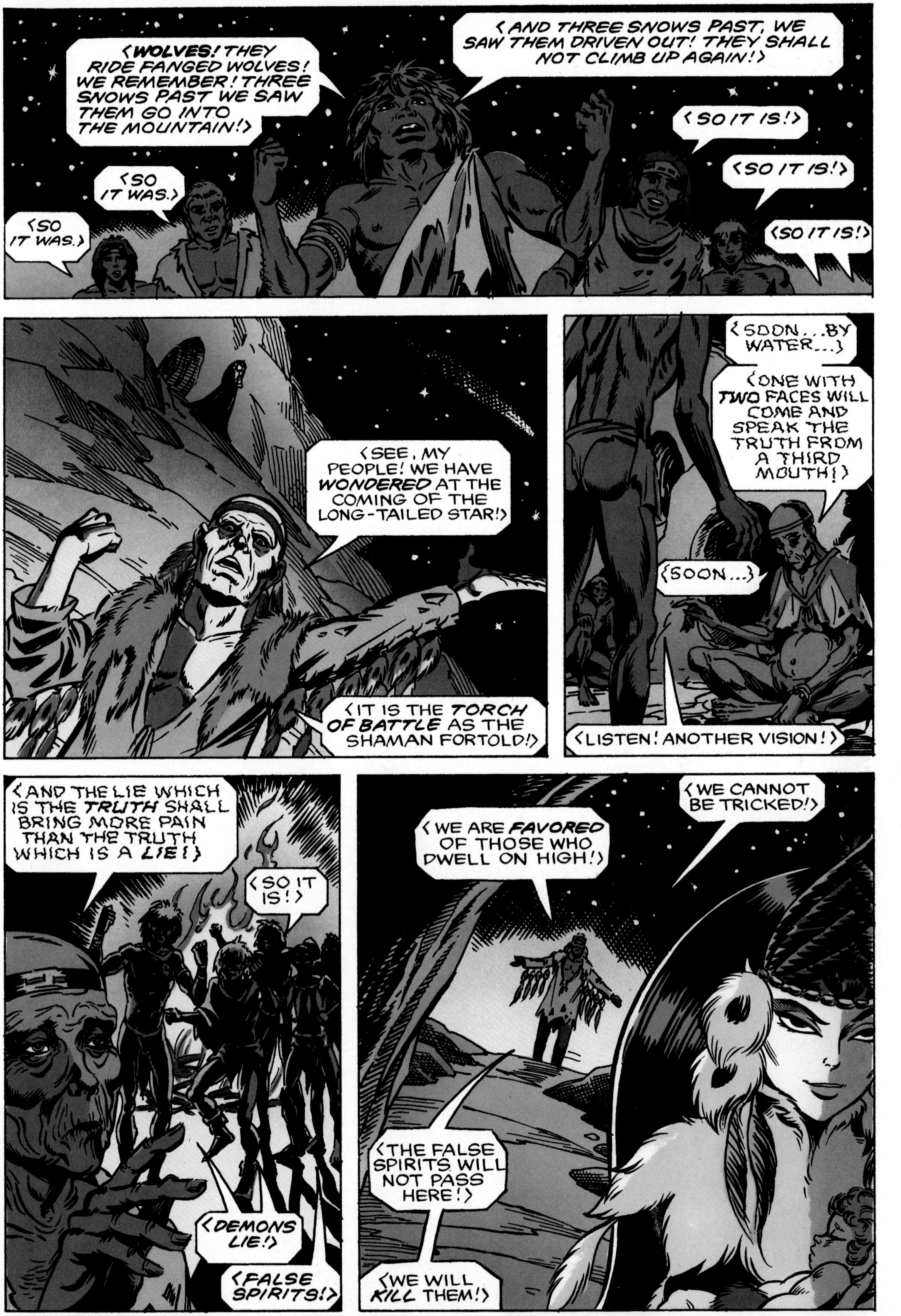
<WOLVES! THEY RIDE FANGED WOLVES! WE REMEMBER! THREE SNOWS PAST WE SAW THEM GO INTO THE MOUNTAIN!>
<AND THREE SNOWS PAST, WE SAW THEM DRIVEN OUT! THEY SHALL NOT CLIMB UP AGAIN!>
<SO IT IS!>
<SO IT WAS.>
<SO IT IS!>
<SO IT WAS.>
<SO IT IS!>
<SEE, MY PEOPLE! WE HAVE WONDERED AT THE COMING OF THE LONG-TAILED STAR!>
<IT IS THE TORCH OF BATTLE AS THE SHAMAN FORTOLD!>
<SOON... BY WATER...>
<ONE WITH TWO FACES WILL COME AND SPEAK THE TRUTH FROM A THIRD MOUTH!>
<SOON...>
<LISTEN! ANOTHER VISION!>
<AND THE LIE WHICH IS THE TRUTH SHALL BRING MORE PAIN THAN THE TRUTH WHICH IS A LIE!>
<SO IT IS!>
<DEMONS LIE!>
<FALSE SPIRITS!>
<WE CANNOT BE TRICKED!>
<WE ARE FAVORED OF THOSE WHO DWELL ON HIGH!>
<THE FALSE SPIRITS WILL NOT PASS HERE!>
<WE WILL KILL THEM!>

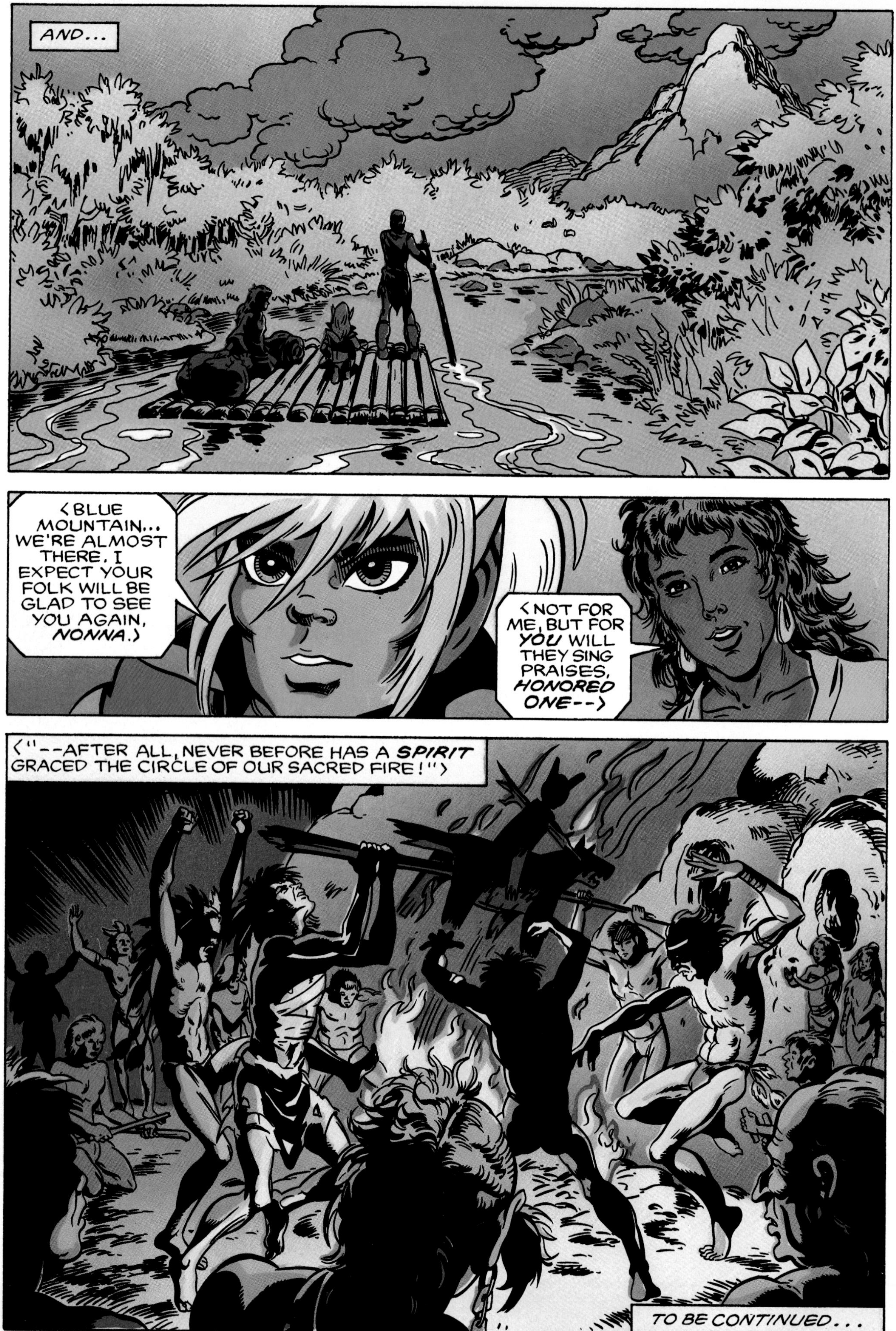
AND...
<BLUE MOUNTAIN... WE'RE ALMOST THERE. I EXPECT YOUR FOLK WILL BE GLAD TO SEE YOU AGAIN, NONNA.>
<NOT FOR ME, BUT FOR YOU WILL THEY SING PRAISES, HONORED ONE-->
<"--AFTER ALL, NEVER BEFORE HAS A SPIRIT GRACED THE CIRCLE OF OUR SACRED FIRE!">
TO BE CONTINUED...

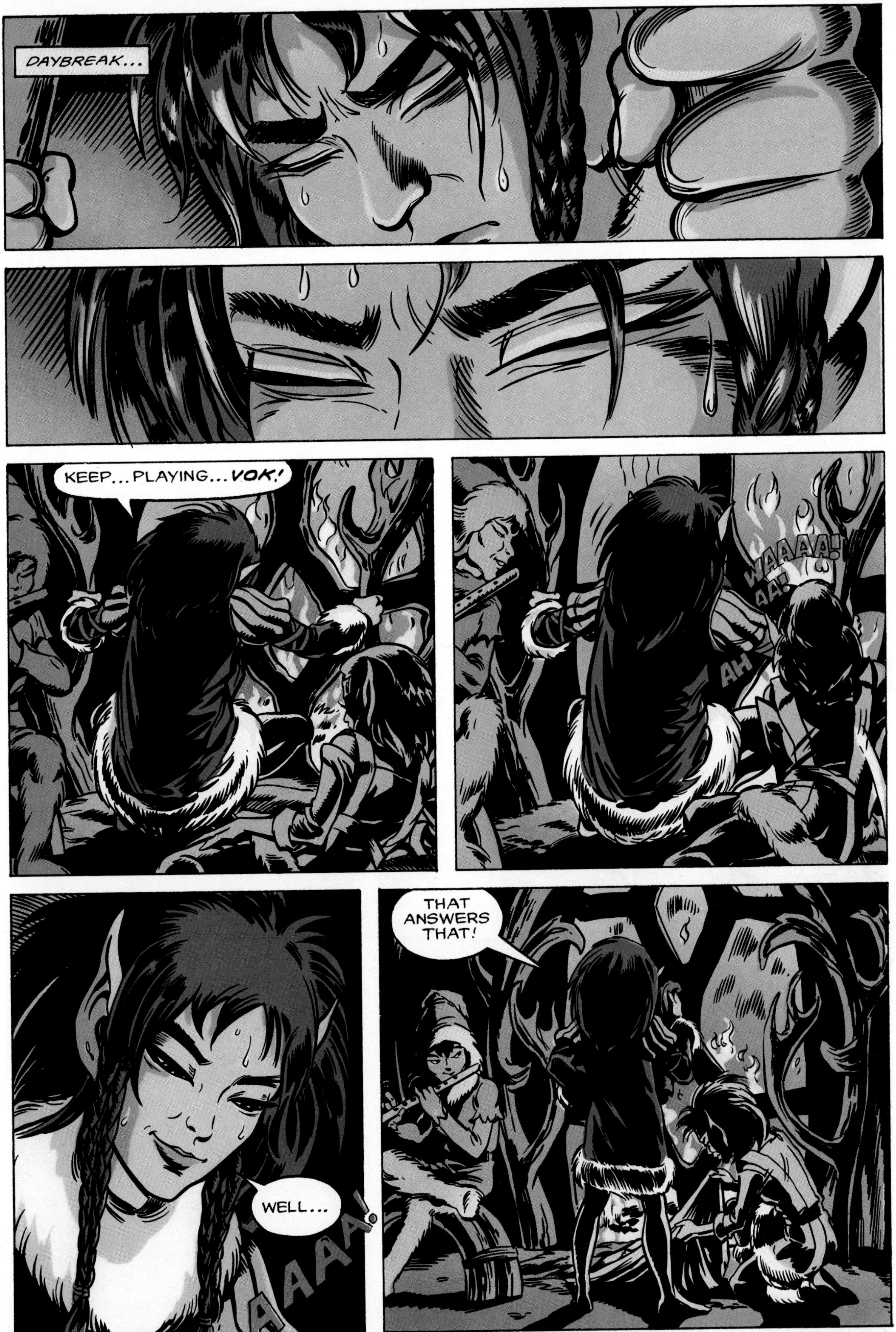
DAYBREAK...
KEEP... PLAYING... VOK!
WAAAAA! AA!
AH
WELL...
AAAA!
THAT ANSWERS THAT!

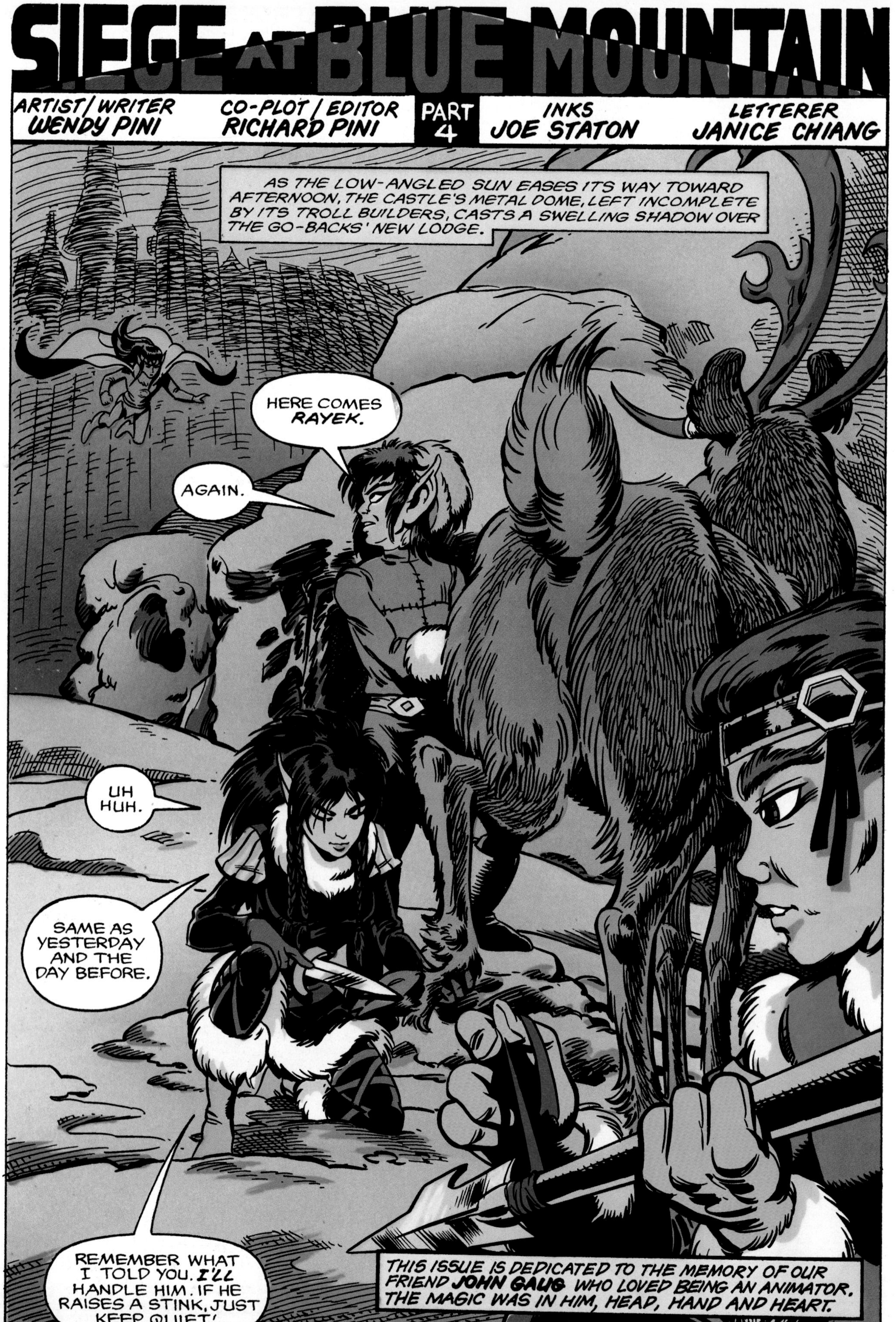
SIEGE AT BLUE MOUNTAIN
ARTIST/WRITER WENDY PINI
CO-PLOT/EDITOR RICHARD PINI
PART 4
INKS JOE STATON
LETTERER JANICE CHIANG
AS THE LOW-ANGLED SUN EASES ITS WAY TOWARD AFTERNOON, THE CASTLE'S METAL DOME, LEFT INCOMPLETE BY ITS TROLL BUILDERS, CASTS A SWELLING SHADOW OVER THE GO-BACKS' NEW LODGE.
HERE COMES RAYEK.
AGAIN.
UH HUH.
SAME AS YESTERDAY AND THE DAY BEFORE.
REMEMBER WHAT I TOLD YOU. I'LL HANDLE HIM. IF HE RAISES A STINK, JUST KEEP QUIET!
THIS ISSUE IS DEDICATED TO THE MEMORY OF OUR FRIEND JOHN GAUS WHO LOVED BEING AN ANIMATOR. THE MAGIC WAS IN HIM, HEAD, HAND AND HEART.

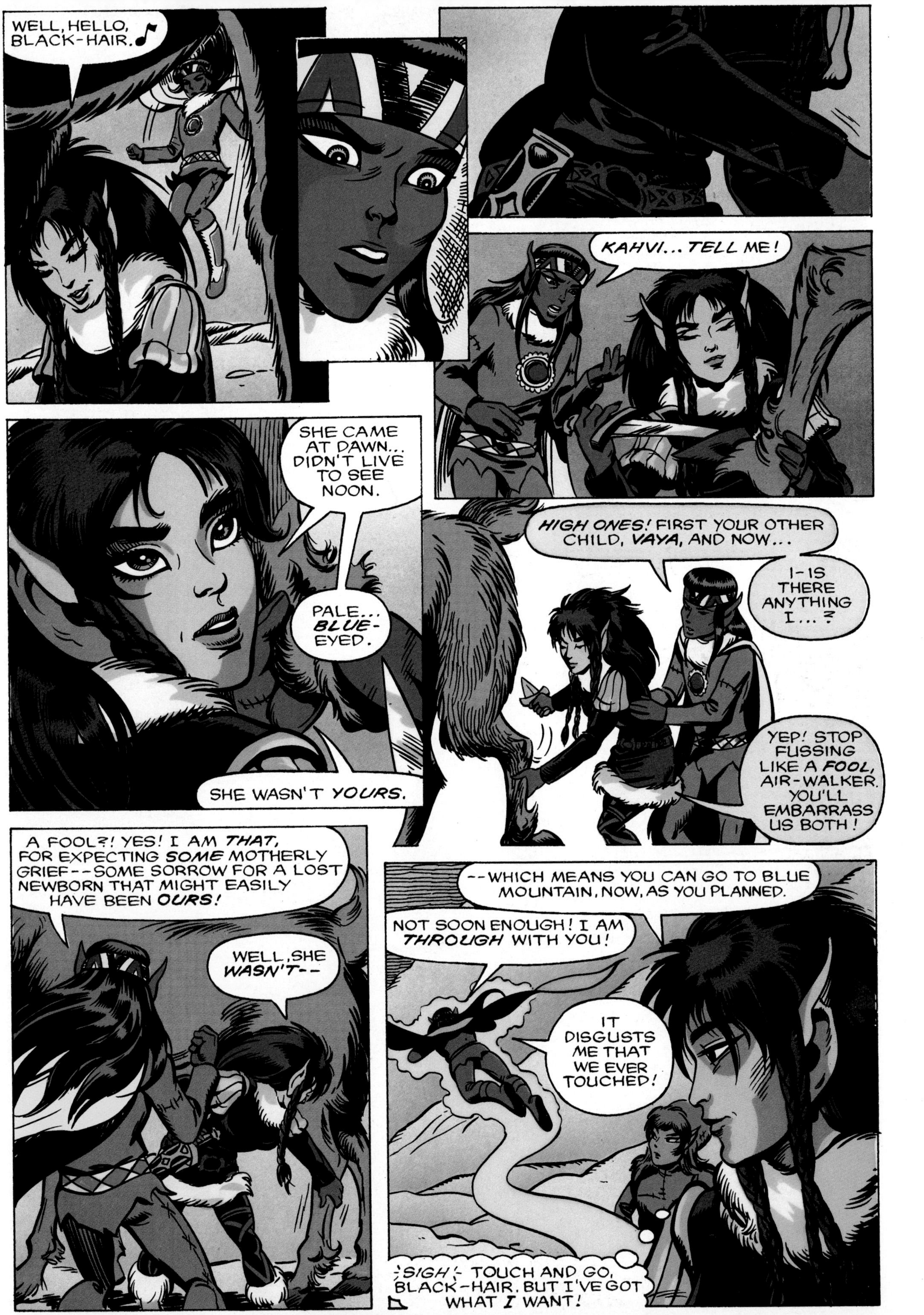
WELL, HELLO, BLACK-HAIR.♪
KAHVI... TELL ME!
SHE CAME AT DAWN... DIDN'T LIVE TO SEE NOON.
PALE... BLUE-EYED.
SHE WASN'T YOURS.
HIGH ONES! FIRST YOUR OTHER CHILD, VAYA, AND NOW...
I-IS THERE ANYTHING I...?
YEP! STOP FUSSING LIKE A FOOL, AIR-WALKER. YOU'LL EMBARRASS US BOTH!
A FOOL?! YES! I AM THAT, FOR EXPECTING SOME MOTHERLY GRIEF--SOME SORROW FOR A LOST NEWBORN THAT MIGHT EASILY HAVE BEEN OURS!
WELL, SHE WASN'T--
--WHICH MEANS YOU CAN GO TO BLUE MOUNTAIN, NOW, AS YOU PLANNED.
NOT SOON ENOUGH! I AM THROUGH WITH YOU!
IT DISGUSTS ME THAT WE EVER TOUCHED!
;SIGH;- TOUCH AND GO, BLACK-HAIR. BUT I'VE GOT WHAT I WANT!

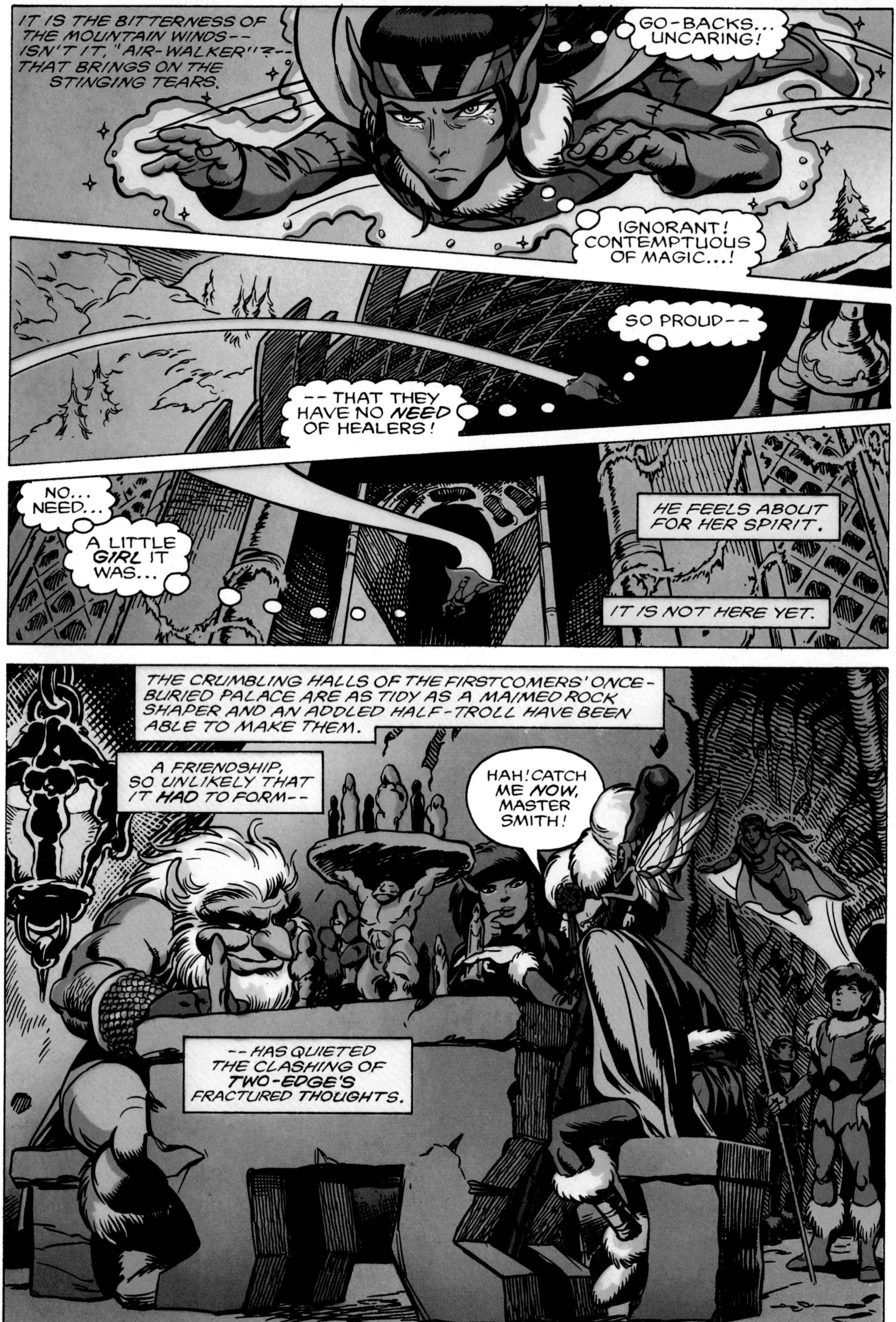
IT IS THE BITTERNESS OF THE MOUNTAIN WINDS-- ISN'T IT, "AIR-WALKER"?-- THAT BRINGS ON THE STINGING TEARS.
GO-BACKS... UNCARING!
IGNORANT! CONTEMPTUOUS OF MAGIC...!
SO PROUD--
--THAT THEY HAVE NO NEED OF HEALERS!
NO... NEED...
A LITTLE GIRL IT WAS...
HE FEELS ABOUT FOR HER SPIRIT.
IT IS NOT HERE YET.
THE CRUMBLING HALLS OF THE FIRSTCOMERS' ONCE-BURIED PALACE ARE AS TIDY AS A MAIMED ROCK SHAPER AND AN ADDLED HALF-TROLL HAVE BEEN ABLE TO MAKE THEM.
A FRIENDSHIP, SO UNLIKELY THAT IT HAD TO FORM--
HAH! CATCH ME NOW, MASTER SMITH!
--HAS QUIETED THE CLASHING OF TWO-EDGE'S FRACTURED THOUGHTS.

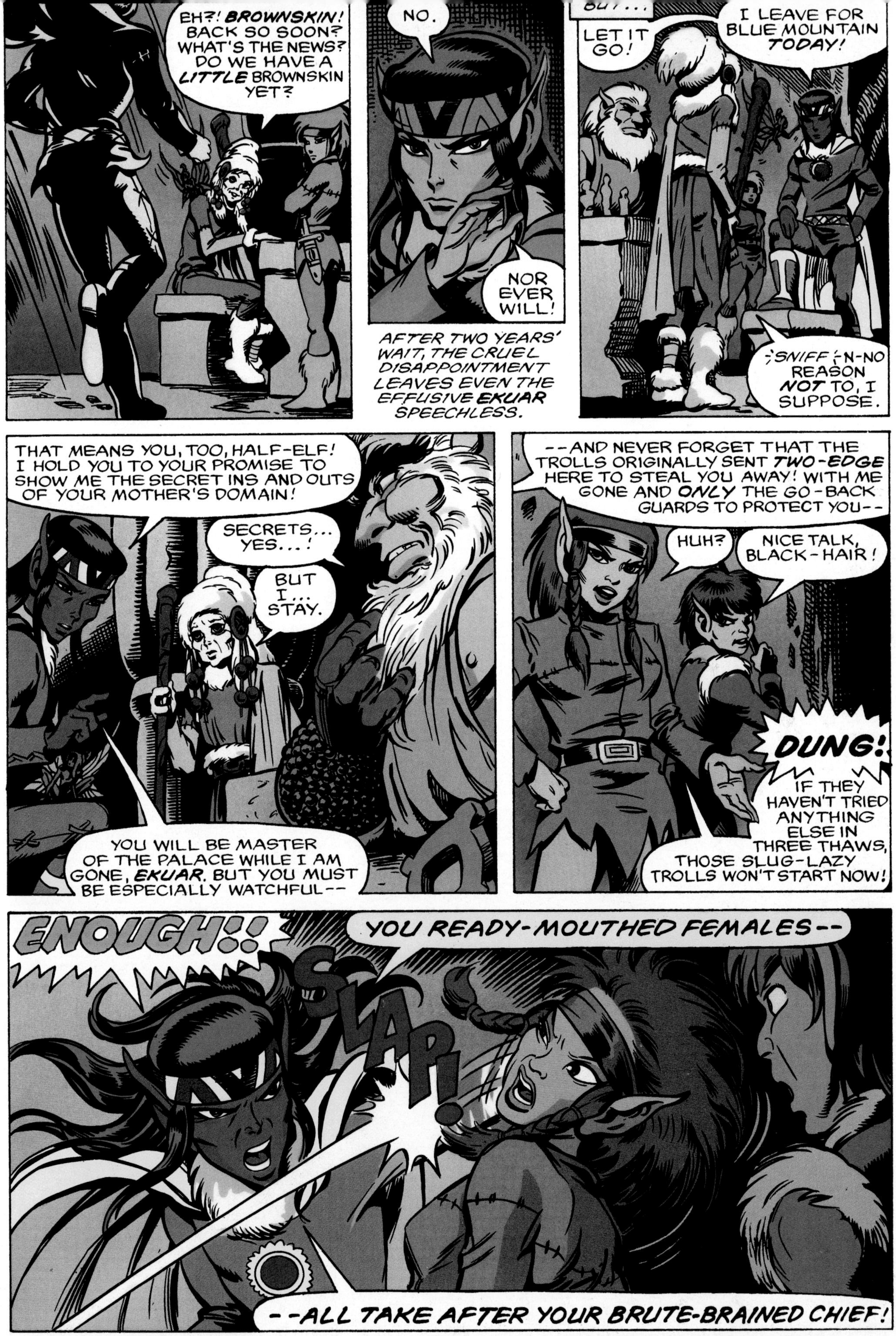

EH?! BROWNSKIN! BACK SO SOON? WHAT'S THE NEWS? DO WE HAVE A LITTLE BROWNSKIN YET?
NO.
NOR EVER WILL!
AFTER TWO YEARS' WAIT, THE CRUEL DISAPPOINTMENT LEAVES EVEN THE EFFUSIVE EKUAR SPEECHLESS.
BUT...
LET IT GO!
I LEAVE FOR BLUE MOUNTAIN TODAY!
-SNIFF- N-NO REASON NOT TO, I SUPPOSE.
THAT MEANS YOU, TOO, HALF-ELF! I HOLD YOU TO YOUR PROMISE TO SHOW ME THE SECRET INS AND OUTS OF YOUR MOTHER'S DOMAIN!
SECRETS... YES...!
BUT I... STAY.
YOU WILL BE MASTER OF THE PALACE WHILE I AM GONE, EKUAR. BUT YOU MUST BE ESPECIALLY WATCHFUL--
--AND NEVER FORGET THAT THE TROLLS ORIGINALLY SENT TWO-EDGE HERE TO STEAL YOU AWAY! WITH ME GONE AND ONLY THE GO-BACK GUARDS TO PROTECT YOU--
HUH?
NICE TALK, BLACK-HAIR!
DUNG!
IF THEY HAVEN'T TRIED ANYTHING ELSE IN THREE THAWS, THOSE SLUG-LAZY TROLLS WON'T START NOW!
ENOUGH!!
YOU READY-MOUTHED FEMALES--
SLAP!
--ALL TAKE AFTER YOUR BRUTE-BRAINED CHIEF!

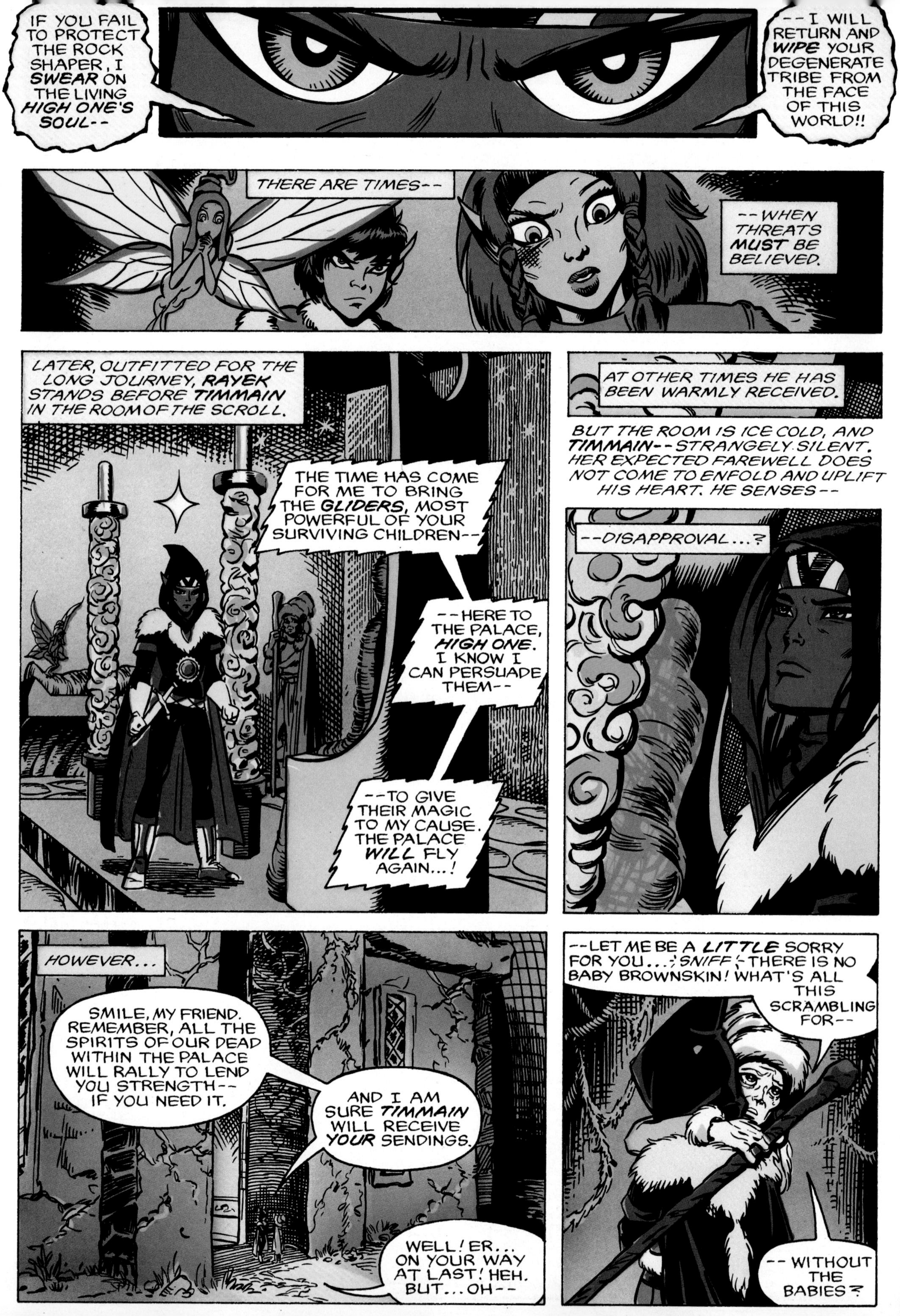

IF YOU FAIL TO PROTECT THE ROCK SHAPER, I SWEAR ON THE LIVING HIGH ONE'S SOUL--
--I WILL RETURN AND WIPE YOUR DEGENERATE TRIBE FROM THE FACE OF THIS WORLD!!
THERE ARE TIMES--
--WHEN THREATS MUST BE BELIEVED.
LATER, OUTFITTED FOR THE LONG JOURNEY, RAYEK STANDS BEFORE TIMMAIN IN THE ROOM OF THE SCROLL.
THE TIME HAS COME FOR ME TO BRING THE GLIDERS, MOST POWERFUL OF YOUR SURVIVING CHILDREN--
--HERE TO THE PALACE, HIGH ONE. I KNOW I CAN PERSUADE THEM--
--TO GIVE THEIR MAGIC TO MY CAUSE. THE PALACE WILL FLY AGAIN...!
AT OTHER TIMES HE HAS BEEN WARMLY RECEIVED.
BUT THE ROOM IS ICE COLD, AND TIMMAIN--STRANGELY SILENT. HER EXPECTED FAREWELL DOES NOT COME TO ENFOLD AND UPLIFT HIS HEART. HE SENSES--
--DISAPPROVAL...?
HOWEVER...
SMILE, MY FRIEND. REMEMBER, ALL THE SPIRITS OF OUR DEAD WITHIN THE PALACE WILL RALLY TO LEND YOU STRENGTH-- IF YOU NEED IT.
AND I AM SURE TIMMAIN WILL RECEIVE YOUR SENDINGS.
WELL! ER... ON YOUR WAY AT LAST! HEH. BUT... OH--
--LET ME BE A LITTLE SORRY FOR YOU...-SNIFF- THERE IS NO BABY BROWNSKIN! WHAT'S ALL THIS SCRAMBLING FOR--
--WITHOUT THE BABIES?

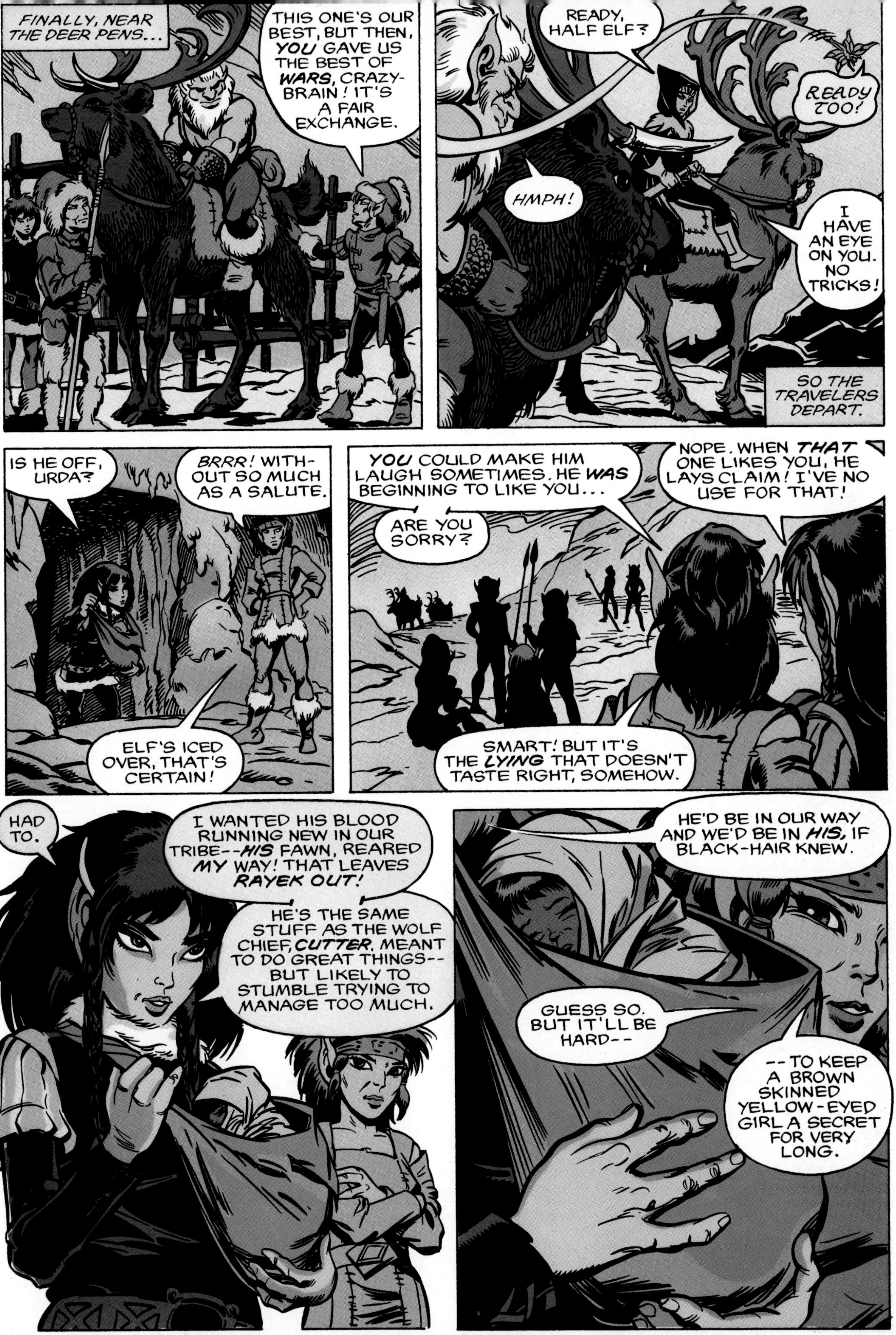
FINALLY, NEAR THE DEER PENS...
THIS ONE'S OUR BEST, BUT THEN, YOU GAVE US THE BEST OF WARS, CRAZY-BRAIN! IT'S A FAIR EXCHANGE.
READY, HALF ELF?
READY TOO!
HMPH!
I HAVE AN EYE ON YOU. NO TRICKS!
SO THE TRAVELERS DEPART.
IS HE OFF, URDA?
BRRR! WITH-OUT SO MUCH AS A SALUTE.
ELF'S ICED OVER, THAT'S CERTAIN!
YOU COULD MAKE HIM LAUGH SOMETIMES. HE WAS BEGINNING TO LIKE YOU...
ARE YOU SORRY?
NOPE. WHEN THAT ONE LIKES YOU, HE LAYS CLAIM! I'VE NO USE FOR THAT!
SMART! BUT IT'S THE LYING THAT DOESN'T TASTE RIGHT, SOMEHOW.
HAD TO.
I WANTED HIS BLOOD RUNNING NEW IN OUR TRIBE--HIS FAWN, REARED MY WAY! THAT LEAVES RAYEK OUT!
HE'S THE SAME STUFF AS THE WOLF CHIEF, CUTTER, MEANT TO DO GREAT THINGS--BUT LIKELY TO STUMBLE TRYING TO MANAGE TOO MUCH.
HE'D BE IN OUR WAY AND WE'D BE IN HIS, IF BLACK-HAIR KNEW.
GUESS SO. BUT IT'LL BE HARD--
--TO KEEP A BROWN SKINNED YELLOW-EYED GIRL A SECRET FOR VERY LONG.

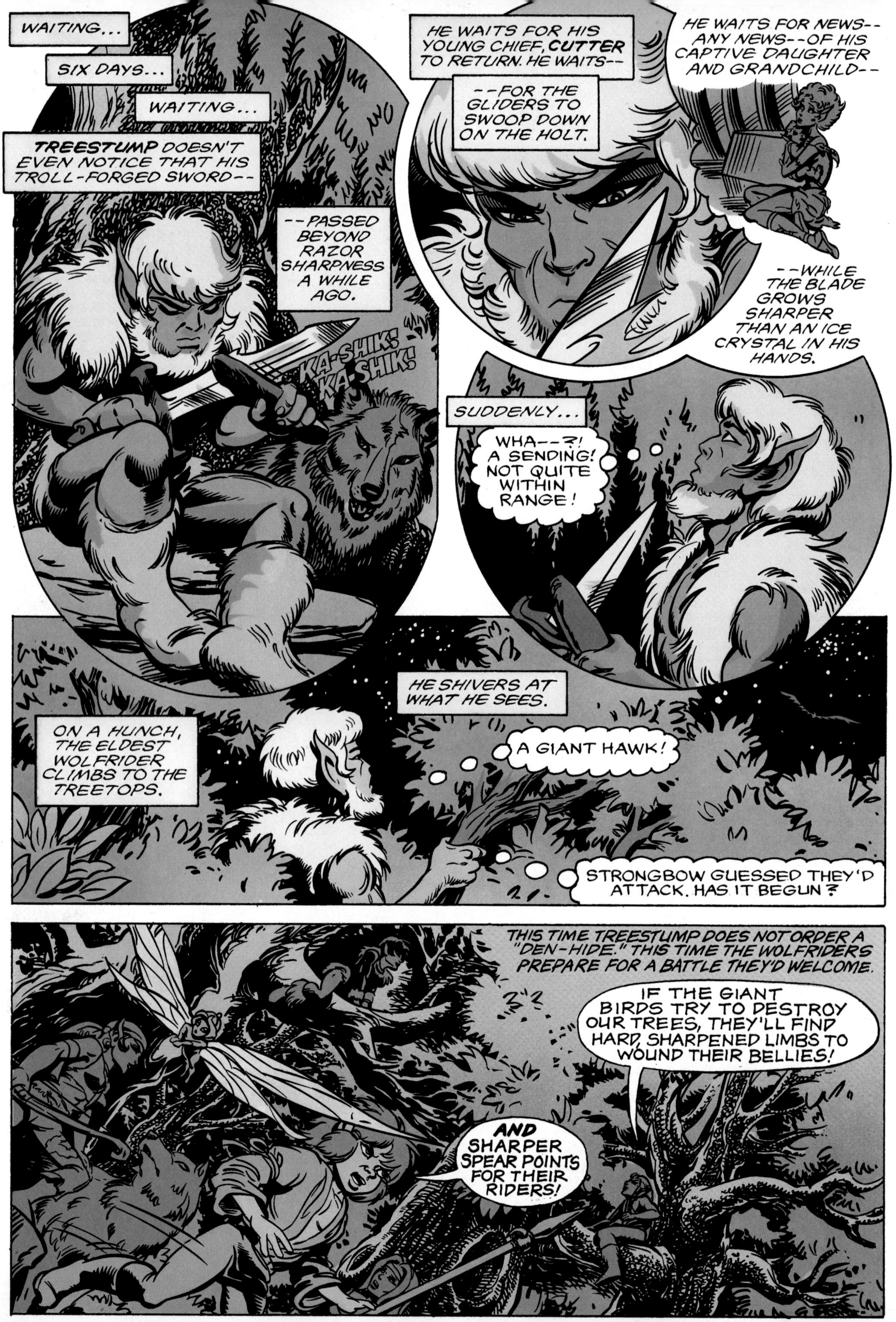
WAITING...
SIX DAYS...
WAITING...
TREESTUMP DOESN'T EVEN NOTICE THAT HIS TROLL-FORGED SWORD--
--PASSED BEYOND RAZOR SHARPNESS A WHILE AGO.
KA-SHIK! KA-SHIK!
HE WAITS FOR HIS YOUNG CHIEF, CUTTER TO RETURN. HE WAITS--
--FOR THE GLIDERS TO SWOOP DOWN ON THE HOLT.
HE WAITS FOR NEWS--ANY NEWS--OF HIS CAPTIVE DAUGHTER AND GRANDCHILD--
--WHILE THE BLADE GROWS SHARPER THAN AN ICE CRYSTAL IN HIS HANDS.
SUDDENLY...
WHA--?! A SENDING! NOT QUITE WITHIN RANGE!
ON A HUNCH, THE ELDEST WOLFRIDER CLIMBS TO THE TREETOPS.
HE SHIVERS AT WHAT HE SEES.
A GIANT HAWK!
STRONGBOW GUESSED THEY'D ATTACK. HAS IT BEGUN?
THIS TIME TREESTUMP DOES NOT ORDER A "DEN-HIDE." THIS TIME THE WOLFRIDERS PREPARE FOR A BATTLE THEY'D WELCOME.
IF THE GIANT BIRDS TRY TO DESTROY OUR TREES, THEY'LL FIND HARD, SHARPENED LIMBS TO WOUND THEIR BELLIES!
AND SHARPER SPEAR POINTS FOR THEIR RIDERS!

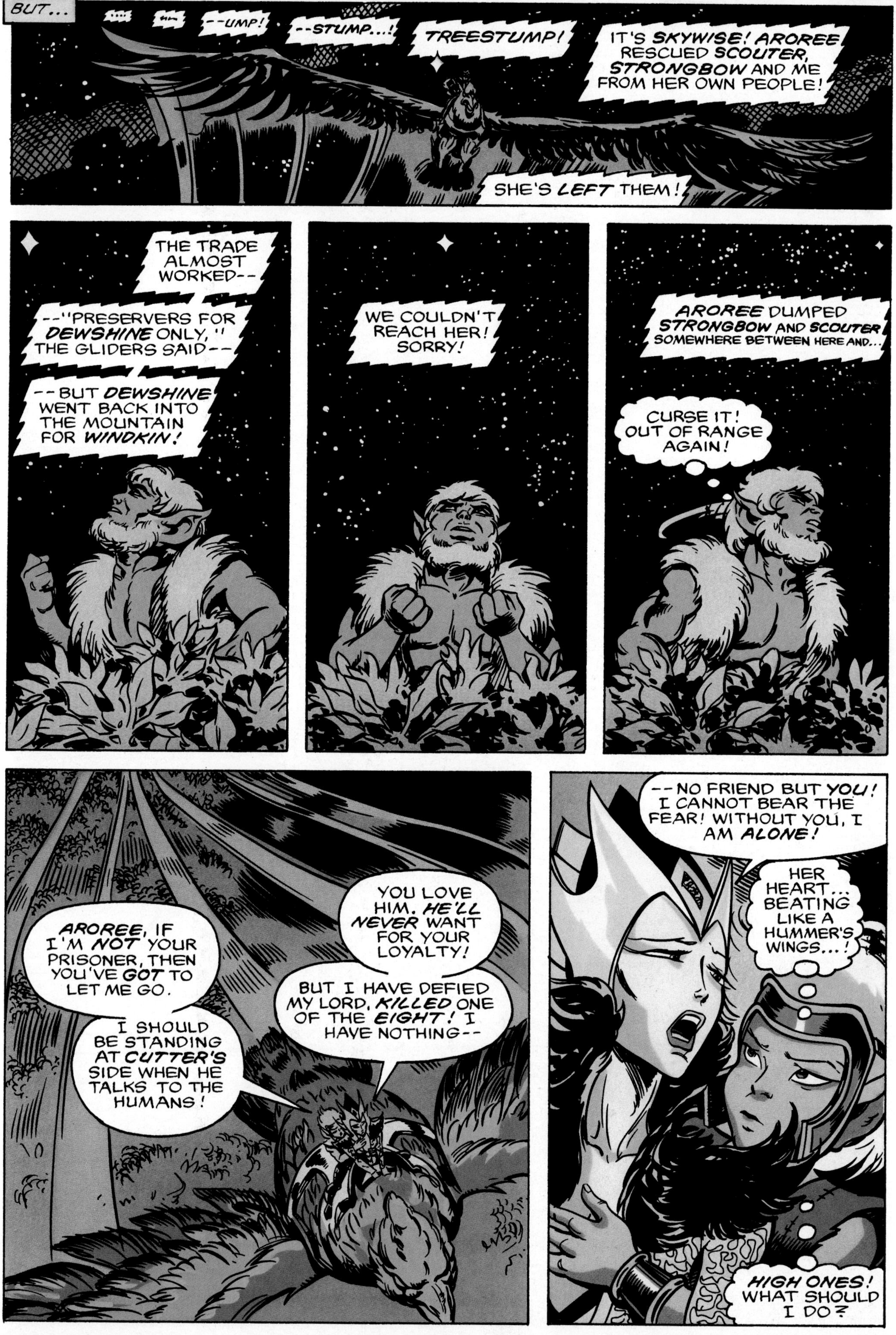
BUT...
--UMP!
--STUMP...!
TREESTUMP!
IT'S SKYWISE! AROREE RESCUED SCOUTER, STRONGBOW AND ME FROM HER OWN PEOPLE!
SHE'S LEFT THEM!
THE TRADE ALMOST WORKED--
--"PRESERVERS FOR DEWSHINE ONLY," THE GLIDERS SAID--
--BUT DEWSHINE WENT BACK INTO THE MOUNTAIN FOR WINDKIN!
WE COULDN'T REACH HER! SORRY!
AROREE DUMPED STRONGBOW AND SCOUTER SOMEWHERE BETWEEN HERE AND...
CURSE IT! OUT OF RANGE AGAIN!
AROREE, IF I'M NOT YOUR PRISONER, THEN YOU'VE GOT TO LET ME GO.
I SHOULD BE STANDING AT CUTTER'S SIDE WHEN HE TALKS TO THE HUMANS!
YOU LOVE HIM. HE'LL NEVER WANT FOR YOUR LOYALTY!
BUT I HAVE DEFIED MY LORD, KILLED ONE OF THE EIGHT! I HAVE NOTHING--
--NO FRIEND BUT YOU! I CANNOT BEAR THE FEAR! WITHOUT YOU, I AM ALONE!
HER HEART... BEATING LIKE A HUMMER'S WINGS...!
HIGH ONES! WHAT SHOULD I DO?

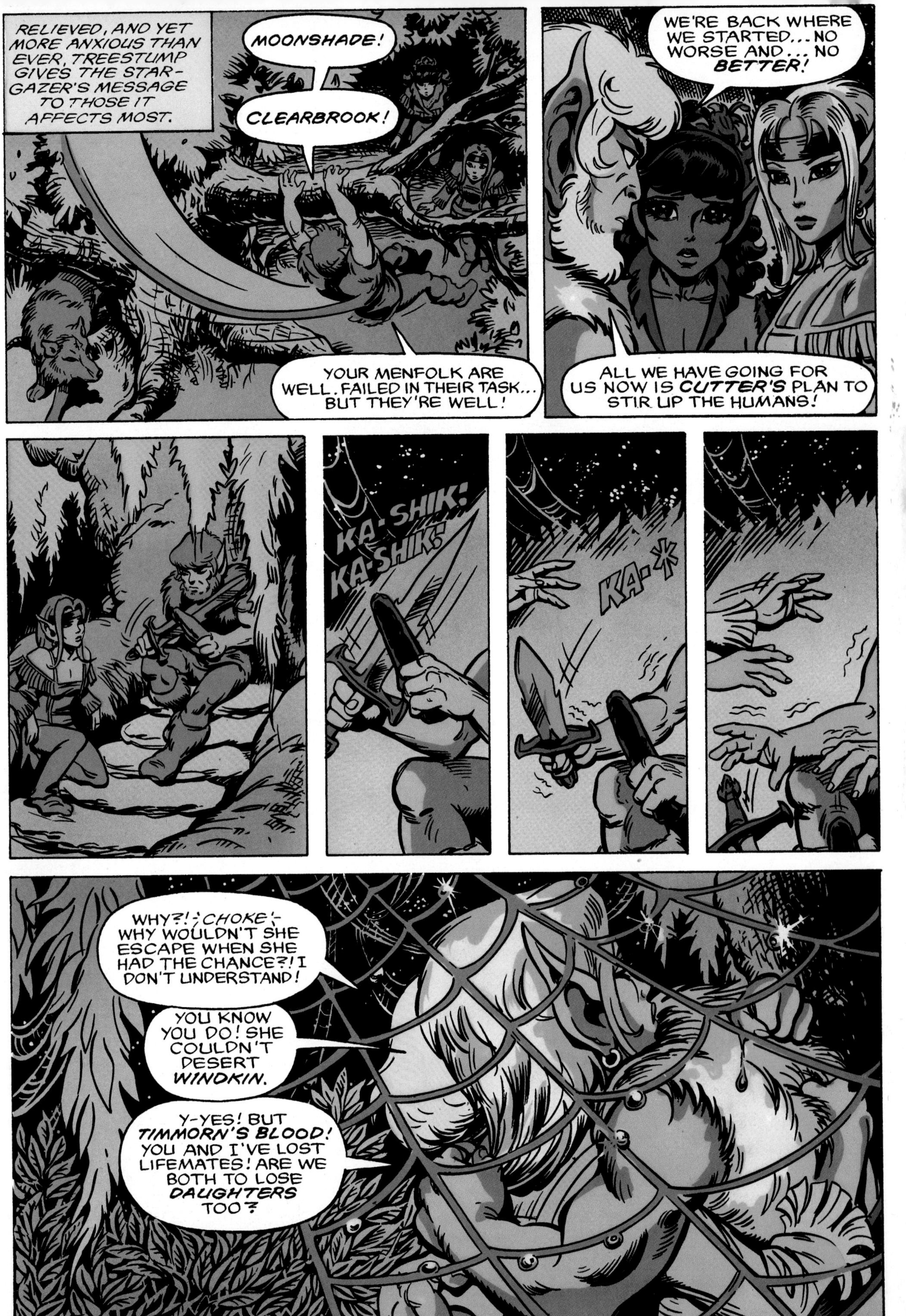
RELIEVED, AND YET MORE ANXIOUS THAN EVER, TREESTUMP GIVES THE STAR-GAZER'S MESSAGE TO THOSE IT AFFECTS MOST.
MOONSHADE!
CLEARBROOK!
YOUR MENFOLK ARE WELL. FAILED IN THEIR TASK... BUT THEY'RE WELL!
WE'RE BACK WHERE WE STARTED... NO WORSE AND... NO BETTER!
ALL WE HAVE GOING FOR US NOW IS CUTTER'S PLAN TO STIR UP THE HUMANS!
KA-SHIK! KA-SHIK!
KA-*
WHY?! -CHOKE- WHY WOULDN'T SHE ESCAPE WHEN SHE HAD THE CHANCE?! I DON'T UNDERSTAND!
YOU KNOW YOU DO! SHE COULDN'T DESERT WINDKIN.
Y-YES! BUT TIMMORN'S BLOOD! YOU AND I'VE LOST LIFEMATES! ARE WE BOTH TO LOSE DAUGHTERS TOO?

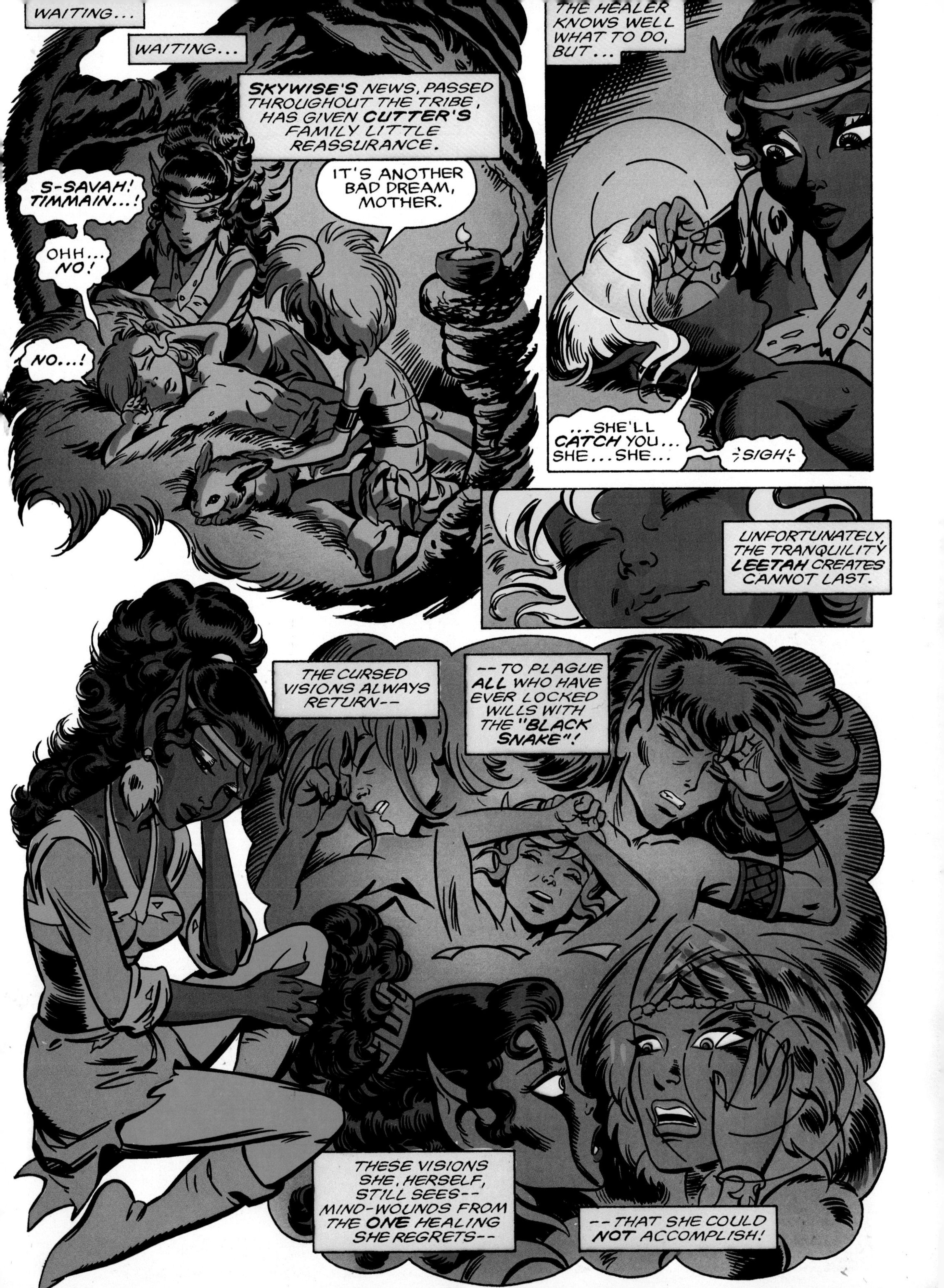
WAITING...
WAITING...
SKYWISE'S NEWS, PASSED THROUGHOUT THE TRIBE, HAS GIVEN CUTTER'S FAMILY LITTLE REASSURANCE.
S-SAVAH! TIMMAIN...!
OHH... NO!
NO...!
IT'S ANOTHER BAD DREAM, MOTHER.
THE HEALER KNOWS WELL WHAT TO DO, BUT...
...SHE'LL CATCH YOU... SHE... SHE...
SIGH
UNFORTUNATELY, THE TRANQUILITY LEETAH CREATES CANNOT LAST.
THE CURSED VISIONS ALWAYS RETURN--
--TO PLAGUE ALL WHO HAVE EVER LOCKED WILLS WITH THE "BLACK SNAKE"!
THESE VISIONS SHE, HERSELF, STILL SEES-- MIND-WOUNDS FROM THE ONE HEALING SHE REGRETS--
--THAT SHE COULD NOT ACCOMPLISH!

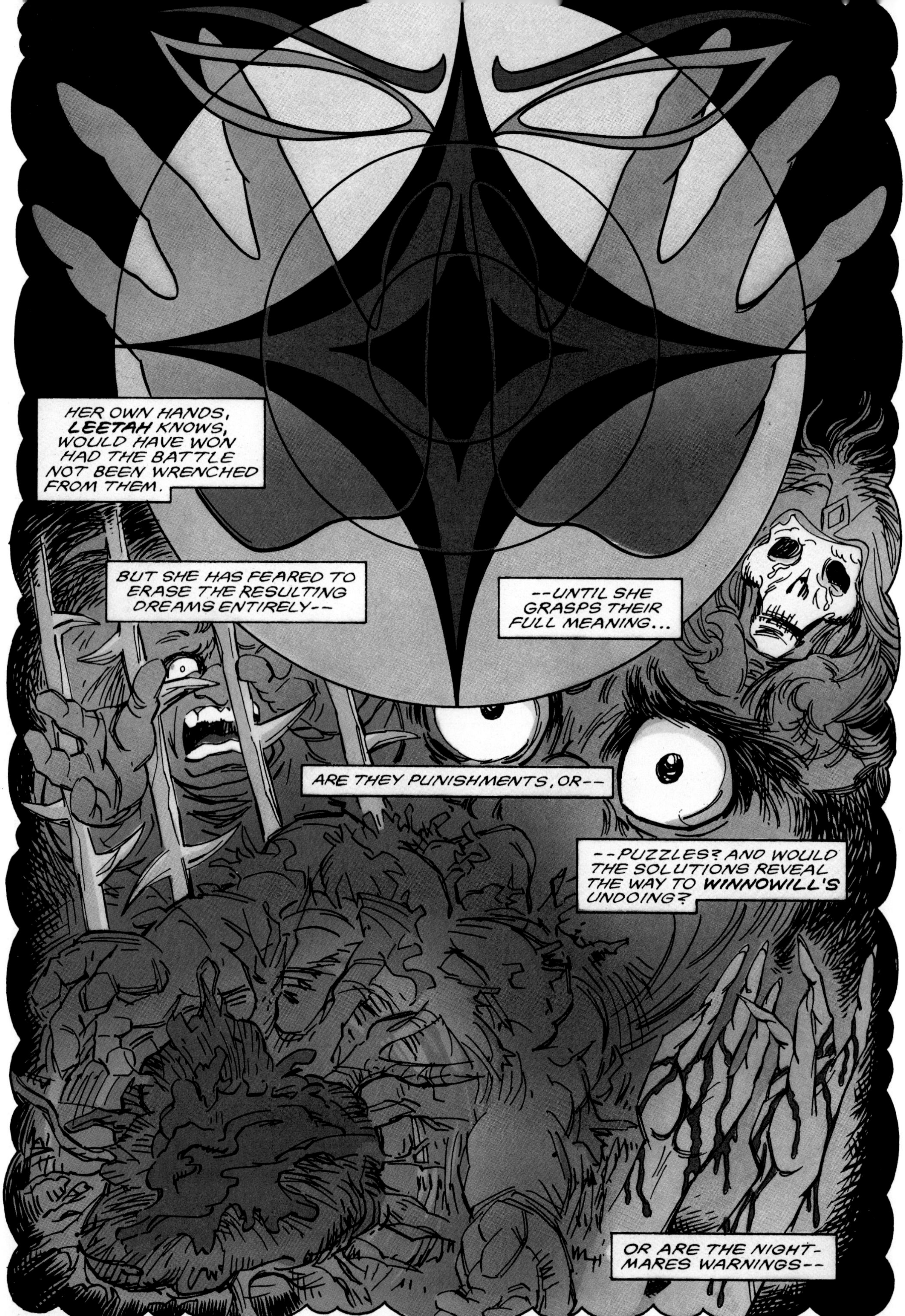
HER OWN HANDS, LEETAH KNOWS, WOULD HAVE WON HAD THE BATTLE NOT BEEN WRENCHED FROM THEM.
BUT SHE HAS FEARED TO ERASE THE RESULTING DREAMS ENTIRELY--
--UNTIL SHE GRASPS THEIR FULL MEANING...
ARE THEY PUNISHMENTS, OR--
--PUZZLES? AND WOULD THE SOLUTIONS REVEAL THE WAY TO WINNOWILL'S UNDOING?
OR ARE THE NIGHT-MARES WARNINGS--

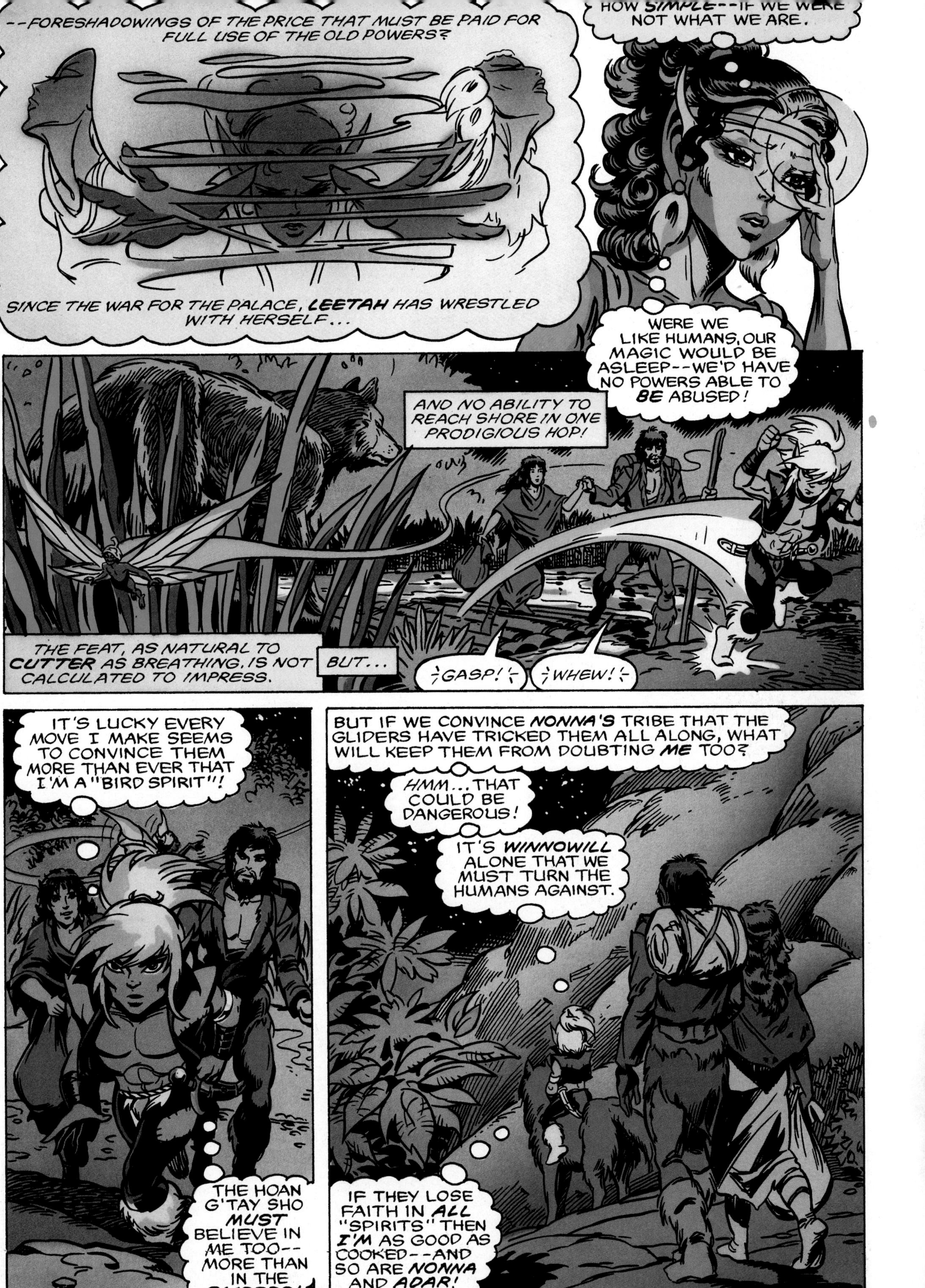
--FORESHADOWINGS OF THE PRICE THAT MUST BE PAID FOR FULL USE OF THE OLD POWERS?
HOW SIMPLE--IF WE WERE NOT WHAT WE ARE.
SINCE THE WAR FOR THE PALACE, LEETAH HAS WRESTLED WITH HERSELF...
WERE WE LIKE HUMANS, OUR MAGIC WOULD BE ASLEEP--WE'D HAVE NO POWERS ABLE TO BE ABUSED!
AND NO ABILITY TO REACH SHORE IN ONE PRODIGIOUS HOP!
THE FEAT, AS NATURAL TO CUTTER AS BREATHING, IS NOT CALCULATED TO IMPRESS.
BUT...
GASP!
WHEW!
IT'S LUCKY EVERY MOVE I MAKE SEEMS TO CONVINCE THEM MORE THAN EVER THAT I'M A "BIRD SPIRIT"!
THE HOAN G'TAY SHO MUST BELIEVE IN ME TOO--MORE THAN IN THE GLIDERS!
BUT IF WE CONVINCE NONNA'S TRIBE THAT THE GLIDERS HAVE TRICKED THEM ALL ALONG, WHAT WILL KEEP THEM FROM DOUBTING ME TOO?
HMM...THAT COULD BE DANGEROUS!
IT'S WINNOWILL ALONE THAT WE MUST TURN THE HUMANS AGAINST.
IF THEY LOSE FAITH IN ALL "SPIRITS" THEN I'M AS GOOD AS COOKED--AND SO ARE NONNA AND ADAR!

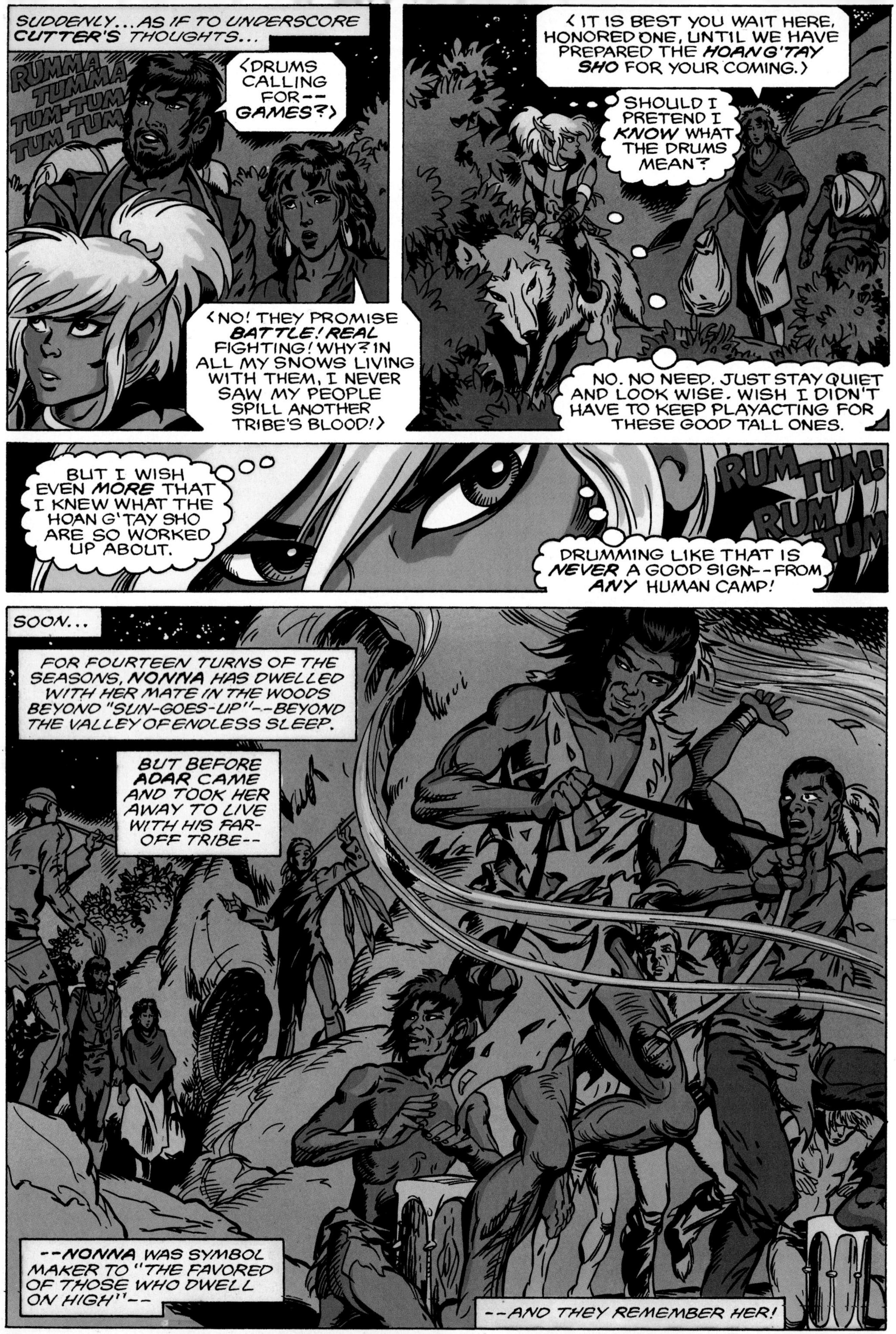
SUDDENLY... AS IF TO UNDERSCORE CUTTER'S THOUGHTS...
RUMMA TUMMA TUM-TUM TUM TUM
‹DRUMS CALLING FOR-- GAMES?›
‹NO! THEY PROMISE BATTLE! REAL FIGHTING! WHY? IN ALL MY SNOWS LIVING WITH THEM, I NEVER SAW MY PEOPLE SPILL ANOTHER TRIBE'S BLOOD!›
‹IT IS BEST YOU WAIT HERE, HONORED ONE, UNTIL WE HAVE PREPARED THE HOAN G'TAY SHO FOR YOUR COMING.›
SHOULD I PRETEND I KNOW WHAT THE DRUMS MEAN?
NO. NO NEED. JUST STAY QUIET AND LOOK WISE. WISH I DIDN'T HAVE TO KEEP PLAYACTING FOR THESE GOOD TALL ONES.
BUT I WISH EVEN MORE THAT I KNEW WHAT THE HOAN G'TAY SHO ARE SO WORKED UP ABOUT.
RUM TUM! RUM TUM
DRUMMING LIKE THAT IS NEVER A GOOD SIGN--FROM ANY HUMAN CAMP!
SOON...
FOR FOURTEEN TURNS OF THE SEASONS, NONNA HAS DWELLED WITH HER MATE IN THE WOODS BEYOND "SUN-GOES-UP"--BEYOND THE VALLEY OF ENDLESS SLEEP.
BUT BEFORE ADAR CAME AND TOOK HER AWAY TO LIVE WITH HIS FAR-OFF TRIBE--
--NONNA WAS SYMBOL MAKER TO "THE FAVORED OF THOSE WHO DWELL ON HIGH"--
--AND THEY REMEMBER HER!

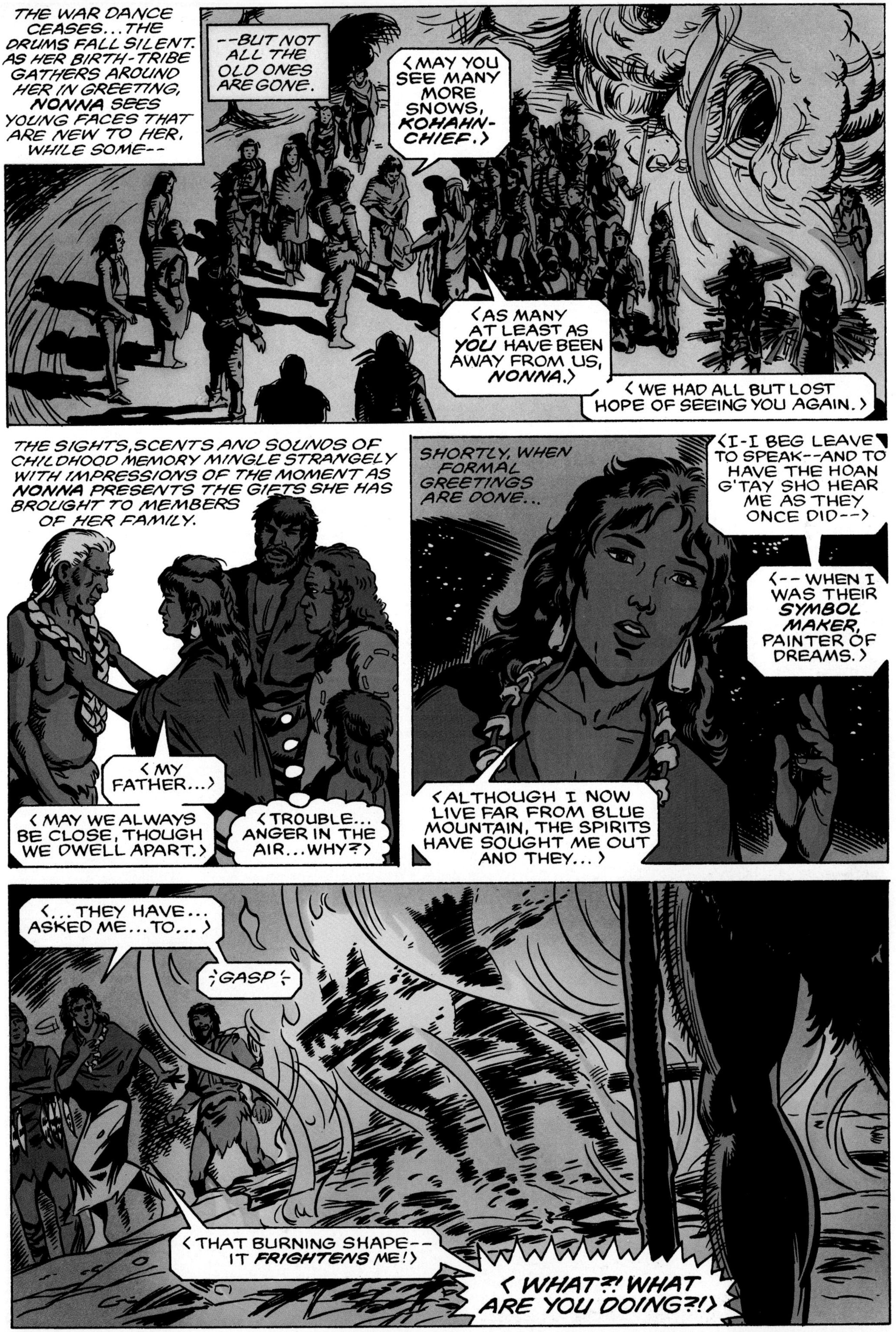
THE WAR DANCE CEASES... THE DRUMS FALL SILENT. AS HER BIRTH-TRIBE GATHERS AROUND HER IN GREETING, NONNA SEES YOUNG FACES THAT ARE NEW TO HER, WHILE SOME--
--BUT NOT ALL THE OLD ONES ARE GONE.
‹MAY YOU SEE MANY MORE SNOWS, KOHAHN-CHIEF.›
‹AS MANY AT LEAST AS YOU HAVE BEEN AWAY FROM US, NONNA.›
‹WE HAD ALL BUT LOST HOPE OF SEEING YOU AGAIN.›
THE SIGHTS, SCENTS AND SOUNDS OF CHILDHOOD MEMORY MINGLE STRANGELY WITH IMPRESSIONS OF THE MOMENT AS NONNA PRESENTS THE GIFTS SHE HAS BROUGHT TO MEMBERS OF HER FAMILY.
‹MY FATHER...›
‹MAY WE ALWAYS BE CLOSE, THOUGH WE DWELL APART.›
‹TROUBLE... ANGER IN THE AIR... WHY?›
SHORTLY, WHEN FORMAL GREETINGS ARE DONE...
‹I-I BEG LEAVE TO SPEAK--AND TO HAVE THE HOAN G'TAY SHO HEAR ME AS THEY ONCE DID--›
‹--WHEN I WAS THEIR SYMBOL MAKER, PAINTER OF DREAMS.›
‹ALTHOUGH I NOW LIVE FAR FROM BLUE MOUNTAIN, THE SPIRITS HAVE SOUGHT ME OUT AND THEY...›
‹...THEY HAVE... ASKED ME... TO...›
GASP
‹THAT BURNING SHAPE-- IT FRIGHTENS ME!›
‹WHAT?! WHAT ARE YOU DOING?!›

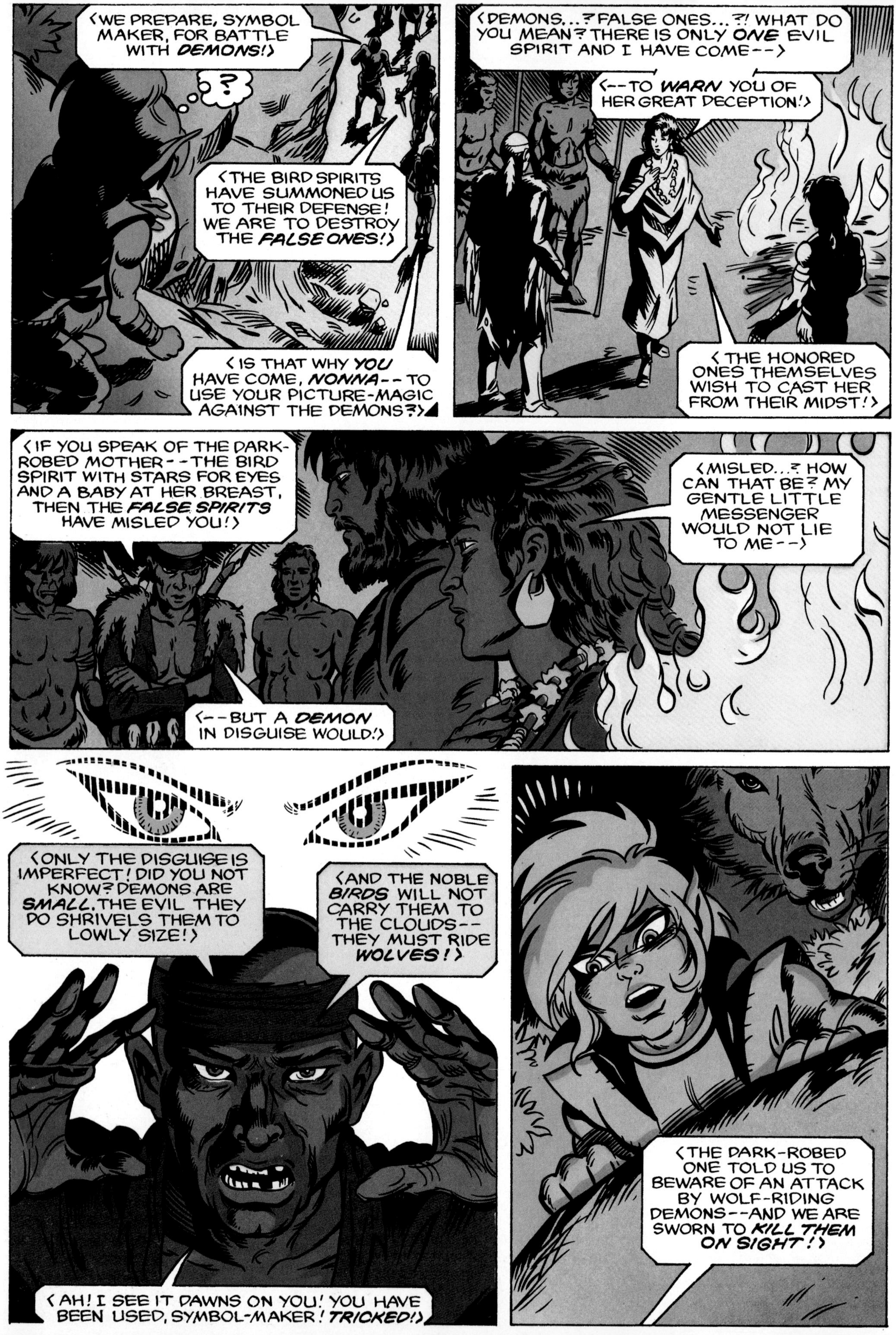
‹WE PREPARE, SYMBOL MAKER, FOR BATTLE WITH DEMONS!›
?
‹THE BIRD SPIRITS HAVE SUMMONED US TO THEIR DEFENSE! WE ARE TO DESTROY THE FALSE ONES!›
‹IS THAT WHY YOU HAVE COME, NONNA--TO USE YOUR PICTURE-MAGIC AGAINST THE DEMONS?›
‹DEMONS...? FALSE ONES...?! WHAT DO YOU MEAN? THERE IS ONLY ONE EVIL SPIRIT AND I HAVE COME--›
‹--TO WARN YOU OF HER GREAT DECEPTION!›
‹THE HONORED ONES THEMSELVES WISH TO CAST HER FROM THEIR MIDST!›
‹IF YOU SPEAK OF THE DARK-ROBED MOTHER--THE BIRD SPIRIT WITH STARS FOR EYES AND A BABY AT HER BREAST, THEN THE FALSE SPIRITS HAVE MISLED YOU!›
‹MISLED...? HOW CAN THAT BE? MY GENTLE LITTLE MESSENGER WOULD NOT LIE TO ME--›
‹--BUT A DEMON IN DISGUISE WOULD!›
‹ONLY THE DISGUISE IS IMPERFECT! DID YOU NOT KNOW? DEMONS ARE SMALL. THE EVIL THEY DO SHRIVELS THEM TO LOWLY SIZE!›
‹AND THE NOBLE BIRDS WILL NOT CARRY THEM TO THE CLOUDS--THEY MUST RIDE WOLVES!›
‹THE DARK-ROBED ONE TOLD US TO BEWARE OF AN ATTACK BY WOLF-RIDING DEMONS--AND WE ARE SWORN TO KILL THEM ON SIGHT!›
‹AH! I SEE IT DAWNS ON YOU! YOU HAVE BEEN USED, SYMBOL-MAKER! TRICKED!›

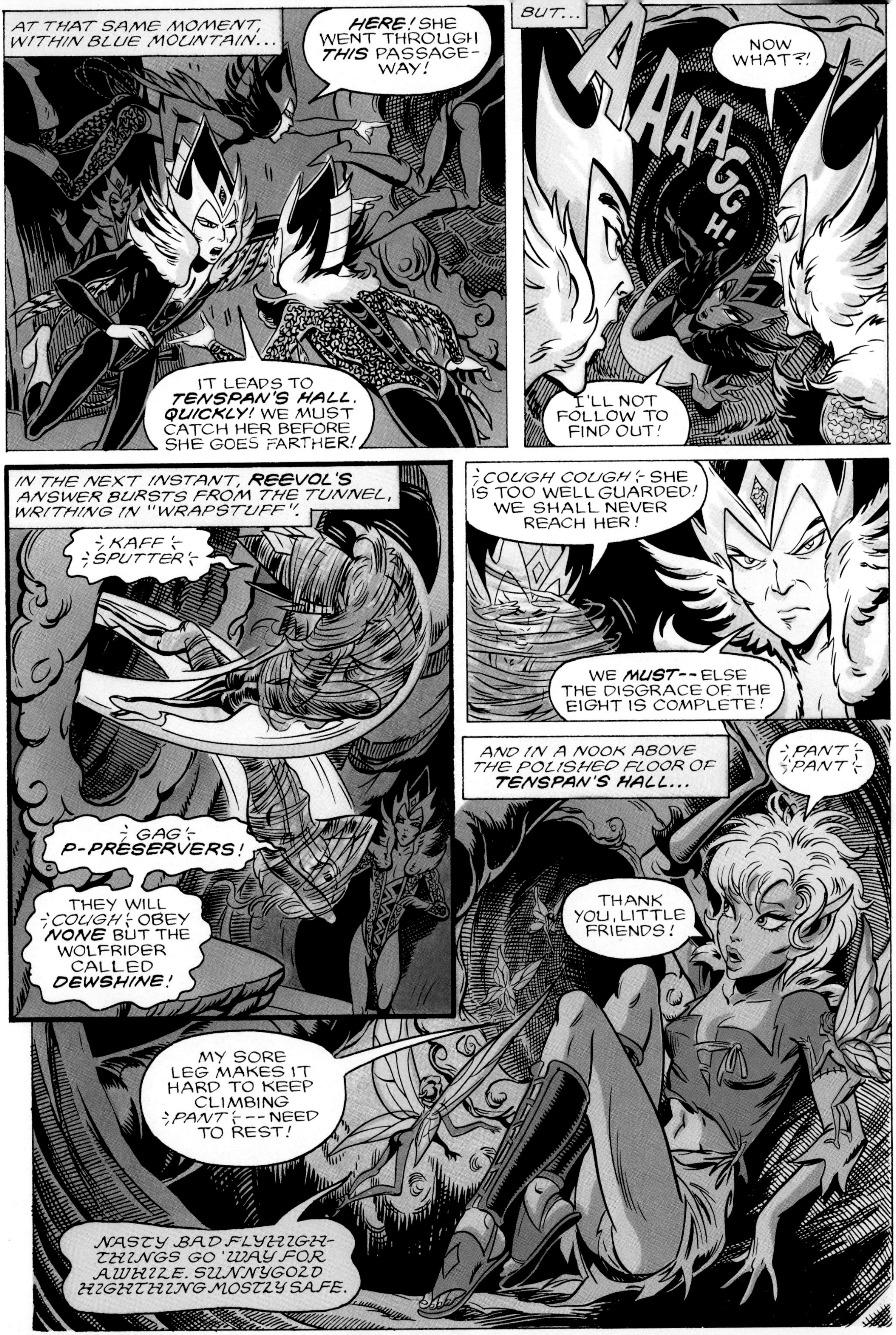
AT THAT SAME MOMENT, WITHIN BLUE MOUNTAIN...
HERE! SHE WENT THROUGH THIS PASSAGE-WAY!
IT LEADS TO TENSPAN'S HALL. QUICKLY! WE MUST CATCH HER BEFORE SHE GOES FARTHER!
BUT...
AAAAAGGH!
NOW WHAT?!
I'LL NOT FOLLOW TO FIND OUT!
IN THE NEXT INSTANT, REEVOL'S ANSWER BURSTS FROM THE TUNNEL, WRITHING IN "WRAPSTUFF".
KAFF SPUTTER
GAG P-PRESERVERS!
THEY WILL COUGH OBEY NONE BUT THE WOLFRIDER CALLED DEWSHINE!
COUGH COUGH SHE IS TOO WELL GUARDED! WE SHALL NEVER REACH HER!
WE MUST--ELSE THE DISGRACE OF THE EIGHT IS COMPLETE!
AND IN A NOOK ABOVE THE POLISHED FLOOR OF TENSPAN'S HALL...
PANT PANT
THANK YOU, LITTLE FRIENDS!
MY SORE LEG MAKES IT HARD TO KEEP CLIMBING PANT--NEED TO REST!
NASTY BAD FLYHIGH-THINGS GO 'WAY FOR AWHILE. SUNNYGOLD HIGHTHING MOSTLY SAFE.

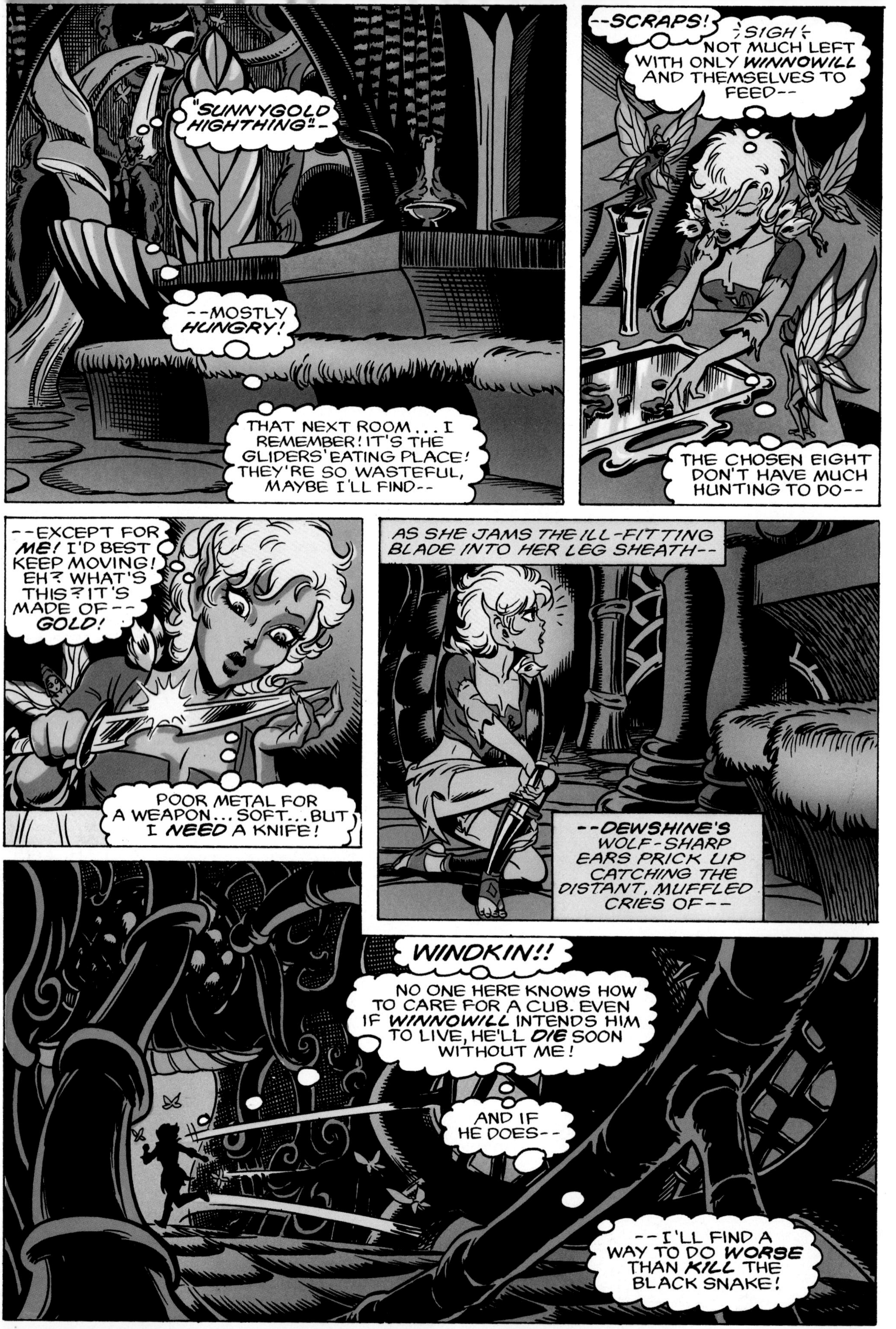
"SUNNYGOLD HIGHTHING"--
--MOSTLY HUNGRY!
THAT NEXT ROOM... I REMEMBER! IT'S THE GLIDERS' EATING PLACE! THEY'RE SO WASTEFUL, MAYBE I'LL FIND--
--SCRAPS!
SIGH
NOT MUCH LEFT WITH ONLY WINNOWILL AND THEMSELVES TO FEED--
THE CHOSEN EIGHT DON'T HAVE MUCH HUNTING TO DO--
--EXCEPT FOR ME! I'D BEST KEEP MOVING! EH? WHAT'S THIS? IT'S MADE OF-- GOLD!
POOR METAL FOR A WEAPON... SOFT... BUT I NEED A KNIFE!
AS SHE JAMS THE ILL-FITTING BLADE INTO HER LEG SHEATH--
--DEWSHINE'S WOLF-SHARP EARS PRICK UP CATCHING THE DISTANT, MUFFLED CRIES OF--
WINDKIN!!
NO ONE HERE KNOWS HOW TO CARE FOR A CUB. EVEN IF WINNOWILL INTENDS HIM TO LIVE, HE'LL DIE SOON WITHOUT ME!
AND IF HE DOES--
--I'LL FIND A WAY TO DO WORSE THAN KILL THE BLACK SNAKE!

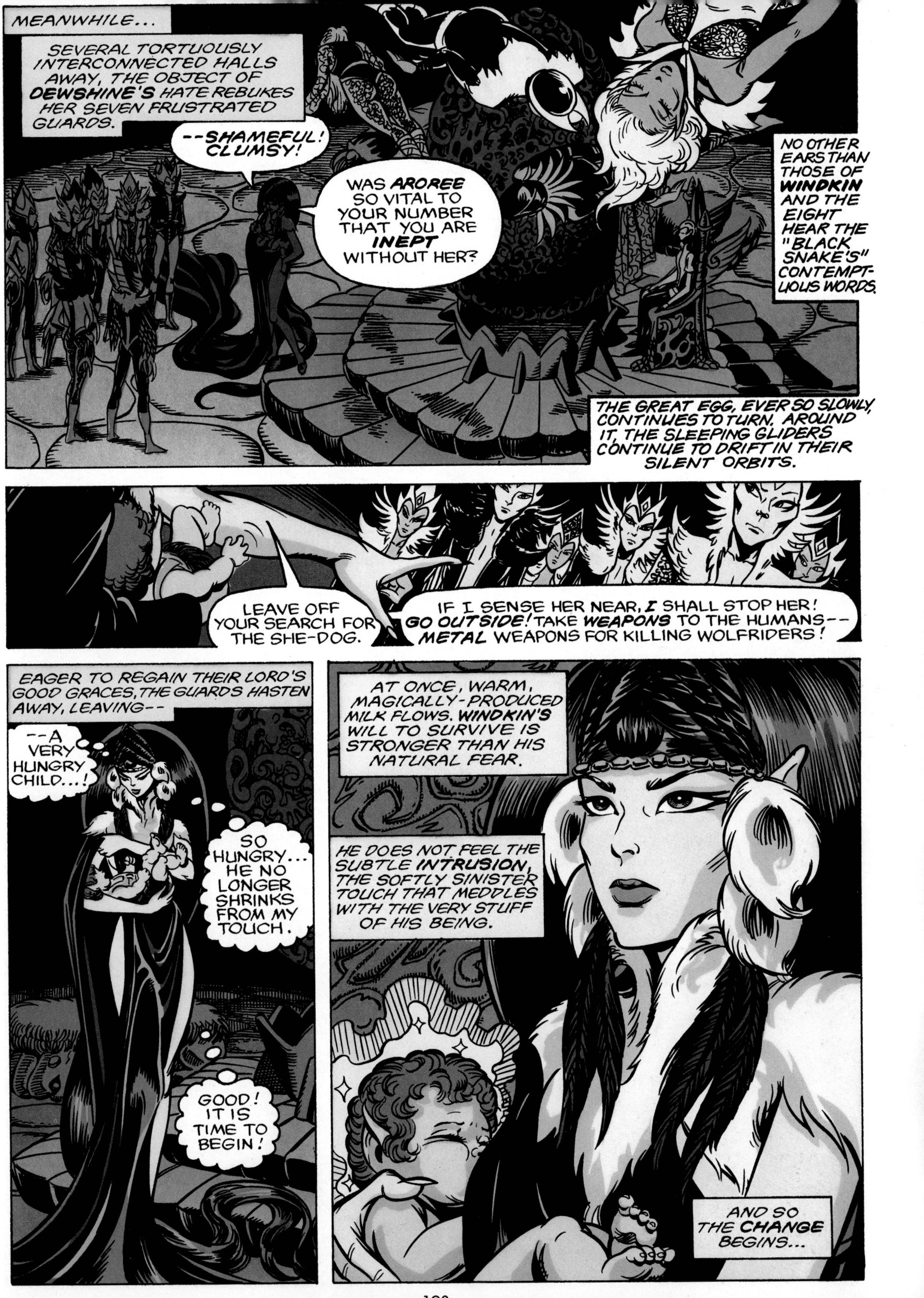
MEANWHILE...
SEVERAL TORTUOUSLY INTERCONNECTED HALLS AWAY, THE OBJECT OF DEWSHINE'S HATE REBUKES HER SEVEN FRUSTRATED GUARDS.
--SHAMEFUL! CLUMSY!
WAS AROREE SO VITAL TO YOUR NUMBER THAT YOU ARE INEPT WITHOUT HER?
NO OTHER EARS THAN THOSE OF WINDKIN AND THE EIGHT HEAR THE "BLACK SNAKE'S" CONTEMPTUOUS WORDS.
THE GREAT EGG, EVER SO SLOWLY, CONTINUES TO TURN. AROUND IT, THE SLEEPING GLIDERS CONTINUE TO DRIFT IN THEIR SILENT ORBITS.
LEAVE OFF YOUR SEARCH FOR THE SHE-DOG.
IF I SENSE HER NEAR, I SHALL STOP HER! GO OUTSIDE! TAKE WEAPONS TO THE HUMANS-- METAL WEAPONS FOR KILLING WOLFRIDERS!
EAGER TO REGAIN THEIR LORD'S GOOD GRACES, THE GUARDS HASTEN AWAY, LEAVING--
--A VERY HUNGRY CHILD...!
SO HUNGRY... HE NO LONGER SHRINKS FROM MY TOUCH.
GOOD! IT IS TIME TO BEGIN!
AT ONCE, WARM, MAGICALLY-PRODUCED MILK FLOWS. WINDKIN'S WILL TO SURVIVE IS STRONGER THAN HIS NATURAL FEAR.
HE DOES NOT FEEL THE SUBTLE INTRUSION, THE SOFTLY SINISTER TOUCH THAT MEDDLES WITH THE VERY STUFF OF HIS BEING.
AND SO THE CHANGE BEGINS...

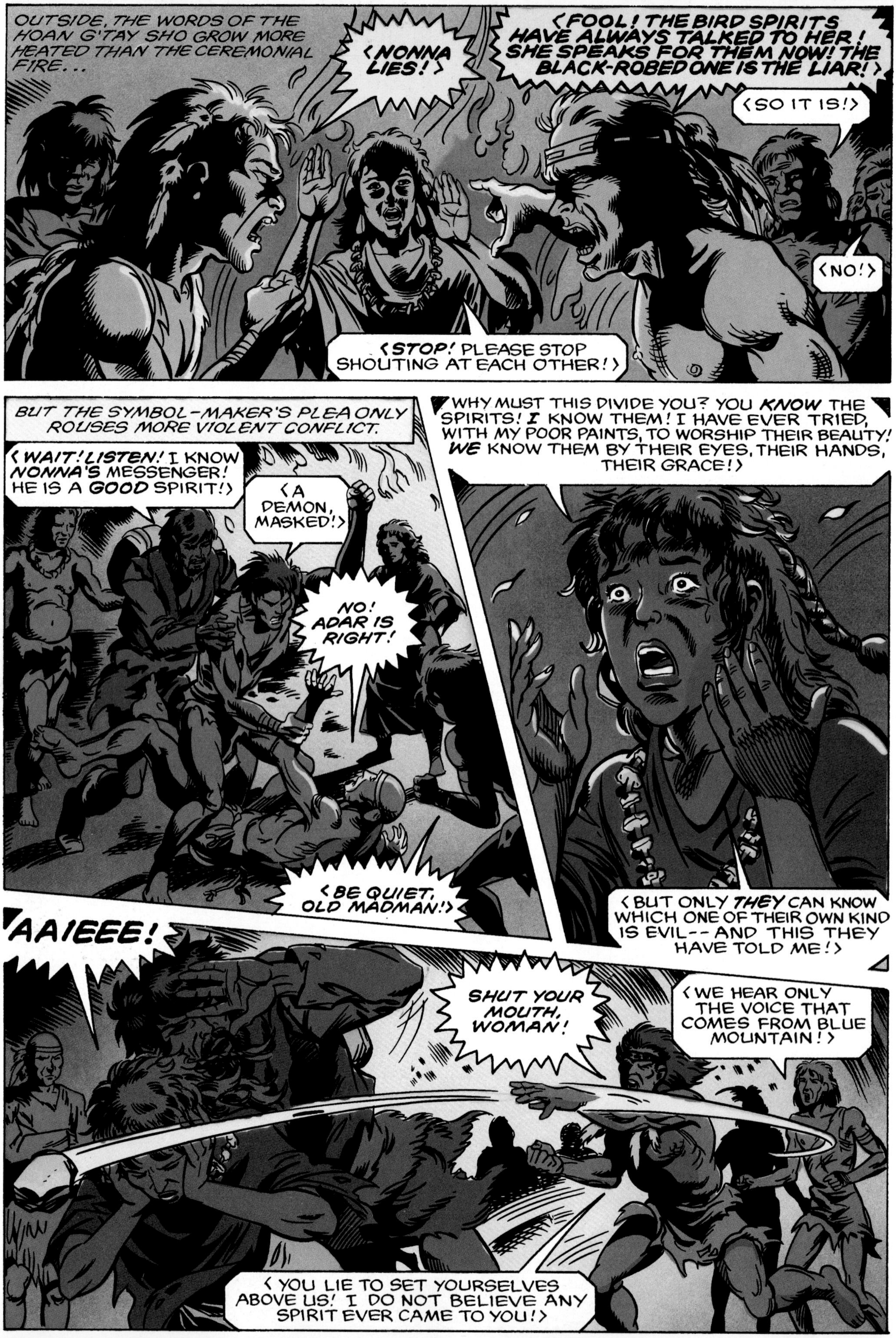
OUTSIDE, THE WORDS OF THE HOAN G'TAY SHO GROW MORE HEATED THAN THE CEREMONIAL FIRE...
<NONNA LIES!>
<FOOL! THE BIRD SPIRITS HAVE ALWAYS TALKED TO HER! SHE SPEAKS FOR THEM NOW! THE BLACK-ROBED ONE IS THE LIAR!>
<SO IT IS!>
<NO!>
<STOP! PLEASE STOP SHOUTING AT EACH OTHER!>
BUT THE SYMBOL-MAKER'S PLEA ONLY ROUSES MORE VIOLENT CONFLICT.
<WAIT! LISTEN! I KNOW NONNA'S MESSENGER! HE IS A GOOD SPIRIT!>
<A DEMON, MASKED!>
NO! ADAR IS RIGHT!
<BE QUIET, OLD MADMAN!>
WHY MUST THIS DIVIDE YOU? YOU KNOW THE SPIRITS! I KNOW THEM! I HAVE EVER TRIED, WITH MY POOR PAINTS, TO WORSHIP THEIR BEAUTY! WE KNOW THEM BY THEIR EYES, THEIR HANDS, THEIR GRACE!>
<BUT ONLY THEY CAN KNOW WHICH ONE OF THEIR OWN KIND IS EVIL--AND THIS THEY HAVE TOLD ME!>
AAIEEE!
SHUT YOUR MOUTH, WOMAN!
<WE HEAR ONLY THE VOICE THAT COMES FROM BLUE MOUNTAIN!>
<YOU LIE TO SET YOURSELVES ABOVE US! I DO NOT BELIEVE ANY SPIRIT EVER CAME TO YOU!>

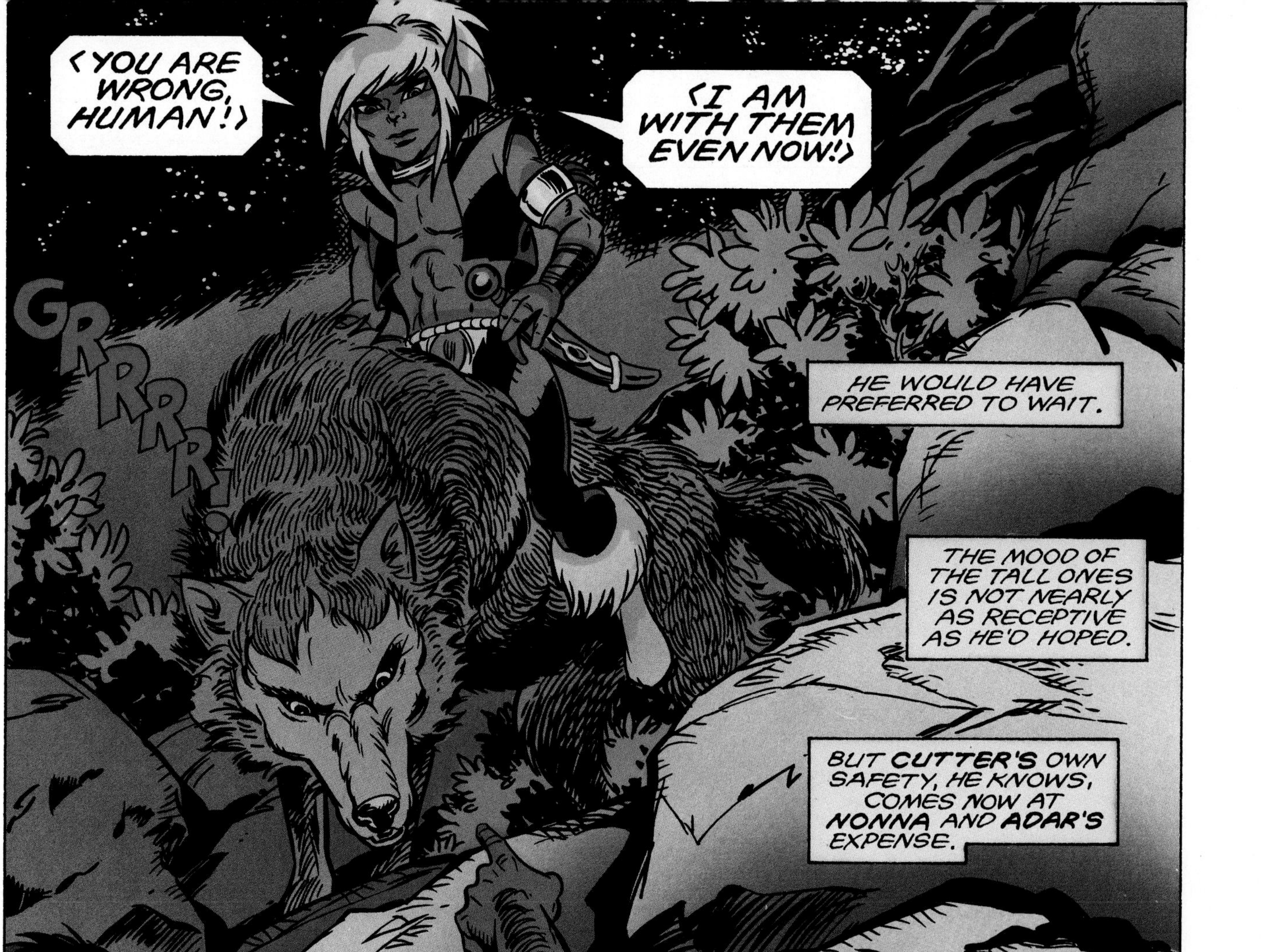

‹YOU ARE WRONG, HUMAN!›
‹I AM WITH THEM EVEN NOW!›
GRRRRR!
HE WOULD HAVE PREFERRED TO WAIT.
THE MOOD OF THE TALL ONES IS NOT NEARLY AS RECEPTIVE AS HE'D HOPED.
BUT CUTTER'S OWN SAFETY, HE KNOWS, COMES NOW AT NONNA AND ADAR'S EXPENSE.
‹D-D-DEMON--!!›
‹--AND A WOLF! THEIR EYES ARE THE SAME! DO NOT LOOK!›

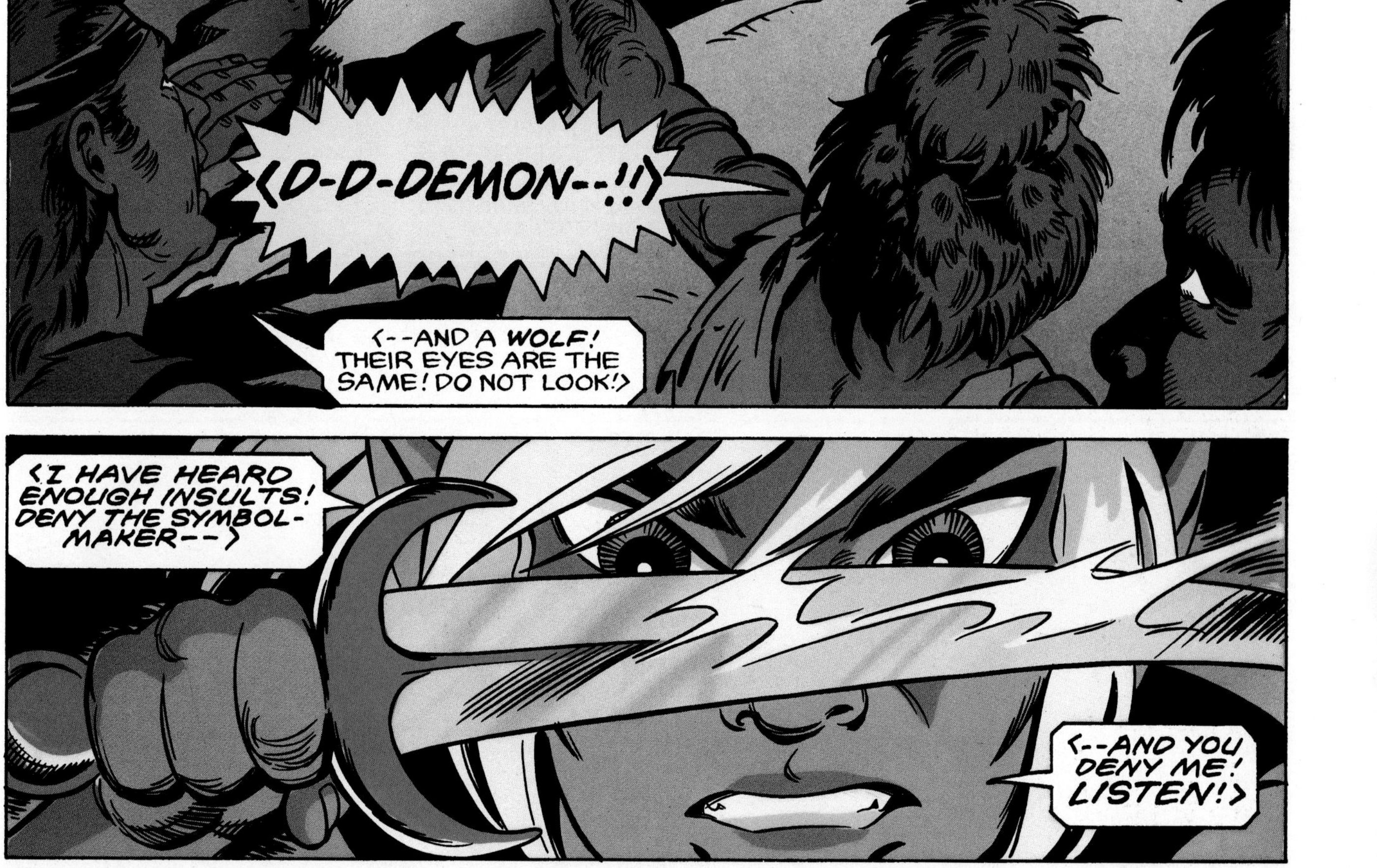

‹I HAVE HEARD ENOUGH INSULTS! DENY THE SYMBOL-MAKER--›
‹--AND YOU DENY ME! LISTEN!›

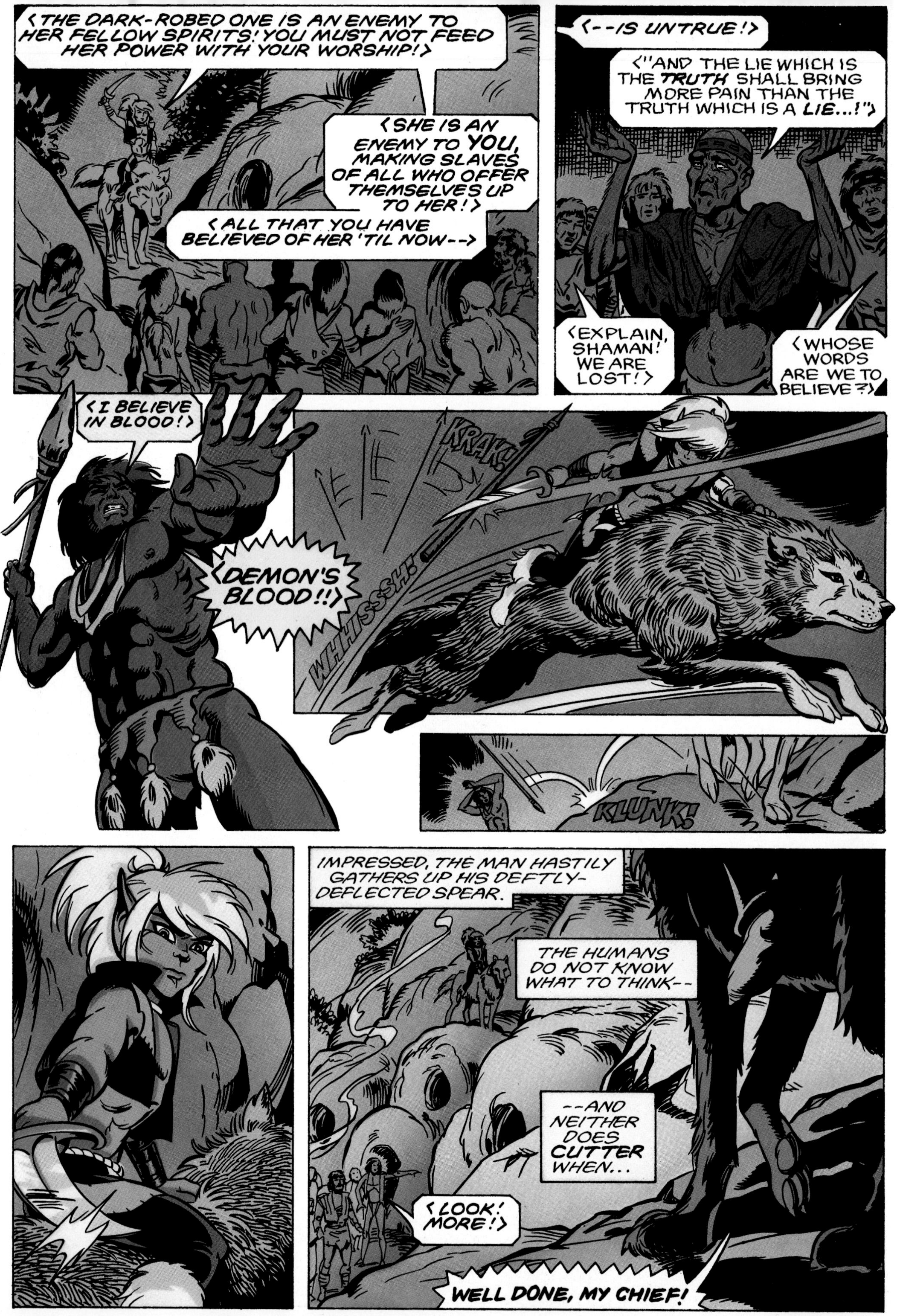

<THE DARK-ROBED ONE IS AN ENEMY TO HER FELLOW SPIRITS! YOU MUST NOT FEED HER POWER WITH YOUR WORSHIP!>
<SHE IS AN ENEMY TO YOU, MAKING SLAVES OF ALL WHO OFFER THEMSELVES UP TO HER!>
<ALL THAT YOU HAVE BELIEVED OF HER 'TIL NOW-->
<--IS UNTRUE!>
<"AND THE LIE WHICH IS THE TRUTH SHALL BRING MORE PAIN THAN THE TRUTH WHICH IS A LIE...!">
<EXPLAIN, SHAMAN! WE ARE LOST!>
<WHOSE WORDS ARE WE TO BELIEVE?>
<I BELIEVE IN BLOOD!>
<DEMON'S BLOOD!!>
KRAK!
WHHISSSH!
KLUNK!
IMPRESSED, THE MAN HASTILY GATHERS UP HIS DEFTLY-DEFLECTED SPEAR.
THE HUMANS DO NOT KNOW WHAT TO THINK--
--AND NEITHER DOES CUTTER WHEN...
<LOOK! MORE!>
WELL DONE, MY CHIEF!

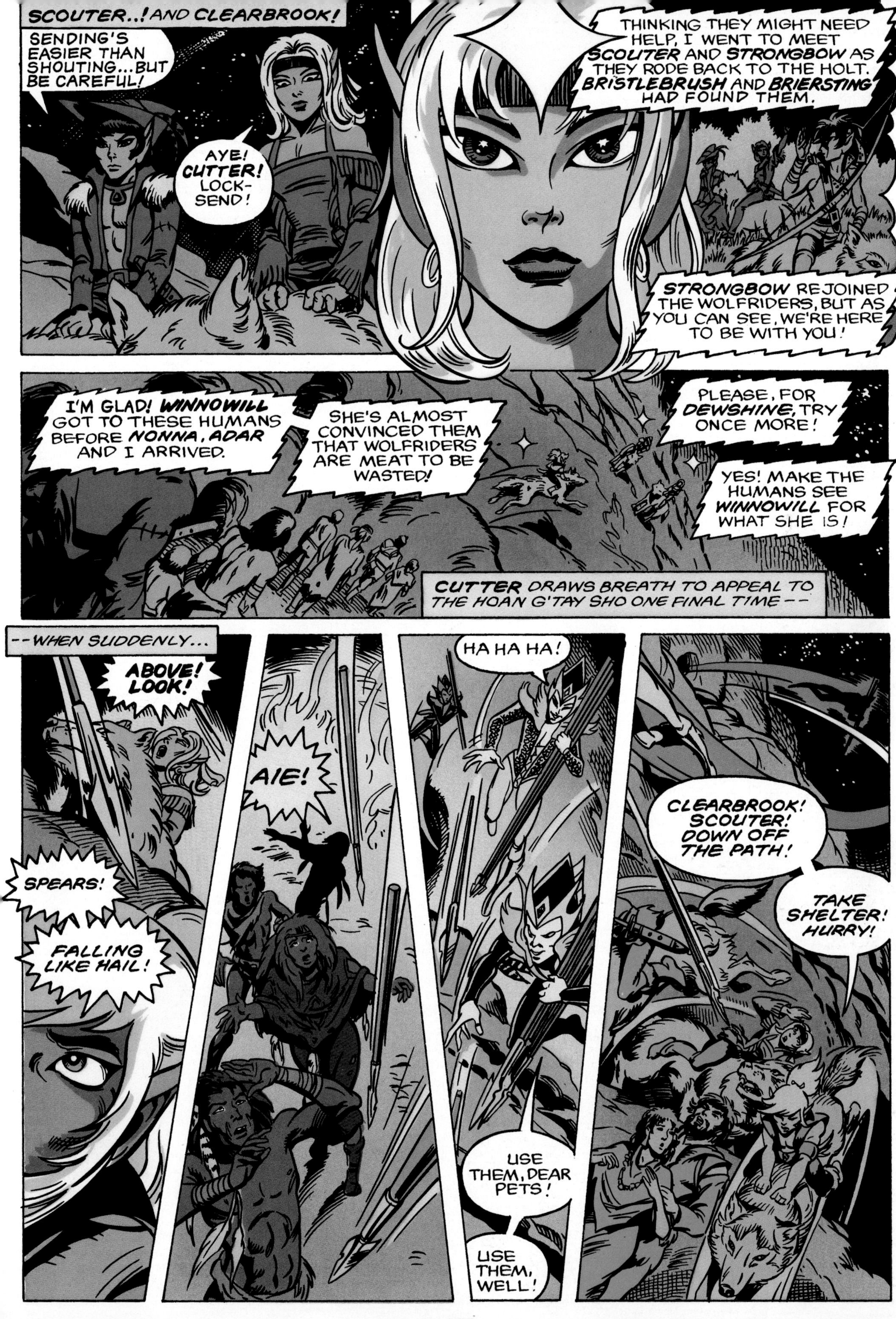
SCOUTER...! AND CLEARBROOK!
SENDING'S EASIER THAN SHOUTING...BUT BE CAREFUL!
AYE! CUTTER! LOCK-SEND!
THINKING THEY MIGHT NEED HELP, I WENT TO MEET SCOUTER AND STRONGBOW AS THEY RODE BACK TO THE HOLT. BRISTLEBRUSH AND BRIERSTING HAD FOUND THEM.
STRONGBOW REJOINED THE WOLFRIDERS, BUT AS YOU CAN SEE, WE'RE HERE TO BE WITH YOU!
I'M GLAD! WINNOWILL GOT TO THESE HUMANS BEFORE NONNA, ADAR AND I ARRIVED.
SHE'S ALMOST CONVINCED THEM THAT WOLFRIDERS ARE MEAT TO BE WASTED!
PLEASE, FOR DEWSHINE, TRY ONCE MORE!
YES! MAKE THE HUMANS SEE WINNOWILL FOR WHAT SHE IS!
CUTTER DRAWS BREATH TO APPEAL TO THE HOAN G'TAY SHO ONE FINAL TIME --
-- WHEN SUDDENLY...
ABOVE! LOOK!
SPEARS!
FALLING LIKE HAIL!
AIE!
HA HA HA!
USE THEM, DEAR PETS!
USE THEM, WELL!
CLEARBROOK! SCOUTER! DOWN OFF THE PATH!
TAKE SHELTER! HURRY!

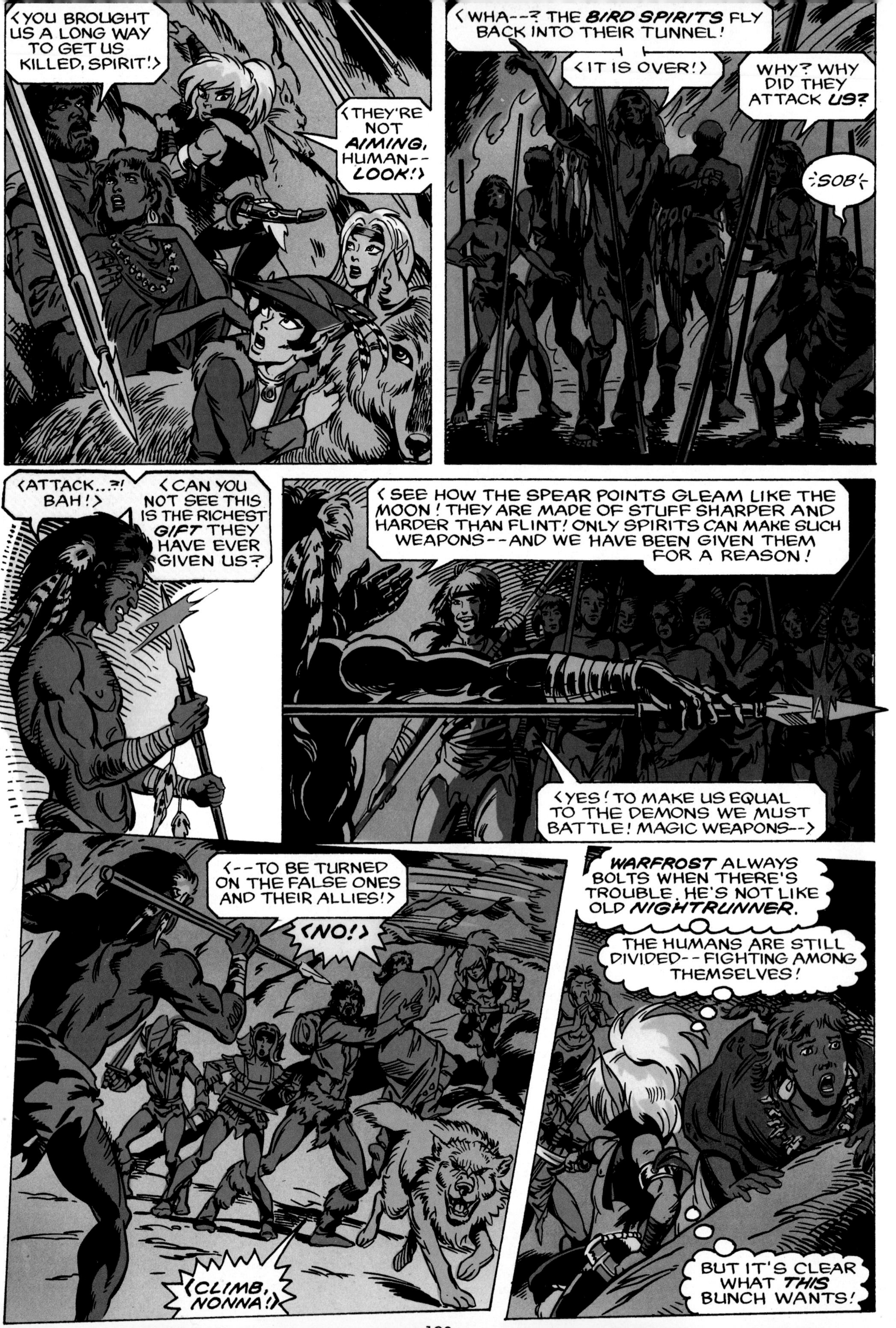

<YOU BROUGHT US A LONG WAY TO GET US KILLED, SPIRIT!>
<THEY'RE NOT AIMING, HUMAN-- LOOK!>
<WHA--? THE BIRD SPIRITS FLY BACK INTO THEIR TUNNEL!
<IT IS OVER!>
WHY? WHY DID THEY ATTACK US?
SOB
<ATTACK...?! BAH!>
<CAN YOU NOT SEE THIS IS THE RICHEST GIFT THEY HAVE EVER GIVEN US?
<SEE HOW THE SPEAR POINTS GLEAM LIKE THE MOON! THEY ARE MADE OF STUFF SHARPER AND HARDER THAN FLINT! ONLY SPIRITS CAN MAKE SUCH WEAPONS--AND WE HAVE BEEN GIVEN THEM FOR A REASON!
<YES! TO MAKE US EQUAL TO THE DEMONS WE MUST BATTLE! MAGIC WEAPONS-->
<--TO BE TURNED ON THE FALSE ONES AND THEIR ALLIES!>
<NO!>
<CLIMB, NONNA!>
WARFROST ALWAYS BOLTS WHEN THERE'S TROUBLE. HE'S NOT LIKE OLD NIGHTRUNNER.
THE HUMANS ARE STILL DIVIDED--FIGHTING AMONG THEMSELVES!
BUT IT'S CLEAR WHAT THIS BUNCH WANTS!

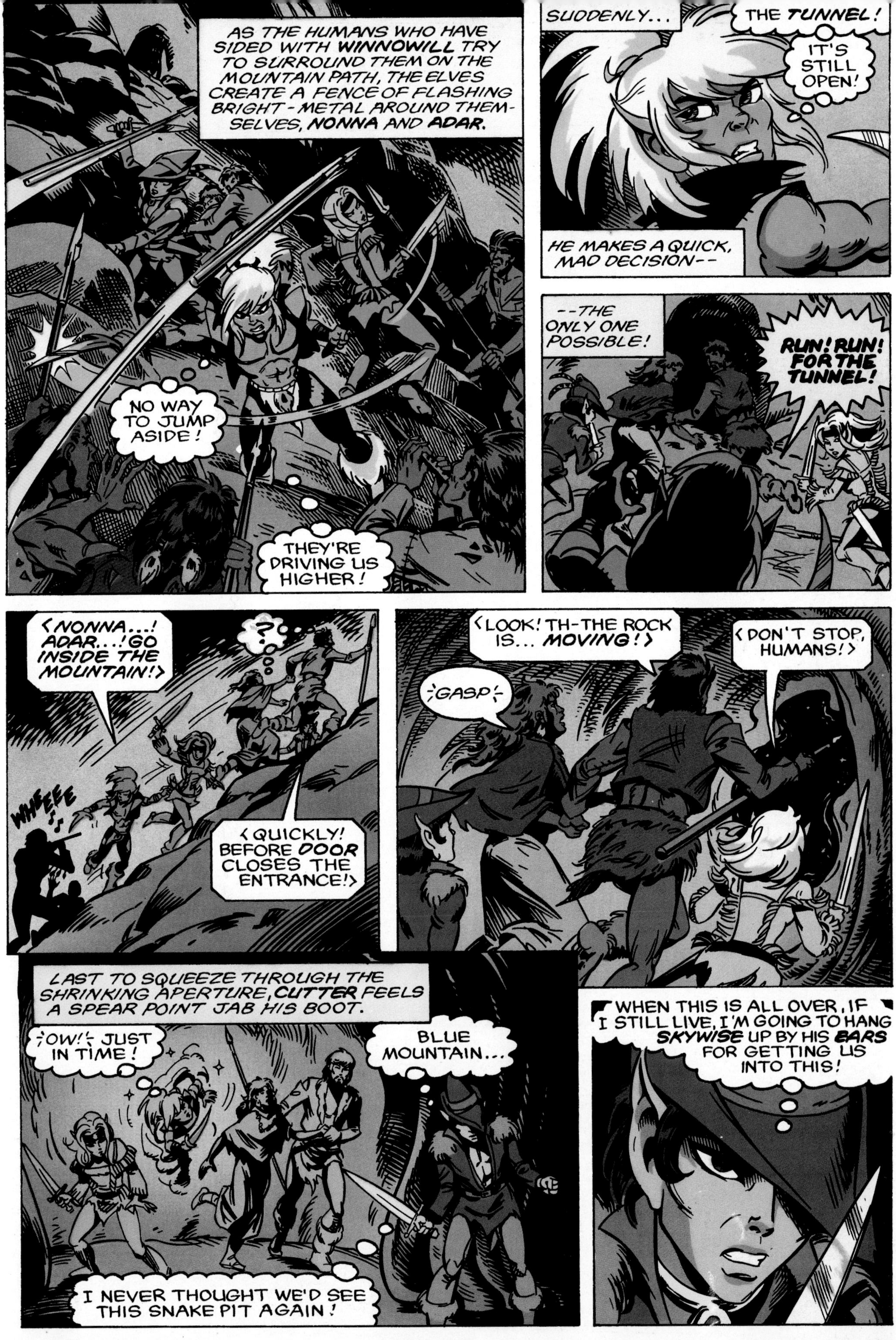
AS THE HUMANS WHO HAVE SIDED WITH WINNOWILL TRY TO SURROUND THEM ON THE MOUNTAIN PATH, THE ELVES CREATE A FENCE OF FLASHING BRIGHT-METAL AROUND THEMSELVES, NONNA AND ADAR.
NO WAY TO JUMP ASIDE!
THEY'RE DRIVING US HIGHER!
SUDDENLY...
THE TUNNEL!
IT'S STILL OPEN!
HE MAKES A QUICK, MAD DECISION--
--THE ONLY ONE POSSIBLE!
RUN! RUN! FOR THE TUNNEL!
<NONNA...! ADAR...! GO INSIDE THE MOUNTAIN!>
?
WHEEEE
<QUICKLY! BEFORE DOOR CLOSES THE ENTRANCE!>
<LOOK! TH-THE ROCK IS... MOVING!>
GASP
<DON'T STOP, HUMANS!>
LAST TO SQUEEZE THROUGH THE SHRINKING APERTURE, CUTTER FEELS A SPEAR POINT JAB HIS BOOT.
OW! JUST IN TIME!
BLUE MOUNTAIN...
I NEVER THOUGHT WE'D SEE THIS SNAKE PIT AGAIN!
WHEN THIS IS ALL OVER, IF I STILL LIVE, I'M GOING TO HANG SKYWISE UP BY HIS EARS FOR GETTING US INTO THIS!

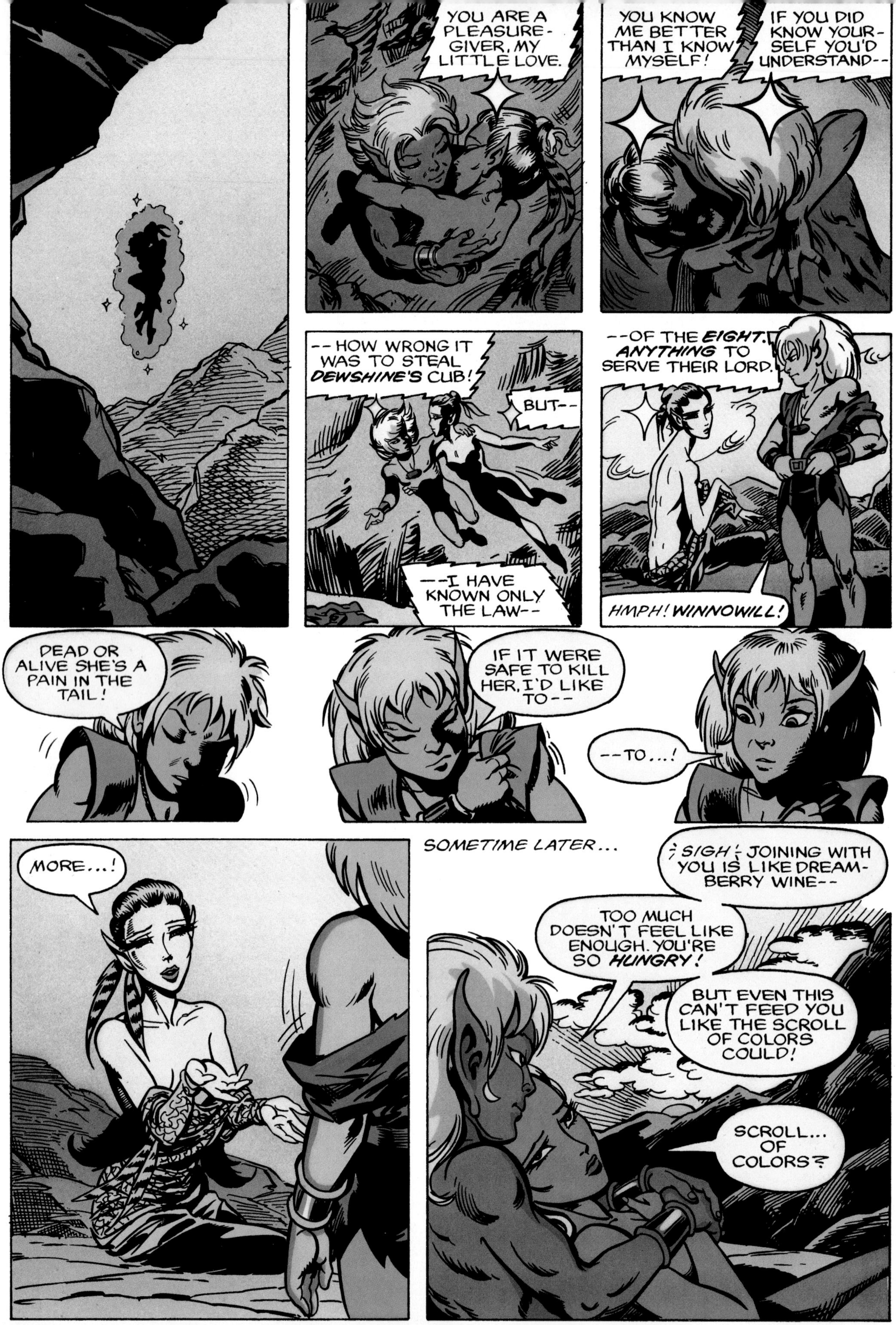
YOU ARE A PLEASURE-GIVER, MY LITTLE LOVE.
YOU KNOW ME BETTER THAN I KNOW MYSELF!
IF YOU DID KNOW YOURSELF YOU'D UNDERSTAND--
--HOW WRONG IT WAS TO STEAL DEWSHINE'S CUB!
BUT--
--I HAVE KNOWN ONLY THE LAW--
--OF THE EIGHT. ANYTHING TO SERVE THEIR LORD.
HMPH! WINNOWILL!
DEAD OR ALIVE SHE'S A PAIN IN THE TAIL!
IF IT WERE SAFE TO KILL HER, I'D LIKE TO--
--TO...!
MORE...!
SOMETIME LATER...
SIGH -- JOINING WITH YOU IS LIKE DREAMBERRY WINE--
TOO MUCH DOESN'T FEEL LIKE ENOUGH. YOU'RE SO HUNGRY!
BUT EVEN THIS CAN'T FEED YOU LIKE THE SCROLL OF COLORS COULD!
SCROLL... OF COLORS?

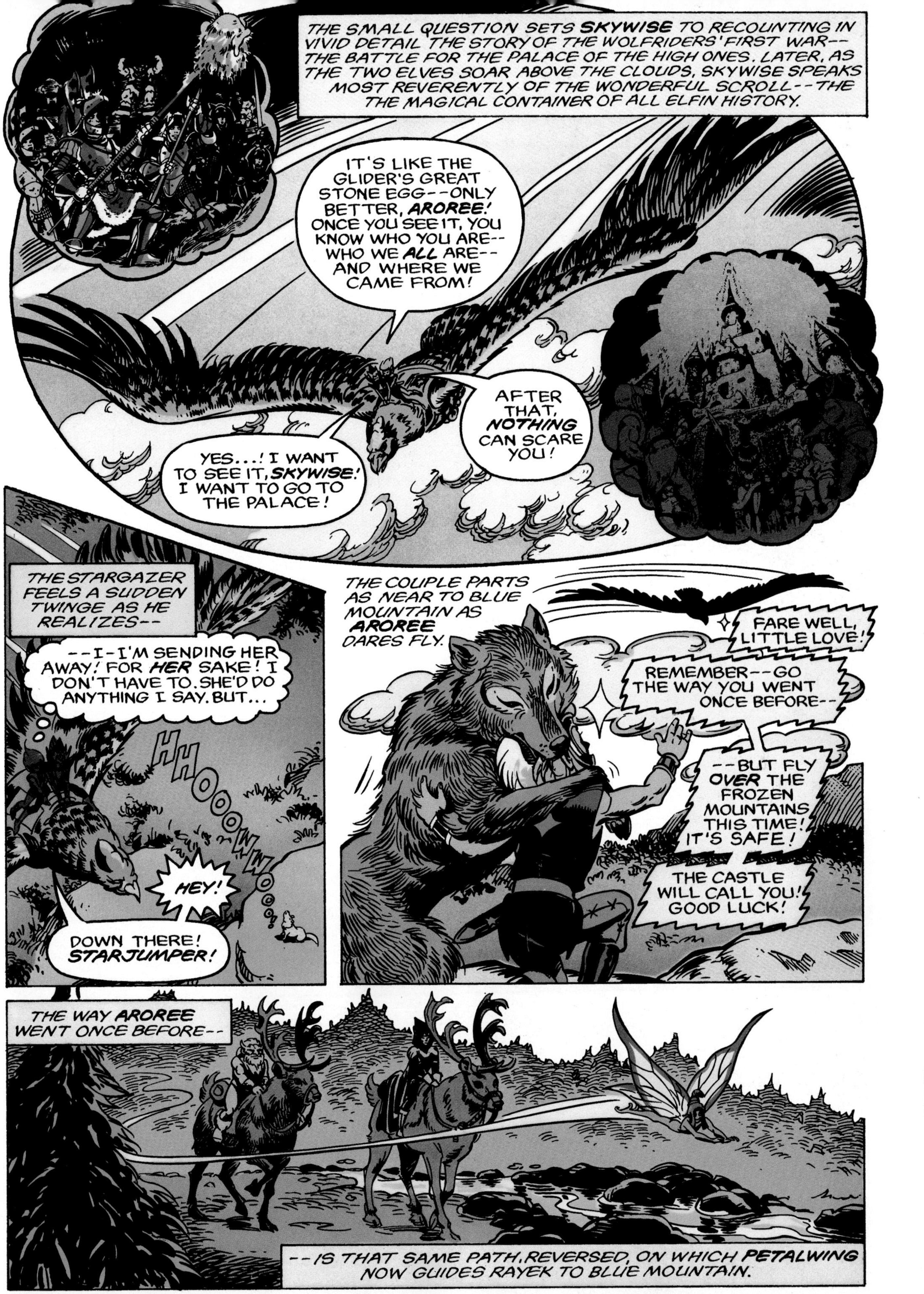
THE SMALL QUESTION SETS SKYWISE TO RECOUNTING IN VIVID DETAIL THE STORY OF THE WOLFRIDERS' FIRST WAR--THE BATTLE FOR THE PALACE OF THE HIGH ONES. LATER, AS THE TWO ELVES SOAR ABOVE THE CLOUDS, SKYWISE SPEAKS MOST REVERENTLY OF THE WONDERFUL SCROLL--THE THE MAGICAL CONTAINER OF ALL ELFIN HISTORY.
IT'S LIKE THE GLIDER'S GREAT STONE EGG--ONLY BETTER, AROREE! ONCE YOU SEE IT, YOU KNOW WHO YOU ARE--WHO WE ALL ARE--AND WHERE WE CAME FROM!
AFTER THAT, NOTHING CAN SCARE YOU!
YES...! I WANT TO SEE IT, SKYWISE! I WANT TO GO TO THE PALACE!
THE STARGAZER FEELS A SUDDEN TWINGE AS HE REALIZES--
--I-I'M SENDING HER AWAY! FOR HER SAKE! I DON'T HAVE TO. SHE'D DO ANYTHING I SAY. BUT...
HHOOOOWWOOOO
HEY!
DOWN THERE! STARJUMPER!
THE COUPLE PARTS AS NEAR TO BLUE MOUNTAIN AS AROREE DARES FLY.
FARE WELL, LITTLE LOVE!
REMEMBER--GO THE WAY YOU WENT ONCE BEFORE--
--BUT FLY OVER THE FROZEN MOUNTAINS THIS TIME! IT'S SAFE!
THE CASTLE WILL CALL YOU! GOOD LUCK!
THE WAY AROREE WENT ONCE BEFORE--
--IS THAT SAME PATH, REVERSED, ON WHICH PETALWING NOW GUIDES RAYEK TO BLUE MOUNTAIN.

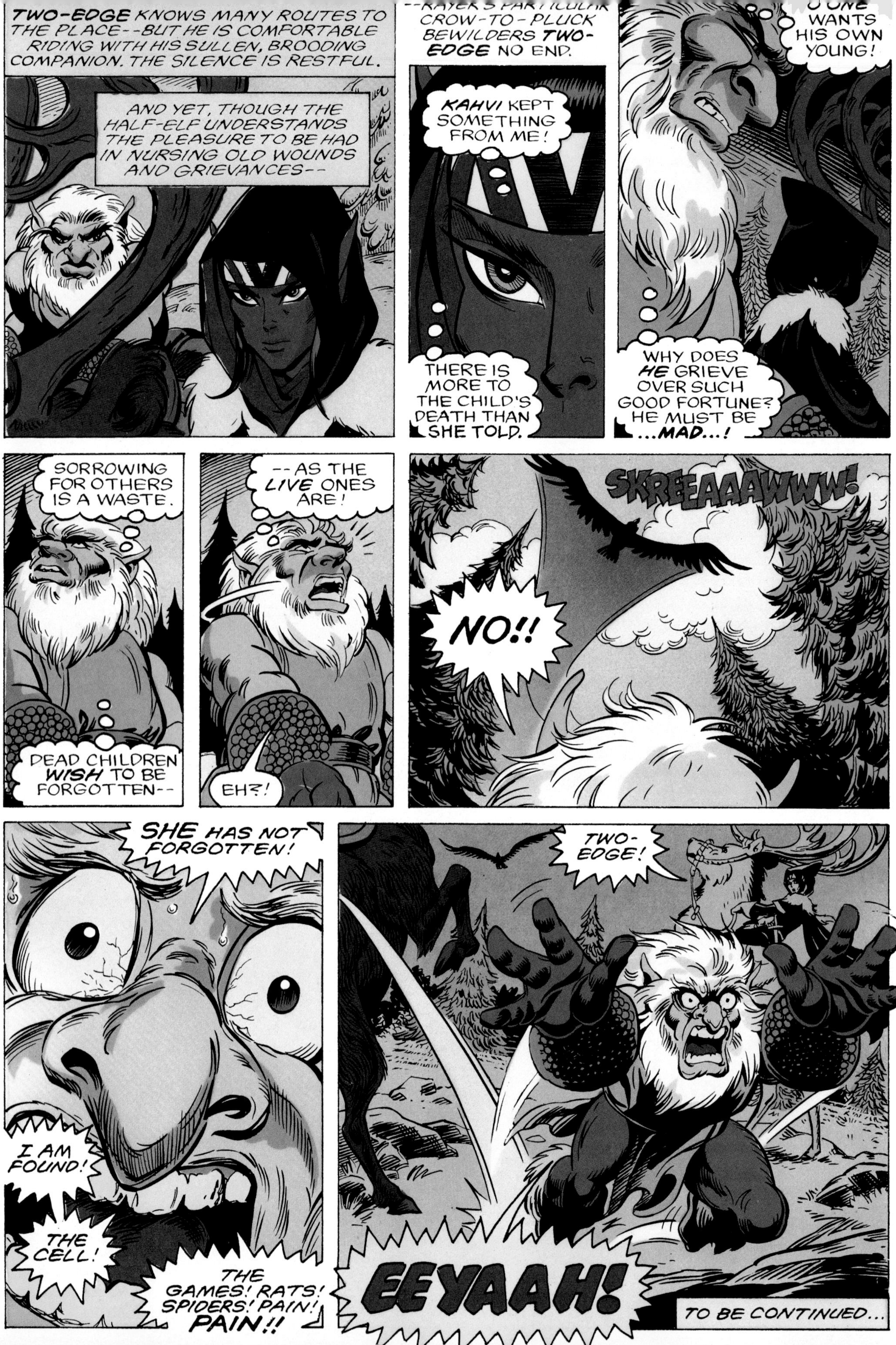

TWO-EDGE KNOWS MANY ROUTES TO THE PLACE--BUT HE IS COMFORTABLE RIDING WITH HIS SULLEN, BROODING COMPANION. THE SILENCE IS RESTFUL.
AND YET, THOUGH THE HALF-ELF UNDERSTANDS THE PLEASURE TO BE HAD IN NURSING OLD WOUNDS AND GRIEVANCES--
CROW-TO-PLUCK BEWILDERS TWO-EDGE NO END.
KAHVI KEPT SOMETHING FROM ME!
THERE IS MORE TO THE CHILD'S DEATH THAN SHE TOLD.
WANTS HIS OWN YOUNG!
WHY DOES HE GRIEVE OVER SUCH GOOD FORTUNE? HE MUST BE ...MAD...!
SORROWING FOR OTHERS IS A WASTE.
DEAD CHILDREN WISH TO BE FORGOTTEN--
--AS THE LIVE ONES ARE!
EH?!
SKREEAAAWWW!
NO!!
SHE HAS NOT FORGOTTEN!
I AM FOUND!
THE CELL!
THE GAMES! RATS! SPIDERS! PAIN! PAIN!!
TWO-EDGE!
EEYAAH!
TO BE CONTINUED...

Gallery 5

In this Volume's Gallery we present a number of items for your enjoyment. First there are the covers from the four issues of the "Siege at Blue Mountain" comic book series that contained the story you've just read. Following that are pastel portraits of several of the characters that appeared in a portfolio published in the early 1980s, when the original *Elfquest* story (presented in Volumes One through Four of this series) was about halfway completed. Then there are the cover and plates from a black and white portfolio — again, published about halfway through the original saga — that drove readers quietly mad, as they tried to pull subtle clues to future storylines from the drawings.

There have, from time to time, been entire additional *Elfquest* stories done for one reason or another. In this Gallery we offer a short tale called "By Any Other Name..." This originally appeared as the lead story in the first issue of the *Warp Graphics Annual*, a showcase of all the comics titles that Warp Graphics was publishing at the time (1984). "Name..." is interesting in that it is the first *Elfquest* story not produced entirely by Wendy and Richard Pini, though it was done under their supervision. Chronologically, it goes before the events that kick off Volume One of the Graphic Novel series, and occurs before — but not long before — the tale of Madcoil in that Volume.

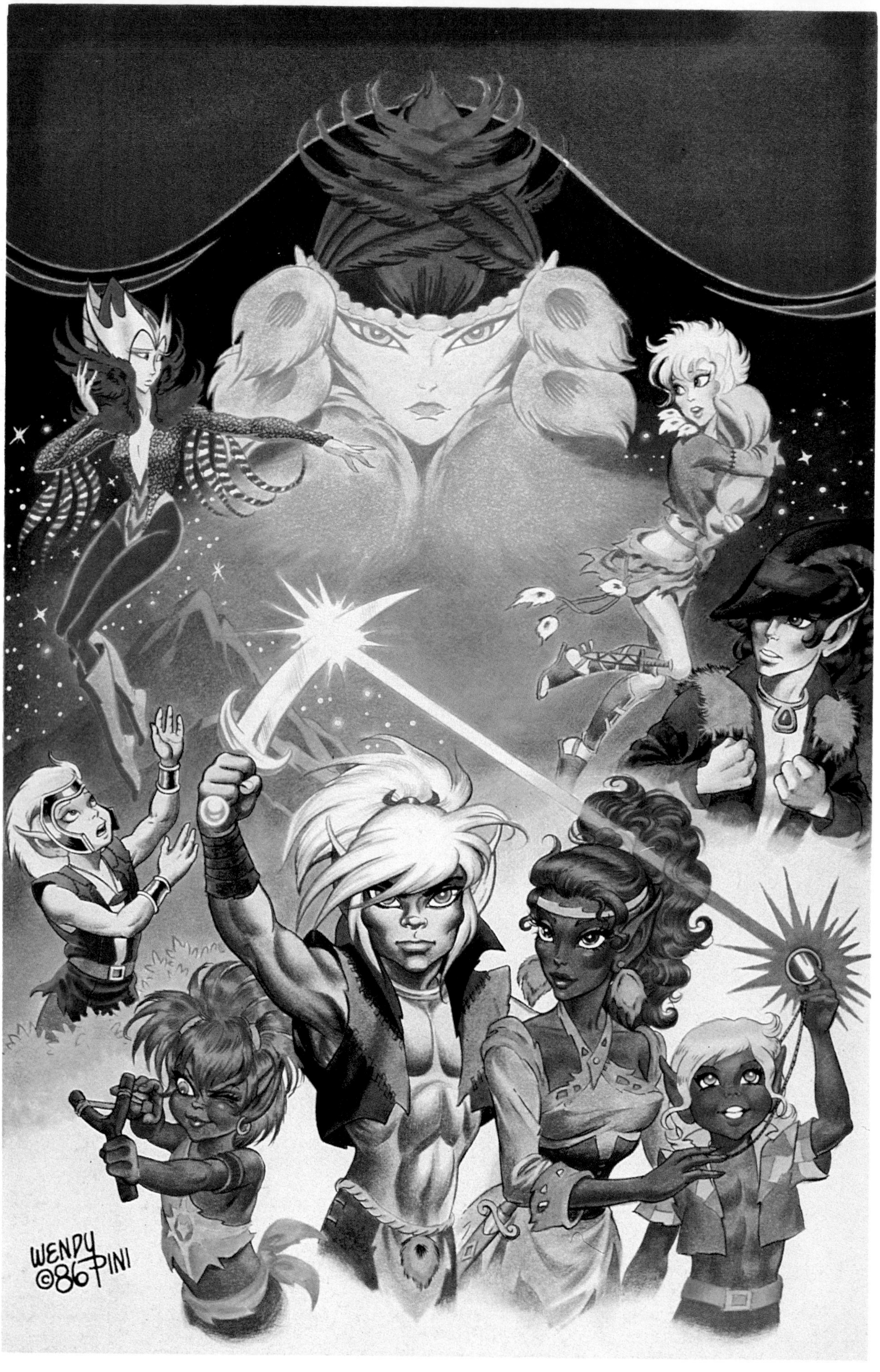
WENDY
©86 PINI

Front cover — Elfquest: Siege at Blue Mountain #1 (Warp Graphics)

Front cover — Elfquest: Siege at Blue Mountain #2 (Warp Graphics)

Front cover — Elfquest: Siege at Blue Mountain #3 (Warp Graphics)

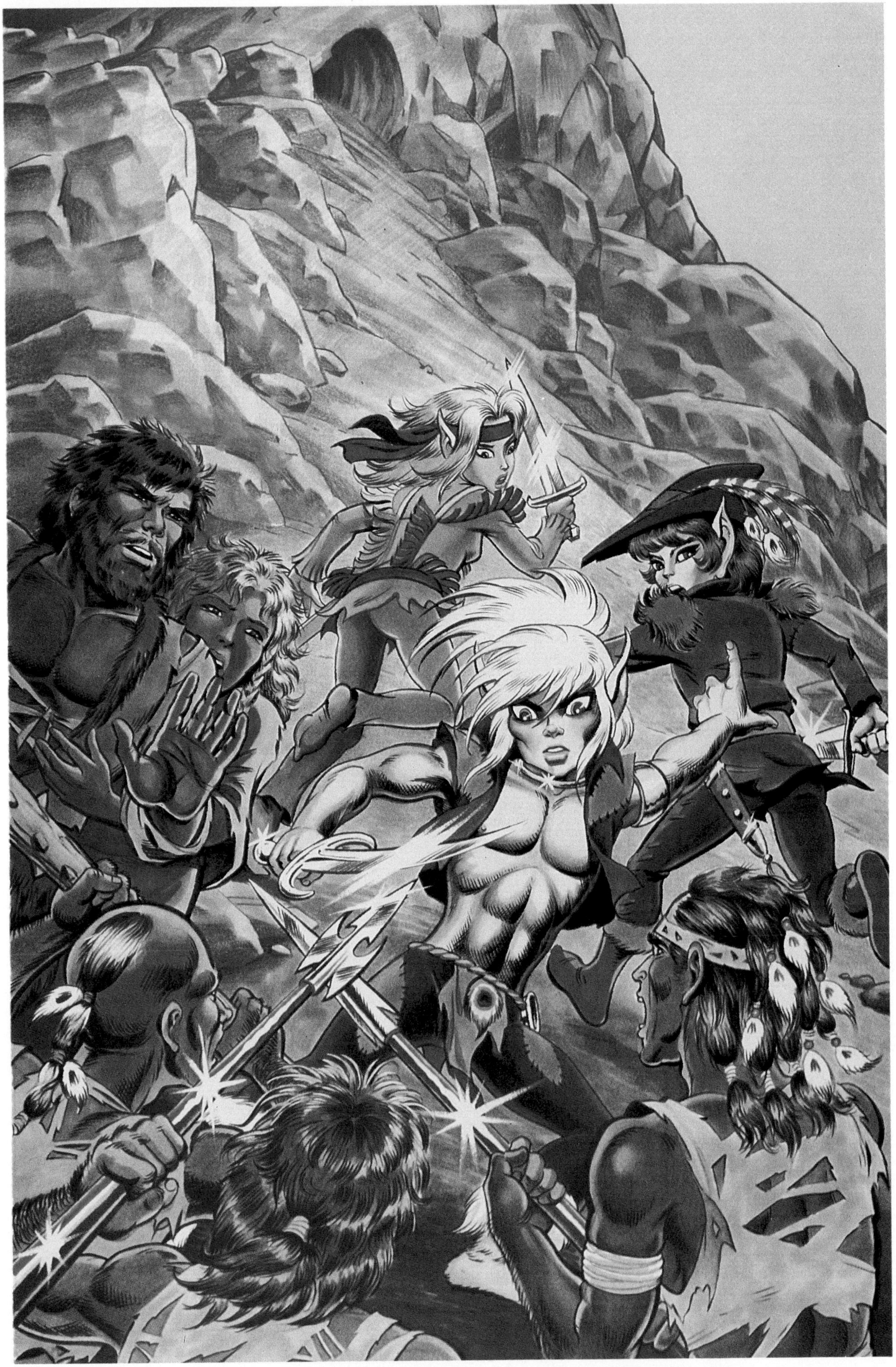

Front cover — Elfquest: Siege at Blue Mountain #4 (Warp Graphics)

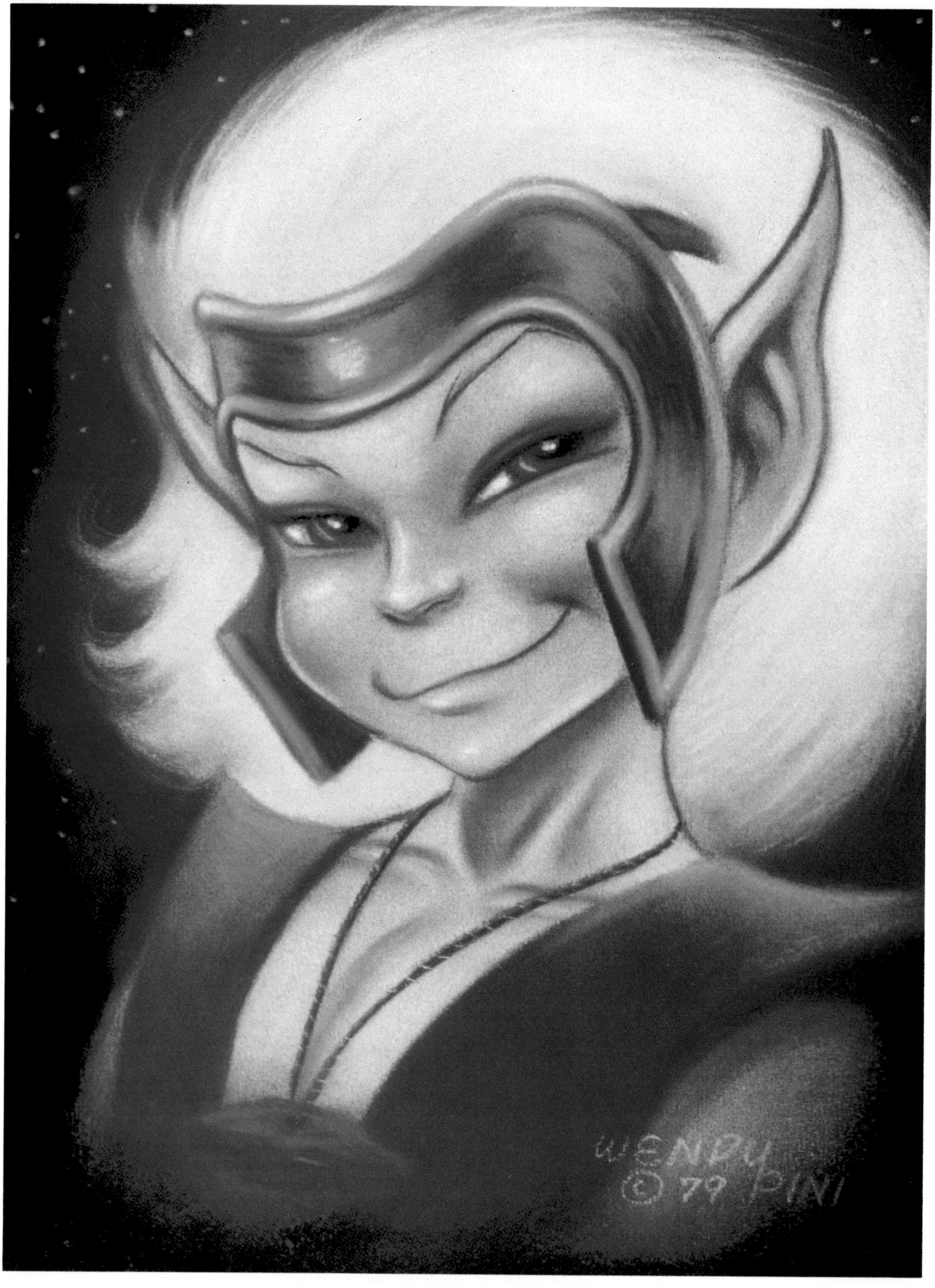
WENDY
© 79 PINI

"Skywise"

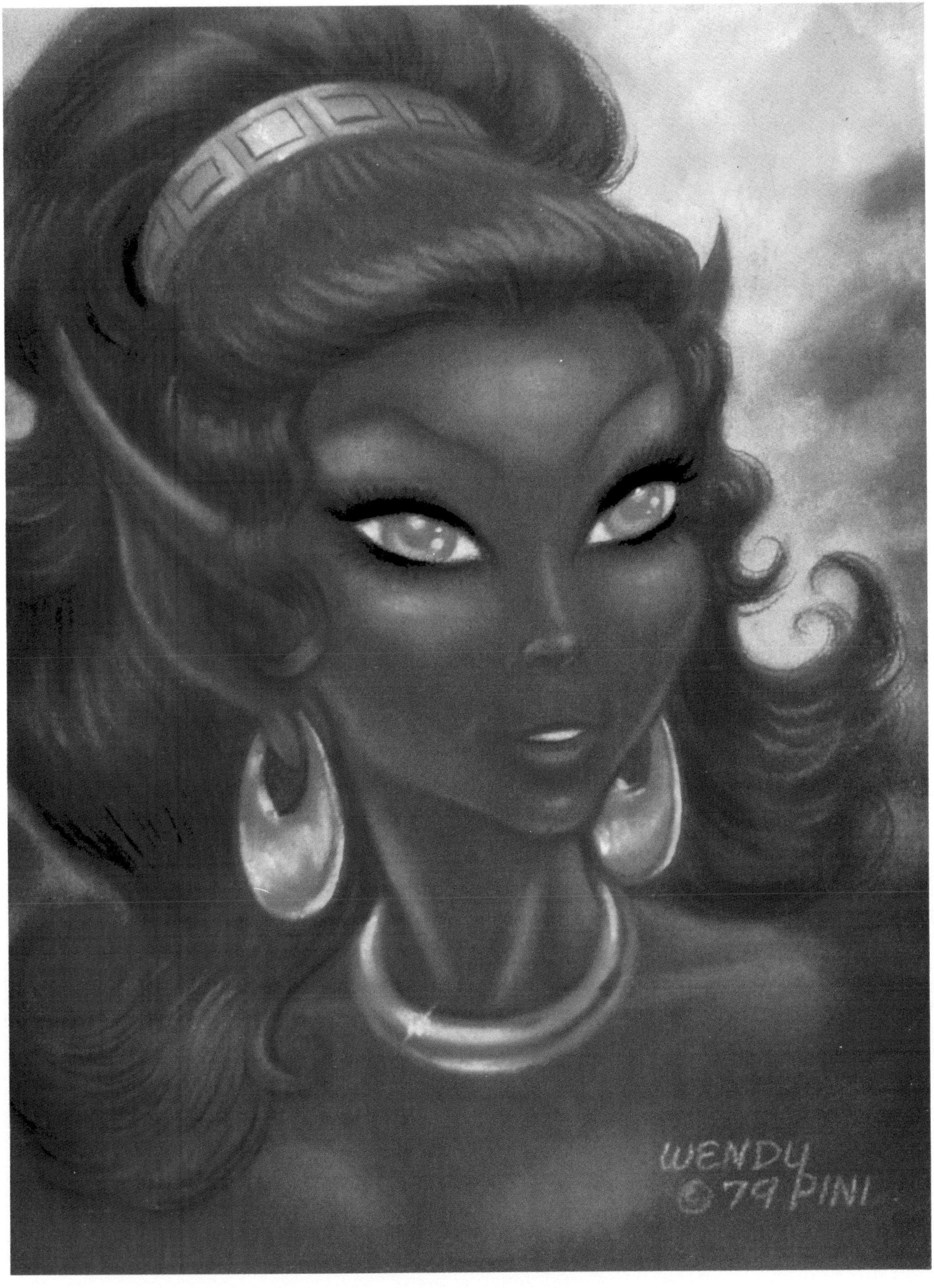
WENDY
© 79 PINI

"Leetah"

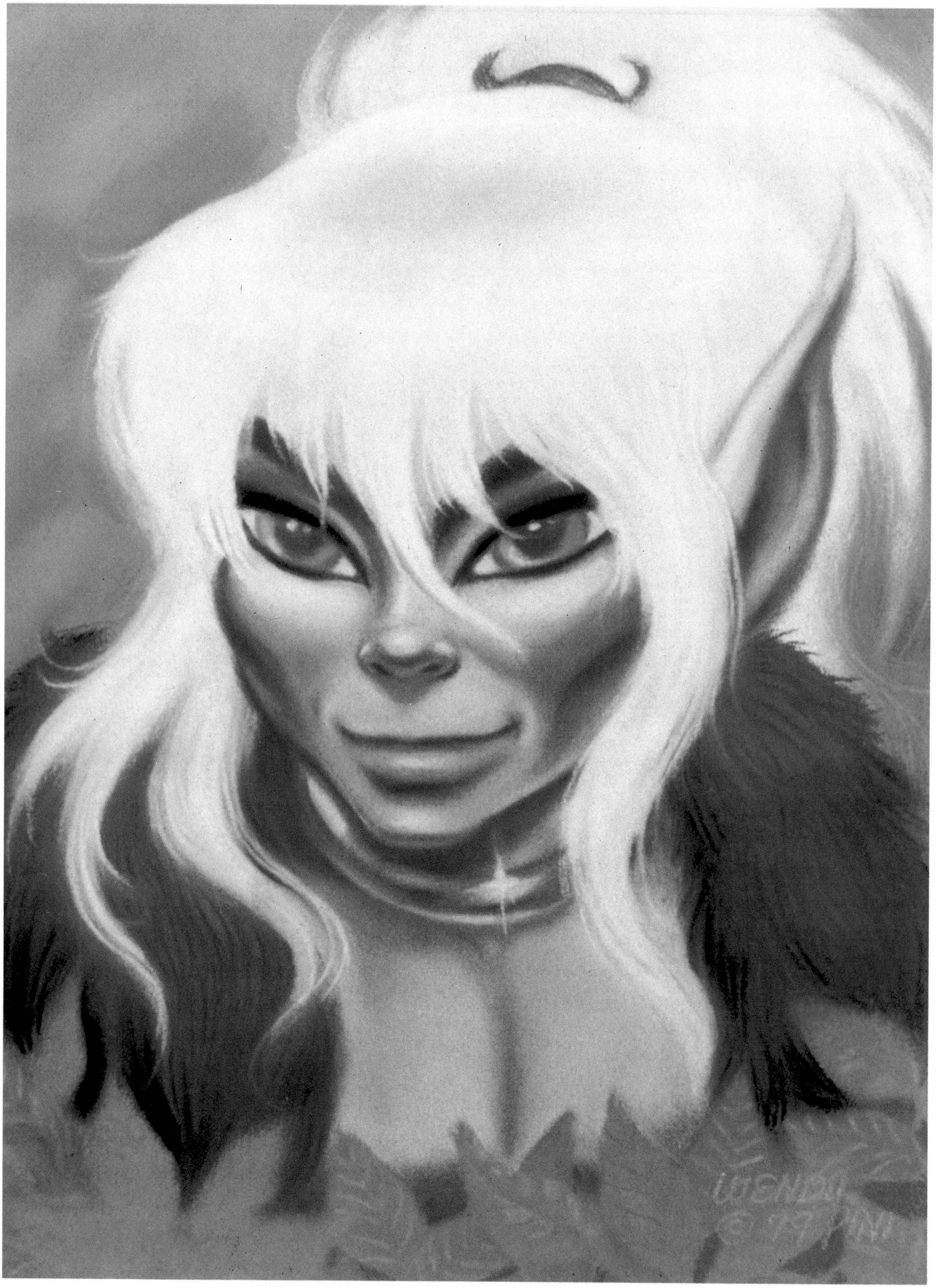

"Cutter"

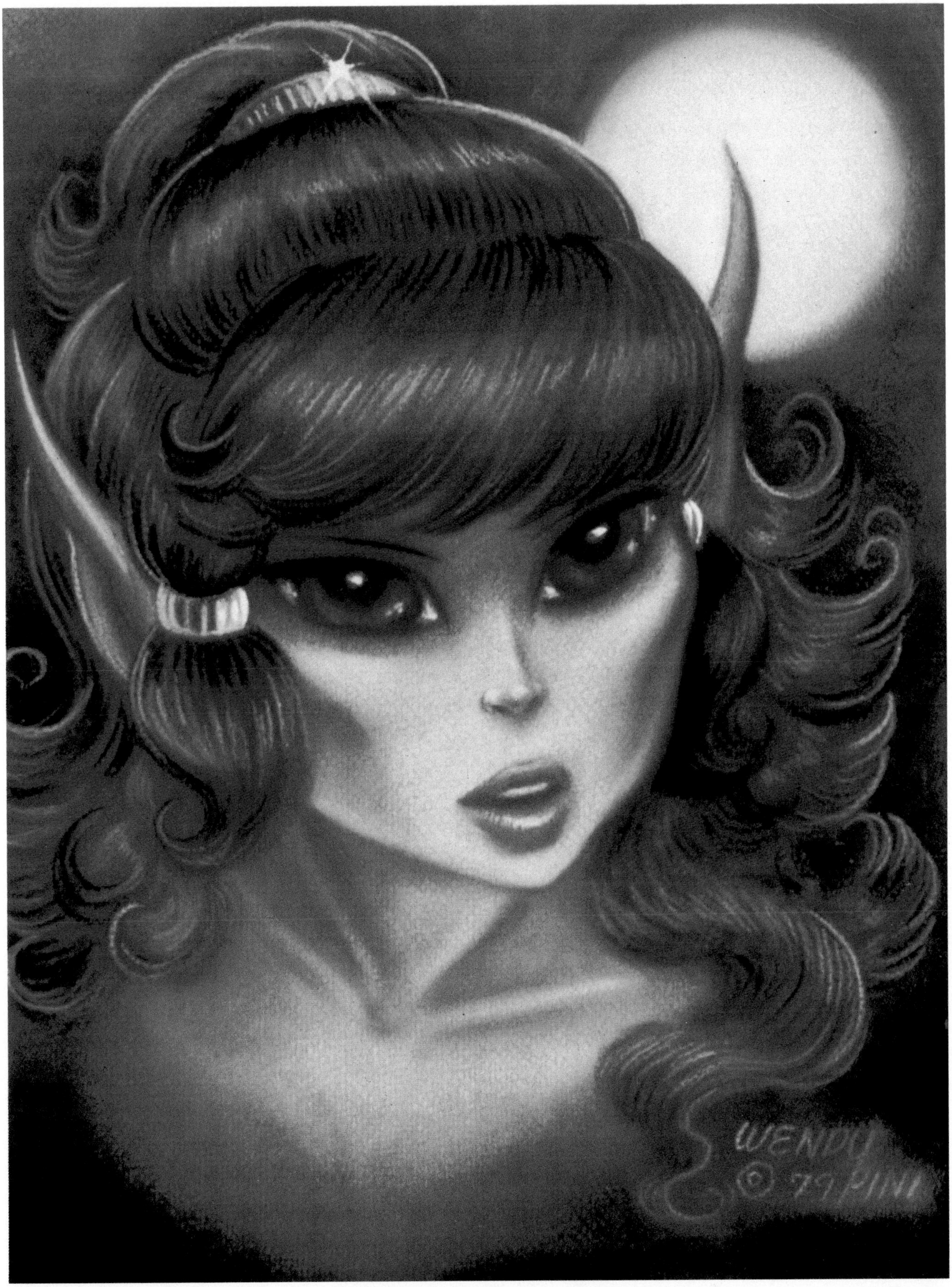
WENDY
© 79 PINI

"Moonshade"

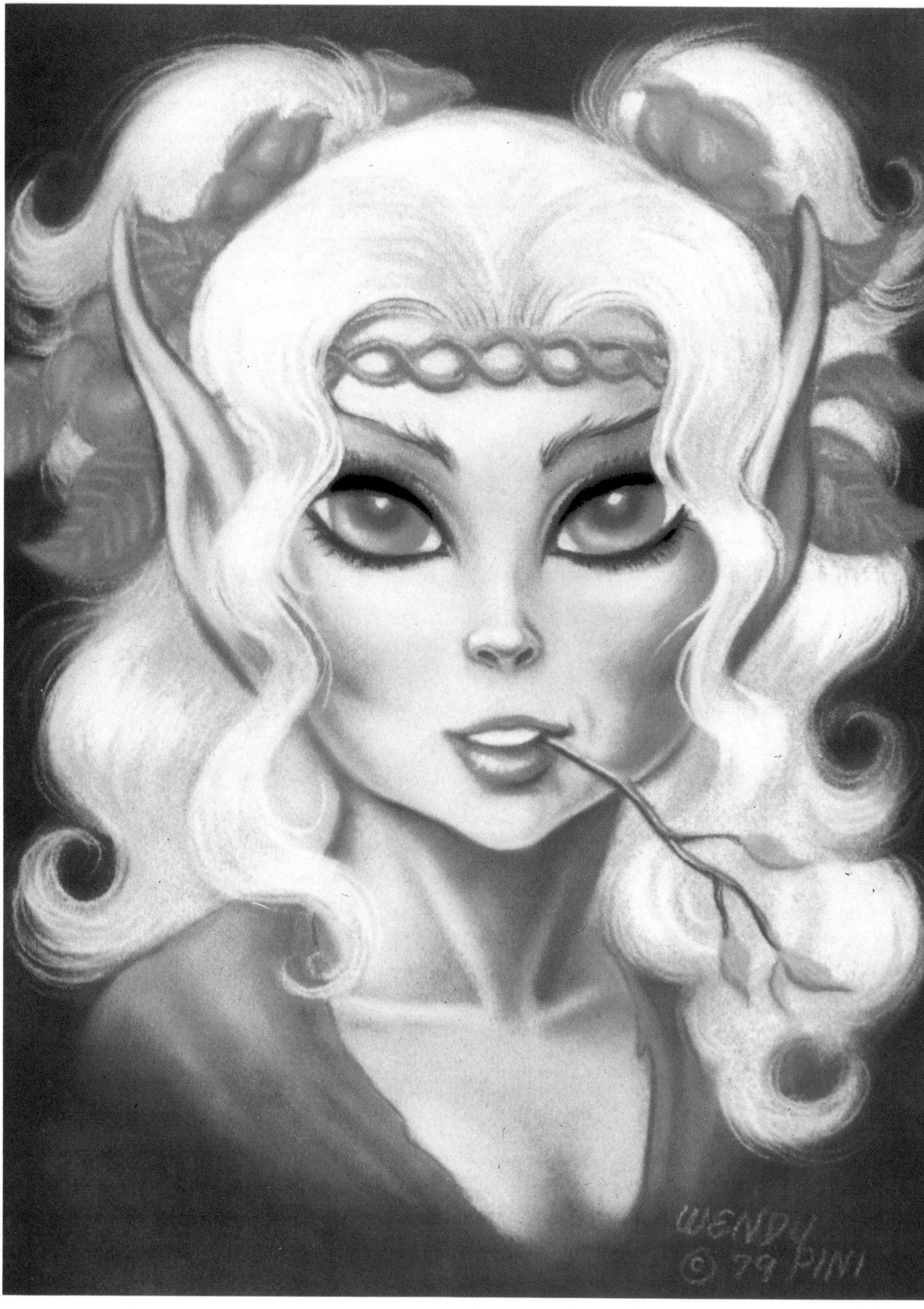
WENDY
© 79 PINI

"Joyleaf"

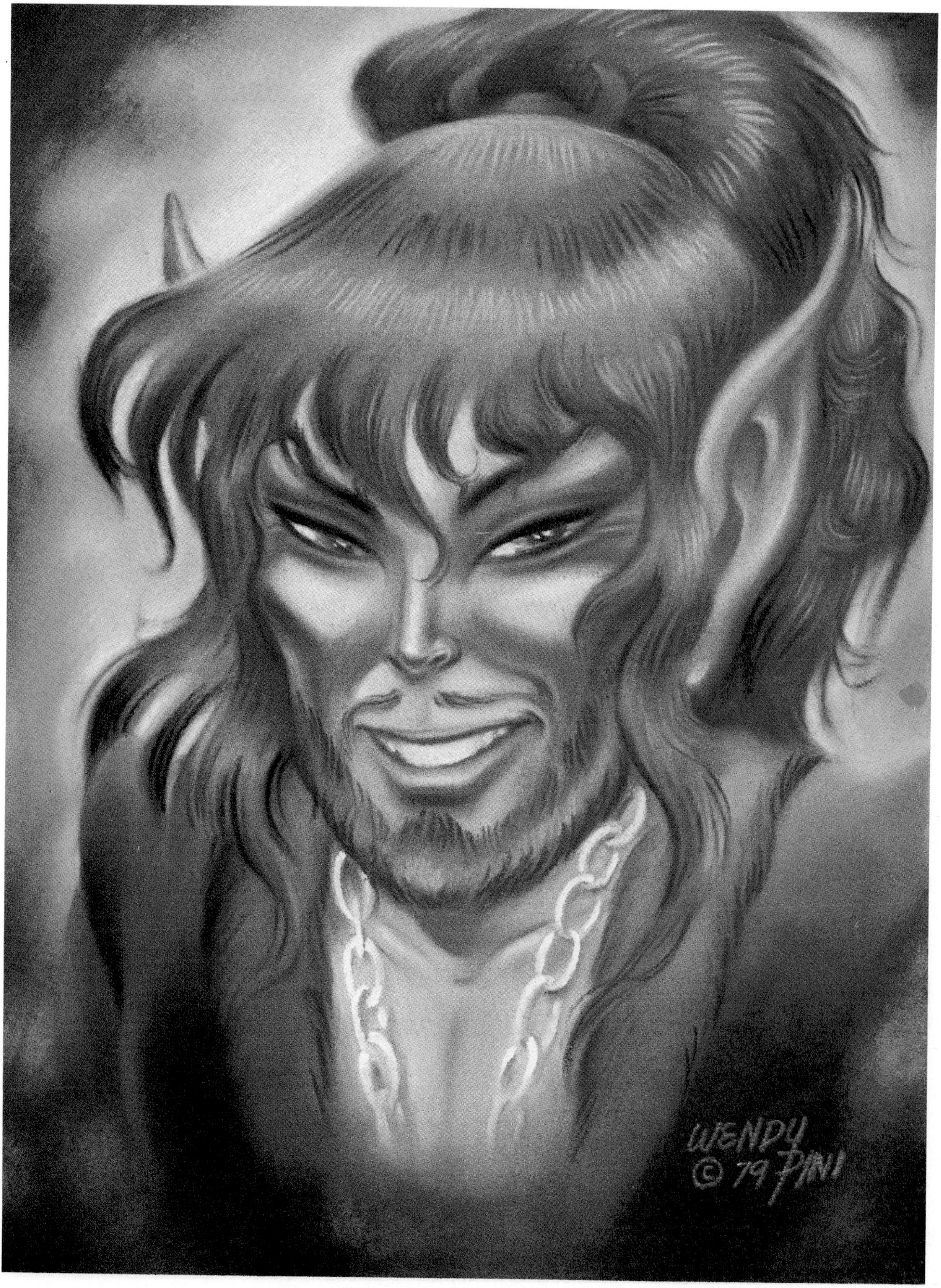
WENDY
© 79 PINI

"Bearclaw"

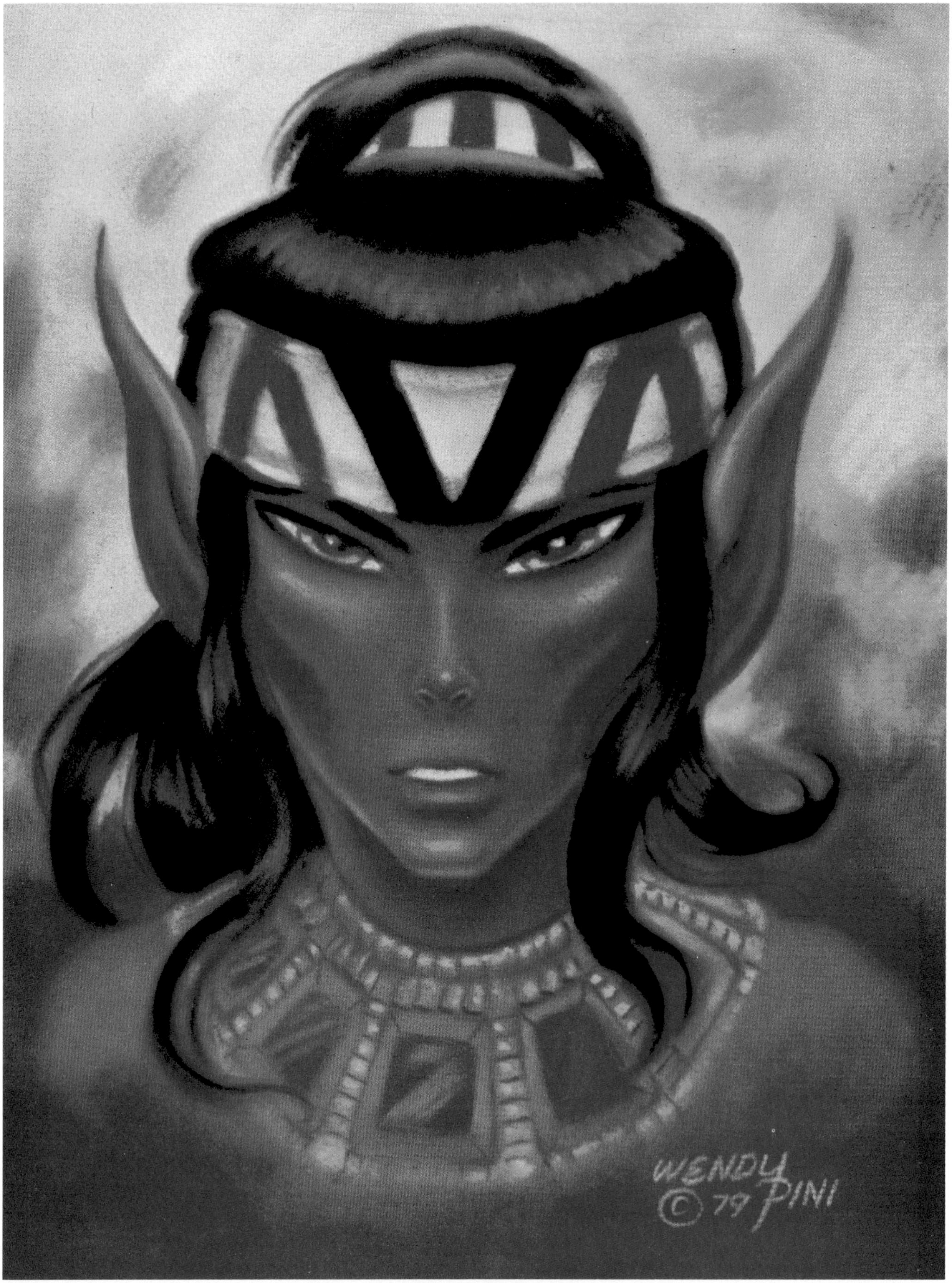
WENDY PINI
© 79

"Rayek"

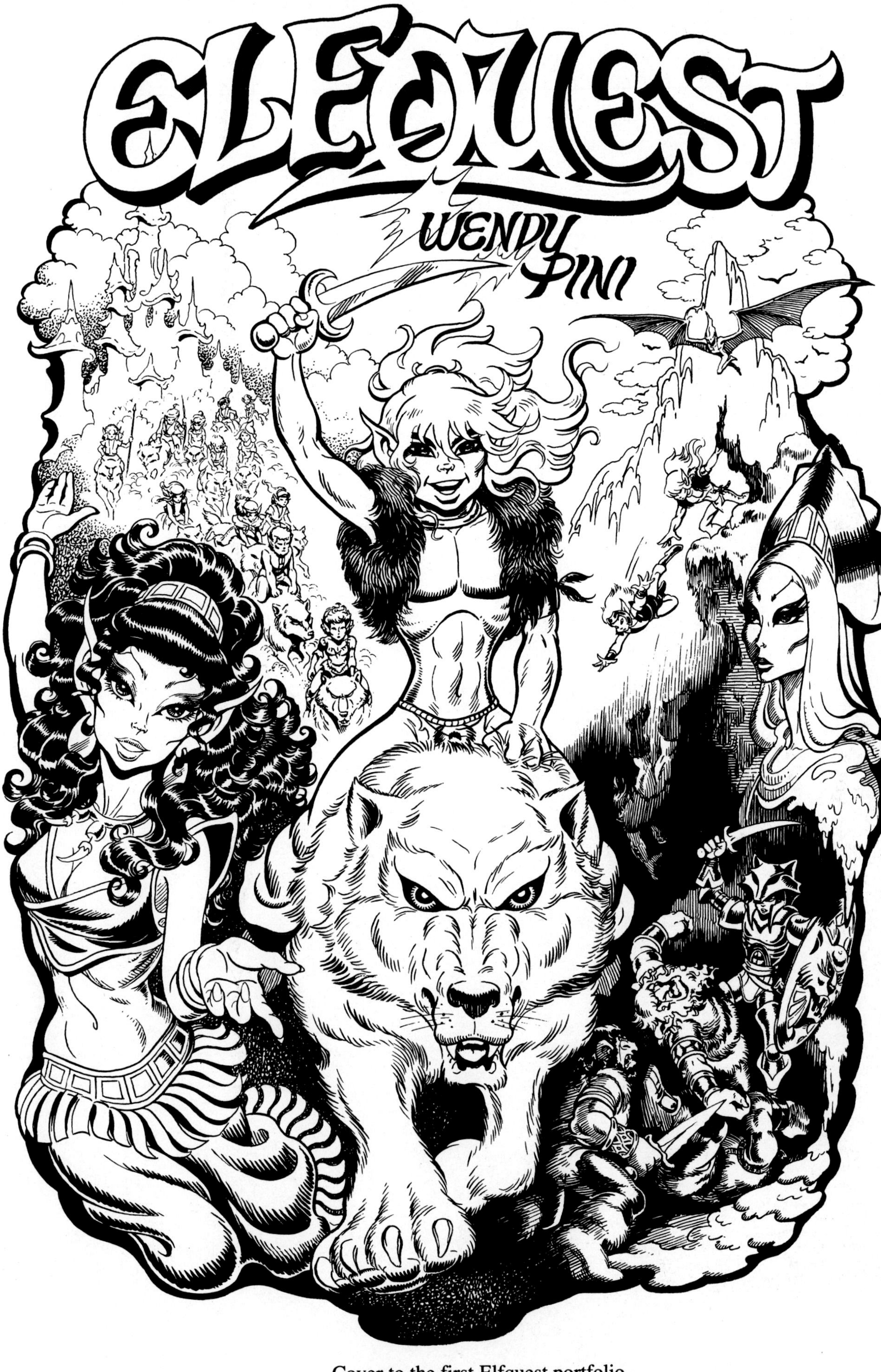
ELFQUEST
WENDY PINI

Cover to the first Elfquest portfolio

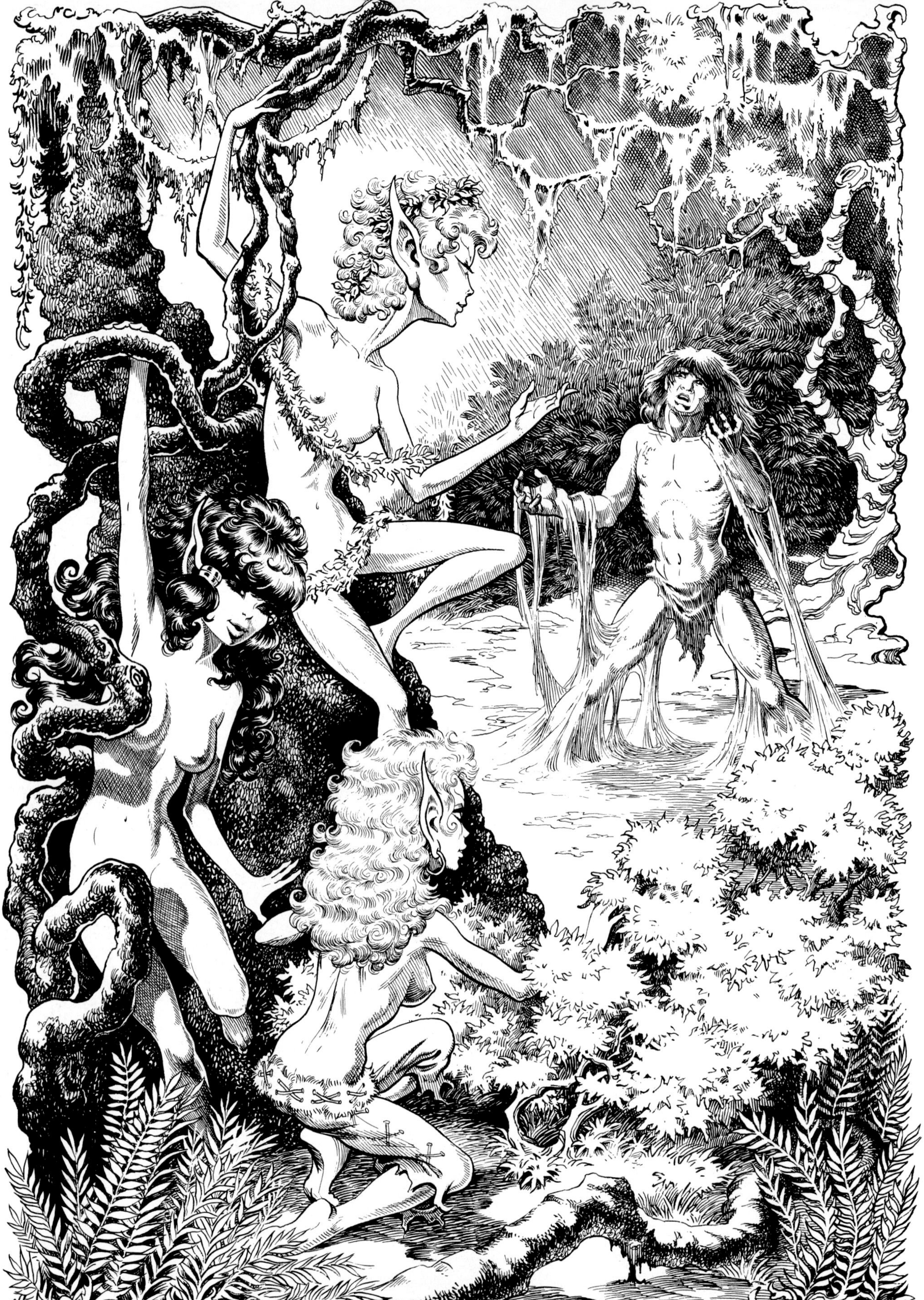
WENDY PINI
© '80

Plate One — "The Lure"

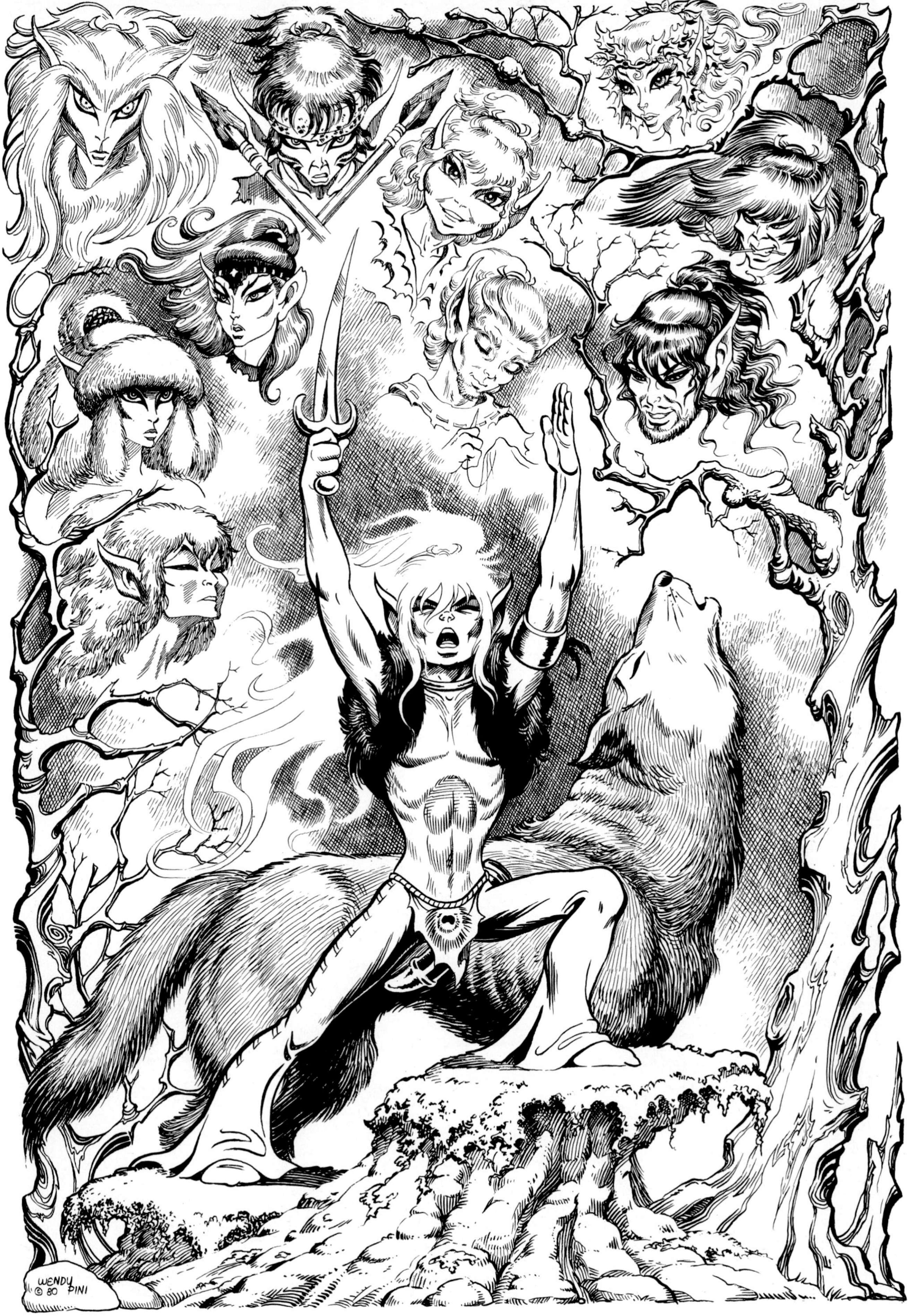
WENDY
© 80 PINI

Plate Two — "Blood of Ten Chiefs"

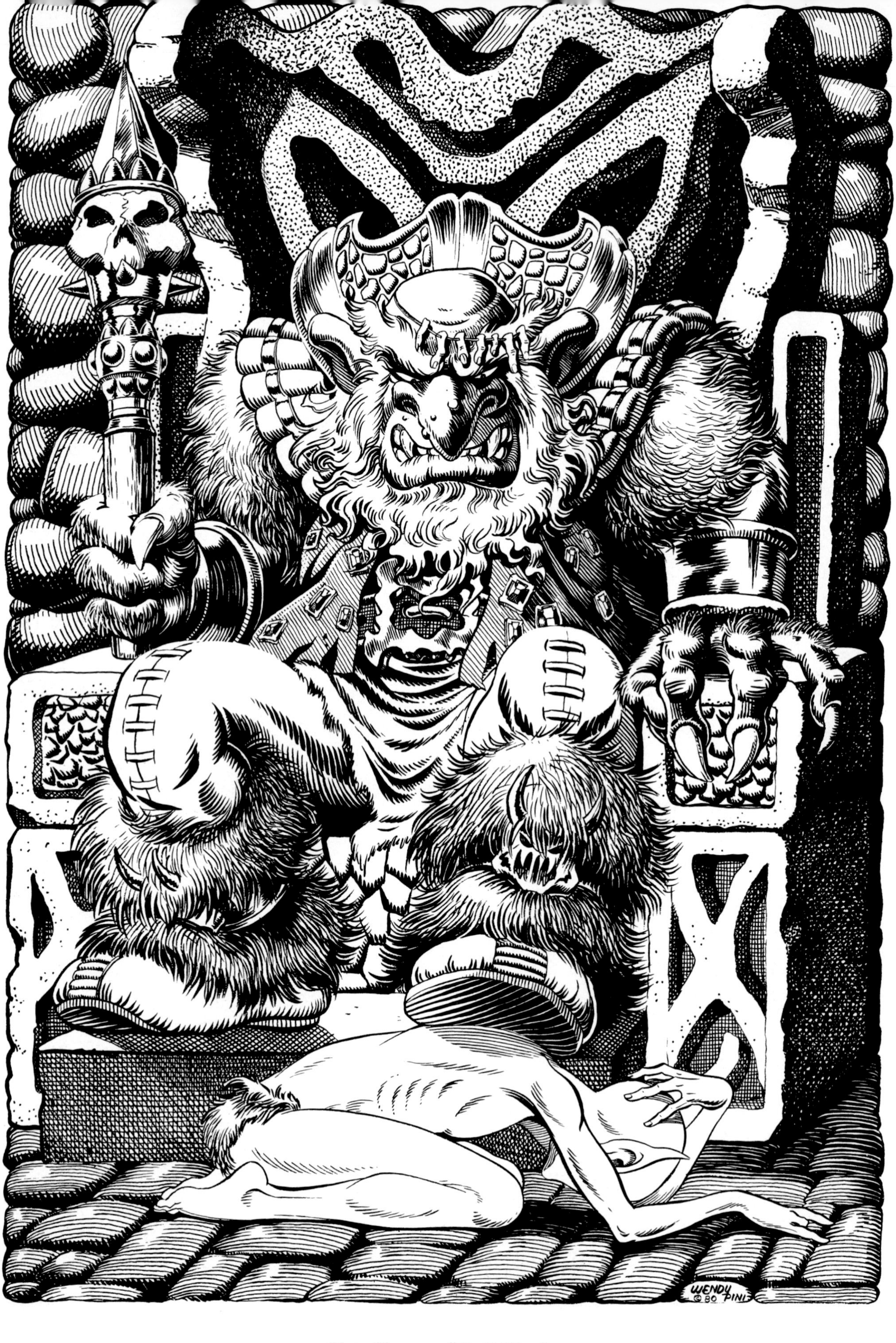
WENDY PINI
© 80

Plate Three — "Troll King"

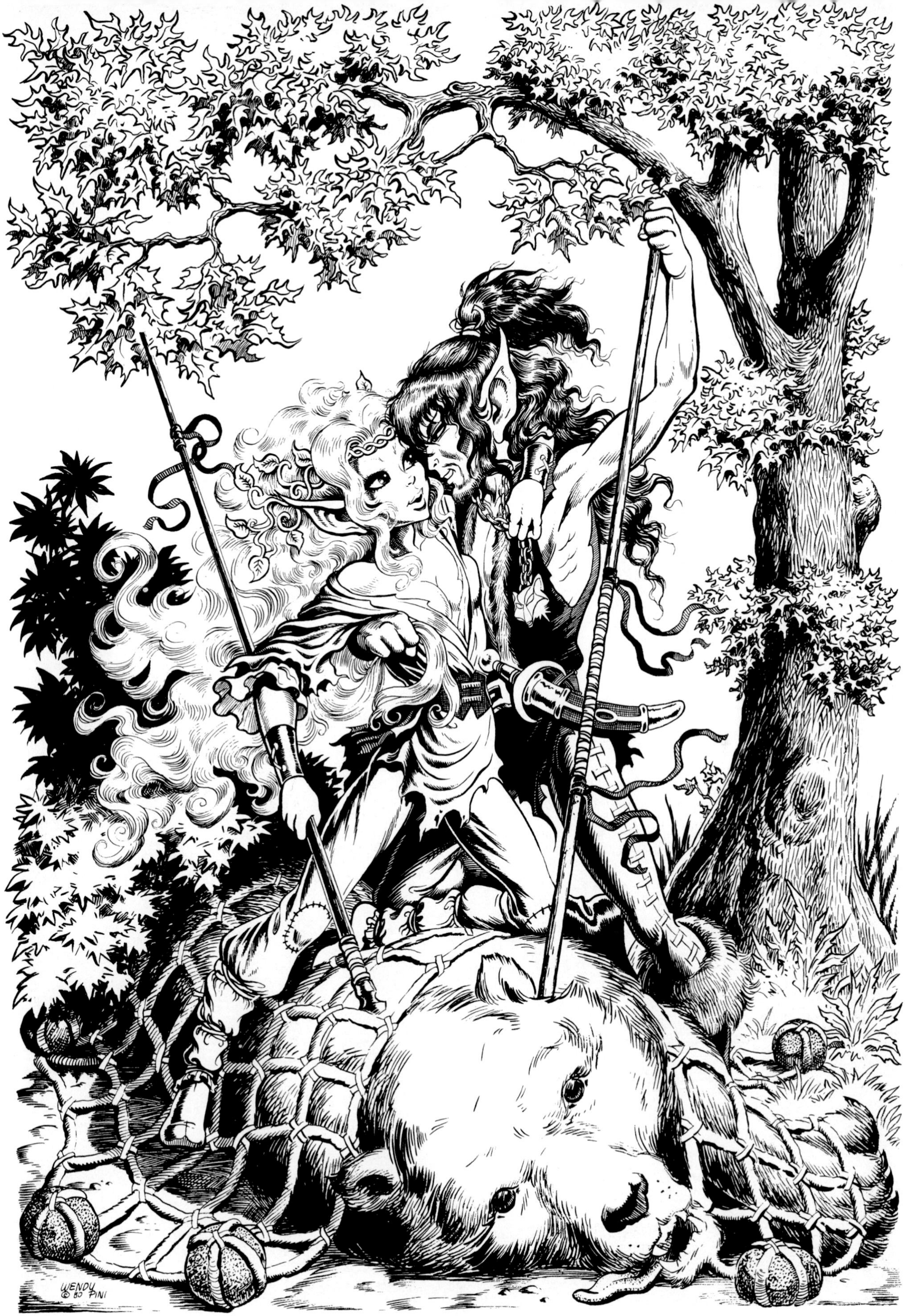
WENDY
© 80 PINI

Plate Four — "Recognition"

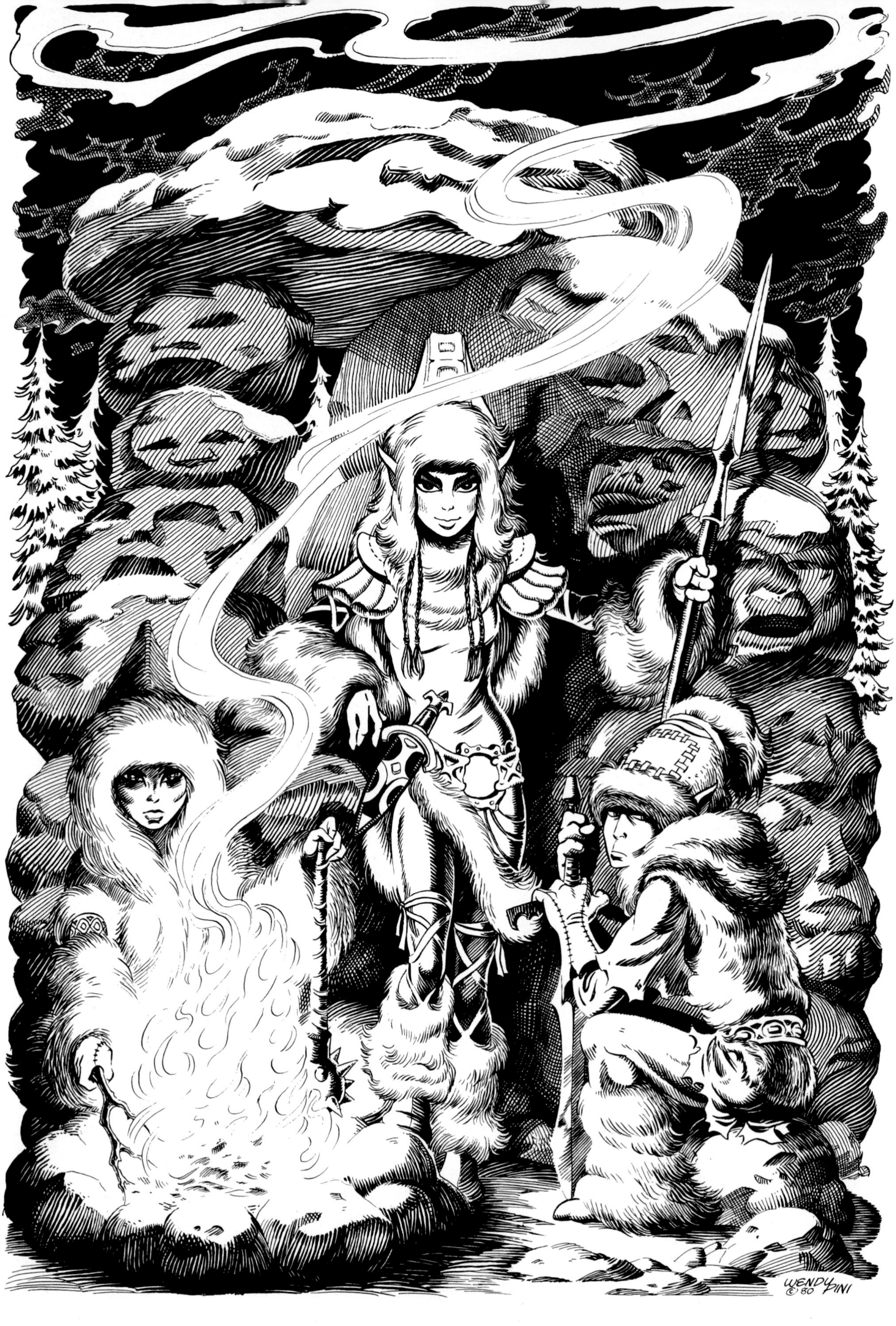
WENDY PINI
© 80

Plate Five — "War-Chieftess"

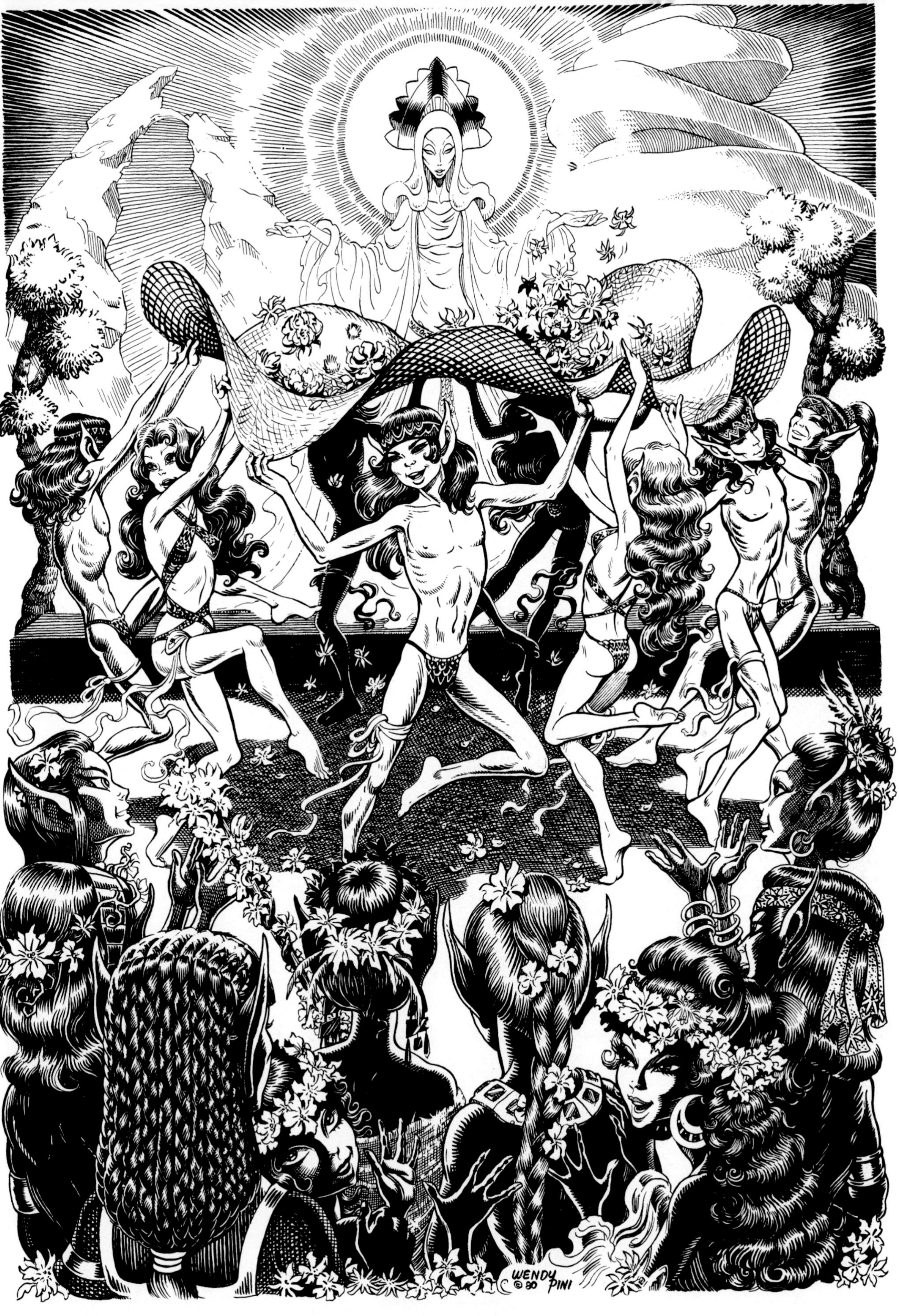
WENDY
©80 PINI
Plate Six — "Festival of Flood and Flower"

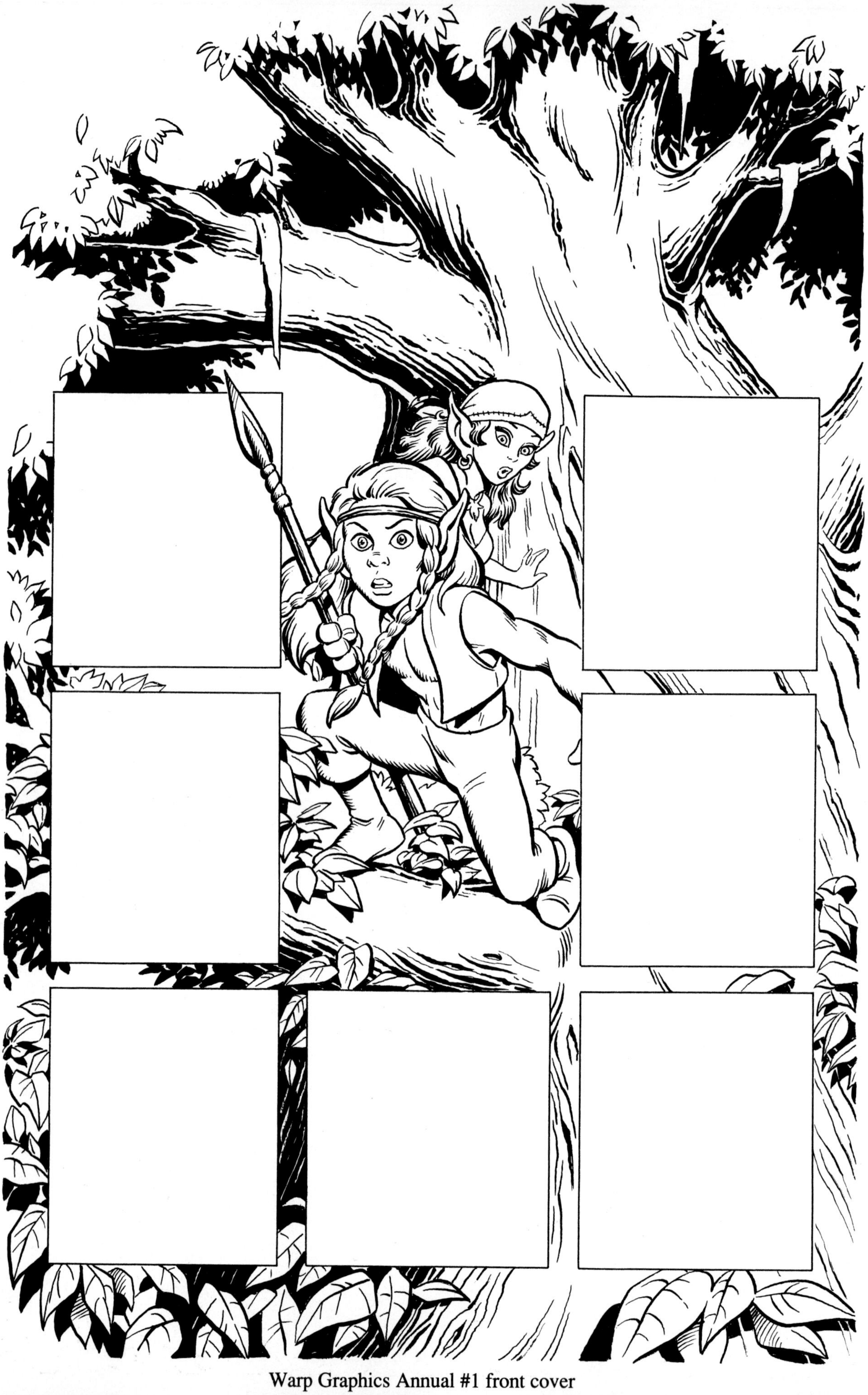

Warp Graphics Annual #1 front cover

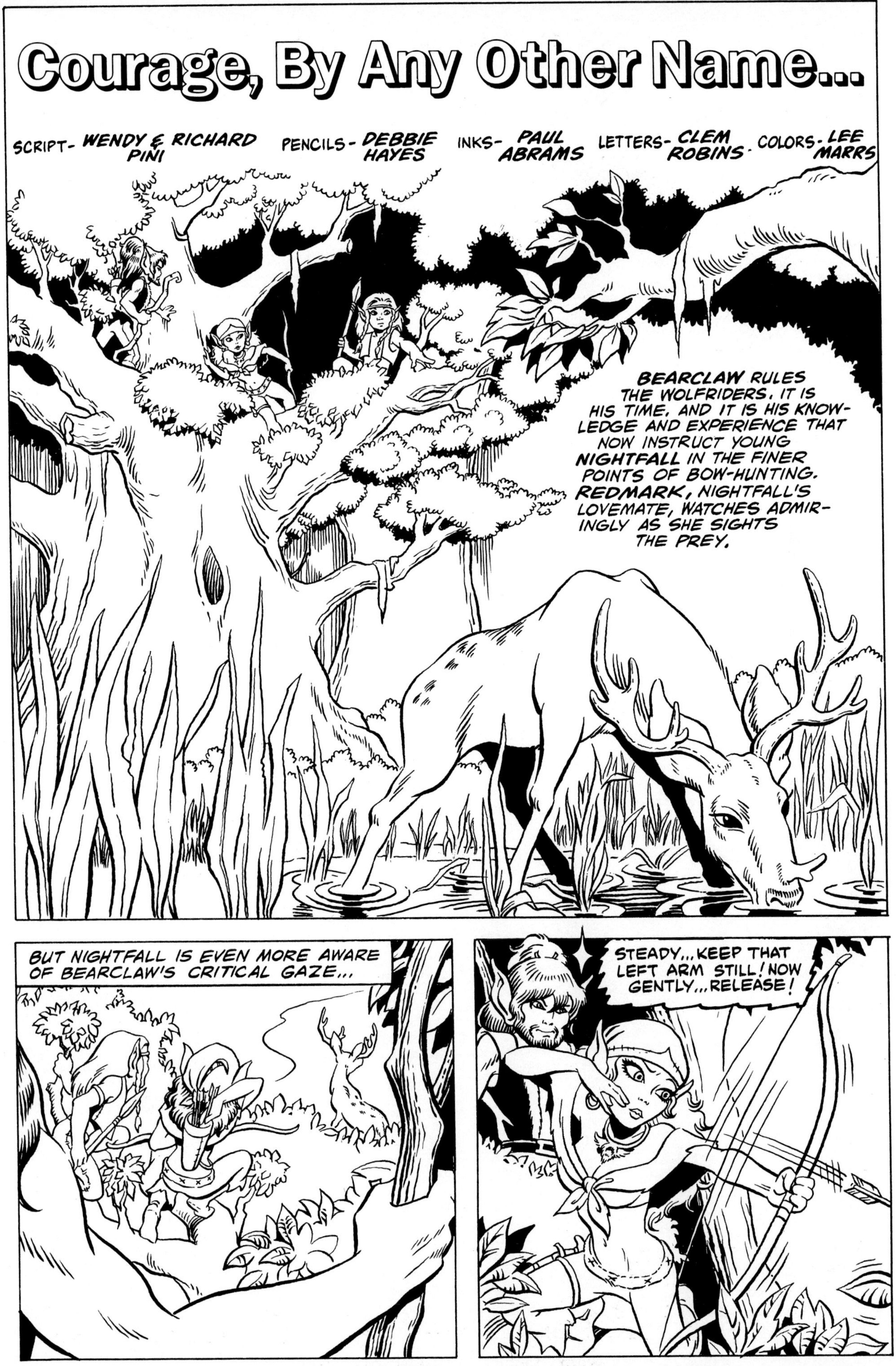

Courage, By Any Other Name...
SCRIPT- WENDY & RICHARD PINI
PENCILS- DEBBIE HAYES
INKS- PAUL ABRAMS
LETTERS- CLEM ROBINS
COLORS- LEE MARRS
BEARCLAW RULES THE WOLFRIDERS. IT IS HIS TIME, AND IT IS HIS KNOWLEDGE AND EXPERIENCE THAT NOW INSTRUCT YOUNG NIGHTFALL IN THE FINER POINTS OF BOW-HUNTING. REDMARK, NIGHTFALL'S LOVEMATE, WATCHES ADMIRINGLY AS SHE SIGHTS THE PREY.
BUT NIGHTFALL IS EVEN MORE AWARE OF BEARCLAW'S CRITICAL GAZE...
STEADY... KEEP THAT LEFT ARM STILL! NOW GENTLY... RELEASE!

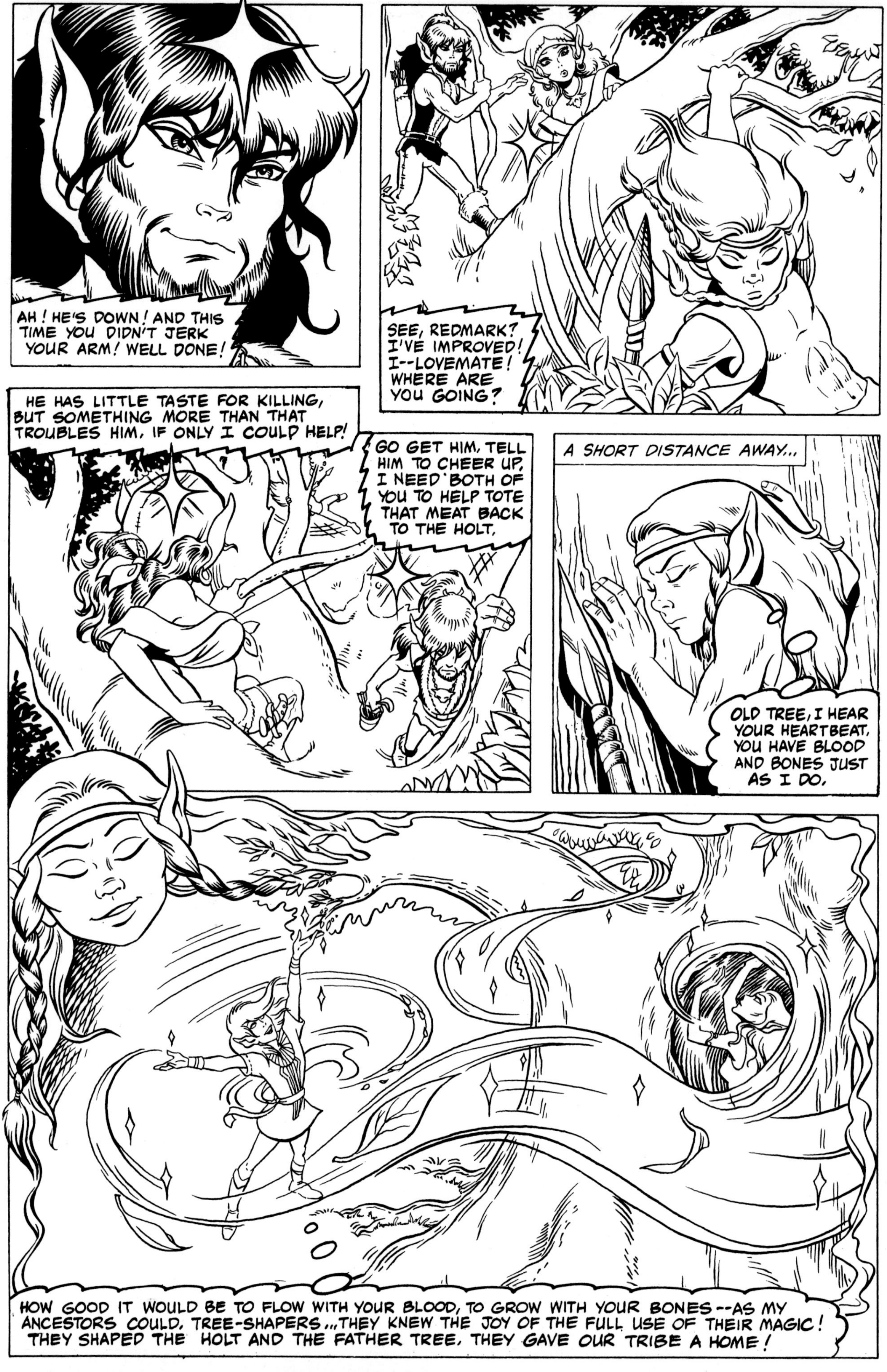
AH! HE'S DOWN! AND THIS TIME YOU DIDN'T JERK YOUR ARM! WELL DONE!
SEE, REDMARK? I'VE IMPROVED! I--LOVEMATE! WHERE ARE YOU GOING?
HE HAS LITTLE TASTE FOR KILLING, BUT SOMETHING MORE THAN THAT TROUBLES HIM. IF ONLY I COULD HELP!
GO GET HIM. TELL HIM TO CHEER UP. I NEED BOTH OF YOU TO HELP TOTE THAT MEAT BACK TO THE HOLT.
A SHORT DISTANCE AWAY...
OLD TREE, I HEAR YOUR HEARTBEAT. YOU HAVE BLOOD AND BONES JUST AS I DO.
HOW GOOD IT WOULD BE TO FLOW WITH YOUR BLOOD, TO GROW WITH YOUR BONES--AS MY ANCESTORS COULD. TREE-SHAPERS...THEY KNEW THE JOY OF THE FULL USE OF THEIR MAGIC! THEY SHAPED THE HOLT AND THE FATHER TREE. THEY GAVE OUR TRIBE A HOME!

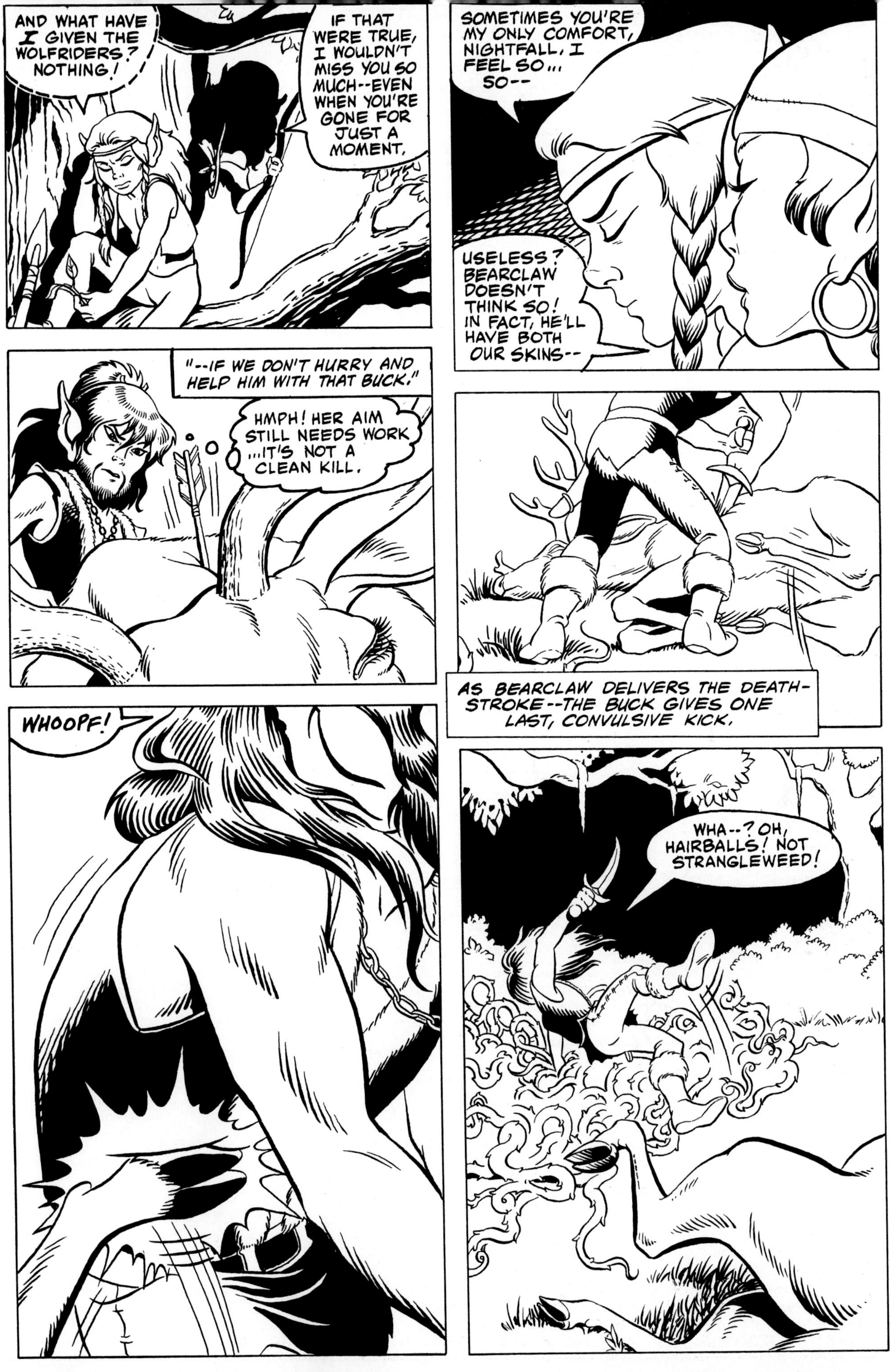
AND WHAT HAVE I GIVEN THE WOLFRIDERS? NOTHING!
IF THAT WERE TRUE, I WOULDN'T MISS YOU SO MUCH--EVEN WHEN YOU'RE GONE FOR JUST A MOMENT.
SOMETIMES YOU'RE MY ONLY COMFORT, NIGHTFALL, I FEEL SO... SO--
USELESS? BEARCLAW DOESN'T THINK SO! IN FACT, HE'LL HAVE BOTH OUR SKINS--
"--IF WE DON'T HURRY AND HELP HIM WITH THAT BUCK."
HMPH! HER AIM STILL NEEDS WORK ...IT'S NOT A CLEAN KILL.
AS BEARCLAW DELIVERS THE DEATH-STROKE--THE BUCK GIVES ONE LAST, CONVULSIVE KICK.
WHOOPF!
WHA--? OH, HAIRBALLS! NOT STRANGLEWEED!

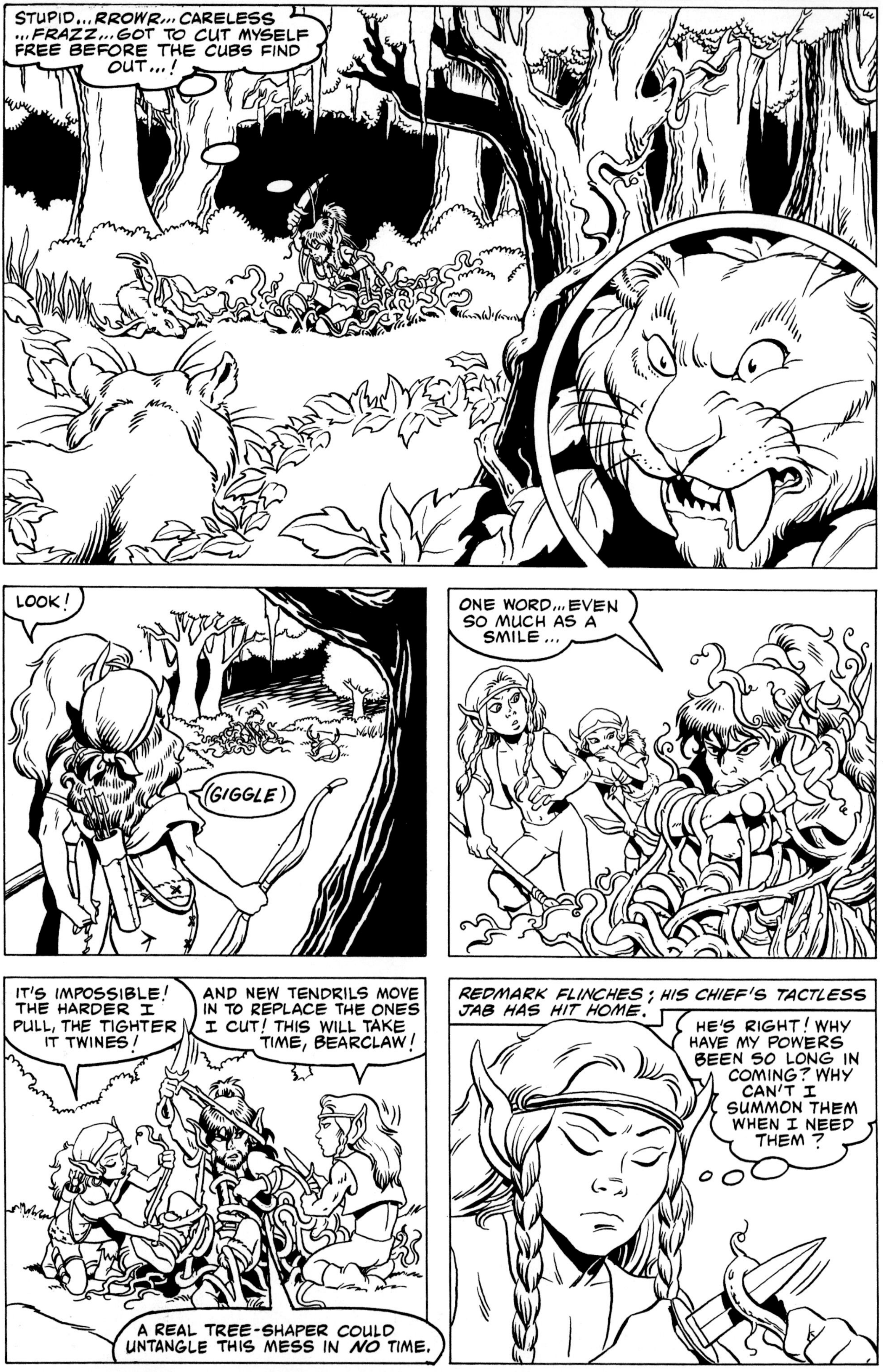
STUPID... RROWR... CARELESS ...FRAZZ... GOT TO CUT MYSELF FREE BEFORE THE CUBS FIND OUT...!
LOOK!
(GIGGLE)
ONE WORD... EVEN SO MUCH AS A SMILE...
IT'S IMPOSSIBLE! THE HARDER I PULL, THE TIGHTER IT TWINES!
AND NEW TENDRILS MOVE IN TO REPLACE THE ONES I CUT! THIS WILL TAKE TIME, BEARCLAW!
A REAL TREE-SHAPER COULD UNTANGLE THIS MESS IN NO TIME.
REDMARK FLINCHES; HIS CHIEF'S TACTLESS JAB HAS HIT HOME.
HE'S RIGHT! WHY HAVE MY POWERS BEEN SO LONG IN COMING? WHY CAN'T I SUMMON THEM WHEN I NEED THEM?

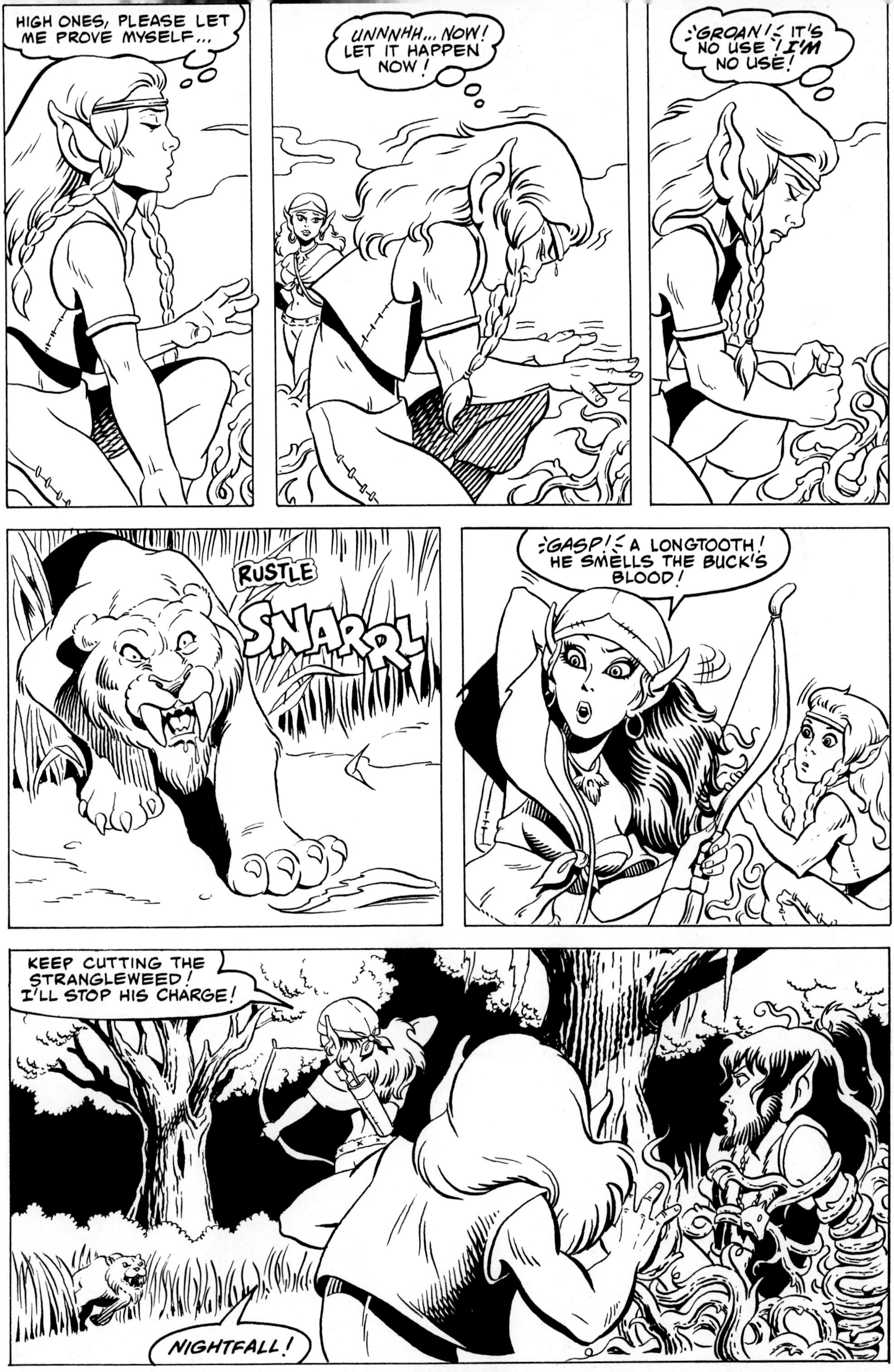
HIGH ONES, PLEASE LET ME PROVE MYSELF...
UNNNHH... NOW! LET IT HAPPEN NOW!
:GROAN!: IT'S NO USE! I'M NO USE!
RUSTLE
SNARRL
:GASP!: A LONGTOOTH! HE SMELLS THE BUCK'S BLOOD!
KEEP CUTTING THE STRANGLEWEED! I'LL STOP HIS CHARGE!
NIGHTFALL!

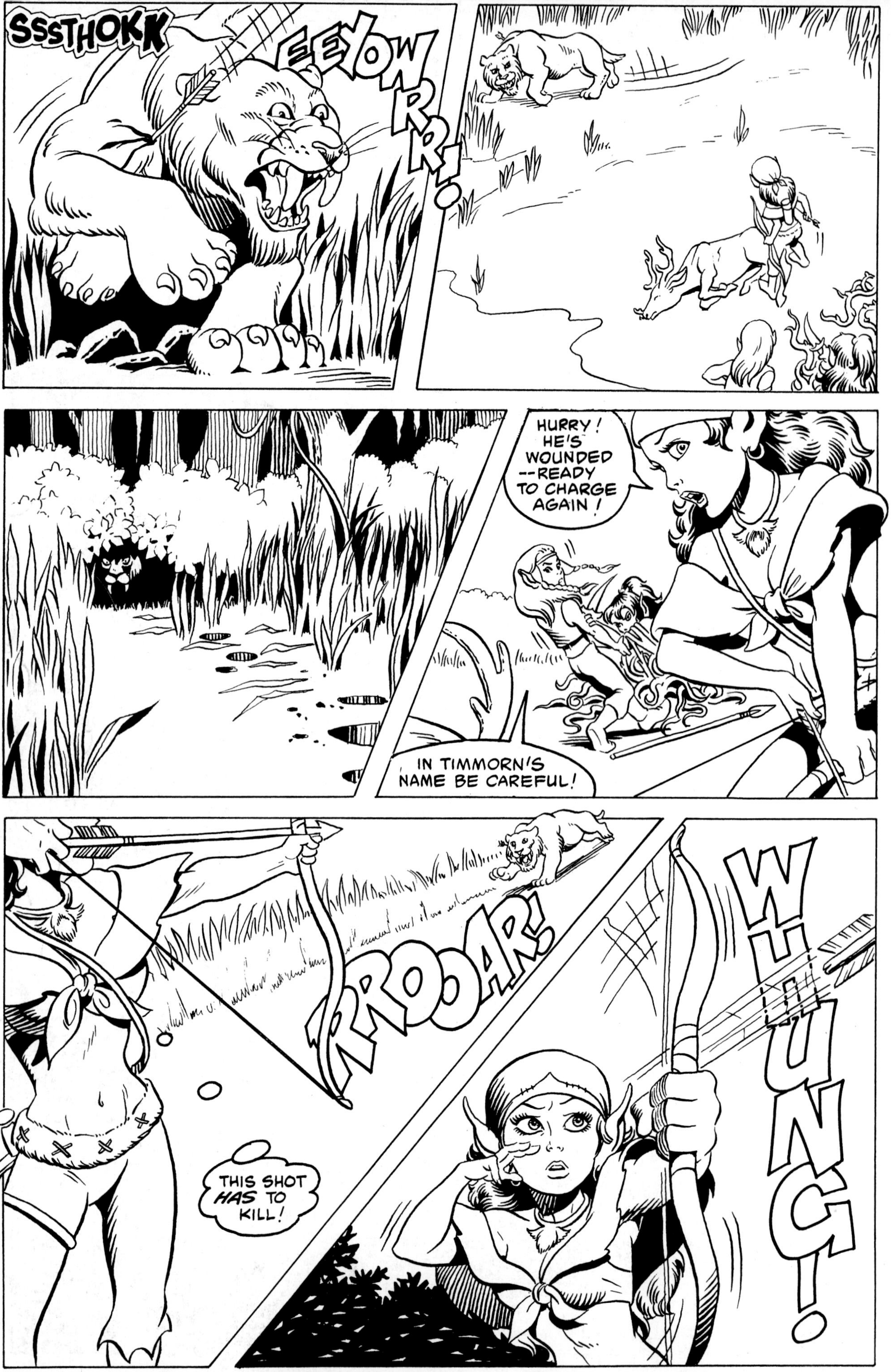
SSSTHOKK
EEYOWRRR!
HURRY! HE'S WOUNDED --READY TO CHARGE AGAIN!
IN TIMMORN'S NAME BE CAREFUL!
RROOAR!
THIS SHOT HAS TO KILL!
WHUNG!

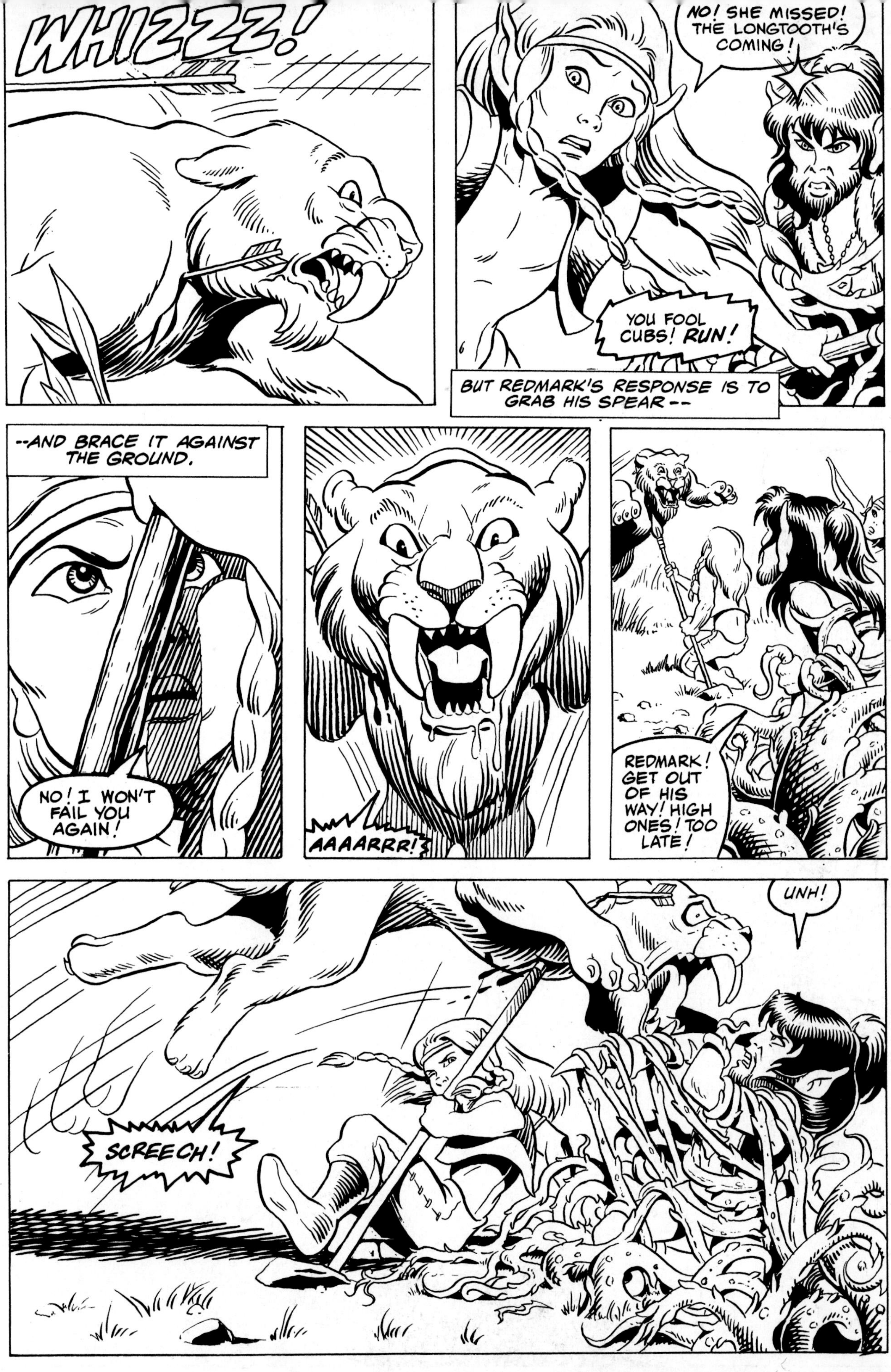
WHIZZZ!
NO! SHE MISSED! THE LONGTOOTH'S COMING!
YOU FOOL CUBS! RUN!
BUT REDMARK'S RESPONSE IS TO GRAB HIS SPEAR --
--AND BRACE IT AGAINST THE GROUND.
NO! I WON'T FAIL YOU AGAIN!
AAAARRR!
REDMARK! GET OUT OF HIS WAY! HIGH ONES! TOO LATE!
UNH!
SCREECH!

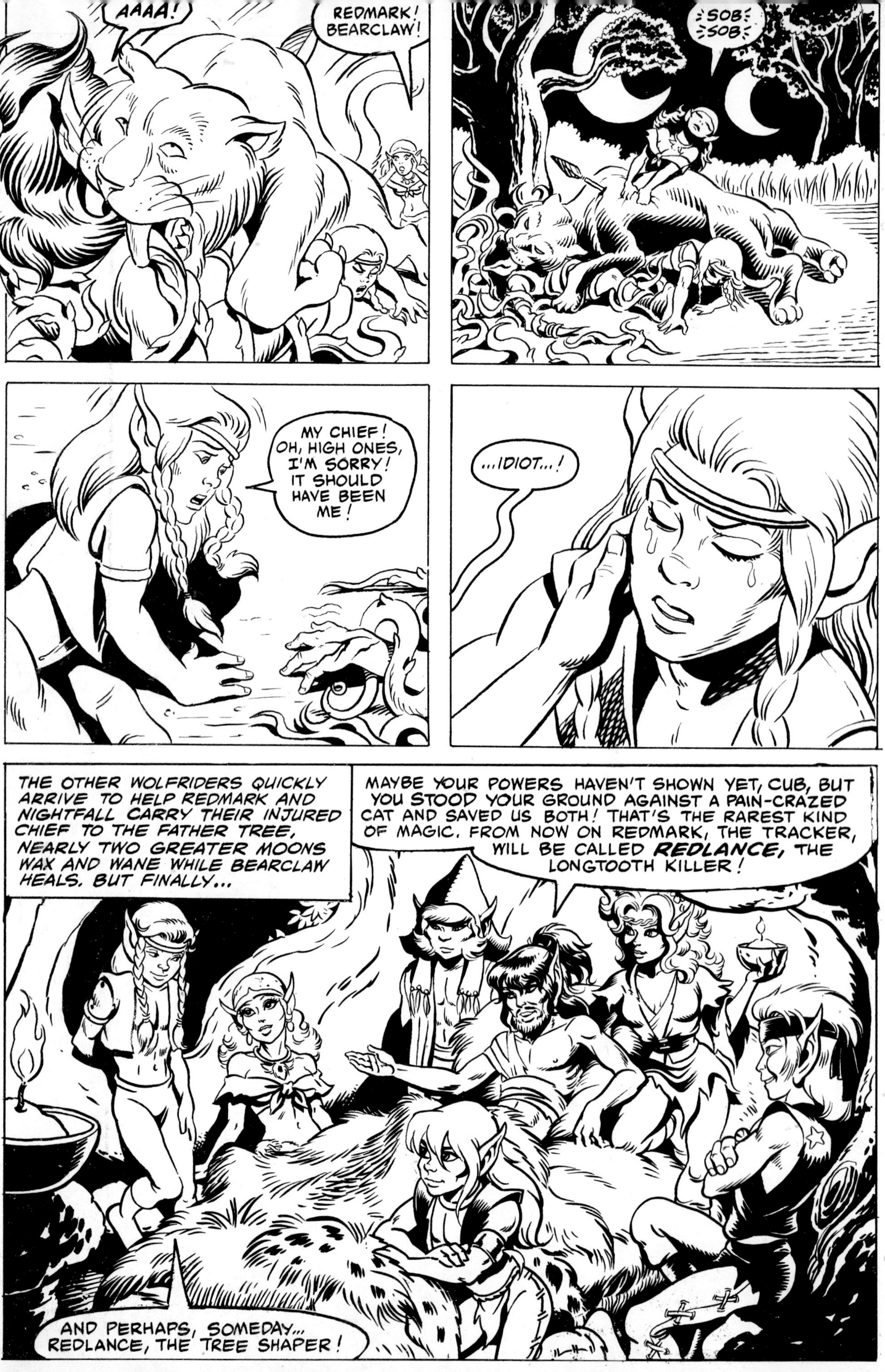
AAAA!
REDMARK! BEARCLAW!
SOB SOB
MY CHIEF! OH, HIGH ONES, I'M SORRY! IT SHOULD HAVE BEEN ME!
...IDIOT...!
THE OTHER WOLFRIDERS QUICKLY ARRIVE TO HELP REDMARK AND NIGHTFALL CARRY THEIR INJURED CHIEF TO THE FATHER TREE. NEARLY TWO GREATER MOONS WAX AND WANE WHILE BEARCLAW HEALS. BUT FINALLY...
MAYBE YOUR POWERS HAVEN'T SHOWN YET, CUB, BUT YOU STOOD YOUR GROUND AGAINST A PAIN-CRAZED CAT AND SAVED US BOTH! THAT'S THE RAREST KIND OF MAGIC. FROM NOW ON REDMARK, THE TRACKER, WILL BE CALLED REDLANCE, THE LONGTOOTH KILLER!
AND PERHAPS, SOMEDAY... REDLANCE, THE TREE SHAPER!